THE GAY
CANON

Great Books

Every Gay Man

Should Read

ANCHOR BOOKS

A Division of Random House, Inc.

New York

THE GAY
CANON

ROBERT

DRAKE

Library of Congress Cataloging-in-Publication Data
Drake, Robert.
The gay canon: great books every gay man should read / by Robert
Drake. —
          p.   cm.
1. Gay men—Books and reading.   2. Homosexuality and literature.
3. Homosexuality in literature.   4. Gay men in literature.   5. Gay
men's writings—History and criticism.   6. Canon (Literature)
          I. Title.
HQ76.D73   1998
028´.9´086642—dc21   98-24581
                        CIP

ISBN 978-0-385-49228-7

Book design by Donna Sinisgalli

www.anchorbooks.com

144903659

ONCE AGAIN

TO

SCOTT

The Canon, a word religious in its origins, has become a choice among texts struggling with one another for survival, whether you interpret the choice as being made by dominant social groups, institutions of education, traditions of criticism, or, as I do, by late-coming authors who feel themselves chosen by particular ancestral figures.

—Harold Bloom,
"Elegy for the Canon,"
The Western Canon

Contents

Part Two: The Age of Enlightenment

Part Three: The Age of Chaos

CONTENTS   xiii

Introduction

> I seek to isolate the qualities that made these authors canonical, that is, authoritative in our culture.
>
> —Harold Bloom
> "Preface and Prelude,"
> *The Western Canon*

In his 1994 bestseller, *The Western Canon*, Harold Bloom explained and defended the cornerstone of contemporary Western education, the perceivable Western Canon, the books that have defined and shaped our culture—our politics, morals and art. Of special concern to Bloom were those among his contemporaries who sought to reshape the Canon along politically correct lines, railing against it as exclusive and arguing for inclusion based on qualities such as gender, race and, conceivably, sexual orientation. *The Western Canon* is arguably a defense of the Canon as it is, and against such suggested modifications.

The Gay Canon does not seek to achieve what Bloom abhors. Frankly, I stand in firm agreement with him that the Western Canon should not be tampered with for reasons of minority bias. *The Gay Canon* seeks to exist outside the Western Canon, touching upon it only where writers and works are in agreement. Yet *The Gay Canon* strives toward a goal similar to Bloom's: to isolate the qualities that made these gay authors canonical—that is, authoritative—in gay culture.

Immediately questions spring to mind, questions that have dogged gay writing since its popularization post-Stonewall. Most obviously: What is a gay book? Must a book have gay content to be a gay book? Must an author evince a gay sensibility in his work to be a gay author, or is the simple nature of his (private) sexuality enough confirmation? What about books with gay content written by heterosexual authors—are they gay books as well?

The responses to such questions are clear, once you brush away the pedant's desire to be obscure. A gay book is a book that addresses issues of same-sex love, or a book written by an author who enjoys his same gender for sexual fulfillment and/or relief. Starting with such a definition, it then follows that content is not a prerequisite, nor is sexual orientation. Gay books may be written by straight people, and vice versa. (A perfect example of the first would be *The Vampire Lestat*; and of the reverse, *A Passage to India*.)

In his "Preface and Prelude," Bloom explains his approach to the selection of canonical texts by saying we must try "to confront greatness directly: to ask what makes the author and the work canonical. The answer, more often than not, has turned out to be a strangeness, a mode of originality that either cannot be assimilated, or that so assimilates us that we cease to see it as strange."

I agree with Bloom in his attribution of an everlasting quality to canonical works: "their ability to make you feel strange at home." As gay readers, we have perhaps become especially tuned to this dilemma—for many of us it is our childhood and adolescence, if not temporally, then psychologically. Until we come out, until we engage in self-acceptance, we always feel strange at home. Afterward there are forever moments of that feeling, a sensation that despite our commonalities with the world at large, there remains for us a separation from the whole. Perhaps this is why many of Bloom's canonical writers have indulged in same-sex love; perhaps it lends a perspective that assists the canonical demand.

Bloom continues to guide us in determining canonical criteria: "Canonical strangeness can exist without the shock of such audacity, but the tang of originality must always hover in an inaugural aspect of any work that incontestably wins the agon with tradition and joins the Canon." We continue to deploy his criteria in assessing the one hundred Great Gay Books that form *The Gay Canon* while acknowledging our limitations. For practical reasons, we have had to limit our considerations to works published in English, either originally or in translation. Doubtless, even though this secures for us the primary sphere of influence for the gay imagination, there are fine and diverse books out there fully capable of being canonical that are not discussed within these pages, simply because they are in great part unknown within the United States or Western Europe. This is a book that concerns itself with works which have shaped a subculture. Like it or not, no matter how exotic or precious certain works may be to us, if they haven't been influential within the United States and Western Europe—arguably the living theater of modern gay culture, of which this book is a part—then they are simply not canonical for our purposes.

So this is not a book of favorites. Given the strictures set forth, many of my favorite works of gay imagination proved impossible to incorporate within the Canon, and so I had to let them go.

It is in the nature of such an effort that some people—perhaps many people—will virulently disagree with my choices and omissions. This is the nature of the beast, and toward that end I can only hope that those with insight to offer will do so, and that the appropriate revisions may take place in future editions. *The Gay Canon* does not aim to present itself as a finished work; rather, it is the beginning of a work hopefully impossible to complete. But that impossibility depends upon the quality of our present and future writers, and their willingness to compete with each other and the writers of the past in their quest to realize the canonical.

The key determining factor for canonical works would appear to be something beyond their ability to physically survive through the ages—many works have managed that feat. With the advent of cyberspace and digital advances, it is conceivable that no text will ever be truly lost again, no matter how arcane. No, the key determining factor would appear to be the work's ability to influence other works—the writer's ability to hold and challenge the imagination and talent of the writers who come after him.

> Contemporary writers do not like to be told that they must compete with Shakespeare and Dante, and yet that struggle was Joyce's provocation to greatness, to an eminence shared only by Beckett, Proust, and Kafka among modern Western authors.
>
> —Harold Bloom,
> "Preface and Prelude,"
> *The Western Canon*

Perhaps most pointedly, *The Gay Canon* asks the question: What does it mean to be a true (gay) writer? In a day when so many works are published because of their commercial appeal alone, or because they serve some political agenda, where does the true writer (as opposed to the convenient writer) fit in?

Answers to this question are found within the Canon. As the quote from Bloom indicates, Joyce was great because he was provoked by the challenges thrown down by canonical writers, by the brilliance of their work. Whom does the gay writer challenge artistically? How does the gay writer find, and determine, his true artistic battle?

Perhaps a personal example will help. I had been an avid reader all my life, but in the late 1970s and early '80s, as an increasingly miserable student, I channeled my teenage energy away from intellectual pursuits and into figuring out my sexuality. A part of this self-determination involved the devouring of literature written by or about gay men, and I think I hit all the high notes of the period: *Dancer from the Dance, Faggots, A Boy's Own Story*, etc. But it all jumbled up inside me; I had no structure through which I might better understand the works in relation to each other, in relation to the new things I read. Or more important, in relation to my life, the meaningful life I was trying to forge and comprehend.

When I began to work with words for a living in 1986—when the fact that I had always been well read and had somehow developed a crude critical faculty led me to a career as a literary agent—I plowed roughly ahead. Understandings were vague to me. Like a dog sniffing the wind, I understood that there was something that related the best works to each other, but I had no idea what that something might be. I managed to function somehow, artistically and commercially, but there was always something desperate about it. In 1990, tired of that desperation, I took a hiatus from agenting and began work on my master's degree at St. John's College in Annapolis, Maryland.

St. John's is one of the Great Books schools: Its curriculum is the Canon of Western Civilization. In a period of two years (four semesters) I studied medicine with Harvey, learned geometry from Euclid and Lobachevsky, ethics from Aristotle, politics from Socrates, literature from Homer and Flaubert, and more. These books— these writers, these people—are your instructors in a Great Books education; the tutors of the college merely facilitate the discussions, and the student's discovery of the work through challenging it.

As the first semester wore on, I found myself referring to texts from one class during discussions in another class.

Suddenly, I understood context.

I began to see patterns emerging, traces of influence shared among Great Works. And as a gay man, as a writer, I began to seek *my* Great Books. *My* cultural challenges. To be honest, this was, and is, in part an act of desperation. I do not believe I am a great novelist, alone. But it is my hope, through coming to an understanding of the Gay Canon, and finding works to challenge my limited talent, that I may produce something which is, if not canonical, at least far better than anything I could have produced had I continued to work in a vacuum, a disorganized, politicized, confusing cultural wasteland.

For that is the present state of gay literature. The gay community has no clear-cut sense of functional literary history. There have been anthologies, but these have served only to give us glimpses of the whole picture, and none of them have addressed or enabled the contextual functionality of those works within the individual.

My hope is that *The Gay Canon* might help to change that. As I write these words, there is no popular framework for understanding gay books and their position within our lives as cultural, societal faggots. There exists no mechanism through which to grasp the interrelationships of these books—perhaps because, before *The Gay Canon,* such interrelationships were an unconscious influence and not (in the main) a wholly realized, conscious, progressive artistic challenge.

The Gay Canon seeks to provide gay writers with a starting place for understanding what it means to be a gay writer, to encounter and come face to face with the works that will challenge them—to separate, in a literary sense, the wheat from the chaff.

And yet writers are not the only ones adrift in modern society. Many gay men young and old frequently complain about the lack of quality or the unavailability of gay culture. They feel adrift, separated, finding queer art muddied by straight culture's co-opting of it. This dilutes our culture within the mainstream and makes it harder to see its specific queer influence, its gay interdependence on other works. *The Gay Canon* seeks to provide gay readers in general with a user-friendly tool through which to understand and consider their culture. It is a device that explains gay passions past and present—gay history, gay hopes, gay mundanities, gay marvels—through a forum where the experience of encounter is not reconstituted or fragmented (as in anthologies or dense scholarly tomes) but is whole, fresh, vibrant and authentic.

The Gay Canon seeks to establish the present bedrock of gay literary culture. It seeks to provide a starting point for understanding. It is half a conversation, with the reader providing the other half in his response. It is designed for popular usage, to foster the idea of community over isolation through the guided formation of reading groups, be they live or cyber. Within these groups, where perceptions of authors and works may do comradely battle through discussion, begins a challenge for gay men to build a cultural awareness that is rooted in the past, yet whose end result is a better, more provocative culture to come.

The Gay Canon is a detective novel with the reader as the protagonist, able in the end to solve the mystery of naming—and intelligently appreciating and discussing with his fellows—his ancestral figures.

My experience at St. John's was revelatory. I bring to *The Gay Canon,* then, an understanding of life without context, together with the mechanics of encountering context and making it one's own. This manifests itself in the entire program of the book, as well as in the readers' group component that is *key but not necessary* for the book's successful deployment. All of this leads to a vital cultural appreciation and to its lively incorporation into one's life when contextual capabilities are realized.

In addition, there has been the staggering amount of reading I've done outside the classics on my own time, or as a result of screening manuscripts by new writers for representation for more than a decade, or while evaluating submissions for the ongoing anthology series I edit with Terry Wolverton for Faber & Faber, *His* and *Hers.*

Balanced against my understanding of the great works of the

past, then, is my informed appreciation for the work that writers are trying to put forward in the present. It is this happy functionality that led to the present book, that brought out in bold relief the need for it, on a staggering scale. Conceivably, every writer, every reader, *every queer person* who has ever felt himself adrift in modern society can turn to *The Gay Canon* for solace and understanding, and walk away not comforted (this is not a self-help book) but challenged, and empowered by an understanding of his place in the scheme of things, the place of things past and the place of things yet to come.

How to Use This Book

The Jews are known as "the People of the Book" because their culture has survived—spiritually and historically—through its preservation in literature.

Queers have a similar resonance with the written word. Because we have had, at times, to suppress the truth of our selves if we were to survive—because, like the Jews, we have often been among the most despised of society—the written word has carried us on, providing a renewed testament for us to turn to and remember that we are not a new invention, we are history—its flesh and blood, its brightest lights.

The Gay Canon is a map through that written history, the texts referenced the longitudes and latitudes of moments in gay culture. It is meant to serve as a *companion* piece to the works discussed; it is hoped that you will go from reading these essays to reading the works themselves. The shorter essays are designed to serve as the basis of a lifetime reading plan for gay men.

Twenty-three chapters are bold-faced in the table of contents and are of a greater length. They form the basis for a bimonthly, yearlong readers' group, or personal reading plan. For the best experience, you should probably read these chapters *after* you've read the Great Gay Books they discuss. (A suggested schedule is provided in the Appendix.) This will ensure that you form your own opinions before encountering those expressed in *The Gay Canon*. At the end of each of these longer chapters are questions for further discussion, but they are meant only to serve as starting points. Certainly, you'll have better questions of your own by the time you've read the work and contemplated its consideration within *The Gay Canon*.

For the works within *The Gay Canon* are works to question, and to let question us—to take inside our lives and be provoked by, intellectually, morally, spiritually, physically. They are books to respect but not revere. Like it or not, the Great Gay Books have earned our respect by shaping our culture and history. For our purposes, however, nothing is sacred but the need for legitimate inquiry. If we limit our ability to question a work, we limit our ability to learn from it.

The Gay Canon's suggested reading program can be carried out at your neighborhood bookstore, or in cyberspace; you can read the texts alone, with just a journal for company, or as part of a group that meets regularly.

The number of longer chapters was set at twenty-three, providing over the course of a year about two weeeks' reading time per title. The titles were selected with that consideration in mind. Obviously, if you are reading on your own, your pace is your own. Should you read privately, you might find it advantageous to keep a journal of your thoughts and responses to the works as you engage them. Not only will this benefit you in the future, when you want to look back to see how you thought at one moment in your life, but it should make the reading itself a bit more fun: having a reaction is one thing; having to tussle with it on paper for a few moments (you might find setting a limit of at least a page per title helpful) is another, and often leads to startling places! These are Great Gay Books in part because they retain their capability to touch our lives today—often hundreds of years after their words were originally written.

But what if you want to read *The Gay Canon* as part of a group?

Whether your group meets in real space or cyberspace, you'll need to address a few basic concerns, such as:

Where will it meet, and when? If you're meeting in cyberspace, check out your options. Using an America Online chat room may limit you to a reading group comprised only of other AOL members; using an Internet chat utility like IRCle (shareware) will broaden your options and allow anyone to participate in your discussion.

Meanwhile, for a more tangible alternative, check out your local bookstore and see if they're interested in hosting the reading group. If you crave a rowdier atmosphere, head down to the neighborhood pub and commandeer a table. Or round-robin it, and each time have a different member host the meeting at his home.

How do I get a good group going? The first thing you want to do is see if you can arouse interest among your friends (and their friends); depending on their response, you may also want to advertise. Take out an ad in the "friends" section of the personals in your community newspaper. Put up a flyer in your neighborhood bookstore, or post it on an on-line bulletin board. Check out the local gay community center as another option for hosting the group or for putting up a flyer for members. Hang a poster at the local gym or coffeehouse; use the new group as an icebreaker with people you've always wanted to chat up before, but for whom you've never quite had a ready opening line.

Okay, I've got some people who are interested. Now what? In many reading groups, there is no set membership. Often the group meets when it meets, and whoever shows up, shows up. This won't really work with *The Gay Canon.* You'll be reading works that will, ideally, begin to suggest their interrelation as the weeks progress, and you'll also find the books challenging you not only intellectually but privately, bringing personal perspectives you've never previously realized you held—or why—to the fore. You need a measure of continuity, you need an atmosphere of trust.

Don't fret. Writers' groups need this too, and many of them

simply have a verbal agreement among all the participants to show up, with readings done and ready to be discussed. Others take a slightly more formal approach, and as the group is forming and it seems clear who will be a part of it and who won't, members sign a kind of promissory note, committing themselves—within reason—to the group and the fulfillment of its purpose.

The latter approach has much to offer. Believe it or not, there's something to that piece of paper you've signed which often makes it harder to blow off a night with the reading group when all you really want to do is watch reruns of *The X-Files* on TV. You may grumble all the way there, but odds are, once you're at the group, you'll be swept up into the conversation, revitalized, and happy you came. The note doesn't have to be complicated either:

> I agree to be a part of *The Gay Canon* reading group, meeting at 7 P.M. at Bookstore X on the second and fourth Wednesday of the month. I understand that the members of the group need to trust they can depend on each other, and toward that end, I agree to attend meetings, keep up with the readings and participate with thoughtful consideration, respecting the opinions of the other members in the group.

That's it, really.

Conversation? How do I run a good conversation? There are a few simple key concepts for running a good discussion group, and they are the same in real space as they are in cyberspace.

- Support your point. It's not enough simply to have an opinion; you've got to have reasons for it. People often don't know why they have a certain opinion; they haven't been made to question it. Ideally, the group will force those questions with a gentle yet determined patience. If someone offers up an opinion—"I hate Anne Rice; she doesn't belong in anything called *The Gay Canon*"—but doesn't support it, ask, "Why?" If his reply is "I just hate her work," try countering with "Why do you hate her work?" A well-run group affords its members the opportunity to quickly sharpen their aptitude for critical thought, as well as a safe place in which to be wrong. The only bad argument is one without reason.

• Don't talk, listen. A bad habit—to which no one is immune—is hearing the first part of something someone says, forming a reaction to it, and failing to hear the rest of what's being said because all we can think about is our bitter riposte.

Stop.

Listen.

Think about what participants are saying and then measure your response. If it helps to take notes while they're talking—key words of key points, especially if they ramble or digress—do so. If they ask what you're doing, tell them you're jotting down notes that will help you follow their argument. Odds are they'll be surprised and flattered that someone's taking them that seriously, and will focus in more on their main thesis.

If someone interrupts you before you've completely made your point, feel free to remind him—politely—that you're not finished yet, and then continue. However, if you've uncomfortably digressed, those who gently nudge you back on track are actually doing you a favor. Learn from them. Pay attention not only to what goes into your ears but to what comes out of your mouth.

Be concise.

Few questions have pat answers. And never treat another member of the reading group with disrespect. Ideas you at first discount as ridiculous may end up leading to profundities. Afford everyone the same respectful consideration you'd like (your ideas) to receive.

• Don't be afraid of the silence. A conversation is only as good as its participants, but sometimes the quality of a dialogue may be measured by the quality of its silence. Silence means people are thinking. Eventually it will break. Let it roll on; don't let it make you anxious. Initially it will feel weird to sit in the silence, but soon you'll find in the quiet interludes rich ore to mine for your contribution to the chat.

• Ask questions. Don't be afraid to offer up an opinion that you might find yourself disagreeing with a half hour later. That's part of coming to terms with the work being discussed, ferreting out the nuggets of (mis-)understanding. Feel free to direct questions—without appearing confrontational, of course—to other members in the group. Check in with people on comments they made on previous Great Gay Books that either complement or don't play with the book you've just read.

This works particularly well in drawing out a reader who has had a lot to say after a previous discussion disbanded and the two of you got together for coffee, but remains silent within the group. At the next meeting, during the discussion period, say that you've been thinking about a particular comment he made about the last meeting's book, while you two had coffee, but still can't quite puzzle it out, though you think it might help your understanding of tonight's book. Restate the basic underpinning of his idea, and your query or point, then ask him to help you; ask him to help the group.

Everyone has something valuable to offer, a new perspective, and a little bit of energy expended in drawing him out often reaps a rich reward. As the books build resonance, so should your conversations.

- Find someone to serve as moderator. This person will have the thankless job of making sure that the conversation stays respectful and that everyone gets heard. Ideally, he'll have nothing to do. But in case you ever need someone to keep the peace or call the group to order, it's good to have an acknowledged central presence. It's also good to rotate the position among the group members so that no one person has a chance to get locked into a position of perceivable authority.

- Stick to the text. This is mentioned last because it's perhaps the most important consideration. Because these books often deal intimately with the very stuff of our lives, it's too easy to let discussions slide out of control and into gossip about current boyfriends, ex-boyfriends, political scandals or parental sins. While each of these topics may have partial relevance to the work under discussion, it is *only* partial relevance, and the readers' group should never confuse itself with group therapy. Asking someone "Excuse me, but I'm lost—how do you get that from the text?" is completely fair. It's not just fair—it's crucial. Asking people to stay connected to the text—again, without being confrontational or embarrassing them—is key to a well-run discussion group, whose focus *is* the text and not some member's inner child.

Mortimer J. Adler and Charles Van Doren wrote a wonderful tome called *How to Read a Book,* which is well worth picking up and taking a look at, if not tackling. It is inevitable, perhaps, that one or more of the titles in *The Gay Canon* reading group will not tickle your fancy, and that someone else will have the exact same difficulty with texts you adore. This is the diversity of taste that keeps literature from being a flaccid monotone; it also means there will probably be a text where you'll just have to grin and bear it. Ideally, there will be nuggets within to invest even the hardest read with bits of charm.

Reading a work from a different time period, or trying to ferret out its meaning, will be new to some of us, and like a first workout at the gym, it can be tough. But as with working out, it gets easier as you go along, until you're laughing with or pinning text you would have run from, pages before. It's incredibly rewarding, and great fun—and it's our history.

These are, after all, the Great Gay Books.

THE GAY
CANON

THE AGE

OF

INSPIRATION

1 Samuel

KING JAMES VERSION OF THE HOLY BIBLE

I am distressed for thee, my brother Jonathan: very
pleasant hast thou been unto me: thy love to me was
wonderful, passing the love of women.

—2 SAMUEL 1:26

David, the first king of the Judean dynasty of Israel, is reputed to
have died between 1018 and 993 B.C.E., and his story as told in the
books of Samuel in the Bible have inflamed the gay imagination
ever since.

Talents as vast as James Baldwin (*Giovanni's Room*),
D. H. Lawrence (*David: A Play*), E. M. Forster (*Where Angels
Fear to Tread*) and William Faulkner (*Absalom, Absalom!*) have
invoked pieces of David's story, the more notable and homoerotic of them often hinging upon the closing words quoted
above: "thy love to me was wonderful, passing the love of
women."

Yet these lines are also the most complicated in making sense
of David's relationship with Jonathan, for it is here that David
names his affection for Jonathan as that for "my brother," and so

defuses much of the romantically charged passion redolent in 1 Samuel, preceding.

A reconsideration is in order.

Although the Bible is without doubt the most influential text in American society—and arguably the one text with the greatest impact on the lives of gays and lesbians—few have given it an intelligent reading. We've encountered it either as children in Sunday school or through our parents' eyes, perhaps we've studied a portion of it in college, but rarely have we sat down without bias and read—as an adult and with an adult's capacity for perception—its words. We rely instead on sound bites and pop commentary to supply our knowledge of this Great Book and our relationship to it.

This is wrong. Given the important, even pervasive, influence of the Bible in our lives (and there is no getting around that simple fact), we must never be satisfied with letting others tell us what to think.

Before we cast our discerning eye toward the relationship of Jonathan and David in particular, some discussion is warranted about the Bible in general. We're not going to haggle over who wrote the Bible and when, and a review of the politics of exclusion that once upon a time separated Biblical from non-Biblical works would be a book in and of itself.

We accept, then, that the Bible simply exists as we have come, popularly, to know it. What Christians call the Old Testament, Jews call the Tanakh. There is a difference between the two collections worth noting, however, because it affects the way we understand Samuel's Prime Mover, the Lord. Where the Tanakh ends in silence, with Daniel's vision of God as the Ancient of Days, the Old Testament ends with the Prophets, a section found in the middle of the Tanakh. When assembling the Bible for their use, Christians simply decided it was more convenient to end the Old Testament this way and give the illusion that it was incomplete—a completion Jesus provides via the New Testament. The Tanakh describes God's arc of activity, from powerful, ready involvement to weary, almost detached observation. It is complete, in and of itself, as far as story is concerned.

Another important consideration: Everything you read in the Bible is a translation (unless you're reading the original Greek and/or Hebrew texts—and this determination of "original" would fill another book). Translations are subject to opinion; in some cases, to repositioning by the translator; or, worse yet, to the entrenchment of perspective by years of unchallenged rhetoric. The story of Sodom and Gomorrah—the destruction of the Cities of the Plain—is one such example. Much has been made of recent claims that previous interpretations erred in emphasizing homosexuality as the sin of Sodom, that the focal point in the text is, and always has been, the inhospitality of the townspeople toward the Lord's messengers. Hospitality was a key concern in ancient times, when people tended to live in nomadic or seminomadic tribes and a stranger's hospitality—his willingness to offer shelter, food and care—was often the difference between life and death.

So we must read the Bible not with a closed, regurgitative mind but with an open, informed one, and with the understanding that its echoes affect our daily lives, our legal standing and, in passages, our tenderest romantic heart.

In the King James Old Testament, 1 Samuel comes well after the destruction of the Cities of the Plain, and after the laws of Leviticus have been laid down—including the (in)famous proscription in 20:13: "If a man also lie with mankind, as he lieth with a woman, both of them have committed an abomination: they shall surely be put to death; their blood shall be upon them."

This is the God of the Old Testament, certainly the God of

1 Samuel: bloodthirsty, harsh and brutal in his ways and his demands.

1 Samuel begins with the conception and birth of Samuel to Hannah, a woman who, barren all her life, has promised to dedicate her child to God if God will grant this miracle, this son.

Samuel's early years bear significant resemblance to those of Jesus: He is born after God's intervention, and at an early age is comfortable ministering to his elders and the priests. Eli, one of God's priests, finds the sons he had hoped would follow in his footsteps pursuing women instead, in a manner displeasing to God. A new priest is needed, and God calls to Samuel and tells him it shall be he.

Samuel grows in faith and reputation not only with God but throughout all Israel. War comes, however, and the Ark of the Covenant is lost to the Philistines, the shock of which kills Eli and plunges the nation into spiritual darkness. Samuel is Israel's last remnant of God's light.

The Ark is eventually returned to the care of the Israelites after it brings nothing but misery to the Philistines, yet God's chosen people have been subjected to Philistine rule for twenty years. Samuel grows to manhood during this time and is instrumental in reconciling God and his people. As a reward, Samuel "judged Israel all the days of his life" (1 Samuel 7:15).

But Samuel suffers from the same problem that plagued Eli: His sons are unworthy to follow in his footsteps. And as he grows old, the people come to Samuel and say, "Behold, thou art old, and thy sons walk not in thy ways: now make us a king to judge us like all the nations" (1 Samuel 8:5).

The work done by Samuel to weave together the Lord and his people is almost undone. For God is clear on this: The Israelites already have a King—God is their King. God is hurt by their request, which he takes as a personal slight, promising Samuel that he will give the Israelites the earthly king they seek, but at the cost of their lives or well-being.

Samuel anoints Saul, "a choice young man . . . there was not among the children of Israel a goodlier person than he . . . from his shoulders and upward [he was] higher than most people" (1 Samuel 9:2).

Saul rules, his method of control perpetuating a fear-based theocracy. Two years into his reign (in 1 Samuel 13), he declares war on the Philistines by ambushing their garrison. It is in this war that we first learn of Saul's son Jonathan, fighting by his father's side.

Jonathan seems firmly entrenched in all things masculine. He is a fighter, always in the company of "the young man that bare his armour" (1 Samuel 14:1), a serving boy so loyal that when Jonathan asks the lad to follow him on a dangerous mission, the reply is "Do all that [is] in thine heart; turn thee; behold, I [am] with thee according to thy heart." Thus bound by their hearts, they go and are victorious over their enemies.

Although capable of staggering cruelty, Saul has vulnerabilities that prove his undoing. When Jonathan, not having heard of an edict his father has laid down, breaks it and is sentenced to die, Saul allows the people to intercede in Jonathan's behalf and the boy lives. When God commands Saul to slaughter everything living in the territory of Amalek, Saul does so—but spares the livestock and Amalek's king, incurring God's wrath.

Saul's softness costs his heirs the kingdom of Israel, as Samuel tells him, "The LORD hath rent the kingdom of Israel from thee this day, and hath given it to a neighbour of thine, that is better than thou" (1 Samuel 15:28).

Upon saying this, Samuel has Saul bring him the still living King of Amalek. Samuel then carves the king up before God, as if to say, "This is obedience." Saul and Samuel do not see each other again until the day of Samuel's death.

For Samuel is charged by God with another mission: He is sent to Bethlehem, to the house of Jesse, where God has said the next King of Israel will be found among Jesse's sons. Eliab, one of Jesse's elder sons, is apparently quite handsome, for Samuel is stunned and, perhaps remembering young Saul's good looks, murmurs that, surely, this must be the Lord's anointed. But God warns Samuel to refuse him, saying that God sees "not as man seeth; for man looketh on the outward appearance, but the LORD looketh on the heart" (1 Samuel 16:7).

At last Jesse's youngest son is brought in from tending the sheep: "Now he was ruddy, and withal of a beautiful countenance, and goodly to look to. And the LORD said, Arise, anoint him: for this is he" (1 Samuel 16:12). Samuel does so, and as the spirit of God descends upon David, it leaves Saul, replaced by a recurring evil spirit of God's making.

God may "looketh on the heart," but in David he finds a man whose "outward appearance" is pleasing as well.

Saul's advisors, noticing the change in their king, suggest he find a skilled harpist whose playing can charm away the evil spirit. Saul tells his servants to find such a man. They point to Jesse the Bethlehemite, who has a son "cunning in playing, and a mighty valiant man, and a man of war, and prudent in matters, and a comely person, and the LORD is with him" (1 Samuel 16:18). Saul sends for the boy: "And David came to Saul, and stood before him: and he loved him greatly; and he became his armourbearer" (1 Samuel 16:21). When the evil spirit falls upon Saul, David and his harp are indeed able to chase away the demon.

And so David enters Saul's household.

Not long after, the Philistines launch an assault against Israel. The armies gather; David is sent home to watch the sheep so that his elder brothers may fight. But the Philistines have a champion, the giant Goliath, whom none will engage, for the Israelites all fear him. The giant has challenged the Israelites with the wager that if they fight him and win, they will have the Philistines as their servants; if they lose, the Israelites will be subjugated instead.

After forty days of this taunt being thrown forth, with no takers, David arrives with food for his brothers and their fellow soldiers. He is appalled that Goliath, a rogue Philistine, should "defy the armies of the living God" (1 Samuel 17:26). He begs Saul to let him take the field against Goliath. David swears that God protected him in the field when he slew a bear and a lion, and that God will protect him now, especially as he goes against one who mocks God's army.

David has the faith, the determined obedience in and to God, that Saul lacks.

David slaughters Goliath. The Philistines flee and the men of Israel chase them, even as David lugs the head of Goliath back to Jerusalem and stores the giant's armor in his tent. The head he offers up to Saul, who seems stunned into insensibility by the boy's success, asking him time and again whose son he is, only to have David at last answer the question simply that he is who Saul must have remembered all along—David, the son of Jesse, the selfsame boy who played the harp and chased away Saul's evil spirit.

But perhaps Saul is after something more; possibly a different answer is begged, for this question foreshadows the questioning of Jesus, where again a certain answer—of divine promise—is sought but not given. Saul here could be fishing to find out if David is the promised neighbor who will take away his kingdom. Wisely, David gives no challenging reply—and is handsomely rewarded:

And it came to pass, when he had made an end of speaking unto Saul, that the soul of Jonathan was knit with the soul of David, and Jonathan loved him as his own soul.

And Saul took him that day, and would let him go no more home to his father's house.

Then Jonathan and David made a covenant, because he loved him as his own soul.

And Jonathan stripped himself of the robe that was

upon him, and gave it to David, and his garments, even to
his sword, and to his bow, and to his girdle.

(1 SAMUEL 18:1–4)

David and Jonathan's union surpasses the physical—and herein lies
the beauty and the problem. Predictive in some ways of Aristophanes' story in Plato's *Symposium*—telling how love is simply the
desire of souls once split in two to find each other and reunite—this
is nevertheless a relationship impossible to dismiss as mere friendship. It is more, even, than simple familial bonding. The words used
are not "loved him as his own brother" (yet) but "loved him as his
own soul."

David, the war hero, quickly ascends to popular power, his
praises sung in towns he visits with the royal family, his accomplishments lauded even as Saul's are denigrated in comparison. Saul
doesn't take this well and, goaded by the evil spirit that has been
about him since David's anointing, lets fly his javelin (representing
his priapic, masculine power) at David not once but twice, missing
each time, but just barely.

Saul finally recognizes David as the man who will take away his
kingdom; David is the heir that Samuel promised God would deliver.

Saul momentarily resigns himself to this, making David a captain over a thousand soldiers. He tries to give David one of his
daughters in marriage, but David has no interest and politely refuses, saying, "Who am I? and what is my life, or my father's family
in Israel, that I should be son in law to the king?" (1 Samuel 18:18).

But Saul has many daughters and tries again, because he wants
his daughter Michal as a spy in David's camp. David again attempts
to discourage him, saying that he couldn't possibly afford the kind
of dowry a king's daughter would require. To which Saul replies,
"The king desireth not any dowry, but an hundred foreskins of the
Philistines . . ." (1 Samuel 18:25).

What the king truly wants as a dowry is David's beating heart stilled in the exercise of this latest slaughter.

David's response is, perhaps, predictable: He returns with *two hundred* foreskins. (Imagine!) Thus further convinced that God has abandoned him for David, Saul gives his daughter Michal to David, only to find his spy useless, for his daughter is truly in love with the man!

At last understanding his predicament, but foolishly believing he can change it, Saul orders Jonathan and his servants to kill David. Jonathan, however, because he "delighted much in David" (1 Samuel 19:2), warns David of his father's intent. He begs David to hide in a field where he himself will bring Saul the next day so that David may eavesdrop as Jonathan pleads David's case. Jonathan is eloquent in his appeal, and David and Saul are momentarily reconciled.

Alas, Jonathan's efforts are ultimately all for naught. The Philistines declare war again, and again Saul hurls his javelin at David and orders his death. And now it is Saul's daughter, David's wife Michal, who tricks the guards, using a model of David covered in bed as a decoy. David makes good his escape and turns to Samuel, his ally and God's.

Saul seeks him out, however, and David runs to Jonathan, who will again try to work the magic of reconciliation he managed before. Jonathan's promise to David echoes that of his own young armor-bearer, quoted earlier: "Whatsoever thy soul desireth, I will even do it for thee" (1 Samuel 20:4). So great is Jonathan's feeling for David that he later exacts his own promise from his friend:

> But also thou shalt not cut off thy kindness from my house
> for ever; no, not when the LORD hath cut off the enemies of
> David every one from the face of the earth.

> So Jonathan made a covenant with the house of
> David, saying, Let the LORD even require [it] at the hand of
> David's enemies.
>
> And Jonathan caused David to swear again, because
> he loved him: for he loved him as he loved his own soul.
>
> (1 SAMUEL 20:15–17)

Under the pretext of target practice, Jonathan will bring the news of his efforts to David in the field the next morning.

Jonathan's efforts result in dismal failure. When Saul finds that his son has spoken with David, he is furious, turning on him, screaming, "[D]o I not know that thou hast chosen the son of Jesse to thine own confusion . . . ?" (1 Samuel 20:30). He tells Jonathan that so long as David lives, Jonathan can never be king. Jonathan doesn't care and continues to stand up to his father on David's behalf, until Saul hurls a javelin—*again* with the javelin!—at Jonathan, nearly piercing him. Jonathan flees the room, now knowing full well his father's only intent toward David, his beloved.

The next day, as scheduled, Jonathan goes to the field, accompanied by a lad to chase his arrows. When the arrows are shot, Jonathan calls out the signaling words that tell David to leave his father's land, then sends the lad back to the city with the quiver.

> And as soon as the lad was gone, David arose out of a
> place toward the south, and fell on his face to the ground,
> and bowed himself three times: and they kissed one an-
> other, and wept with one another, until David exceeded.
>
> And Jonathan said to David, Go in peace, forasmuch
> as we have sworn both of us in the name of the LORD,
> saying, The LORD be between me and thee, and between my
> seed and thy seed for ever. And he arose and departed: and
> Jonathan went into the city. (1 SAMUEL 20:41–42)

David flees to a priest who knows that David is a wanted man. David asks him for bread, and the priest replies, "There is no common bread under mine hand, but there is hallowed bread; if the young men have kept themselves at least from women" (1 Samuel 21:4). To which David replies that the holy bread will do just fine.

And having received from the priest the captured sword of Goliath, which had lain waiting for him there, David sets off again, a hunted man, with only three friends in the world: his wife, his lover, his God.

They will prove enough.

Saul, torn by Jonathan's betrayal, goes mad. Learning of David's visit to the priest, he orders all the priests slaughtered after a brief inquisition. Still not satisfied, he razes their city, butchering men, women, children and livestock. David learns of the killing, even as he learns of yet another Philistine attack upon Israel. He begs God for guidance—and goes off to engage the Philistines on Israel's behalf.

Saul learns of this and runs to where David has fought, again hoping to capture or kill the future king, but to no avail. God protects David and hides him in a forest.

But God does not hide David from Jonathan:

And Jonathan Saul's son arose, and went to David into the wood, and strengthened his hand in God.

And he said unto him, Fear not: for the hand of Saul my father shall not find thee; and thou shalt be king over Israel, and I shall be next unto thee; and that also Saul my father knoweth.

And they two made a covenant before the LORD: and David abode in the wood, and Jonathan went to his house.

(1 SAMUEL 23:16–18)

At last David and Saul confront each other. At a time when David is in a position to kill Saul—and indeed his soldiers urge him to do so—he cannot, admitting to Saul that he will not murder the Lord's anointed: It is not respect for Saul that stays his hand, but respect for God.

This kindness—for Saul perceives it only as a kindness—stuns Saul. He grants that David is a better man than he and takes him back into the fold of Israel with one easily sworn oath, echoing his son Jonathan's request: "Swear now therefore unto me by the Lord, that thou wilt not cut off my seed after me, and that thou wilt not destroy my name out of my father's house" (1 Samuel 24:21).

And they are reconciled, even as Samuel dies.

A new time begins in David's life. Able to live openly as heir to the throne of Israel, he almost slaughters a man and his male slaves for not knowing his name and refusing him hospitality, having determined to slay "any that pisseth against the wall" (1 Samuel 25:22, 34). David spares the man when the fellow's wife hears what her husband has done—from the mouth of one of David's men—and runs to bring David and his soldiers food.

He covets her, and shortly thereafter God kills her husband. David takes her as his wife, along with another woman, even as Saul takes his daughter Michal, David's first wife, and gives her to another man.

Relations tense up again between Saul and David; each has loyal soldiers who stand ready to kill the other, and eventually David realizes he must hide himself yet again. For Saul is God's anointed, after all; his life is only God's, or his own, to take.

David first turns to the neighboring country of Gath, hiding himself in the home of Achish, son of its king. Achish gives him a town, Ziklag, and David goes there to live, and Saul leaves him alone.

David hides himself in the country of the Philistines for a year and four months, during that time slaughtering every inhabitant of the towns he comes across, taking their livestock and grain as his own, never leaving man, woman or child alive to tell of his butchery. All the while he is friends with Achish, who suspects nothing other than that David is a good soldier, yet a man without a country—a man who can serve Achish well.

The Philistines again mass for war against Israel, terrifying Saul, who, in Samuel's absence, prays to God but receives only silence in response. David, meanwhile, rides with Achish to fight against the Israelites but is turned back when he is recognized by some of the Philistine princes. He returns to find Ziklag sacked, its women and children taken captive. Torn, David reaches out to God for advice and is told, "Pursue: for thou shalt surely overtake them, and without fail recover all" (1 Samuel 30:8).

And David does; and it is so. He rides out with four hundred men, two hundred staying behind because they are too weak. All that was carried away is recovered, wives and children are freed, and those who had razed Ziklag—Amalekites, preying on both Israel and Philistine—are slaughtered except four hundred young men, who escape on camelback.

Yet even as David is returning to restore peace to his city and its neighbors, the Philistines are pressing hard upon Israel. They kill Saul's sons, including Jonathan.

Saul, wounded by archers, begs his armor-bearer to run him through with his sword, but the man refuses, presumably from fear of God's vengeance, should he kill God's anointed. Saul takes a sword and falls upon it, killing himself, and his armor-bearer does likewise.

And all of Saul's soldiers perish.

The Philistines cut off Saul's head, strip off his armor and fasten his body to the wall, and apparently doing the same with the bodies of Saul's sons, for the loyal men in the city of Jabesh go at night and retrieve all the bodies, cremating them, burying the bones beneath a tree in their city and then setting to fast for seven days.

So ends 1 Samuel.

It would perhaps be convenient to end the matter of David and Jonathan there, but it would be prejudiced. We opened this chapter with 2 Samuel 1:26: "I am distressed for thee, my brother Jonathan: very pleasant hast thou been unto me: thy love to me was wonderful, passing the love of women."

By far, the argument for David and Jonathan being lovers is stronger *before* this quote than after. They claim to be the same soul, establishing a covenant—a marriage?—in 1 Samuel 23:18, an escalation of the covenant made in 1 Samuel 18:3, as here it is made expressly before God.

It is never said that David and Jonathan were lovers—there is no "and Jonathan and David did know each other," the kind of language the Bible so fondly deploys to describe sexual acts. Neither is there similar language invoked in discussions of Michal, David's wife, or any of his successive wives to that point. Yet when David takes the bread from the priest, there is a nod to the fact that David is not exactly chaste when he does so—he has simply not been with a woman for the time it takes to hallow his body (a time, admittedly, David conveniently reduces to three days, though the priest asks for five).

So: Were David and Jonathan lovers?

Apparently, only their hairdresser knows for sure.

It would be irresponsible to end this discussion without noting that the love of David and Jonathan stands out in such sharp relief against the tableau of 1 Samuel because it is a book of almost relentless brutality. Above the blood-dark sea of violence that is this portion of Jewish history, the love of the two men for each other gleams as a beacon of goodness and humanity—the saving light of the holy in the midst of hell.

Reading 1 Samuel—reading the Old Testament—raises disturbing notions about the nature of God, and about his relationship toward his chosen people in particular. We have grown used to questions such as "Why did God let the Holocaust happen?"—as if the God of the Jews is, at all times, a sheltering God, tender in his mercies.

He is not. Perhaps the most disturbing thing about 1 Samuel, far overwhelming the redemptive power of the love between David and Jonathan, is that it makes the unthinkable possible. God's history with his people *as it is written* is one of harsh punishment for failing to obey his commands. And given this track record, maybe the only way we can escape blaming God for the Holocaust, as some sort of reprisal for the wavering, fragmented faith that is Jewry in the twentieth century, is to posit that he's gone: God is an absentee landlord in our modern world.

As 1 Samuel makes clear, God's invasive bloodthirst is legendary—and virtually unquenchable. And the Jews' readiness to prove feckless—to abandon God's laws for the laws of the land or the intrigue of the moment—is, apparently, equally timeless. Examining God's reaction to the Israelites' request for an earthly king in 1 Samuel, we can readily imagine his sense of disappointment in the modern nation of Israel, a nation that tries to straddle realms not only sacred but also secular in its rule.

God takes no prisoners. God cares not for international diplomacy.

Reading 1 Samuel leads us to understand just how men the world holds as good and decent, such as Prime Minister Rabin, can be gunned down by zealots in their own camp, men convinced they are doing God's work.

Horribly, perhaps they are.

FIVE QUESTIONS

1. How are women valued or not valued in David's time, and what does that say about the possibilities of David and Jonathan's relationship?

2. What similarities are there between the relationship of David and Jonathan and of other great figures in history and/or literature, such as Hadrian and Antinous or *Roderick Hudson*'s Mallet and Hudson? Do such comparisons help us to understand the possibilities of their relationship? Why or why not?

3. Given his anger toward Jonathan in 1 Samuel 20:30, does Saul think that Jonathan and David have a love "passing the love of women"?

4. What separates a friend from a lover? Are Jonathan and David friends or lovers?

5. How often are we appropriating our twentieth-century experiences to justify or explain Jonathan and David's feelings for each other? Is that valid? Why or why not? (What else are we to do?)

Homer

The Iliad

TRANSLATED BY SAMUEL BUTLER

Now Patroclus, so long as the Achaeans and Trojans were fighting about the wall, but were not yet within it and at the ships, remained sitting in the tent of good Eurypylus, entertaining him with his conversation and spreading herbs over his wound to ease his pain. When, however, he saw the Trojans swarming through the breach in the wall, while the Achaeans were clamouring and struck with panic, he cried aloud, and smote his two thighs with the flat of his hands. "Eurypylus," said he in his dismay, "I know you want me badly, but I cannot stay with you any longer, for there is hard fighting going on; a servant shall take care of you now, for I must make all speed to Achilles, and induce him to fight if I can; who knows but with heaven's help I may persuade him. A man does well to listen to the advice of a friend."

—BOOK XV

As with the Biblical scribes, there is no certainty that "Homer" ever existed. Nevertheless, the lore that has sprung up around him includes the famous, intimate attribute that he was blind. On the Greek island of Chios, the "Stone of Homer" sits in an open-air sanctuary at Vrontades, where legend has it the poet sat and recited his lines to students, known as the Homeridae, a league of professional reciters. No fewer than four Greek city-states claim to hold Homer's birthplace.

If he existed at all, it is believed he lived in the second half of the eighth century B.C.E. Evidence of his epic poem *The Iliad* appears around 700 B.C.E. (with *The Odyssey* to follow), roughly five hundred years after the end of the Trojan War, the inspiration for his works.

It is further believed that Homer's lifetime coincided with the introduction of writing into the Greek world and that he was among the first to take advantage of this new artform. Certainly, the notion that the poems began as oral works, to be repeated in serial portions night after night, makes sense when one reads *The Iliad* and *The Odyssey*. There appear to be frequent repetitions of key passages—in *The Iliad,* most notably the listing of the black ships—that a reader would remember but an audience might not.

For gay readers, *The Iliad*'s queer heart beats within the breast of its ultimate hero, Achilles.

Achilles, son of a god, the best soldier among the Greeks, is driven to rage at the opening of *The Iliad* when Agamemnon, his king, impinges on Achilles' honor and takes away his prize slave girl, a war trophy, for Agamemnon's use. Achilles' response, in effect, is to pout, to absent himself from the war until his honor—the woman, his property—is restored.

That his petulance will result in the death of his beloved companion, Patroclus, is the pivot of our affection for Achilles. Despite his rampant egotism, and his penchant for revenge, his sorrow at Patroclus' death is heartbreaking. And coupled as this grief is with Achilles' decision to sacrifice his own life to revenge his friend's murder, it lends credence to the argument that Patroclus was more than just his friend, that Patroclus was his companion, his lover.

There are problems in establishing Achilles and Patroclus as lovers: Neither of them fits the man-boy love relationship structure common at the time, although Patroclus is clearly Achilles' inferior. They share an affinity for slave women, but this only suggests a portrait of men wildly in love with their own maleness: fucking and fighting together, fighting for each other and fucking each other. Besides, the women they toy with are literally just that: toys. Captured booty (as it were).

But the argument that the men were simply friends is also hampered by the evidence of the text. Particularly moving is Patroclus' last request, when he comes to Achilles in a dream after his death and says:

> But one thing more. A last request—grant it, please.
> Never bury my bones apart from yours, Achilles,
> let them lie together . . .[1]
> (BOOK XXIII, LINES 99–101)

Of course, Achilles assents, without hesitation. As he bears his friend's body to the funeral pyre, he slips a lock of his hair into Patroclus' hand. He heaps his friend's bier with sacrifices. The pyre itself is a hundred feet in length and breadth, piled high with skinned sheep and cattle, jars of honey and oil, the bodies of four massive stallions, two of Patroclus' faithful dogs (their throats slit) and, as a last touch, "a dozen of the proud Trojans he hacked to pieces with his bronze" (Book XXIII).

Achilles stays up all night beside the fire, pouring libations to the gods and calling out to his friend's ghost, falling asleep only as the flames subside and rosy-fingered dawn makes its appearance. After Achilles has hosted a series of games in his friend's honor, and the ritual of mourning is complete, the last book of *The Iliad* opens with:

---

[1] This excerpt is from the translation by Robert Fagles.

The assembly now broke up and the people went their ways each to his own ship. There they made ready their supper, and then bethought them of the blessed boon of sleep; but Achilles still wept for thinking of his dear comrade, and sleep, before whom all things bow, could take no hold upon him. This way and that did he turn as he yearned after the might and manfulness of Patroclus; he thought of all they had done together, and all they had gone through both on the field of battle and on the waves of the weary sea. As he dwelt on these things he wept bitterly and lay now on his side, now on his back, and now face downwards, till at last he rose and went out as one distraught to wander upon the seashore.   (BOOK XXIV)

As mentioned earlier, his grief will be the death of him.

As with David and Jonathan, we have neither confirmation nor denial that Achilles and Patroclus shared each other sexually. But what we certainly do have is a love story as passionate and powerful as anything ever again created in Western literature. That Achilles and Patroclus were lovers cannot be doubted, but as for how their love manifested itself within their hearts and bodies, we have only our intuition, and our erotic leanings, to guide us.

Homer

The Odyssey

TRANSLATED BY SAMUEL BUTLER

Ulysses looked sternly at him and answered, "If you were their sacrificing priest, you must have prayed many a time that it might be long before I got home again, and that you might marry my wife and have children by her. Therefore you shall die."

With these words he picked up the sword that Agelaus had dropped when he was being killed, and which was lying upon the ground. Then he struck Leiodes on the back of his neck, so that his head fell rolling in the dust while he was yet speaking.

—BOOK XXII

It is impossible to present any kind of authoritative overview of Western literature, regardless of subcultural fixation, without mentioning Homer's *The Odyssey*.

Although lacking the specific homoeroticism of an Achilles or a Patroclus in its heart or belly, as a work of literary influence, it ranks second only to the Bible.

The Odyssey is the story of a man, the wily Greek soldier Odysseus, trying to make his way home to Ithaca after the fall of Troy.

He has been away for over ten years, and his wife has waited patiently as his house fills with suitors for her hand. In Ithaca he is a king, and many of the young men there are eager to usurp his power, his residence, his wife.

The Odyssey has served as a template for all stories that involve a journey as their main concern—in some of them explicitly, such as James Joyce's Ulysses, and in others implicitly, perhaps even subconsciously. For so ingrained in our minds is the fable of this adventurer that his name has come to mean journey (odyssey) in our language. The obstacles he encounters—the Cyclops, the Sirens— have also entered our sphere of common knowledge.

But The Odyssey is more than the story of a man's journey home. It is also the story of a boy's coming of age. Odysseus' son, Telemachus, becomes a man in his father's absence. His reunion with Odysseus, and their ensuing effort to reconcile their past memories of each other with their present realities, form the template not only for every coming-of-age novel ever written but, arguably, for every coming-out novel as well. In fact, the coming-out novel was based on the coming-of-age novel, which preceded it, whereas the sympathies of The Odyssey are unthwartedly rich and original. This renders, then, the bulk of coming-of-age novels—and coming-out novels, by extension—more derivative than canonical. This is true even though, in its emergence in the two decades following 1969's Stonewall Riot, the coming-out novel proved so momentarily popular within the world of gay letters that it came to constitute a genre all its own, one as pervasive as erotica or mystery. The best examples of such works are probably found in John Fox's The Boys on the Rocks and Frank Mosca's All American Boys, heartfelt novels of young men in love. The genre eventually became so common that it suffered the first backlash in modern queer letters when the plaintive refrain of "Is that all there is?" began to waft above the newly burgeoning shelves of gay bookstores—until AIDS proved a sufficient juggernaut to distract us from the coming-out story as the preeminent theme of our lives.

So most of these coming-out yarns pale beside Telemachus' passion in *The Odyssey*—and this is what separates the derivative from the canonical. It is, possibly, an unfair comparison. *The Odyssey* has perhaps had the greatest resonance of any of the old Greek and Roman writings, remaining—especially in Robert Fagles' brilliant translation—a stunningly evocative reminder of the power of literature in history and in our lives. Few writers—Joyce, again—can plumb its depths and emerge Homer's peer. But this is the challenge inherent in the canonical, in which simply trying to measure up to an all but immeasurably Great Book improves the quality of our literary effort—perhaps, in that rare, fantastic instant, even creating one of our own.

Archilochus

The Fragments

TRANSLATED BY GUY DAVENPORT

H e comes, in bed,
As copiously as
A Prienian ass
And is equipped like a stallion.
—FRAGMENT 36

In *The Fragments of Archilochus,* the politely restrained same-gender sexual attraction present in 1 Samuel and *The Iliad* is given full voice—and that voice is rough, throaty, visceral and orgasmic.

Archilochus is Sappho for gay men. Not only are his poems explicit in their objects of desire, they are also all but lost, surviving in fragments culled from Alexandrine scrap paper used to wrap lower-class mummies, and in a few slices preserved for posterity by critics.

Born on Paros in the Cyclades in 714 B.C.E., Archilochus—his name means "First Sergeant"—was known by the ancients as "The Satirist." Plato called him "The Very Wise." Archilochus' hometown erected a public monument in his honor that noted his ascerbic wit. His companion was a lad named Glaukos—"Gray Eyes"—and their relationship held paternal overtones.

During a war between Paros and Naxos in 676 B.C.E., legend has it that Archilochus was killed by a man named Crow; Apollo banned Crow from all the temples for this slaughter of a favored poet. Archilochus' tomb bore the inscription HASTEN ON, WAYFARER, LEST THOU STIR UP THE HORNETS.

One of those who repeatedly felt Archilochus' sting was the man who was to be his father-in-law, Lycambes. The marriage with Lycambes' daughter Neobule might well have provided a settlement that would have allowed Archilochus to stop soldiering. Lycambes broke his word, however; the wedding was called off. Up until the time the routine study of Greek was removed from classrooms, Lycambes' name became synonymous with a lack of honor, thanks to Archilochus' verses. A good example of this is found in Fragment 262, wherein the warrior-poet hopes, among other things, for Lycambes to be kidnapped, imprisoned in a faraway land, served food fit only for slaves, endure the plague and freezing weather, and rot with the filth of the ocean.

The ready and unapologetic bawdiness and intense lechery of Archilochus' lighter poetry is complemented by his ability to render, with the briefest of words, an image of stunning erotic power (Fragment 130: "Every man / Stripped naked" holds all the cock-hardening resonance of Whitman's simple yet delicious poem written millennia later, "The Runner") and by his disarming candor. As rough as he may be on some (as when he writes, in Fragment 9, "With ankles that fat / It must be a girl"), he spares no kindness for himself (Fragment 266: "I've worn out / My dick").

Archilochus prefigures as well the work of World War I poets such as Wilfrid Owen, who found in poetry a place to grapple with the horrors of war. They serve as a reminder (with Stephen Spender and Rupert Brooke) that war has been unreservedly triumphant only for those who did not have to fight, but led, instead, from the safe bunker of a bureaucrat's desk.

Sîn-Leqi-Unninnì

Gilgamesh

TRANSLATED BY HERBERT MASON

It is an old story
But one that can still be told
About a man who loved
And lost a friend to death
And learned he lacked the power
To bring him back to life.
It is the story of Gilgamesh
And his friend Enkidu.

—"PROLOGUE"

There are several wonderful versions of *Gilgamesh* available: David Ferry's verse translation is a favorite of some; John Gardner's penchant for historical accuracy makes his sexually explicit translation another's pet; but Herbert Mason's translation best lends itself to a straightforward—and often campy—reading.

Unknown to Western readers until the late nineteenth century, the epic of Gilgamesh quickly seized the imagination and intellect of its latter-day readers. Was there a "real" Gilgamesh? Yes, there was. He ruled the ancient Mesopotamian city of Uruk around 2700 B.C.E. His story existed as disparate legends, but sometime in the years 1600–1000 B.C.E., the Sumerian exorcist-priest Sîn-Leqi-Unninnì wove the tales together into one magnificent poem. It is from the fragments available of this work that we are able to discern what is perhaps the oldest surviving piece of narrative literature.

From the outset, Gilgamesh and Enkidu are incomplete creatures, living simple, single-minded lives. Gilgamesh is a hedonistic, all-but-feckless leader of his people, banging his subjects' wives on their wedding night before the husbands can enjoy them (as was the right of the king), as well as dabbling in the arts. Enkidu runs about the forest, at one with the other animals (whom, as the ur-PETA activist, he frees from the traps of hunters), a creature of nature such as Adam was in Eden before the Fall.

Enkidu's undoing is sex. A prostitute is sent from the city to seduce him so that he will leave behind the world of animals and embrace the world of man: self-knowledge through sex. At once Biblical serpent and tempting fruit, the prostitute

> came close to him and the animals withdrew.
> She took his hand and guided it
> Across her breasts and between her legs
> And touched him with her fingers
> Gently and bent down and moistened
> Him with her lips then drew him
> Slowly to the ground.

After, Enkidu rises and looks for his friends, the animals, feeling "a strange exhaustion, / As if life had left his body," and moreover, feeling himself estranged from his former companions. Separate from them now, he is utterly alone and empty.

The fine line between childhood and nascent sexuality, suddenly and by a single act irretrievably changed, is explicit to the modern reader. For gay readers, there is pointed relevance in Enkidu's pain as we recall the sense of wholeness in childhood, that

time—however brief—before the recognition of our innate difference separated us from feeling at one with our peers.

Meanwhile, back at the palace: Gilgamesh, given to indulging
his dreams and sharing them with his mother, Ninsun, has a dream
of a falling star—Enkidu—that comes to him and from which he
cannot be separated. His mother explains the star to him:

> It will be a person, she continued,
> Speaking in her somber monotone,
> A companion who is your equal
> In strength, a person loyal to a friend,
> Who will not forsake you and whom you
> Will never wish to leave.

Gardner is more explicit throughout his translation, here having
the mother close by prophesying, "you lay him down at my feet /so
that I compared him with you; / like a wife you hugged him."

Again Gilgamesh dreams, this time of an unliftably heavy ax,
also interpreted by his mother as representing "a graceful man," a
peer who will come and lift Gilgamesh from his wearying life.

Gilgamesh's response is ecstatic:

> O Ninsun, I want your words to be true.
> I have never known such weariness before,
> As if some life in me has disappeared
> Or needs to be filled up again.
> I am alone and I have longed
> For some companionship.

Gilgamesh is hurting. His life is empty. Sex with new brides doesn't
satisfy him; his life as a king is empty ritual and duty. Although
comfortable, and satisfied in material needs, he feels as though he
has nothing.

This compulsion in people, this feeling that we are incomplete until joined, emotionally and soulfully, with another, was as prevalent in ancient times as it is in today's world. Although addressed most imaginatively in Plato's *Symposium,* it realized in *Gilgamesh* its most painful clarity: Sex alone is not satisfying; the best love is between equals.

The prostitute continues to sleep with Enkidu until he is used to her; in essence, she is taming him. She speaks Gilgamesh's name to him and he feels weak. She clothes him and grooms him, bringing out his physical resemblance to Gilgamesh; and with the shepherds who used to trap his friends, he eats bread—the food of man—and drinks liquor. Soon he is out in their fields, trapping wolves for them.

Enkidu remains in the countryside until a man from Uruk passes by, talking of Gilgamesh and his habit of sleeping with every man's new bride. The thought makes Enkidu tremble—"He felt a weakness in his body / At the mention of their king"—and he goes with the prostitute to Uruk, where

> People said: he looks like Gilgamesh
> But he is shorter and also stronger . . .
> They hailed him as the equal of their king.

Some readers use the physical resemblance between Gilgamesh and Enkidu to slight the love between them—and, by extension, its homoerotic overtones and homosexual desire in general—calling it an exercise in narcissism. This is at best a meretricious observation. The physical similarity is nothing more than an outward reflection of their internal compatibility, a tangible manifestation of their souls' resonance, the one with the other.

Enkidu has but one thought in mind: to keep Gilgamesh from his latest appointed liaison with a new bride. Is his motive moral, in that he perceives what Gilgamesh does to be wrong, or one of primal jealousy? The text is unclear.

What is clear is Enkidu's anger at Gilgamesh's intention to

sleep with this woman, as well as Gilgamesh's anger at being told what to do by another, even by another who resembles him, as Enkidu does, and who proves equally strong when the two men wrestle in the doorway of the bride's house, with screaming children and barking dogs underfoot.

Their fighting is desperate and animal, yet short-lived:

And quiet suddenly fell on them
When Gilgamesh stood still
Exhausted. He turned to Enkidu who leaned
Against his shoulder and looked into his eyes
And saw himself in the other, just as Enkidu saw
Himself in Gilgamesh.
In the silence of the people they began to laugh
And clutched each other in their breathless exaltation.

Again, we are back in a land of middling clarity. Gone is the jism-spurting misogyny of Archilochus and in its place is the delicately worded passion of one man for another. Here, however, important as it is to acknowledge the heterosexual prowess Gilgamesh and Enkidu displayed prior to their meeting, it is equally important to note that both of them found these acts of heterosexual congress deeply unsatisfying. Their only emotional satisfaction comes when they look into each other's eyes and each realizes he is looking at his only, true beloved.

Having "embraced and made their vow / To stay together always, / No matter what the obstacle," Gilgamesh and Enkidu set off on a quest to slay the Evil One, Humbaba. They go against Enkidu's better judgment, for even as he is thinking of the dread that kept the animals from Humbaba's wood, Gilgamesh is thinking only of the cedars he might climb. Enkidu fears death, having brushed against it in his time with the animals; Gilgamesh accepts it as man's lot in life, saying, "Only the gods are immortal anyway . . ."

The two men visit Gilgamesh's mother for a blessing, and she adopts Enkidu as her own. They set off, sharing their fears in order to ease them and always drawing solace from each other's company. That night, on the edge of Humbaba's wood, they both dream, Gilgamesh of victory, and Enkidu that only one of them will survive the impending onslaught.

Gilgamesh is our oldest surviving work of literature, but it is also the perfect template for the hero's journey, perhaps best described in Joseph Campbell's *The Hero with a Thousand Faces*. The quest and the notion of sacrifice are staples of myth, lending to the reader a sense of the inevitability Enkidu feels after his dream that night and, later, upon hearing Gilgamesh's dream.

Using teamwork, the two men kill Humbaba, a giant. And as with Goliath, the giant in 1 Samuel, they chop off his head. They hang it from a tree high above them, as a war trophy, and then rest. Enkidu has been battered badly in the battle, having engaged the giant first while Gilgamesh stood by frozen in fear at the terrific sight of the Evil One.

In the morning, as they prepare to return to Uruk, they are visited by Ishtar, the primary goddess of Gilgamesh's city. The gods are upset that Humbaba has been killed, but if Gilgamesh agrees to marry Ishtar, she will intercede on his behalf with her father, Anu, and the other gods to keep the peace.

Gilgamesh refuses her offer, calling her "a fat whore" in the process, "[a]nd turned away to his friend / Enkidu."

Ishtar is enraged. She goes to Anu and asks him to unleash the Bull of Heaven on Gilgamesh and his people. Anu assents, and three hundred people are slaughtered before the bull finds Gilgamesh and attacks him.

Seeing Gilgamesh so attacked, the battle-weary Enkidu "to protect his friend / Found strength." He sticks his sword cleanly into the nape of the bull's neck, then tears the "thigh"—a word often used as a euphemism for "genitals"—from the bull, throwing the bloody meat in Ishtar's face.

That night, the wounds Enkidu received from Humbaba

worsen, aggravated by the fight with the Bull of Heaven. Enkidu is feverish—worse, Enkidu is dying.

Gilgamesh has never seen death before; his soft life as a king has sheltered him. His earlier acceptance of death was like that of a child's: innocent, and false. Now, however, death confronts him in his soul's twin, and he is rendered silent. Enkidu, his mind as ever focused on those he loves, is worried about the animals he ran with—"Who will be kind to them?"—and about Gilgamesh:

> You will be left alone, unable to understand
> In a world where nothing lives anymore
> As you thought it did.

Enkidu understands that once a person has seen death, everything in life is changed. If before, sex took Enkidu from childhood to adolescence, death takes Gilgamesh from adolescence—that heady time of invulnerability and inconceivable mortality—to adulthood. Not surprisingly, Enkidu lashes out, blaming the prostitute:

> He became bitter in his tone again:
> Because of *her*. She made me see
> Things as a man, and a man sees death in things.

He warns Gilgamesh that this is to be his lot in life now too, and prophesies Gilgamesh's yearning to recover the feeling of life before death's shadow loomed.

And then, his vision fading, Enkidu reaches out to draw Gilgamesh's face close to his and says:

> You are crying. You never cried before.
> It's not like you.
> Why am I to die,
> You to wander on alone?
> Is that the way it is with friends?

Gilgamesh sat hushed as his friend's eyes stilled.
In silence he reached out
To touch the friend that he had lost.

There is a cultural parallel to be drawn here, for gay men in the
1970s could well be said to have indulged themselves as adolescents
do, in a heady euphoria of liberation and invulnerability. We found
ourselves able to recognize pieces of kindred souls in others' bodies
and, through sex, to press our hearts together, working to make one
man from two, as Gilgamesh and Enkidu almost do.

Yet, like Gilgamesh, we were stymied. By death.

Gilgamesh's grief is all but unbearable, and the rest of the narrative
resolves itself into the epic's true quest: Gilgamesh's search for the
secret of immortality, through which he hopes to bring Enkidu
back to life.

He goes in search of Utnapishtim (Noah), the man who survived the flood, for if anyone will know the secret of resurrection,
Utnapishtim will. The old man lives on the other side of the waters
of death, and Gilgamesh crosses that sea naked, thin with grief,
using his clothing for a sail. But Utnapishtim has no comforting
words of immortality for him, only the story of Utnapishtim's own
familiarity with loss through surviving the flood. Utnapishtim ad-
vises Gilgamesh to go home, to return to the world of the living,
and abandon his quest. Gilgamesh despairs, and Utnapishtim's wife
nudges her husband:

He has come so far.
Have you forgotten how grief fastened on to you
And made you crave some word, some gesture, once?

Utnapishtim hasn't, and he softens, telling Gilgamesh of a thorny
plant at the bottom of the river that will, indeed, bring new life.

Gilgamesh, grateful, hurries off and dives for the plant, tying stones around his feet to help him sink. When he grasps the plant, its thorns loose his blood into the water. Then

> He cut the stones loose from his feet and rose
> Up sharply to the surface and swam to shore.
> He was calling out, I have it! I have it!

He returns to the shore of the living with the plant, stopping only to refresh himself in a clear pool he encounters, setting the plant at the water's edge, unguarded. A serpent slithers up and devours it. Gilgamesh returns after washing to where he left the plant, but finds only a shed snakeskin to tell him where Enkidu's new life has gone. Defeated, "He sat / Down on the ground, and wept."

Gilgamesh recognizes this loss as the end of his quest. He returns to Uruk, only to find that Enkidu's name—he who slew the Bull of Heaven—is no longer remembered by his people. Gilgamesh is alone in the city he rules, filled with people who honor but do not love him:

> All that is left to one who grieves
> Is convalescence. No change of heart or spiritual
> Conversion, for the heart has changed
> And the soul has been converted
> To a thing that sees
> How much it costs to lose a friend it loved.

FIVE QUESTIONS

1. How are women regarded in Gilgamesh's kingdom? How do Ishtar, Ninsun (Gilgamesh's mother), the prostitute who initiates Enkidu into the world of men, and Utnapishtim's wife serve to

illustrate our understanding of the role of women in Gilgamesh's world?

2. How do Gilgamesh and Enkidu complete each other? Are they truly incomplete before they meet? Is everyone incomplete without some Other?

3. Are you a "Gilgamesh" or an "Enkidu"? Why, and how?

4. Is Gilgamesh's decision to accept the snake's devouring of the plant of new life the right one? Should he have continued his quest to find a way to bring Enkidu back to life? Was there more than one of these plants in the river, and if so, should he have gone back and gotten another one? Why? If he could, if he did, how would that have changed Gilgamesh and the book?

5. What is to be learned from Gilgamesh's life and struggle? What is man to make of life, of death, of the purpose of—and reason to—love?

Plato

The Dialogues

READING:

Symposium

TRANSLATED BY W. H. D. ROUSE

"Here we are again," said Alcibiades, "the usual thing; where Socrates is there is no one else can get a share of the beauties!"

—*SYMPOSIUM*, 223A

What do we know of Plato? It is estimated he lived from 428 to 348 B.C.E. History has it that he was the pupil (if not the associate) of Socrates, as well as the teacher of Aristotle, who would later teach Alexander the Great. It is believed, although little is known about his childhood, that Plato was from a wealthy Athenian family.

After Socrates was sentenced to death—for politically corrupting the minds of Athenian youth—Plato traveled widely in Greece, southern Italy and Sicily, where he met Dion, a relative of Dionysus I, ruler of Syracuse. The boy was arguably the love of Plato's life. When Dion was assassinated shortly after a successful political rebellion, Plato wrote this epitaph: "[Now] in your wide-wayed city, honored at last you rest, / O Dion, whose love once maddened the heart within this breast."

Unlike Socrates, Plato never married.

It was with Dion's help that Plato had founded the Academy in Athens, circa 387 B.C.E. The Academy was to become a famous center for mathematical, scientific and, of course, philosophical research. Plato would preside over the Academy for the rest of his life—a legacy of his lover's interest.

Despite Plato's early and middle dialogues extolling the virtues of same-sex attraction—the most notable being *Lysis*, on friendship; *Phaedrus*, on romantic love and rhetoric; and *Symposium*, here discussed—he ended his life a bitter fascist. In *Laws* he writes of an ideal state where all but martial poetry is banished and sexual activity between men forbidden. To be sure, the seeds of this fascism are found in the earlier writings, including *Republic*, but in *Laws* its sterile nastiness finds full voice. A bitter noise, indeed, with which to end so enthralling, so rapturously idealistic a career.

But we are not concerned with *Laws*. We are concerned with *Symposium*, a happier work from an earlier time. Certainly, it was a more humanly honest one.

The format of the symposium was a popular literary device at this time in history; as we'll see, both Xenophon and Plutarch deployed it to their benefit in later works. Simply put, a symposium was a dinner party where men met to drink, eat and talk.

The dinner party in Plato's *Symposium* took place in 416 B.C.E. in the home of a man named Agathon. Thirty-one when he gave the banquet, Agathon was on the brink of becoming a popular tragic poet. A few days before the meal, he had won the poetry laurel in a dramatic festival performed in the Theater of Dionysus—located at the foot of the Athenian Acropolis—before an estimated crowd of 30,000.

Socrates, fifty-three at the time, attended the symposium with Aristodemus. Rounding out the night's companions were Phaedrus, after whom another Socratic dialogue on love is named; a man called Pausanias, who was a disciple of Prodicos, a Sophist; Eryximachos, a physician; and thirty-two-year-old Aristophanes, the comic playwright, many of whose works survive in our time. Joining them last at Agathon's table would be Alcibiades, thirty-five at the time and best remembered nowadays for being Socrates' most notable crush.

Yet we should remember that rather than a straightforward "you are there" approach, Plato instead has chosen to filter his account through a fifteen-year-old veil of memory. Perhaps this was a wise choice, given that the evening under discussion involved much drinking; claiming accuracy of representation when it comes to drunken evenings is risky business, and memory allows for the same sort of error as alcohol—a certain fluidity of the facts. As it stands, Aristodemus had told Apollodoros—who would later appear in the dialogue *Phaedo*—of the night in question, and now, a decade and a half later, Apollodoros tells a nameless friend—arguably, the reader.

And the topic of discussion that famous night? Why, love!

Symposium is wonderfully rich not only in substance but in minutiae. Socrates usually went about barefoot, but here he honors the occasion by wearing a pair of fancy-dress shoes. Before the evening has even started, Socrates has already lost himself in thought. Upon arriving at Agathon's, he walks not into the house but onto the porch next door, oblivious to the calls of the servant for him to join Agathon at supper. Someone who apparently knows Socrates better than the others, a friend of Aristodemus', urges that they get on with the dinner, that such intellectual distraction is common with Socrates. They do, and Socrates indeed manages to join them halfway through the meal.

They talk of drinking, and Eryximachos launches them into a conversation based on something Phaedrus had said: that love has yet to receive the praise it is due. And so, at the physician's prompting but under Phaedrus' guidance, the men set about making speeches to praise—and explain—love.

As the instigator of the topic, Phaedrus goes first. He makes the case that Love is the oldest of the gods, and of the greatest good for man: "For I cannot say what is a greater good for a man in his youth than a lover, and for a lover than his beloved" (178c). His reasoning is that Love leads one toward what is good, what is beautiful and virtuous, and this cannot help but be beneficial.

Then it is the Sophist's turn. Pausanias takes the one Love that Phaedrus speaks of and divides it into two: Common Love and Heavenly Love, the latter being the purview of the goddess Aphrodite. Of Common Love, Pausanias says, "[T]his is the love which inferior men feel. Such persons love women as well as boys; next, when they love, they love bodies rather than souls . . ." (181b). He argues further that they do not care how well they love, only that they love, and this deficiency in virtue is attributed to the fact that the minor goddess, who is Common Love, "in her birth had a share of both female and male" (181c). But Heavenly Love springs, perplexingly, "from the Heavenly goddess, who firstly has had no share of the female, but only of the male." Is his argument that Aphrodite, goddess of Love, knows not the heart of women, despite her being a woman herself, albeit one of godly stature?

That is insensible. Ah, these Sophists! Must we suffer fools gladly? And yet, before we dismiss Pausanias too quickly, it is worth noting that the point of the Homeric hymn to Aphrodite—in which the goddess is finally made to feel the same desires that she has inflicted upon others—gives credence to his argument.

Pausanias goes on to say that Heavenly Love is the elder of the two loves and is without violence—the more knowledgeable, the more peaceable—and "consequently those inspired by this love turn to the male because they feel affection rather for what is stronger

and has more mind" (181c). Pausanias chooses to ignore the violence inherent in Attic masculinity, embodied in his time by war
exercises (the men at the table have already referenced *The Iliad*).

Interestingly, Pausanias' description of Heavenly Love hinges
on a violation of the concept of love between men in Athenian
times—that it was never a love between peers but always between
someone who had to learn and someone who offered to teach;
traditionally, a boy and a man. But here Pausanias argues for a love
between peers, even as in his earlier speech Phaedrus worked to
make sense of the love of Patroclus and Achilles, naming them as
lovers, not friends. Pausanias allows an out for the "pederast"
through the transformative pubescent window of ephebophilia—
that time when boys begin to develop minds and so become attractive to the Heavenly Lover.

Pausanias spins on for quite some time, discussing how the
lessons of love may be useful in politics, how the world of the
despot is a world without love, and making diverse arguments,
some sound—"it is called better to love openly than secretly"
(182d)—and some questionable—"especially to love the highest
and noblest born, even if they are uglier than others" (182d)—
along with the conceit that vows made in love are as no vows at all,
merely words, unleashed at the moment. Pausanias works himself
up into a whirl of redundancy as he closes, breathless and self-
impressed.

The idea of holding a symposium of one's own is often a
tempting one, and it is only the rhetoric of a Pausanias that keeps
one from doing it at times. The idea of being trapped there, sitting,
having to feign attention while listening for the occasional pearl of
truth sunk in scummed-over pools of weak, Sophistic thought, as
evidenced by Pausanias, leads us to consider the modern words this
school of thought—a school despised by Plato—has spawned:
sophomoric (idiotic) and sophisticated (stylish but not necessarily
substantial), among others.

Aristophanes is to go next, but he has the hiccups and passes the torch to Eryximachos, who starts by saying, "Pausanias began well, but ended feebly" (185e), and expands on his predecessor's idea that love is dual, as opposed to singular. Only for the physician, "there is one love in the healthy and another in the diseased" (186b). He makes his case that both kinds of love are necessary, the Heavenly and the Common, using examples from medicine, music and nature to illustrate his central thesis that what is sought—what is good—is balance.

Aristophanes is next. And his comic tale is the stunning centerpiece of *Symposium*.

As it was the physician's inclination to use the tools of his understanding—the sciences of medicine and meteorology, the mathematics behind harmony and polyphonic discordance—to describe love, it was the Sophist's inclination to spin out a perfectly good idea that he then drowned in a soup of excess. As the initially curious Phaedrus provided a simple yet well-thought-out basis from which to springboard the discussions, so Aristophanes invokes his trademark literary skill. He spins for the men a fable of imagination unsurpassed until Blake sought to carve out for himself an independent mythology.

Aristophanes posits that at first there were three sexes, not two: male, female and hermaphrodite. Man at that time was a great round creature whose spine and ribs forged the framework of a circular body from which extended four arms, four legs, one head with two faces looking front and back, four ears and two sets of genitals. Man was strong in this incarnation and he walked upright; but when he wanted to run, he did so by becoming a sort of fleshly tumbleweed, rolling over and over, propelling himself on his eight limbs.

Man was strong, and man was full of ambition. It was this ambition that got him (and us) into trouble. He attacked the gods. The gods met to decide what to do. They liked the tributes offered up to them by man too much to wipe him off the face of the earth. At last Zeus, King of the Gods, came up with the solution: He would weaken man by cutting him in half. This brought an added benefit to the gods because, instead of destroying man and leaving no one to worship them, it actually increased man's numbers and so doubled the worshipful crowd! And Zeus, caught up in the moment, said that if halving men didn't work, didn't stave off their arrogance, he'd slice them into quarters so that they might "hop about on one leg!" (190d).

It was done. And man's face was turned toward the cut to remind him of his punishment, and the navel was where the gods fastened man's skin about him.

What does this have to do with love?

Everything:

> "So when the original body was cut through, each half wanted the other, and hugged it. They threw their arms around each other desiring to grow together in the embrace, and died of starvation and general idleness because they would not do anything apart from each other."
> (191B)

This continued, and Zeus took pity on them and so moved their genitals to the front so that they might make love with each other and bring forth children, whereas previously they had brought forth children within the ground, "like the cicadas" (191c), and their love was sufficiently self-contained in a round eight-limbed physical whole—two hearts, one soul.

The union of the male with the female is designated for procreative purposes, while the union of male with male leads to satisfaction, and rest, and allows each man, afterward, to turn toward "the general business of life." Eloquently shifting his tale from the comic to the genuinely romantic, Aristophanes says:

"So you see how ancient is the mutual love implanted in mankind, bringing together the parts of the original body, and trying to make one out of two, and to heal the natural structure of man."   (191B–D)

". . . to heal the natural structure of man." Beautiful, and true.

Aristophanes then spends some time discussing the nature of the divisions of the three original sexes, and what their result was in man as he has come to be.

Those who were of the sex that held both man and woman in them (hermaphrodites) became men who are fond of women, "and adulterers generally come of that sex, and all women who are mad for men, and adulteresses" (191d). Women who came from the sex that had only the female about it now manifest themselves in two-legged form as lesbians and, Aristophanes tells us—perhaps having burst a blood vessel in his head from all his earlier sneezing, for this makes no sense—"strumpetesses" (191e).

As for men who were of the sex that was all man, they now pursue the love of other men, even as boys, and Aristophanes equates this love with the best of men, and the bravest. He argues that proof of this is found in the life these lads go on to lead as adults, invariably becoming political leaders and pillars of the community. And when at last they find their other half, whether there be a generation in age between them or not, they recognize it and are lovers from that point on, for always.

In Aristophanes' myth, Gilgamesh and Enkidu, David and Jonathan, you and your lover or the lover out there for whom you search and who searches for you, are all incomplete, literally and physically, and our embrace is the desire to be one again, to press as close to that instinctive reality as we possibly can.

Next is Agathon, our host and recent prizewinner. He starts by positing Love as the youngest, not the oldest, of the gods, as some of the others have argued. He goes on to Love's embodiment of justice, temperance and courage before turning to the last quality he attributes to Love, wisdom:

> "Love is so wise a poet that he can make another the same; at least, everyone becomes a poet whom love touches, even one who before that, had 'no music in his soul.' This we may fittingly use as a proof that Love is a good poet or active maker in practically all the creations of the fine arts." (196E)

Admittedly, Agathon is working here to secure the province of Love in his field, as Eryximachos did before him, using the sciences. Agathon's speech, while lacking the sophistry of Pausanias' and yet surpassing in honest eloquence the simplicity of Phaedrus', comes as something of an anticlimactic exercise after the fabulous yarn spun out by Aristophanes. And it is with Agathon's speech that Socrates begins to pick apart the words of the others, en route to his own conclusion, which he wraps in the presentation of memory: a speech made to Socrates on the topic by Diotima, a prophetess.

Diotima's speech provides, in a sense, a synthesis of all the other speeches of the symposium, redirected toward a logic and a cohesion that are not without the gloss of romance. Love is a "helper for human nature" (212b), directing it toward the Beautiful, something wholly incomprehensible to man, limited as he is by the physical world.

On the heels of this eloquence Alcibiades, Socrates' lover, stumbles in, drunk off his ass. At first he's angered to find Socrates sitting next to Agathon, the handsomest man at the gathering, instead of someone like Aristophanes, whose coveted talent is his comedy and not his looks. But as it is with drunks, Alcibiades' anger passes quickly. He wreaths Socrates' head in ribbons, plops himself down beside his lover, orders more drinks—a half gallon of wine for himself alone—and reveals that Socrates, no matter how much the old man drinks, never gets drunk.

The men entreat a speech from Alcibiades on love, as everyone, including Socrates, has just given. Alcibiades protests, first because he is too thick with wine to make a speech before sober men; then, railing at them, he says (with all apparent good humor):

> "And at the same time, bless you my dear! do you really believe anything of what Socrates has just said? Don't you know that the truth is exactly the opposite of what he stated? For if *I* praise anybody in his presence, god or man other than himself, this man will not keep his two hands off *me*."
>
> "Won't you shut up?" said Socrates. (214D)

Alcibiades doesn't, instead maneuvering himself into a speech that ostensibly praises Socrates but in actuality displays Socrates in action as a lover, enabling a comparison between Socrates' words—and those of the others, earlier—and deeds. The evidence? His affair with Alcibiades.

So, what is the result? Alcibiades describes Socrates as a kind of Pied Piper, his philosopher's words the music he uses to attract those he desires. And yet, despite his early recognition of Socrates the seducer, Alcibiades found himself tricked at the outset of their relationship into playing the lover (active) while Socrates played the beloved (passive)—though the reverse was true. Socrates engenders such role-playing in those he desires, for he loves on his terms, and it is up to the beloved to submit to them if he wants Socrates as a lover.

At their earliest meeting, Alcibiades invited Socrates to dinner. Socrates accepted, but then shamed his host by leaving immediately thereafter. Alcibiades tried again, and this time Socrates did stay the night and they did talk. Alcibiades made his move, which Socrates dodged, yet the boy climbed into bed with the man and they slept together without having sex. (At the time, Socrates was roughly thirty; Alcibiades, in his late teens.)

Despite recognizing and admiring Socrates' philosophical discipline, Alcibiades still felt himself distanced from the man he respected so much. Soon, however, he and Socrates were thrown together as part of a military campaign, and again, the boy had a chance to observe the man—his stamina, his bravery, his semicomic capacity for stunningly focused philosophical reverie (as earlier evidenced by Socrates' sojourn on the neighbor's porch). Later, Socrates and Alcibiades returned to Athens and to a normal life that included, between them, a kind of chaste lovers' intimacy. In Athens, Alcibiades has seen other, fresher acolytes suffer fates similar to his, for Socrates is a man who, like St. Paul after him, lauds not physical love but spiritual love, love of the mind and heart rather than of the groin.

And this is Platonic love.

And it is nonexclusive.

FIVE QUESTIONS

1. Having read *Symposium,* which of the offered speeches strikes at your heart most strongly, and describes the understanding of love you, presently, want to hold? If you could, would you extend that perception universally? Why or why not, and what would be the results?

2. Given Aristophanes' story, what is to be said of bisexuals? Is it possible to fit them into the myth without creating another gender from the outset? How? And what is the end result of such an exercise upon the fable and, by extension, its world? Is Aristophanes' yarn meant to be taken seriously, or is it all a big joke?

3. What is to be made of Platonic love? Is love without sex satisfactory (Socrates apparently found it so) or hollow (as Alcibia-

des perhaps found it, though able to admire the Platonic lover's discipline), and why? Is Socrates' view of love parallel or in conflict with his manner of teaching? How?

4. Is there virtue—Beauty—in casual sex, and if so, what is it?

5. What is wrong with pedophilia and/or ephebophilia? What is right with it? Is the act itself right or wrong, or is that judgment overcast by the perspective of the greater society? If it is all in the latter, what meaning does that leave terms like "healthy" and "unhealthy"?

Xenophon

Symposium

TRANSLATED BY HUGH TREDENNICK
AND ROBIN WATERFIELD

"That you, Callias, are in love with Autolycus is known to the whole of our city and, I expect, to a good many foreigners too, the reason being that you are both sons of famous fathers, and distinguished men yourselves. I have always admired your nature, but now I admire it much more, because I see that the person you love is not pampered by luxury or enervated by effeminacy, but displays to the eyes of all his strength, endurance, courage and self-discipline. To be attracted by these qualities is evidence of the lover's own character."

—SOCRATES, SPEAKING IN
XENOPHON'S *SYMPOSIUM*

It is thought that Xenophon lived from 435 to 354 B.C.E. He was a soldier and a disciple of Socrates. He was the son of an Athenian knight, and after years of his own military exercises—which, for the most part, were to reward him well—he settled with his wife and two sons at an estate in Scillus, near Olympia, in 391 B.C.E. The estate was a gift to him from the Spartans: Xenophon and his soldiers had, years before, joined the Spartan army, an act that secured Xenophon's banishment from Athens.

Xenophon lived at his estate for the next twenty years, and it is there that he wrote his books. Most notable of these would prove to be *Anabasis,* the chronicle of his expedition in Persia to secure the overthrow of the king by his younger brother. (The attempt failed.)

Ultimately, Xenophon's sentence of banishment was lifted when the Athenians joined with the Spartans in a war against Thebes. After being forced to leave his estate as a result of a military overthrow in the region, Xenophon would settle—and live out his remaining years—in Corinth.

Compared with the *Symposium* of Plato, Xenophon's *Symposium* is a work of less flash but of greater, focused purpose: to refine and establish the superiority of Platonic love in relations between lovers and their beloveds. It is perhaps more comic than Plato's effort. Socrates, when asked what his life's calling is, replies it is that of "a pimp," and he later accuses a dinner partner of being inspired by his "beautiful body," a self-deprecating if good-naturedly sarcastic comment if ever there was one: Socrates was not known for his physical attractiveness.

Xenophon's symposium differs from Plato's not only in its substantially redirected focus but in a number of other ways as well. First, it describes a wholly different evening. Also, instead of filtering his story through a veil of memory as a thrice-told tale, Xenophon claims to recount first-hand a dinner he attended with Socrates, as well as the conversation that ensued. However, given that the event is set in 422 B.C.E., when Xenophon was eight years old at best, this claim seems rather fictive.

No less a source than Edmund Spenser, author of the bafflingly immense yet half-completed poetical exercise *The Faerie Queene,* noted that Xenophon was read far more widely than Plato by Renaissance English scholars. This entrenches Xenophon's sphere of influence, however overshadowed he might be today by Plato. When the two *Symposium*s are read side by side, Plato's is clearly superior: more lively, more intellectually combative. Yet Xenophon's work is an important footnote, if for no other reason than it shows the changing diversity of attitudes toward love between males in Grecian thought at the time. (In Xenophon's *Symposium,* the argument is strenuously made—and not refuted—that Achilles and Phaedrus' were merely friends: worlds apart from Phaedrus' opening stance in Plato's effort.)

Xenophon's *Symposium,* for its influence upon Renaissance writers and for the compelling depth it lends our understanding of the sexual politics of ancient Greece, as well as for the richer resonance it gives to Plato's dialogue, preserves its place on our bookshelves even as it begs us to consider where the line is drawn between homosexuality and homoaffectionalism, and whether one is superior to the other or simply more socially feasible.

Aristotle

Ethics

TRANSLATED BY HIPPOCRATES G. APOSTLE

Young men are also amorous, for the greater part of amorous friendship occurs by passion and for the sake of pleasure; and it is in view of this that they become friendly and soon end that friendship, and often do these the same day. But they do wish to spend their days and live together, for what friendship means to them is living in this manner.

—BOOK Θ, SECTION 3, 1156B

What is the purpose of life? How do we live well?

Some would boil these questions down to biology, saying the purpose of life is reproduction, evolution, continuing the gene stock, and that we live well if we have plenty of food, shelter and fuckables. But where are queers in that equation?

Seeking only a biological answer equates living well with mere satisfaction, or primitive happiness, and thereby opens a floodgate of difficulty. For the ability to experience pleasure, rather than serving endlessly as a mindless slave to nature's whim, complicates the search for the definition of the good life, rendering the biologist's answer incomplete. For man, life is more than good food, good housing and good sex. Something has to string all these together, to sustain them, and allow us to feel permanently that satisfaction, that happiness, of which these things form a part.

Henri Bergson put forth a remarkable, wondrous theory in *Creative Evolution:* as there is a physical evolution in life, so there is a spiritual evolution, and neither one is completely possible without the other. In his *Letters on the Aesthetic Education of Man,* Friedrich von Schiller, Goethe's pal, suggested that the purpose of Man is union with Beauty through Art. Both these theories—and others— find their roots in Aristotle's *Ethics,* a wrestling for the basic pur- pose of man's life.

The sum of the parts is the whole.

Aristotle begins his argument in search of a definition of happiness and what is good, tackling the problematic nature of the universal good that Plato proposed. From there, he moves on to a consider- ation of how a man acts and of the resulting discernment of virtue. This is followed by a discussion of actions and their consequences, as well as an examination of the resulting vices or virtues in practi- cal society. He addresses justice and injustice, and posits that ethical virtues are ethical habits, launching into a listing of these and the ways in which they may be attained, before settling into a contem- plation of man's character. This segues readily into Aristotle's ex- amination of friendship, which concerns us most, and wraps up with a review of *Ethics.* The review serves as a prologue, in essence, to a reading of Aristotle's *Politics,* a text in search of the good in laws, of the institution and preservation of the rightly virtuous state.

BOOK θ

> After what has just been said, a discussion of friendship
> would follow, for friendship is a virtue or something with
> virtue, and besides, it is most necessary to life; for no one
> would choose to live without friends, though he were to
> have all the other goods.   (SECTION 1, 1155A)

In *Ethics,* Aristotle says that there are three reasons for friendship:
pleasure, such as the friendship of young men, living for today with
little thought of tomorrow; compatibility, which hinges upon recognition by one man in another of a similar degree of virtue; and
utility, wherein the friendship serves some useful purpose for each
party, separate from the concerns of virtue and momentary satisfaction.

Of these, Aristotle clearly prefers the friendship of compatibility. He argues that friendships of utility and of pleasure are the
friendships that men who are truly virtuous—truly capable of understanding the primary pleasure and utility of shared virtue—
spurn, leaving less virtuous men to pursue them in their wanton
way. While this may smack of elitism, it is important to remember
that what makes a man bad or good for the purposes of this discussion is not his class or education but his ability to be virtuous, an
ideally innate quality beyond money's grasp.

Aristotle goes on to state the reasons why young men are more
willing to befriend someone new than someone old: Youth, as a
rule, tends toward flexibility in understanding. He adds that perfect
friendship, like love, is the product of focused intimacy and concern. When it's diluted by numbers, as with love, it loses its value.
Really, this is nothing more than the common twentieth-century
observation that we tend to have many acquaintances but few
friends—only that Aristotle holds this up as a blessing, where we
often hear it as a complaint.

Aristotle's second choice is for the friendship of pleasure, because it boasts a mutual generosity, as opposed to the stingy are-they-getting-more-from-this-than-I-am friendship of utility.

He also claims that all the friendships he is concerned with depend upon a successful realization of parity between the involved friends, and further claims that friendship between superiors and inferiors is difficult, if not impossible to achieve. Further, he states that "if the interval is great, as between a man and God, there can be no friendship at all" (9, 1159a). Perhaps this is because, for Aristotle, the best of friendships consummate in cohabitation. Men who are sympathetic to each other but do not live together are really nothing more than casual acquaintances; true friendship invests itself in a shared lifestyle. In truth, this promotes the idea of virtuous support: It is easier to maintain our faith, our morals, with rigor if we share them with someone who lives with us, whose life falls into our pattern of existence, and ours into theirs. By this definition, Aristotle establishes the friendship of men and women living together as husband and wife, though this is only one option. And he states that this intimacy, this lived-in friendship, is qualitatively separate in its sense of justice, "for what is just towards a friend does not appear to be the same as what is just towards a stranger, or a comrade, or a classmate" (14, 1162a).

BOOK I

But in the friendship of love, sometimes the lover complains that his excess of love is not returned in kind (though he may happen to have nothing lovable about him), while often the beloved complains that the lover promised everything before but now fails to fulfill his promises; and such things happen when the lover loves the beloved for the sake of pleasure while the beloved loves the lover for the sake of usefulness, but they do not both have what is expected of them. (SECTION 1, 1164A)

Aristotle clearly believes that a happy friendship is dependent on two things: equality, with regard to the parties involved and their investment in the friendship; and honesty, with regard to each person's expectations from and for the friendship.

Accordingly, should these expectations change, especially in the case of friendships based on utility or pleasure, the friendships may well end, and it is not necessarily wrong that they do so. Aristotle argues convincingly throughout that honesty is to be directed not solely toward your friend but also toward yourself. If a friendship changes and reveals itself always to have been based upon pleasure and never upon companionable empathy, it's important to assess whether you were self-deceived in this regard or whether your (former) friend willfully deceived you. The answer determines the outcome, and the emotions, of the changing friendship.

Yet friendship is not something to be easily walked away from. While Aristotle admits that one should never seek out the friendship of men who are lacking in virtue or, more pointedly, who are evil, he also cautions against rash actions, saying that the friendship should be ended "only when one's friend is incurable in his evil habits" (3, 165b). A friend's first obligation is to help another friend, and Aristotle makes the keen point that often we are quicker to help friends financially than we are to help them morally. And yet to help a friend get back on his feet ethically is far more important than simply loaning him cash to tide him over one crisis or another. It's all very reminiscent of the adage that if you buy a man a fish, he eats for a day, but if you teach a man to fish, he eats for a lifetime.

So yes, change is possible, and yes, friendships do end. But it shouldn't be an easy, or immediate, sundering.

Aristotle argues that in cases where the change is one of an increase in sensibility (he cites boyhood friendships as the best example of this scenario), rather than simply ignoring a former friend, "[p]erhaps he should keep remembrance of the earlier intimacy; and just as we think that we should favor our friends rather than strangers, so we should show some regard for those because of our earlier friendship, if the friendship did not end because of excessive evil habits" (3, 1165b).

For Aristotle, true friendship would also serve to enhance man's capacity for being good, in that it is impossible for those who are bad to meet the demands of true friendship, even at its most basic. The concept of friendship, however, can vary from man to man. Some believe that friendship is based always upon what's in the best interest of the person you're friends with; always wanting what is best for him, and so on. Others believe a good friend is one who follows their advice and lives life accordingly, a setup echoing that of parents and their children. Still, there are those who define friendship simply as companionability, those you hang out with, while to others, only those they can turn to in times of trouble are truly friends.

Aristotle believes that even bad men know right from wrong and that their hateful actions, at some level, tear them apart. Bad people are never completely happy; once the moment of wrong-doing that brings pleasure has passed, they are left only with the knowledge that they've done wrong. This is why satiety is well nigh impossible for criminals, as the act itself becomes a sort of addiction, pleasurable only for the moment. Is it an unfair extension to claim that Aristotle is arguing that man is basically good at heart? That man's happiness is innately drawn toward what is good? When it comes to friendship, certainly, Aristotle believes that it is possible only between men who are good, saying, "[W]e should make every effort to avoid evil habits and try to be *good*, for it is in this way that a man can be friendly to himself and become a friend to another man" (4, 1166b).

Aristotle then wends his way through the nature of friendship with oneself and with others. He discusses compatibility and the need to love oneself, which one does if one is virtuous and loves in oneself and in others that which is virtuous. He then reminds us that man is a social animal, that even if we are given all the worldly goods we crave, we still need the companionship of a few good fellows in happy times and in sad, albeit for different reasons.[2]

Aristotle ends his discussion of friendship with a consideration of community, an extension of his previous argument that friends should live together. And here, as with the definitions of friendship discussed above, friends will be drawn to live together for different reasons, some simply because their social circles and habits are compatible. When evil people form friendships with one another, the result itself is invariably greater evil. Yet "[t]he friendship of *good* men, on the other hand, is *good*, and it grows as their companionship continues; and they seem to become even better men by acting together and correcting each other, for each models himself on what he approves of the other. Whence the saying, 'Good men from good things learn'" (12, 1172a).

So: What is the purpose of life? How do we live well?

The purpose of life is to be virtuous, to be *good*. We live well by surrounding ourselves with those things and people that bring us closer toward the goal of being *good*.

Aristotle's *Ethics* is not a self-help book, although perhaps it is the root from which all self-help books stem. It addresses the concerns of modern pop psychology (self-love, love of others, codependency, being *good* versus being bad, the nature of evil) but does so in a manner that, rather than being superficial and gimmicky, is shamelessly determined to result in a virtuous, *good* work.

[2] Inevitably, the case of America's most famous twentieth-century heterosexual hermit, Howard Hughes, comes to mind. Yet it can be said that Hughes, who had all the worldly goods he could desire yet turned his back on companionship, watching *Ice Station Zebra* over and over in his room, turned as well from virtuous friendship and hence entombed himself in solitude. He lost the capacity for any friendships other than those of utility and pleasure, and as he had no immediate use for them, he did without. An aberration, certainly, but wholly within Aristotle's considerations.

While *Ethics* can be read from a distance, it's better to read it unguardedly, to find yourself shifting with discomfort as you explore your community, your friendships, yourself in the hard light of Aristotle's resolve that everything should tend toward the *good*.

And you know what? He's right.

Ethics is also a comforting text in troubled times, for it reminds us that not all friendships are meant to last; those whose foundation is utility or pleasure probably won't, unless they shift to become friendships of moral compatibility. The book reminds us that there is evil in the world, but that we ourselves are not hopelessly given over to it. That, if nothing else, a *good* friendship may save us.

Aristotle's *Ethics* is, in sum, a moral primer from a time when being gay—loving someone of your own gender—was not considered an immoral act. Although at this writing politically conservative pundits are quick to spew forth loose, self-ingratiating names for what is moral behavior and what is not, *Ethics* stands as a reminder that their words are mere fashion, a thin crying down the wind; and, more happily, that true ethics—true virtue, morality and goodness—is a timeless concept that, no matter how hard a few men might try in their reactionary times to change it, is stubbornly immutable.

Cheers to the *good*, friend.

FIVE QUESTIONS

1. Aristotle rarely mentions religion in *Ethics*. Is this surprising to you or not? Why?

2. Think of those friendships that have had the biggest impact on your life. What type of friendships were they? How did they function in your life?

3. What kind of impact could the practical application of *Ethics* have on your life, or your community, or the worlds of religion and politics? Should it have such an impact? Are you willing to redirect

your life according to *Ethics,* or is that simply too hard? And if so, what does that say about yourself, and can you live with that?

4. Are you a *good* person? Why or why not?

5. Is this book wrong? Are scientists right? Is there no moral drive in man? Is it all instinct? Why? Why not?

Aristotle

Poetics

TRANSLATED BY HIPPOCRATES G. APOSTLE,
ELIZABETH A. DOBBS AND MORRIS PARSLOW

Since the poet is an imitator, like a painter or any other maker of likenesses, he must always imitate one of three [kinds of] objects: (a) things such as they were or are, or (b) objects such as they are said or thought [to be or have been], or (c) objects such as they should be.

—1460B

Accustomed as we are to thinking of Aristotle as one of the great minds in human history, all we have of that brilliant mind is the bright reflection from broken shards: notes taken by students, patched together into something resembling a whole. Aristotle never wrote down any of his thoughts, or if he did, those writings did not survive history. So we make do.

We do know, with relative certainty, that Aristotle lived from 384 to 322 B.C.E. He was the son of the court physician to the King of Macedon.

When Aristotle was just seventeen, he went to Plato's Academy and began his studies. He would eventually teach there, staying for twenty years until Plato's death, when Aristotle was twenty. When Plato's nephew took over, Aristotle left Athens. He would stay away until he was forty-nine.

He traveled. In Asia Minor he met his wife-to-be and they married. When he was forty-two, he began tutoring the son of Philip of Macedon. The lad was the grandson of the king Aristotle's own father had served, and would grow up to become Alexander the Great.

Upon his return to Athens, Aristotle founded the Lyceum. He taught there until he was in his early sixties, in 323, when Alexander the Great died and a strong anti-Macedonian sentiment ran rampant through Athenian society and politics. In light of his former connections, Aristotle found himself accused of impiety and fled the city, though he would live but a year in exile, dying at last in Chalcis, Euboea.

Aristotle's *Poetics* is not explicitly homoerotic. Its canonical qualities rest within its sphere of influence: *Poetics* remains the basis for every later work on the craft of writing. So complete was Aristotle's breadth of inquiry that it is impossible to find a practical school of thought which it does not anticipate, and yet the end result, instead of seeming jumbled, is orderly. *Poetics* is the wellspring, the core text for all literary theory. However, its importance derives from its still-vivid real-world potential: its exercises in application. (E. M. Forster's book on writing, *Aspects of the Novel*, is practically a crib of *Poetics*. This is testament to the latter's inexorable primacy and influence. For although Forster hoped his book would prove its counterpoint, *Aspects of the Novel*, alas, succeeded only in being complementary.)

A spin through the summary provided in the Apostle, Dobbs and Parslow edition quickly bears this out: Aristotle terms the realization of literary capability a "productive science," and he holds the production of art up to the same rigorous standards he applied to physics, providing a clean, incisive examination of the body of creative literature. And these standards are applicable to today's literary output—or should be:

> The best of all recognitions is that which arises from the events themselves, when the striking event comes through probabilities . . . Such recognitions are the only ones that occur without the contrived use of signs or amulets. The next best are recognitions which arise from inference. (1455A)

plus:

> The poet should elaborate the diction of his poem in the parts in which there is no action but not in those which manifest character or *thought,* for highly brilliant diction conceals both character and *thought.*   (1460B)

add up to: Don't tell, show. And:

> Now it is possible that what arouses fear and pity come from the spectacle, but it is also possible that these feelings come from the very structure of the events; and indeed this is a better imitation and a mark of a better poet. For the plot should be so constructed as to make the one hearing the events shudder and feel pity as a result of what happens, even without seeing the tragedy performed. (1453B)

simply says: Substance over style.

As Aristotle examines tragedy, so, too, comedy and rhetoric. *Poetics,* itself the cobbled together notes from a creative writing workshop millennia ago, remains the Rosetta stone for literary output of any cultural, moral or entertainment value whatsoever. It is also intriguing in that its proposition—that emotions must be vented through literature—runs distinctly counter to Plato's view that literature evoking an emotional response was too dangerous to be allowed, unless, of course, that emotional response served the country's patriotic good.

Catullus

Poems

TRANSLATED BY JAMES MICHIE

Just now I saw a young lad fucking his girl,
So I arose, and, by the grace of Venus,
Transfixed him then and there with my own stiff prick!

—POEM 56

Born in 84 B.C.E. and living for only thirty years, Catullus wrote some of the most spirited poetry of his time, pungent love poems and vicious political attacks among them.

The son of a wealthy and well-connected family, he came from Verona. He started writing poetry in 68 B.C.E. In his twenty-second year he settled in Rome, but maintained villas both in Tibur and Sirnio.

It was in Rome that he would meet "Lesbia," a married woman who was indisputably the love of his life. He composed poems to her until their falling out in 57 B.C.E., at which time his heartbreak compelled him to flee Rome and he traveled with the governor to the province of Bithynia. (Catullus' brother had died near Troy, and the poet probably visited his tomb during this journey.)

Catullus had hoped to enrich himself in Bithynia, but such was not to be the case. He returned to Rome, only to hurl himself into the arena of politics, armed with wicked, often brilliantly derisive poetic invective, much of it aimed at his father's friend, Julius Caesar.

Still, for gay and lesbian readers, Catullus' unabashed erotic and emotional ardor is of primary importance. The love he holds for Lesbia is also extended to certain lads—albeit in a slightly watered-down form—especially a boy named Juventius, who, in Poem 48 in particular, Catullus dreams of kissing tenderly, even the boy's "honeyed eyes."

Yet, as tender as he could be, he did not save all his bile for political opponents. He unleashed it on those he found an embarrassment to Rome, or perhaps, as in Poem 33 when he excoriates Vibennius and his "pansy son," the dishonest, the pretentious, the undesirable.

There's something wildly refreshing in the ease with which Catullus spins forth his hate, echoing the manful bitchiness of Archilochus, which we seem to miss today. Modern sarcastic poetry rarely lifts itself above doggerel, and certainly even the idea of the poet-politician seems a hard one for us to grasp these days.

Catullus, like many of the Greeks and Romans, seeks to remind us that politics is in itself an art—but not an exclusive one. His poems show us that the passion of the human soul resides not only in the heart but in the body politic as well.

We know nothing of how Catullus died. His poetry was thought lost during the Dark Ages, until unearthed in his native Verona in the fourteenth century.

Virgil

Eclogues

TRANSLATED BY BARBARA HUGHES FOWLER

The shepherd Corydon was burning for lovely Alexis,
who was his master's love. There was no hope for him.
—ECLOGUE II, LINES 1–2

With Publius his given name, Vergilius his family name and Maro
the name of his clan, Virgil was born in 70 B.C.E. in Andes, by
Mantua in Cisalpine Gaul. His father owned a small piece of property there. Virgil studied at Cremona and Milan, leaving for Rome
in 54 B.C.E. to study philosophy and rhetoric. Men from this area
did not acquire Roman citizenship until 49 B.C.E., when Julius Caesar extended that opportunity to the region.

In 41 B.C.E., after Virgil had finished his education and settled
into the life of a pastoral bachelor, victorious Roman lieutenant
governors settled disbanded soldiers on confiscated lands throughout Italy. Virgil's farm and that of his father were seized. On Governor Asinius Pollio's advice, and prepared with special recommen-
dations to the emperor Augustus, Virgil went to Rome to plead for
the restoration of the family land. Although his plea was not fully
successful, Virgil managed to have his father's farm restored and

was handsomely compensated for the land he lost. The gratitude of Eclogue I suggests this sort of compromise.

Pollio was Virgil's earliest patron, and it was in his care that the poet would write his *Eclogues*. Pollio owned a slave named Alexander, and the boy would prove to be Virgil's artistic passion, serving as the model for Alexis in Eclogue II.

Virgil published his *Eclogues* in 37 B.C.E., and they were well received. He was awarded a sort of government grant as court poet to the Roman statesman Maecenas. Virgil, now wealthy, established additional homes for himself: a villa in Naples and a country house near Nola. Perhaps the country house, coupled with boyhood memories, inspired him: Seven years after *Eclogues* was published, Virgil's *Georgics,* or *Art of Husbandry,* appeared, in four books. These poems, dealing with the work of the field and the stable, the beekeeper and the winemaker, were also well received, so much so that they confirmed Virgil's position as the foremost poet of his time.

Virgil's poetry soars, but on earth the man was a country bumpkin for most of his life: shy, often awkward, and a virtual recluse who would hide in the nearest available house whenever he was recognized in public. He was in ill health, though it is said he was tall and dark and, one would think, not unattractive. It is also said he had a fine reading voice. In an appendix to the *Commentary* of Donatus, a fourth-century critic, he is described as "inclined to passions for boys," which is striking only because it positions him as having a set gender preference when fluidity of desire was the Roman cultural norm—as reflected in *Eclogues*. Virgil never married, and what romantic apocrypha there is about him is generally homosexual in nature.

Although five of the *Eclogues* feature same-gender desire as an unabashed part of their storytelling, it is Eclogue II, the "Corydon"

Eclogue, that has proved to be the most famous homoerotic or homoaffectional poem in Latin writing—even though Virgil himself would try to supplant the work with portions of *The Aeneid*.

Yet it is the "Corydon" Eclogue that challenged Christopher Marlowe, among others, and nestled deep in the heart of the gay imagination, to be critically resurrected at the dawn of the twentieth century by André Gide with his publication of four dialogues in defense of homosexuality, entitled *Corydon*.

Why? What is so appealing about Corydon?

Simply this: He is a lover, wonderfully human, wonderfully flawed.

For example, in lines 26 through 28, when Corydon tries to reassure himself that he is, at least, better looking than some, we find well illustrated the lover's combination of insecurity and bravado at the moment of loving. It is this subtle, resonant richness that positions Corydon's desire in our hearts, even as his gentle longing to homestead with his partner secures our sympathetic affections. All he wants, after all (and as he says so clearly in lines 29–31), is for Alexis to live with him in a plain hut, and hunt with him, and herd his goats.

Yet Alexis spurns Corydon's advances, his high-strung proffering of love, leading to self-deprecation in line 57—"Corydon, you're a boor"—and giving vent to a helpless comparison of his devotion to the boy to a devotion forced by nature. He compares himself to the lioness who chases after the wolf, who in turn has hunted the baby goat, which has chewed raw the clover. All of them are driven, mindlessly almost, by desire, by instinct.

This leads, though, to a moment of helplessness. It is a surrender in which lies hope, the nascent recognition that work occupies the romantically tormented mind and soothes it. It is also the admission that there are other fish in the sea besides Alexis, that eventually another will give rise to Corydon's passion.

The further recognition that homoaffectionalism and homosexuality are entwined, that there is a desire not simply to build a friendship but to build a life between fellows, and the cruel historical turn that would make unrequited love the currency of passion in the homosexual realm for centuries after Virgil, combine to deepen Corydon's ability to serve, in his outspoken longing and eventual resignation, as the model for same-sex affection and desire—and truth in love.

Virgil

The Aeneid

TRANSLATED BY JOHN DRYDEN

Nigh where the foes their utmost guards advance,
To watch the gate was warlike Nisus' chance.
His father Hyrtacus of noble blood;
His mother was a huntress of the wood,
And sent him to the wars. Well could he bear
His lance in fight, and dart the flying spear,
But better skill'd unerring shafts to send.
Beside him stood Euryalus, his friend:
Euryalus, than whom the Trojan host
No fairer face, or sweeter air, could boast—
Scarce had the down to shade his cheeks begun.
One was their care, and their delight was one:
One common hazard in the war they shar'd,
And now were both by choice upon the guard.

—BOOK IX

Nicknamed "the Virgin" for his modesty and lack of aggressiveness, at the end of his life Virgil would produce a poetic work whose muscularity could find rivals only in its predecessors: Homer's *The Iliad* and *The Odyssey*.

Augustus commissioned *The Aeneid* following Virgil's success with his *Georgics*. Greece had *The Iliad;* Rome needed a mythological spine as well. It fell to Virgil to provide it.

Virgil worked for a decade on *The Aeneid* and then hoped to travel to the Near East to see the sites of his poem. He fell ill in Greece, however, and had to turn back, barely reaching Italian soil before dying. (He is buried in Naples, on the road to Pozzoli, and for hundreds of years after his death, the tomb was considered a sacred place.)

He had planned three more years of work on *The Aeneid*. When he realized that death would finish him before he finished it, he ordered the poem burned. Augustus ignored Virgil's dying request, however, and published the poem two years after Virgil's demise. There are, accordingly, places where the work seems a tad rough, where the virile flow of words we have enjoyed thus far weakens. Yet these places are few and far between, and as a whole *The Aeneid* remains a solidly literary work of majesty, power and propriety—as well as a stunning invention of a national psyche.

The Aeneid has been described as part *Odyssey,* part *Iliad,* and this is superficially apt: The first half of the poem concerns the voyages of the valiant Aeneas and his crew in their flight from Troy in hopes of finding a new home; the second half deals with the wars they must wage to establish themselves in their new, god-decreed land. Yet in a sense, this violence merely echoes the violence at the end of *The Odyssey,* where, in order to secure his home, a man must throw out all those who seek to disturb his hoped-for peace. *The Aeneid,* then, is more aptly described as the Trojan *Odyssey,* the flip side of Homer's work.

Aeneas is part god himself, the son of Aphrodite. As such, he is a stunner to behold: strapping, yellow-haired, a *Colt* stud. But this should come as no surprise, for the Greeks (and so the Romans) argued that true virtue made itself known externally as well—and thus Aeneas, the most virtuous of Trojans, could only be the most beautiful of men. When our story opens, he is at sea, together with men who have fought beside him in the Trojan War, which ended when they saw their city fall to the crafty Greeks' ruse of a vast wooden horse, its secret belly filled with soldiers. This story—the tale of Troy's fall—is recounted with explicit horror in Book II, after Aeneas and his crew have landed in Carthage.

Within *The Aeneid* are nestled several other tales that have inspired fine homoerotic moments in art and literature. Before Troy falls, there are signs of ominous portent, perhaps none more so than when Laocoön steps up to serve as priest to the sea god Neptune. After he sacrifices a bull, two serpents stream from the sea, moving side by side. They have fire-bright crests, and the sea seems to hiss where they pass, boiling in the monsters' wake. Their lashing tails are speckled, and slowly, surely, they move onto the land.

Their tongues flick, their eyes are red as blood, their very spit sizzles in their mouths as the crowd that has gathered for the sacrifice flees in horror. The serpents:

And to Laocoon and his children make;
And first around the tender boys they wind,
Then with their sharpen'd fangs their limbs and bodies
    grind.

The wretched father, running to their aid
With pious haste, but vain, they next invade;
Twice round his waist their winding volumes roll'd;
And twice about his gasping throat they fold.   (BOOK II)[3]

---

[3] A stunning ancient marble statue of this moment offers something for everyone in the straining beefy torso of Laocoön and the willowy, lithe bodies of his boys struggling against the serpents' press.

They crush him dead against the bodies of his sons, then slither away up the hill to the temple of Athena. There they coil, protected by the goddess's shield and spear.

This kind of explicit horror is brought home time and again in *The Aeneid*, always startling, gripping in its brutality—even to the modern reader. We have grown jaded to the violence of cop shows on TV, it's true, but the violence of the mythic imagination is shockingly new to us, especially when deployed as vividly, as skillfully, as Virgil manages in his masterwork.

Violence isn't spared in the sacking of Troy either, though none of it is gratuitous. King Priam falls, slipping in a pool of his son's blood on an altar step, and is slaughtered. The heroes of *The Iliad* and *The Odyssey* are invoked or make appearances—Ulysses, most notably—but here they are villains, intent on the slaughter of families in their homes, the destruction of a civilization.

Aeneas, however, escapes with his father and son, and makes for the open sea with several shiploads of Trojans.

The world of the supernatural is known to Aeneas and his followers; he is beset by anguished ghosts and pleads with gods and goddesses for care and safekeeping. Many of the gods, spurred on by Aeneas' mother, take up his cause, but Juno remains here as big a "bitch" as she was in Homer's works, the perpetual instigator.

Emotions run high in *The Aeneid;* it is in all respects as passionate a work as either of Homer's epics, and on as grand a scale. The Queen of Carthage, Dido, falls for Aeneas, and when he slips away from her, she takes her own life, viciously stabbing herself in the chest, so that the life whistles out of her.

But Aeneas sees the queen again when he journeys into the underworld in search of his father's ghost. He spies her in the Fields of Mourning, so called "[s]ince here are those whom pitiless love consumed / With cruel wasting, hidden on paths apart / By myrtle

woodland growing overhead. / In death itself, pain will not let them
be"[4]   (Book VI).

It is important to note that while Aeneas as a personage resonates with all the flesh-and-blood poignancy Virgil managed to
create in Corydon, his is emphatically a story not of love but of
duty and obedience: to the will of the gods and the demands of
fate—in this case, the responsibility of a father to his country-to-be.
For it cannot be forgotten that Aeneas is the father of Rome and
that the Trojans, with their newfound Italian allies, will provide the
mythic underpinning for the glory of the Roman people. Establishing the heroic root of Rome is the purpose of Virgil's entire effort,
his creative engine, his ultimate drive:

> Arms, and the man I sing, who, forc'd by fate,
> And haughty Juno's unrelenting hate,
> Expell'd and exil'd, left the Trojan shore.
> Long labors, both by sea and land, he bore,
> And in the doubtful war, before he won
> The Latian realm, and built the destin'd town;
> His banish'd gods restor'd to rites divine,
> And settled sure succession in his line,
> From whence the race of Alban fathers come,
> And the long glories of majestic Rome.
>
> (BOOK I)

Virtually every verse of *The Aeneid* is slickened with a veneer of
homoeroticism, much of it in the description of rough-and-tumble
soldiers. Yet explicit instances erupt, none more so than in the fine
moments and key plot point spun out to be shared by the lovers
Nisus and Euryalus.

Virgil draws our attention to the pair in Book V when he has
the runners line up for a race:

---

[4] This excerpt is from the translation by Robert Fitzgerald.

First Nisus, with Euryalus, appears;
Euryalus a boy of blooming years,
With sprightly grace and equal beauty crown'd;
Nisus, for friendship to the youth renown'd.
(BOOK V)

But the race does not go smoothly. Nisus stumbles, slipping in blood spilled during the slaughter of the animals for sacrifice. Even in his loss, however, he finds the will to help his lover and reaches out to trip another runner, enabling Euryalus to win first place.

It is a deceptively lighthearted harbinger.

It has been argued that Nisus and Euryalus are willful creations of Virgil, an attempt to justify homosexuality between peers at a time when the only men to be used by other men for sex were slaves— and also an attempt to graft Achilles and Patroclus into the Roman mythos.

There has been no quibbling, however, over these comrades' relationship. No opportunity for a Xenophon to come along and argue, "But they were only friends!"

Virgil took pains to ensure that such an argument would prove impossible to make. Clearly, in passages such as the one that opened this chapter and others in *The Aeneid,* not only are Nisus and Euryalus lovers, they are acknowledged as such by their fellow warriors, and their love is respected, honored, even admired for the loyalty it inspires between the two.

Brothers could not be more closely bound.

Perhaps here Robert Fitzgerald's assertion that Virgil may have been part Celt takes hold, for certainly this episode of *The Aeneid* is not a Roman story but an Irish one, in its willful, horrific avoidance of the happy ending in its slavish drive toward tragedy.

Nisus and Euryalus make a nighttime sortie to inflict slaughter on opposing troops while they sleep; the two are successful and pick

up booty in their retreat, including a brilliant helmet Euryalus
dons. The metal of the helmet catches the gleam of the moonlight
and alerts the till-then-unaware guards to the presence of the invad-
ing team. Nisus and Euryalus are set upon. In a dark wood the
lovers are separated. When Nisus realizes this, despite the danger to
himself he turns back to find Euryalus:

> He winds the wood, and, list'ning, hears the noise
> Of tramping coursers, and the riders' voice.
> The sound approach'd; and suddenly he view'd
> The foes inclosing, and his friend pursued,
> Forelaid and taken, while he strove in vain
> The shelter of the friendly shades to gain.
> What should he next attempt? what arms employ,
> What fruitless force, to free the captive boy?
> Or desperate should he rush and lose his life,
> With odds oppress'd, in such unequal strife?
> (BOOK IX)

Nisus contemplates his options and hurls his javelin at the soldiers
holding his beloved, killing one; then another of his javelins claims
a second. In the darkness Volcens, leader of the men holding Euryalus, cannot find the dark avenger and so turns back to Euryalus:

> "But thou," he cries,
> "Shalt pay for both," and at the pris'ner flies
> With his drawn sword. Then, struck with deep despair,
> That cruel sight the lover could not bear;
> But from his covert rush'd in open view,
> And sent his voice before him as he flew:
> "Me! me!" he cried—"turn all your swords alone
> On me—the fact confess'd, the fault my own.
> He neither could nor durst, the guiltless youth:
> Ye moon and stars, bear witness to the truth!

His only crime (if friendship can offend)
Is too much love to his unhappy friend."
Too late he speaks: the sword, which fury guides,
Driv'n with full force, had pierc'd his tender sides.
Down fell the beauteous youth: the yawning wound
Gush'd out a purple stream, and stain'd the ground.
His snowy neck reclines upon his breast,
Like a fair flow'r by the keen share oppress'd;
Like a white poppy sinking on the plain,
Whose heavy head is overcharg'd with rain.
(BOOK IX)

Virgil's ready poetic tenderness at the passing of Euryalus is palpable, and it moves us. This is a horrible, horrible murder, yet we read on. Desperate, blinded by rage and sorrow, Nisus plunges into the circle of men who have slaughtered his lover, exacting vengeance on Volcens before Nisus, too, is felled:

Dying, he slew; and, stagg'ring on the plain,
With swimming eyes he sought his lover slain;
Then quiet on his bleeding bosom fell,
Content, in death, to be reveng'd so well.
O happy friends! for, if my verse can give
Immortal life, your fame shall ever live,
Fix'd as the Capitol's foundation lies,
And spread, where'er the Roman eagle flies!
(BOOK IX)

Returning from the sacrifice of the lovers to the purpose of his epic—the securing of a heroic Roman mythos—Virgil clearly positions Euryalus and Nisus at the physical heart of the work, launching the action that will shape itself into the last battle the Trojans will fight before they know this land as their home. Moreover, Virgil positions them as the moral heart of the work: Nisus and

Euryalus are loyal men, beyond reproach in a devotion to duty equaled only by their devotion to each other.

Heroes indeed. And Virgil's Roman ideal.

Virgil's writings are among the few literary works to have a steady effect upon our civilization. In their longevity, they have taken bizarre twists and turns of influence, as their more fantastic elements were sometimes celebrated over the poet's skill.

In brief, soon after Virgil's death, his works became the textbooks of Western Europe. In the third century his poems ranked as sacred books and were used for purposes of divination. (Let's not forget: His tomb was worshipped upon as holy ground.) In the Dark Ages he was revered more as a magician than as a poet.

With the advent of the Renaissance and a return to learning, Virgil's poetic worth was at last fixed as his legacy. Later, Byron published his own translation of the story of Nisus and Euryalus while still in his teens, finding in their passion an emotional balm for his same-gender adolescent sexual burnings. And we have previously discussed the purposes to which the *Eclogues* have been put.

Virgil was perhaps the first queer writer who realized in his art the power of activism, and sought to shape the morals of his society into a world where not mere tolerance but acceptance was the heroic due to him and his kind.

FIVE QUESTIONS

1. Is there such a thing as a homosexual sensibility in art?

2. Are we less inclined to admire Nisus and Euryalus (even Aeneas, for that matter) as heroes for their keen willingness to take life? If so, is that a fair judgment on our part? Why or why not?

3. Should *The Aeneid* have been destroyed, as Virgil requested? Why or why not?

4. What is the purpose of art?

5. What equivalents to *The Aeneid* are there, if any, in your country's culture? If there are equivalents, how do they compare? If there are none, do you think your culture is richer or poorer for its lack of a mythological spine?

Ovid

The
Metamorphoses

TRANSLATED BY SIR SAMUEL GARTH

You when alive were Phoebus' darling boy;
In you he plac'd his Heav'n, and fix'd his joy:
Their God the Delphic priests consult in vain;
Eurotas now he loves, and Sparta's plain:
His hands the use of bow and harp forget,
And hold the dogs, or bear the corded net;
O'er hanging cliffs swift he pursues the game;
Each hour his pleasure, each augments his flame.

The mid-day sun now shone with equal light
Between the past, and the succeeding night;
They strip, then, smooth'd with suppling oyl, essay
To pitch the rounded quoit, their wonted play:
A well-pois'd disk first hasty Phoebus threw,
It cleft the air, and whistled as it flew;
It reach'd the mark, a most surprizing length;
Which spoke an equal share of art, and strength.

Scarce was it fall'n, when with too eager hand
Young Hyacinth ran to snatch it from the sand;
But the curst orb, which met a stony soil,
Flew in his face with violent recoil.
Both faint, both pale, and breathless now appear,
The boy with pain, the am'rous God with fear.
He ran, and rais'd him bleeding from the ground,
Chafes his cold limbs, and wipes the fatal wound:
Then herbs of noblest juice in vain applies;
The wound is mortal, and his skill defies.

—"ORPHEUS," BOOK X
(HYACINTHUS TRANSFORM'D INTO A FLOWER)

Born on March 20, 43 B.C.E., in the Abruzzi, the Roman poet Ovid was originally intended for a career in law. He had a brother, who died young; both boys were educated in Rome. Ovid showed great promise as a lawyer, but it had been his brother's passion; after his death, Ovid turned to his real love, poetry, and quickly established himself there as well. Ovid admits that he "only caught a glimpse of Vergil," though they shared the same patron in Maecenas.

All this was not enough, however, to keep him on the good side of the emperor Augustus, who banished Ovid to Tomi, on the Black Sea, in 7 C.E. The reasons behind this action remain unclear. Ovid died in exile at the age of seventy-four.

In addition to *The Metamorphoses,* Ovid is chiefly remembered for his *Loves* (short poems about his mistress) and the self-explanatory *Art of Love.* Among his incomplete and lost works is a how-to poem to help women apply makeup properly. Ovid, a master of metrical form, was perhaps the most voluminous of the Roman poets, but compared to Virgil's, his work is the lesser. This may be an unfair comparison, but it is nevertheless a true one.

There are similarities between *The Metamorphoses* and *The Aeneid*. Ovid, too, includes the voyages of Aeneas as a part of his work (in Books XIII and XIV) and shares a similar relationship with Homer: Heroes from *The Iliad* also appear within these pages (Books XI through XIV).

The Metamorphoses is an invaluable resource for any writer hoping to peer into the classical mindset, for it gathers together diverse legends and lore centering around the transformation of men, women, nymphs, etc., into something other than what they were before: Hyacinthus the boy into Hyacinth the flower is a fine example.

So we have an invaluable collection of myths, fantastic stories and fables. In many ways, the myths echo the ones set forth in the Tanakh, for there is a flood and a creation story (Book I), as also found in our Old Testament. Book X features another horrific echo of the Book of Genesis, when daughter Myrrha seduces her father, Cinyras, when he is drunk—much the same way Lot's daughters seduce him after the destruction of Sodom and his wife's *metamorphosis* into a pillar of salt. There are other crosscultural echoes, which may be nothing more than the desire of the Roman Ovid to place his culture at the root of all others: In one such instance, the virgin nymph Io—raped by Jove and then turned by him into a bovine creature (resulting in the hopefully intentionally funny line "this heifer was no cow," Book I, lines 621–647[5]) to protect his adultery from the jealous Juno's prying—ends up in *The Metamorphoses* as Isis, Egypt's celebrated goddess.

But all this is nothing new. Creation stories are standard in virtually all cultures—as are stories of a great flood—and this desire to establish everything good as everything Roman we have also seen before, though, here again, Virgil did it better, quite possibly because he had a more clearly defined sense of purpose.

---

[5] From the Mandelbaum translation.

Ovid left behind wife number three when he was sent into exile, so it needs to be said: Ovid preferred women to boys for sex. Basically, to say even that Ovid was bisexual would be fudging a bit. His *Art of Love* poems pretty much take heterosexual lust as their province, so while Ovid occasionally tosses us a bone, as in the allusion to "no boy to sing of" at the outset of *Loves,* we should remember that boys really weren't his thing. He said that it was because women get more pleasure from sex than boys, and although that point is certainly arguable, it is best to let it rest and simply acknowledge his preference without trying to twist it for our purposes. Perhaps, however, this is why his works fail to excite us as much as Virgil's: For the gay reader, they simply lack resonant sexual tension.

Yet Ovid did not shy away from homosexual themes in *The Metamorphoses,* and where they come into play, they are rendered faithfully: Apollo's love for Phoebus and Jove's yearning for Ganymede (in Book X), and of course, Narcissus' yearning for himself (Book III). (Cast against the redundant whisperings of the nymph Echo, who also loved Narcissus, this is a particularly poignant tale; though to be fair, the reader's sympathy is all with her. Narcissus is an annoying git, perhaps the first circuit queen in literary history. Long before he succumbs to his own reflection in the pool, we are ready to press his lips to those of his reflection and hold him under just a wee bit longer than necessary, ending our torment, along with his—and Echo's.)

There's also a tasty tidbit of a gender-walloping story in Book IV, of Salmacis and Hermaphroditus; and in Book IX, the story of Iphis and Ianthe is a lesbian nightmare. Perhaps the best gay evocation in *The Metamorphoses* belongs to Orpheus, who in Book X, having lost his wife to the realm of the dead as a result of his own foolish doubt, forswears other women but, apparently, not boys. But many of the earlier translations suppressed this aspect entirely. Garth's says only:

And now his yearly race the circling sun
Had thrice compleat thro' wat'ry Pisces run,
Since Orpheus fled the face of womankind,
And all soft union with the sex declin'd.
Whether his ill success this change had bred,
Or binding vows made to his former bed;
Whate'er the cause, in vain the nymphs contest,
With rival eyes to warm his frozen breast:
For ev'ry nymph with love his lays inspir'd,
But ev'ry nymph repuls'd, with grief retir'd.
(BOOK X)

Yet Mandelbaum's recent translation restores the truncated verse:

. . . Indeed, he was the one who taught
the Thracian men this practice: they bestow
their love on tender boys, and so enjoy
first fruits, the brief springtime, the flowers of youth.

Horace

The Complete
Odes and Epodes

TRANSLATED BY W. G. SHEPHERD

. . . she goes through the crowd of obstructive youths.
A heroic duel must decide which one of you two
shall have the prey . . .
—*ODES*, BOOK III, NO. 20, "NON VIDES QUANTO"

According to Suetonius, the Roman lyric poet Horace was born
Quintus Horatius Flaccus in Venusia on December 8, 65 B.C.E., and
died on November 27, 8 B.C.E. He left everything to his friend the
emperor Augustus and was buried at the far end of the Esquiline
Hill, close to the grave of his friend and patron Maecenas, who had
died but a few months earlier and who had claimed to love Horace
(again, according to Suetonius) "more than my own bowels."

Short, fat and balding, Horace nonetheless had a "thousand
passions for girls, thousand passions for boys." He lived mostly in
the country, where, Suetonius wrote, "he had his women placed in
a room lined with mirrors in such a way that wherever he looked he
could see a reflection of his love-making." Horace called Virgil "the

half of my soul" *(Odes,* I, 3), and his poetry indeed suffers little in comparison with that of his friend: it is redolent with a steamy, at times voyeuristic sexuality, making up for what it lacks in narrative tension or character development with a stylistic daring Virgil typically shied away from.

Horace was inspired by Archilochus in terms of style and content, and took from Sappho the ability to write intimately of personal matters—though, anticipating Shakespeare, he was not above slipping into character now and again and writing from an imagined perspective as well. In sum, his talent was wildly brilliant, brave and saucy. That, coupled with the brevity of much of his work, has made him a popular favorite throughout history, though his stylistic risks often wore down schoolboys when they had to translate him, as Byron did while at Harrow.

Born the son of a freed slave, Horace was educated in Rome instead of Venusia, a studied move on his father's part to avoid the local snobbery of the sons of the free-born. In Rome, Horace studied well, progressing to the Academy in Athens. There he met up with Brutus, fresh from his work as Caesar's assassin, and formed an alliance with him that found flower in war against Rome. Horace was twenty-one at the time, and his military flourish was short-lived: In their second battle he and Brutus were defeated. Brutus killed himself, and the campaign essentially came to an end.

Horace returned to Italy, but his treason had led to his farmland being confiscated; his esteemed father was dead. When he was twenty-six, amnesty was granted to those who had fought against Rome in Brutus' rebellion, and he became a treasury clerk, a position he would hold for some time.

Yet his situation soon improved. On Virgil's advice, Maecenas offered Horace a patronage, establishing him with his own farm and estate in the Sabine Hills. It was everything Horace wanted.

In 35 B.C.E. Horace published his first book of *Satires;* four years later would come the *Epodes.* In 23 B.C.E. he brought out three books of *Odes;* these were poorly received, and he abandoned lyric writing for six years, returning to the staid hexameters he'd deployed with such success in the *Satires*.

Still, he was well connected. He became Rome's poet laureate, holding the position until his death, and wrote the "Centennial Hymn" for Augustus, also publishing the *Epistles* and a last book of *Odes*.

Petronius

Satyrica

TRANSLATED BY R. BRACHT BRANHAM
AND DANIEL KINNEY

Well, use it or lose it, I thought, as I made an attempt to breach her brother's virtue, while he was watching his sister's antics through the keyhole. The well-schooled boy did not shun my advances but even there the gods were against me.

—''CIRCE''

The gayest thing about Petronius' book is Fellini's movie. That said, *Satyrica* is hailed by many as the first gay novel. For what it's worth, it's an unsuccessful one: What remains of the book are fragments, and while these piece together as a dazzlingly tempting sequence of sexual misadventures, they fail to coalesce into anything resembling the modern novel. (Archilochus' poetry suffers from time's fragmentation as well, true; but poetry, tightly woven as it is, survives such shattering better than prose.)

It would be a mistake, however, to dismiss *Satyrica* so glibly. While it may not succeed as well as we would like, it remains a work of enormous influence. Robert Louis Stevenson, D. H. Lawrence,

Lytton Strachey, Oscar Wilde and T. S. Eliot are but a few of the writers who have read it and found it remarkable.

And remarkable it is. For at a time when all other literary works (that we know of) took themselves very seriously, *Satyrica* took only one thing seriously: pleasure, and its pursuit.

This is probably a reflection of its author. Petronius was Arbiter of Elegance at the court of the young emperor Nero, but little is known about his life. Much is known about his death, however: When a rival, Tigellinus, turned Nero against Petronius, the former Arbiter was banished and ordered to commit suicide.

He complied—fabulously.

He slit his wrists, then chatted with friends about things superficial, setting down an account for Nero of the emperor's own debauches—partners male and female—and sealing it with his signet ring, which he proceeded to shatter so that it could never be used again. Before death he napped, and ate heartily, so that his body might retain a lifelike appearance afterward.

It was a send-up, of course, of graver suicides, such as Socrates', mocking them even as the voice of its star participant fell silent. One show only; a last extravagant theatrical dig at the society that had fed, then scorned him. Clearly, little mattered to Petronius other than being fabulous, and when such seemed no longer possible—well, life was over.

Some people have read *Satyrica* as a literal description of general Roman depravities, but that denies the human memory's predilection for exaggeration. Yet, if not a resolute historical depiction of a society as a whole, what is *Satyrica*?

It is a glimpse at excess and indulgence within a world of money, power and decadence. In this realm, the hair upon a slave boy's head is used for a towel after pissing, and the only failing is impotence—which our novel's hero, Encolpius, suffers from as he pursues his beautiful lover, the boy Giton, through a variety of risqué scenarios.

Satyrica is a teasing surrender to the lustful glutton that is the animal base of man.

Mixed in are incredible tales of the supernatural—werewolves and spirits—and the captivating exercises of a character named Trimalchio, the ultimate reveler, the defining host of extravagant feasts. So peerless was his ability to disgorge wealth in the entertainment of others that F. Scott Fitzgerald, while shaping *The Great Gatsby*, called it *Trimalchio at West Egg*, a nod to the excesses and pretensions of Fitzgerald's aborning hero, and an echo of the impact of Petronius' *Satyrica*, still rippling through the ages.

Martial

Epigrams

TRANSLATED BY ANONYMOUS

Give me a boy whose tender skin
Owes its fresh bloom to youth, not art.
—15, 205 (PARTIAL)[6]

Martial, Martial, Martial!

Marcus Valerius Martialis was born in Spain in the year 40 C.E. At the age of twenty-four he moved to Rome and fell under the influence of fellow Spaniard Seneca, who helped him secure a patron in Lucius Calpurnius Piso.

His patron, however, plotted to assassinate the statesman Cicero, and when the attempt failed, Martial lost his best friends in the fallout: not just Piso but Seneca and Seneca's nephew, the writer Lucan.

Martial became in essence a writer-for-hire, crafting verses to fit special events and courting patronage by their deployment. When the emperor Titus dedicated the Colosseum in 80 C.E., Martial's epigrams in honor of the occasion brought him equestrian

[6] This epigram translated by Brian Hill.

rank. Yet as tender as his poetry can be—witness the above ex-ample—Martial's focus was more often crude, as in "To Polycharmus":

> When you lie with a woman, at least so girls say,
>   You shit the same moment you come.
> But what do you do, Polycharmus, I pray,
>   When a lover's stiff prick stops your bum?
>
> (9, 58)

The first twelve books of *Epigrams* appeared between the years 86 and 98 C.E. As he aged, Martial found himself increasingly alone. His palace friends were variously lost to him; for example, the emperor Domitian, who succeeded his elder brother Titus in 81 C.E. and was the recipient of some of Martial's most vulgar flattery, was ousted in a conspiracy in 96 C.E.

Homesick and all but alone, Martial borrowed money from another writer, Pliny the Younger, to return to Spain, where he lived until his death at the age of sixty-four.

Ripe with the flavor of Horace but with the more focused disdainfulness of Archilochus, Martial's epigrams lack Horace's so-phistication but deliver in their own way a bawdy, if misogynistic, wisdom:

> My better half, why turn a peevish scold,
> When round some tender boy my arms I fold,
> And point me out that nature has designed
> In you as well a little hole behind?
> Has Juno ne'er said this to lustful Jove?
> Yet graceful Ganymede absorbs his love.
> The stout Tirynthian left his bow the while, as
> The lusty hero drove his shaft in Hylas.
> Yet think you Megara had not her bulls-eye?
> And starting Daphne turning round to fly,

Her bottom lit a lust for virile joys
Phoebus needs quench in the Oebalian boy's:
However much Briseis towards Achilles
Turned her white buttocks, fairer than twin lilies,
He found below the smooth Patroclus' waist
Enjoyment more congenial to his taste.
They give no manly names to back or front.
A woman everywhere is only cunt.

(11, 43)

Reading Martial—indeed, reading most of the ancient Greeks and Romans—brings to mind a disturbing parallel: It is often said that modern gay men have never felt much of a need to ally themselves or concern themselves with women in general, and lesbians in particular. But even at a time when bisexuality was the societal norm, men tended to undervalue their relationships with women and to underplay the concerns of women.

Perhaps some will take comfort that such tendencies are still evident today; others will wonder how it can be that civilization could claim to have advanced over the past millennia and yet remain in key structural ways—the treatment of women and sexual minorities (remember Virgil's sense of being different, which caused him to graft homoerotic myth at the heart of *The Aeneid*)—very much the same.

"The Cut Sleeve"

NO TRANSLATION AVAILABLE

In the first decade of the twentieth century, the pseudonymous Ameng of Wu edited an anthology of Chinese homosexuality in fiction and fact, and called it *The Cut Sleeve.*

The title comes from a historical fable of the first century C.E. One day, Emperor Ai of the Han Dynasty and his favorite boy, Dong Xian, lay down together. Dong Xian fell asleep, with his head resting on the emperor's sleeved arm. The emperor needed to get up but did not want to disturb his lover. Dong Xian's happiness was so important to the emperor that he slit open the sleeve and slipped out his arm without disturbing the sleeping lad.

A tender story, it has come to serve as the identifying episode of Chinese same-gender love between men. Despite the fact that Ameng of Wu's anthology ranged from the fifth century B.C.E. to the nineteenth century C.E., it was the story of the cut sleeve that proved central to the Chinese understanding of male homosexuality.

At the time Ai slit his sleeve for Dong Xian, it started a fashion trend. It is hard for us, perhaps, to reconcile this embracing attitude toward same-gender love in light of our understanding of modern China's repressive Communist regime. Yet despite the suppression of a recognizable gay identity in China at

THE GAY CANON 97

the end of the millennium, and despite the fact that there exists no printed version of the fable, the story itself survives, a tenacious historical artifact preserved by word of mouth, marking an identity and saying, without shame, "We were here. We are here. We exist."

Plutarch

Lives

TRANSLATED BY JOHN DRYDEN

After they were twelve years old, they were no
longer allowed to wear any undergarments, they had
but one coat to serve them a year; their bodies were
hard and dry, with but little acquaintance of baths and
unguents; these human indulgences they were allowed
only on some few particular days in the year. They
lodged together in little bands upon beds made of the
rushes which grew by the banks of the river Eurotas,
which they were to break off with their hands without
a knife . . . By the time they were come to this age
there was not any of the more hopeful boys who had
not a lover to bear him company.

—"LYCURGUS"

Plutarch said in his "Alexander" that his design was "not to write
history, but lives." Toward that end, his collected *Lives*—from *Parallel Lives*, first published as pairs of biographical essays, followed
by contextual essays comparing the two lives under discussion; and
from miscellaneous biographies published independently of each
other—contains a wealth of minutiae mixed with facts of great

import. Plutarch's concern, which would be finally and best realized by Lytton Strachey in *Eminent Victorians,* was to render a three-dimensional portrait of the individual and not merely recite a listing of his accomplishments.

Born in Boetia in the year 46 C.E., Plutarch began pursuing his higher education in Athens in 66 C.E. Although he would visit Rome more than once, and even lecture there on matters of philosophy, Boetia would remain his lifelong home.

He married and fathered five children; at least two of his sons lived to adulthood. He founded a school of philosophy and eventually served at Delphi as a priest of Apollo. He would die in 120 C.E., and although no one set out to write his life, as he had done for so many others, Plutarch's personality—his familial attitudes, his sense of humor—may be pieced together in the essays that form his *Moralia* (of which *The Dialogue on Love* is one).

Thanks to an English translation by Sir Thomas North in 1579, Plutarch's *Lives* would influence arguably the greatest playwright of Western history, William Shakespeare. His *Coriolanus, Julius Caesar* and *Antony and Cleopatra* owe a clear debt to Plutarch's exhaustive yet entertaining biographies—and with good reason.

Plutarch's *Lives* goes behind the scenes, reaching past the veil of history and myth to touch the warm skin of its subjects. In examining the life of Alexander the Great, Plutarch notes that while the boy may have been tutored by Aristotle, his greatest contribution to history—the idea of world conquest—wasn't, at heart, Aristotelian. Plutarch also explores the life of Alcibiades, remembered from Plato, and fleshes out that portrait in great detail.

Alcibiades, noted in Plato's *Symposium* for his handsomeness, is confirmed in Plutarch's portrait as one of those people who are handsome at every stage of their lives. But despite Alcibiades' achievements as a soldier and statesman, and

> with all this sagacity and eloquence, he intermingled exor-
> bitant luxury and wantonness, in his eating and drinking

and dissolute living; wore long purple robes like a woman, which dragged after him as he went through the market-place. ("ALCIBIADES")

Plutarch also describes Alcibiades' chameleon-like ability to immerse himself in each society he encountered: "At Sparta, he was devoted to athletic exercises, was frugal and reserved; in Ionia, luxurious, gay, and indolent; in Thrace, always drinking; in Thessaly . . ." ("Alcibiades"). An indiscreet philanderer, he impregnated the wife of one country's king, a sour turn that may have precipitated Alcibiades' assassination. Whether it was by this king's order, or by the hand of the brothers whose sister he had defiled, Plutarch makes it clear that the one constant in the rumors surrounding Alcibiades' death was that it resulted from his wanton, passionate self-indulgences.

Plutarch's essays on Solon, the man who gave the Law to Athens and whose only unfinished work at his death was a history of Atlantis, and Lycurgus, who founded the moral Spartan state, with its naked dancing youth and separate societies for men and women, are a compelling blend of the political and the personal. Within each of these essays—and indeed, all the essays—same-sex love, where discussed, is neither shied away from nor trifled with but, rather, honestly recognized for its place and purpose in the life of the individual and society under discussion.

Plutarch

The Dialogue on Love

TRANSLATED BY W. C. HELMBOLD

"Love, on the other hand, has a function as holy as any you could mention, nor is there any competition more fitting for a god to preside over than the pursuit and tendance by lovers of handsome young men."

—758

Plutarch's symposium—*The Dialogue on Love* (from *Moralia)*—borrows heavily from Plato and Xenophon, certainly, but is far from a merely derivative exercise.

To begin with, *The Dialogue on Love* concerns itself not simply with love but with love's purpose and its part, if any, in marriage between a man and a woman. The speeches are set into motion when a young widow—she's thirty—attempts to take a boy of eighteen or twenty as her husband.

Perhaps this was progress; perhaps it was merely a consequence of Plutarch himself having been well married, and of the symposium's being recorded by Plutarch's son Autobulus. Regardless, *The Dialogue on Love,* while heaping plenty of praise on the love of men for each other, also gives women more happy credit than they have previously been allotted in the Greco-Roman tradition.

So the widow Ismenodora is to take the boy—by Roman standards, still a minor—as her spouse. The boy—"Bacchon who was called The Handsome" (749)—cannot decide what to do. The widow's intentions are honorable, but her mother fears Bacchon will be marrying too far above his class; the widow is well positioned socially, thanks to her previous marriage. Meanwhile, Bacchon's hunting companions rib him about marrying such an older woman. In his confusion, he leaves the decision to his lovers, Pisias and Anthemion. But even they cannot agree! Pisias believes Anthemion has led the boy astray even to allow him to consider the possibility of marriage to Ismenodora; Anthemion accuses Pisias of acting in self-interest, of still wanting the beautiful boy for his pleasure.

They choose Plutarch and his friends to serve as their arbiters, and the battle begins in earnest:

> "When you say foulest," asked Daphnaeus, "are you referring to marriage, the union of man and wife, than which there has not existed, now or ever, a fellowship more sacred?"
>
> "Why, of course," said Protogenes, "since it's necessary for producing children, there's no harm in legislators talking it up and singing its praises to the masses. But genuine love has no connexion whatsoever with the women's quarters. I deny that it is love you have felt for women and girls—any more than flies feel love for milk or bees for honey or than caterers and cooks have tender emotions for the calves and fowls they fatten in the dark."
>
> (750)

The love of a man for a woman is equated with softness and indolence, while "there is only one genuine Love, the love of boys" (750). The love of boys leads to virtue and honor.

Daphnaeus manages a defense, saying that boy love is cloaked with pseudomorality and public benefit, when the underlying goal is the same: sexual release. Plutarch sides with Protogenes with an outburst of disbelief: "So marriage is to be a loveless union, devoid of god-given friendship!" (750).

The conversation meanders. An examination of women who have come to power is in order to show what happens if they are allowed to independently realize their desires. Always, men involved with these women come to bad ends—the reader waits for a vivid discussion of *vagina dentata,* but alas, this never takes place.

Ismenodora, meanwhile, has grown tired of waiting for the men to finish chatting. She abducts Bacchon, sending Pisias into a panic—screaming about the "emasculation" (755) of the city and dashing off for town, loyal Protogenes trailing after.

The remaining discussion centers around the place of Eros and Aphrodite in human relations—familiar ground that we have trod before with Plato and Xenophon. But here, we end up with a previously unmentioned result, with echoes of Aristotle: Love is a form of friendship, friendship is a part of marriage, marriage is then imbued with love—and rightly so.

Various discussions follow, reaffirming the practical purposes of pederastic desire (including its necessity for producing sperm) and, later, reviling the passive partner in sex:

> That is why we class those who enjoy the passive part as
> belonging to the lowest depth of vice and allow them not
> the least degree of confidence or respect or friendship.

Inevitably, of course, this leads to the question: If these men are not to have another man in passive sexual congress because it denigrates the participant, whom are they to have sex with?

The preceding discussions have returned us to the realm of Platonic love, where homoaffectionalism is good, homosexuality (the act) is not.

Hm. Thank the gods for women!

Women are lauded as capable of virtue and designed by "nature" (769) to be sexually attractive to men, and also emotionally attractive in the friendship that springs from the intimacy of marriage.

The discussion would continue, but the men are called away to a wedding: Bacchon and Ismenodora's. And all are in agreement—Pisias reconciled to events and now set to lead the wedding procession—that the god of love "approves and is graciously present at this affair" (771).

We are left, then, happy that Ismenodora and Bacchon have found each other, but uncomfortable that any potential for virtuousness and friendship with women appears to carry with it the price tag of sexual relations between men and/or boys. And we ask ourselves: Why?

John

The Gospel

KING JAMES VERSION OF THE HOLY BIBLE

Then Peter, turning about, seeth the disciple whom Jesus loved following; which also leaned on his breast at supper, and said, Lord, which is he that betrayeth thee?

Peter seeing him saith to Jesus, Lord, and what shall this man do?

—21:20–21

John was one of the twelve apostles, the younger brother of the apostle James, both of them the sons of Zebedee. His mother may have been Salome, Jesus' aunt. He was probably a native of Bethsaida and a Galilean fisherman.

Early stories tell of his slaughter by Jews, the same fate that befell his brother James. But from 150 on, he has been named as the author of Revelations, and from 175 on, the lore changed so that John now lived a long life, scribbling away in Ephesus. In addition to this Gospel and Revelations, there are three epistles that bear his name.

It is impossible to write about the Gospel of John with even the pretense of objectivity. No text in Western civilization has been used in the demonization of queers—and, indeed, Jews—as often as the New Testament. (It should be noted that the New Testament is a collection of books. Not taking into account the Apocrypha, only the four Gospels concern the life of Jesus; the rest is simply inspirational text.) But how much of our response to the words of this Gospel—be they relief or revulsion—is based on what we have read over what we have been told?

For a long time following Jesus' death, it was the custom for the sacred Christian texts to be interpreted for the people by priests or ministers—similar to the Jewish tradition, where scriptural authority was weighed by learned elders. The King James Version of the Bible—and the invention and promotion of the printing press—changed all that, rendering the Bible from indecipherable Greek, Latin or Hebrew into English and making it available to anyone who could read. Still, for most Christians, their ministers and priests remained a source of interpretive wisdom, and this is true today.

There's nothing wrong with this, really. Or there wouldn't be if that animal urge for self-interest didn't influence so keenly the way sacred texts are often interpreted. We establish ministers and priests in positions of power and then act surprised when they seek to manipulate the words of the Bible for their own benefit. And in truth, it may be that as long as the minister's interests are aligned with ours, we see no reason to complain; it's only when he diverges from our self-interest that we complain. (The same is true for pagans and atheists, who have their own priests and ministers, though they go by different names.)

Like anyone else, it is easiest for gay men, if we are part of the well-living majority, to preserve the status quo. How do we preserve the status quo? By beating down that which threatens us. Let's not make the mistake of thinking that since queers are discriminated against, we therefore hold some sort of noble, exalted-by-suffering position in the true socialist pantheon. Queers are as eager to discriminate as anyone else, and often do. Some lesbians are separatists; some gay men are misogynists; and a whole bunch of "us" are racist. And the gay community—such as it is, defined by self-interest—has often shown itself eager to close ranks against bisexuals, the transgendered, or men who are loved by boys.

Rather than embrace the diversity of the human sexual minority experience, we selectively approve subsets of it, those who are most likely to align with our self-interest. When offered the chance to choose between a readily classifiable if slightly repugnant individual who fits within the status quo and a man whose action flays open our sense of safety in the pursuit of honesty, those of us who are comfortable—the majority—call out, "Not this man, but Barabbas" (18:40).

Who was Jesus?

He was a passionate Jew who believed he was living in the time of the world's end. The apostles shared this sense of apocalypse, and certainly, so did Paul. It was only as time marched on, and the world failed to end, that Christianity evolved from being a religion of the apocalypse to what it is today: an absorptive mishmash of previous world religions and traditions (the cult of Osiris, the Egyptian sun god, who was butchered, only to rise again on the third day; the celebration of the winter solstice; the Greek rites of Bacchus; etc.) whose success maybe owes as much to any "truth" as it does to the Roman example of domination by assimilation prevalent at the time of Jesus and the writings of the early Christian church.

> In the beginning was the Word, and the Word was with God, and the Word was God.
>
> The same was in the beginning with God.
>
> All things were made by him; and without him was not any thing made that was made.
>
> In him was life; and the life was the light of men.

> And the light shineth in darkness; and the darkness
> comprehended it not.   (1:1–5)

Opening before Time, the Gospel of John has but one purpose: to establish Jesus as the Christ, the Messiah, the redemptive power through which unity with God may be realized after death. The words of Jesus annex themselves to the words of the Tanakh: "For the law was given by Moses, but grace and truth came by Jesus Christ" (1:17).

Moving quickly, John the apostle proceeds to tell about another John, who baptizes with water, a shadow of "he which baptizeth with the Holy Ghost" (1:33).

Throughout the Gospel run several recurring devices: the metaphors of "light" and "seeing," and the promise that Jesus is leading up to something big, which can be completed only after his physical death. And perhaps most amusingly—for Jesus responds with increasing aggravation—Jesus is forever having to explain and justify himself and his words to people who want more than he can give, even as they refuse what he offers.

Jesus begins to gather his disciples and attends a wedding where he changes water to wine, in a fit of pique, at the request of his mother. He kicks the moneychangers out of the temple, saying, as he tosses out their wares, "Take these things hence; make not my Father's house an house of merchandise" (2:16). Moments later, being questioned by the Jews, Jesus tells them, "Destroy this temple, and in three days I will raise it up" (2:19). The Jews misunderstand him, thinking he is talking of the synagogue that took forty-six years to build, "[b]ut he spake of the temple of his body" (2:21).

Jesus is then visited at night by a Pharisee named Nicodemus, who questions him. (Nicodemus will bring spices to anoint Jesus' body for burial after he is crucified.) Here begins a dialogue that Jesus will later enter into with other Pharisees (with less success) and in which he sets forth some key points: "For God sent not his Son into the world to condemn the world; but that the world through him might be saved" (3:17); and "For every one that doeth evil hateth the light, neither cometh to the light, lest his deeds should be reproved" (3:20). Here we have Jesus stating plainly that his part is not one of condemnation, and offering a nod to man's innate desire for self-preservation at the expense of what is right and just.

Women play an interesting part in John's Gospel. While Jesus is snappish with his mother at the wedding (saying, in 2:4, when she complains their hosts are out of wine, "Woman, what have I to do with thee? mine hour is not yet come"), he is kind to the Samaritan woman he meets at Jacob's well. This is all the more surprising because Jews did not associate with Samaritans in Jesus' time. Yet she is honest with him and receives what he has to say with curiosity instead of hostility:

> The woman saith unto him, I know that Messias cometh, which is called Christ: when he is come, he will tell us all things.
> Jesus saith unto her, I that speak unto thee am he.
> (4:25-26)

How women are viewed by Jesus' contemporaries may be best revealed by what happens immediately after Jesus' revelation to the woman by the well, as John tells it:

> And upon this came his disciples, and marvelled that he talked with the woman: yet no man said, What seekest thou? or, Why talkest thou with her?   (4:27)

That he simply deigns to talk with a woman seems marvel enough for the apostles. Jesus lived in a patriarchal society, and the word of women was not worth much. (This makes all the more interesting the role women are given to play in the Gospel; later, it will be a woman who makes the key discovery that Jesus' tomb is empty.)

The Samaritans are excited by what the woman has said, and beg Jesus to stay with them a few days, which he does; and during this time they embrace him as the Christ. And as a result, upon his return to his own people, ". . . Jesus himself testified, that a prophet hath no honour in his own country" (4:44).

Jesus works miracles, healing a man's sick child from miles away. On the Sabbath he makes it possible for a lame man to walk—warning him to "sin no more, lest a worse thing come unto thee" (5:14)—and when the healed man tells the Jews who it was that made him able to walk again, they chastise Jesus for healing the man on the Sabbath day. "But Jesus answered them, My Father worketh hitherto, and I work" (5:17).

By his actions, Jesus is basically desanctifying the Sabbath day as a special day for rest and prayer. This is a primary tenet of the Jewish faith, that the Sabbath day be kept holy. But for Jesus, God's work is not to be denied on any day.

As he heals people, however, Jesus posits that physical ailments happen to us because we sin. Shortly thereafter, in response to queries raised by the Jews, Jesus says, "For the Father judgeth no man, but hath committed all judgment unto the Son" (5:22) and "I can of mine own self do nothing: as I hear, I judge: and my judgment is just; because I seek not mine own will, but the will of the Father which hath sent me" (5:30).

By his own words now, Jesus admits to being able to judge, but not condemn, and that through him is made manifest God's will.

He admonishes the Jews, accusing them of not believing even in Moses, "[f]or had ye believed Moses, ye would have believed me: for he wrote of me. But if ye believe not his writings, how shall ye believe my words?" (5:46–47).

Is this fair? (And does it matter if it is fair?) A man comes up to you, disregards key tenets of your faith and then tells you that he is the fulfillment of that faith's promises. Do you believe him?

Would you if it happened today?

Jesus trots off, feeds five thousand men with five barley loaves and two small fishes, later walks upon the water, then returns to state that he is the bread of life, "the bread which came down from heaven" (6:41). (John's Gospel avoids the idea of virgin birth; there is no reason to think Joseph is not Jesus' father, and so these pretensions of coming down from heaven seem, well, to those who know Jesus' family, a bit wacko.) Jesus moves on to establish that he will give up his fleshly existence "for the life of the world" (6:51) and then, in the synagogue at Capernaum, invokes cannibalistic ritual:

> Then Jesus said unto them, Verily, verily I say unto you, Except ye eat the flesh of the Son of man, and drink his blood, ye have no life in you.
>
> Whoso eateth my flesh, and drinketh my blood, hath eternal life; and I will raise him up at the last day.
>
> For my flesh is meat indeed, and my blood is drink indeed.
>
> He that eateth my flesh, and drinketh my blood, dwelleth in me, and I in him.   (6:53–56)

His followers in the temple, hearing him, take it literally at first and say, "This is an hard saying; who can hear it?" (6:60). Jesus is appalled at their literal-mindedness and says to them, incredulously, "Doth this offend you?" (6:61), before reminding them:

> It is the spirit that quickeneth; the flesh profiteth nothing: the words that I speak unto you, they are spirit, and they are life.   (6:63)

Many of his followers in the synagogue walk away, unable any longer to follow him, either literally or figuratively, but the twelve disciples remain steadfast, assuring Jesus of their devotion, even as he reveals to them that one among them "is a devil" (6:70).

He is speaking of Judas.

The news of Jesus spreads throughout the land. There are more confrontations with Jews and Pharisees, in which ideas are refined and positions clarified, including the admonition by Jesus to "Judge not according to the appearance, but judge righteous judgment" (7:24). Nicodemus tries to plead Jesus' case, but is rebuffed, and Jesus goes to the Mount of Olives.

The next morning Jesus strolls into the temple, and again the people gather around him, "and he sat down, and taught them" (8:2). The scribes and Pharisees bring him a woman caught in the act of adultery, a sin punishable by death by stoning, according to Mosaic law. Jesus admonishes, "He that is without sin among you, let him first cast a stone at her" (8:7). This frustrates the people, unable to bear false witness to their own consciences, and when Jesus next looks to the woman, he sees her standing alone and says, "Woman, where are those thine accusers? hath no man condemned thee?" (8:10).

> She said, No man, Lord. And Jesus said unto her, Neither do I condemn thee: go and sin no more.   (8:11)

As Jesus and the Pharisees go at it again, Jesus tells them, "Ye judge after the flesh; I judge no man" (8:15), and "Whosoever committeth sin is the servant of sin" (8:34). This discussion resolves itself in Jesus' most fiery denunciation of the Pharisees yet, language sure to entrench their position against him, for he reviles them, scourging them with words as he himself will be scourged later with the whip—

Jesus said unto them, If God were your Father, ye would love me: for I proceeded forth and came from God; neither came I of myself, but he sent me.

Why do ye not understand my speech? even because ye cannot hear my word.

Ye are of your father the devil, and the lusts of your father ye will do. He was a murderer from the beginning, and abode not in the truth, because there is no truth in him. When he speaketh a lie, he speaketh of his own: for he is a liar, and the father of it. (8:42–44)

—and ends with a startling statement that strikes at the root of Judaism:

Before Abraham was, I am. (8:58)

Jesus escapes the Pharisees' clutches and is next seen performing another miracle on the Sabbath, making a man born blind see by applying to his eyes a clay mixture from the mud of the road and spit. Again, this grates against the will of the Pharisees, and Jesus lectures them—playing off the man's blindness—to no avail, though some begin to ask, "Are we blind also?" (9:40), which, one supposes, could be called progress.

Jesus establishes himself as "the good shepherd" (10:11) and moves on to say, echoing his work in Samaria:

And other sheep I have, which are not of this fold: them also I must bring, and they shall hear my voice; and there shall be one fold, and one shepherd. (10:16)

This is key because it is Paul who is often hailed as the man who opened up Christianity to non-Jews. Yet here it would appear that Jesus' faith-full passion is of a spiritual nature and not a racial one.

While Paul extrapolates from that, and takes it further than Jesus does, it's clear the message Jesus spouts is not meant only for the Jewish race but for the Jewish spirit, the spirit of God, coming through Jesus to be ignited in all.

In a sense, Jesus was for accessible Judaism, the first reform Jew.

Some have found a nascent homoeroticism in Chapter 11 of John, where Jesus raises Lazarus from the dead. Lazarus is the brother of Mary—who will anoint Jesus with ointment and wipe his feet with her hair—and Martha. These women sent for Jesus, saying, "[H]e whom thou lovest is sick" (11:3).

But John follows this with "Now Jesus loved Martha, and her sister, and Lazarus" (11:5). And it appears that Jesus purposely waits until he understands that Lazarus is dead before he travels from Jordan, where he is revisiting the place where John baptized him, to Bethany, a journey of four days.

Martha greets him as he approaches her house, saying, "[I]f thou hadst been here, my brother had not died" (11:21), but without anger or resentment, and stating clearly in the next breath her faith that her brother will be raised up at "the last day" (11:24).

> Jesus said unto her, I am the resurrection, and the life; he
> that believeth in me, though he were dead, yet shall he
> live . . . (11:25)

Martha agrees, readily and wholeheartedly, so sure is her faith that Jesus is the Christ. When Jesus comes across Mary, however, all is not so quick and easy, for Mary is sobbing with grief, as are the Jews—friends and family—around her, and Jesus "groaned in the spirit, and was troubled" (11:33).

Why is he troubled? Earlier, he knew his friend was sick, but he did not go to him. It was only when he realized his friend was dead that he went to Mary and Martha's house. It is only reasonable to ask: Why did he wait?

Was it because, as the text earlier implies, Jesus thought some PR miracle could be wrought from Lazarus' resurrection, a metaphor exercised on a grander scale than that of the man blind from birth he made to see? Is his groan not from sorrow at his friend's death but from sorrow that his selfish pursuits have caused someone he cared for, Mary, great pain? It would not be out of character, especially if we take Jesus at his word that like Father, like Son. For remember the story of Job, wherein God slaughters a man's family and tortures him to win a bet with the devil. Compared to that, what Mary is suffering is just a scratch.

Regardless:

Jesus wept.
    Then said the Jews, Behold how he loved him!
(11:35–36)

Jesus again groans as he approaches the cave. He orders the stone rolled away from the entrance to the tomb, and he raises Lazarus from the dead.

Then comes the Passover supper. After eating, Jesus strips naked. He wraps a towel about his waist and washes the feet of the disciples, drying them with the towel he wears. He tells them when he is finished that he does this as "an example, that ye should do as I have done to you" (13:15). Then:

Verily, verily, I say unto you, The servant is not greater than his lord; neither he that is sent greater than he that sent him.   (13:16)

And then Jesus is troubled and announces that one of those gathered there that evening will betray him.

> Now there was leaning on Jesus' bosom one of his disciples, whom Jesus loved.
>   Simon Peter therefore beckoned to him, that he should ask who it should be of whom he spake.
>   He then lying on Jesus' breast saith unto him, Lord, who is it?   (13:23–25)

When Jesus indicates Judas, Judas "went immediately out: and it was night" (13:30).

Again, John is using images of light and darkness here to signify what is good and what is bad. Yet how bad is Judas? Can a man be called bad whom fate (God) has decreed shall play a pivotal role in bringing Jesus' plan to fruition? Perhaps it is simpler if we ask the question this way: Without Judas, where would Jesus be?

Jesus seems to relax once Judas has left. Having symbolically washed the feet of his disciples, and with this as yet unnamed boy's head nestled upon his chest, he turns from the use of (what has often been, for the apostles) puzzling metaphor to speak clearly of what his disciples are to do, how they are to recognize each other and what law they are to follow:

> A new commandment I give unto you, That ye love one another; as I have loved you, that ye also love one another.
>   By this shall all men know that ye are my disciples, if you have love one to another.   (13:34–35)

Jesus repeats this time and again through the next two chapters. At the same time, he also begins promising to visit them after his death. He promises further that he shall send to them a "Comforter." Even as he tries to provide them with these balms, there looms the repeated and inescapable fact that first he must die, which casts a certain pall over the remnants of the supper.

Then, in Chapter 15, he says something that is more startling than his work on the Sabbath day and his desire to make God accessible to non-Jews:

> If ye keep my commandments, ye shall abide in my love;
> even as I have kept my Father's commandments, and abide
> in his love. (15:10)

Where before he has seen fit to violate individual aspects of Jewish (Mosaic) law, here he tosses it all out the window: Gone are the Ten Commandments, gone are the Levitican codes, only to be replaced by:

> This is my commandment, That ye love one another, as I
> have loved you. (15:12)

Everything is to stem from that now. Not a complex series of "shall" and "shall not"; not a rating of abomination and death penalties but one rule against which all else is to be judged.

The radical nature of this exercise cannot be underestimated. And where there is radical change, there is resistance. Jesus knows this and comforts his disciples with:

> If the world hate you, ye know that it hated me before it
> hated you. (15:18)

and:

> They shall put you out of the synagogues: yea, the time
> cometh, that whosoever killeth you will think that he
> doeth God service. (16:2)

All this, with a boy's ear pressed above his heart, the smell of the lad's hair in his nostrils, the tenderness of their love the love of Christ.

Jesus is well aware of the duality of his message. Even as he gives the disciples love and hope—"I have overcome the world" (16:33)—he does not let them forget that first he must suffer something horrible. He tells Peter that before the rooster's cry greets the new dawn, Peter will thrice deny knowing Jesus. Peter is horrified to hear this.

And Jesus goes to the garden with his disciples.

And Judas meets him there and betrays him.

Jesus is brought before the Jewish high priest Caiaphas' father-in-law, Annas. Caiaphas had previously been among the Pharisees when Jesus spoke or was tested, and Caiaphas sees in Jesus a great threat to his power and their rule.

Jesus is struck by a Roman soldier for not answering Annas' questions satisfactorily. Peter denies Jesus thrice and the cock crows. Annas sends Jesus to Caiaphas, who delivers him to Pontius Pilate.

Pilate is one of the few figures who fares better than he should in John's recounting. A horrible man, paradoxically both weak and powerful, he comes off here as well-meaning. Perhaps there was something politically expedient in John's description of Pilate at the time of the Gospel's first writing and circulation; regardless, it is not accurate. Historically speaking, Pilate was a pig.

Pilate sees no fault in Jesus and offers the Jews the choice of releasing either him or a habitual criminal named Barabbas, as it is the custom to liberate a prisoner on Passover.

But Barabbas doesn't threaten the status quo.

Jesus is whipped, crowned with thorns and covered in a purple robe by Roman soldiers, who beat him up while saying, "Hail, King of the Jews!" (19:3). Pilate tries time and again to have Jesus released, but the crowd calls for Jesus' crucifixion. Ultimately, Pilate accedes to their wishes.

Jesus is taken to Golgotha and hung on a cross between two thieves. In Hebrew, Greek and Latin, Pilate writes a sign to be hung above Jesus' head: "JESUS OF NAZARETH THE KING OF THE JEWS" (19:19).

The Pharisees press him to add an attribution which says that this is what Jesus claimed, but Pilate rebuffs them, saying, "What I have written I have written" (19:22).

While Jesus hangs on the cross, the soldiers below him divide up his garments, except for his cloak, which is of one piece of cloth, and this they gamble for.

> Now there stood by the cross of Jesus his mother, and his mother's sister, Mary the wife of Cleophas, and Mary Magdalene.
>
> When Jesus therefore saw his mother, and the disciple standing by, whom he loved, he saith unto his mother, Woman, behold thy son!
>
> Then saith he to the disciple, Behold thy mother! And from that hour the disciple took her unto his own home.
> (19:25–27)

Jesus says only two more things: He calls out that he is thirsty, and is given vinegar from a sponge; he says, "It is finished" (19:30), and dies.

Because the Jews would not tolerate the bodies hanging on the crosses on the Sabbath, the legs of those being crucified are broken and they are taken down. But when the soldiers come to Jesus, having already snapped the legs of the thieves, they find him dead. They pierce his side, and out pours blood, and water.

Joseph of Arimathea, a secret disciple of Jesus, gets Pilate's permission to receive the body of Jesus and takes it from the cross.

There is a garden on Golgotha with a virgin tomb, and after being wrapped in spices and linen by Nicodemus and Joseph, Jesus is placed inside the sepulchre, its entrance covered with a stone.

His mother finds shelter in the home of his beloved.

The first day of the week cometh Mary Magdalene early, when it was yet dark, unto the sepulchre, and seeth the stone taken away from the sepulchre.

Then she runneth, and cometh to Simon Peter, and to the other disciple, whom Jesus loved, and saith unto them, They have taken away the Lord out of the sepulchre, and we know not where they have laid him.

Peter therefore went forth, and that other disciple, and came to the sepulchre.

So they ran both together: and the other disciple did outrun Peter, and came first to the sepulchre.

And he stooping down, and looking in, saw the linen clothes lying; yet went he not in.   (20:1–5)

Simon Peter does go in, however, and sees, lying separate from the linen wrappings, the cloth head covering.

Then went in also that other disciple, which came first to the sepulchre, and he saw, and believed.   (20:8)

The men return home. But Mary stays, and cries, and then at last, when she looks inside the tomb she sees two angels, one at the head and one at the foot of where Jesus' body has lain. They ask her why she cries, and she tells them it is because Jesus' body has been taken.

And she turns around to go, only to see Jesus standing there before her in the shadows.

She does not recognize him at first, thinking him to be the

gardener. Then she recognizes and speaks to him, but before she runs off to tell the disciples what she has seen and heard:

> Jesus saith unto her, Touch me not; for I am not yet ascended to my Father: but go to my brethren, and say unto them, I ascend unto my Father, and your Father; and to my God, and your God.   (20:17)

Jesus appears to the disciples that night as well, bringing them the Comforter, the Holy Ghost and the power to forgive sins. But one disciple is missing from this encounter, Thomas, who doesn't believe what the other disciples have said, that Jesus is again among them. So Jesus appears a second time, and Thomas' doubts are quelled:

> And after eight days again his disciples were within, and Thomas with them: then came Jesus, the doors being shut, and stood in the midst, and said, Peace be unto you.
>
> Then saith he to Thomas, Reach hither thy finger, and behold my hands; and reach hither thy hand, and thrust it into my side: and be not faithless, but believing.
>
> And Thomas answered and said unto him, My Lord and my God.   (20:26–28)

Jesus appears a third time, to just a few of the disciples, who have been out fishing. They do not know him at first—until the disciple whom Jesus loved recognizes him. They've had a miserable time of fishing; Jesus helps them increase their catch, and they eat together.

And after his third appearance, Jesus is wholly risen from the dead.

But Simon Peter is also among the disciples fortunate to share this last meal with Jesus, and it is here that perhaps the tenderest moment—after that of the beloved disciple resting his head on

Jesus' breast following the Passover meal—occurs in the Gospel of John:

> So when they had dined, Jesus saith to Simon Peter, Simon, son of Jonas, lovest thou me more than these? He saith unto him, Yea, Lord; thou knowest that I love thee. He saith unto him, Feed my lambs.
>
> He saith to him again the second time, Simon, son of Jonas, lovest thou me? He saith unto him, Yea, Lord; thou knowest that I love thee. He saith unto him, Feed my sheep.
>
> He saith unto him the third time, Simon, son of Jonas, lovest thou me? Peter was grieved because he said unto him the third time, Lovest thou me? And he said unto him, Lord, thou knowest all things; thou knowest that I love thee. Jesus saith unto him, Feed my sheep.
>
> (21:15–17)

Three times does Peter deny he knew Jesus; three times is he allowed to profess his love to Jesus. This is a gracious act of forgiveness and closure, and a reminder that far greater than the ability to forgive sins is the ability to redeem them.

As for the identity of the beloved disciple, coyly kept secret to the very end of this Gospel, John reveals with a flourish:

> This is the disciple which testifieth of these things, and wrote these things: and we know that his testimony is true.
>
> (21:24)

Before moving on, it is important to note that Jesus' ability to be considered raised from the dead is paralleled by his ability to rediscover his fleshly form. When Mary Magdalene sees him, he cannot be touched—he must not be touched! By the time he appears to Thomas, he may be touched—but isn't—and when he shows up on the beach, he's a man once more, able to enjoy the pleasures of life such as food, and love.

FIVE QUESTIONS

1. Can it be argued convincingly that Jesus and John were not lovers? Why or why not?

2. What does it mean that, in order to conquer death, one must become fully human?

3. Is the Gospel a spiritual testament or a work of propaganda? If the latter, toward what end? If both, why and how?

4. Is John an anti-Semite? Prove or disprove it, using the text, in the process resolving whether or not John was himself a Jew and how that affects your argument.

5. The Ten Commandments and the proscriptions of Leviticus are detailed and exact. Is Jesus' commandment? Which is more feasible for a society to live by? Which is easier? Which do you choose?

THE AGE

OF

ENLIGHTENMENT

Michelangelo

Poetry

TRANSLATED BY JAMES M. STASLOW

. . . Hence love walks with a limp,
so unbalanced is the burden he transports,
bringing me light, and carrying away my darkness.

—30 (EXCERPT)

Michelangelo di Lodovico Buonarroti Simoni—Michelangelo—was born in 1475 at Caprese in Tuscany, Italy. The primary focus of his career and his life was the visual arts, though he realized poetical fame during his lifetime as well. In fact, his poetry was held up as exemplary in a series of lectures on literary criticism delivered shortly before his death in 1564.

He is probably best known for his statue of David, or perhaps his frescoes on the ceiling of the Sistine Chapel (a project he tried to palm off on Raphael, complaining to the Pope that he, Michelangelo, was only a sculptor), or possibly his statue of Moses, or the *Pietà;* no, it is impossible to cite any single work for which Michelangelo is best known.

But when it comes to his literary work, there are two clearly distinguishable, notable—and timeless, in that they are also wholly modern—drives: passion and shame. Bluntly put, Michelangelo lived in a repressive Christian age and, significantly, made the now "classic" mistake of falling in love with a straight boy.

His statements about art make it clear that much, if not all, of Michelangelo's work is in some way a self-portrait. Not all of it is as explicitly—and nakedly—rendered as his self-cast role in the Sistine Chapel's *The Last Judgment,* where he appears in the guise of the flayed martyr St. Bartholomew. His poems, in places, are certainly as revealing.

Michelangelo would give his beloveds drawings as tokens of his affection. His greatest love was Tommaso de Cavalieri, twenty-three when he met Michelangelo, who was then fifty-seven. Their relationship would never be consummated, and Michelangelo would occasionally turn his affections toward other young men. These, too, may have gone unfulfilled: There is no evidence that Michelangelo was ever sexually active. This supposition is not wholly implausible, if he was not at all physically attracted to women (he even used male models for all his female figures) and sexual congress with another male would have brought condemnation from society and God. Without the act, he was simply an artist, able to appreciate beauty—or at least, able to use that aspect of his craft as an attempted dodge for his true nature.

Michelangelo was ashamed of his homosexuality; the rapture that his passion for Tommaso brought him warred with an equally fiery anguish. Publicly, Michelangelo denied his sexuality, and several drafts of romantic poems show changes of gender from "he" to "she" in their final forms.

Yet his poetry is often as candid as his Bartholomew self-portrait, and in his sonnets and madrigals and fragments, we have the work of a brilliant artistic mind, one that, arguably, sculpted his emotions as well with words as with marble: genius cut loose from repression.

Christopher Marlowe

Complete Plays
and Poems

READING:

Edward the Second

EDITED BY E. D. PENDRY AND J. C. MAXWELL

MORTIMER SENIOR. Nephew, I must to Scotland; thou
   stay'st here.
Leave now to oppose thyself against the king.
Thou seest by nature he is mild and calm,
And seeing his mind so dotes on Gaveston,
Let him without controllment have his will.
The mightiest kings have had their minions:
Great Alexander lov'd Hephaestion;
And conquering Hercules for Hylas wept;
And for Patroclus stern Achilles droop'd;
And not kings only, but the wisest men.
The Roman Tully lov'd Octavius;
Great Socrates, wild Alcibiades.

Then let his grace, whose youth is flexible
And promiseth as much as we can wish,
Freely enjoy that vain light-headed earl,
For riper years will wean him from such toys.
—*EDWARD THE SECOND*, ACT I, SCENE 4

Christopher Marlowe was born in Canterbury in 1564, the son of a shoemaker. From Kings School he went to Benet (now Corpus Christi) College, Cambridge, graduating with a B.A. in 1583 and an M.A. in 1587, the same year *Tamburlaine the Great* was first produced, in two parts. Three years later, it was published. It was the first play to discover the flexibility and power of blank verse, coupling with this impressive use of language a horrific violence. Marlowe had studied for the priesthood but spurned holy orders, and his life would reflect a religious sensibility that despised the faith that gave birth to it, despised its rigid-mindedness and repressive effect.

Other plays followed *Tamburlaine the Great* in rapid succession, though none would be published during Marlowe's lifetime: *Dr. Faustus* was probably the next Marlowe play performed, followed by *The Jew of Malta* in 1588, *Edward the Second* in 1590 and then *The Massacre at Paris* and *The Tragedy of Dido*.

Ascertaining the authorship of these plays is sometimes troublesome, an uncertainty characteristic of the era in which they were written. For instance, Marlowe probably had a hand in revising Shakespeare's *Henry VI* and *Titus Andronicus*, and other writers certainly pitched in at times on Marlowe's creations. *Dr. Faustus* is the earliest play to bear these signs, reading as a series of stylistically incompatible vignettes rather than as a unified work. We are at a loss to explain the original quality of *The Massacre at Paris*, which must have been written after 1589, judging from its concerns, yet has descended to us horribly mutilated. And *The Tragedy of Dido*, whose opening scene features Ganymede on Jupiter's knee, was probably left in fragments by Marlowe, to be finished by Thomas Nashe, another dramatist and satirist of the time.

Marlowe wrote translations of the better-known classical Roman writers such as Ovid, and poetry of his own—most notably, "Come Live with Me, and Be My Love," after Virgil's Eclogue II, and "Hero and Leander," wherein the Roman god Neptune finds himself unable to resist the charms of the mortal boy Leander. Marlowe is perhaps the second-most-famous writer of epigrams in English letters (after Oscar Wilde), saying, "That all they that love not tobacco and boys were fools" and, of the relationship between Jesus and the beloved disciple, "That St. John the Evangelist was bedfellow to Christ and leaned always in his bosom; that he used him as the sinners of Sodoma."

Marlowe lived roughly, and he was probably an agent in Sir Francis Walthingham's Elizabethan spy network, but his connections could protect him only so far. In 1593, Marlowe's explicit antireligious opinions led him to be charged with atheism, an offense then as serious as heresy and blasphemy, but he was stabbed through the eye in a Deptford tavern brawl and died before he could be arrested.

At the time Marlowe was writing, plays had to be approved by the Church and the royal censors before they could be put on. Thus, what he got away with, in presenting homosexual characters with a hitherto unheard-of sympathy and development, is remarkable.

> GAVESTON. My father is deceas'd, come Gaveston,
> And share the kingdom with thy dearest friend.
> (ACT I, SCENE 1)

So opens *Edward the Second*. A portion of the play is a love story, and an equal portion—perhaps the greater part—concerns itself with power: who has it, who claims to have it, who wields it. In

Edward the Second, there are diverse answers to each of these questions.

As a love story, *Edward the Second* is primarily about one man's love for another: Edward's love for Piers de Gaveston. Gaveston is a handsome but social-climbing fop of a Frenchman. Barring his love for Edward, there is little to recommend Gaveston—and even his love is overshadowed by the power such a romance brings him. In the eyes of those who surround the king, it is not so much his love for another man that his subordinates find deplorable but, rather, Edward's love for this particular man. Edward's father, while alive, had simply banished Gaveston and so, in the short term, had solved the problem of his son's obsession. But with his father dead, Edward summons Gaveston back from exile and into the heart of the court.

An early exchange between the Earl of Lancaster and Edward sets the tone, and foretells the resolution of the tragedy:

> LANCASTER. And northward Gaveston hath many friends.
> Adieu my lord; and either change your mind,
> Or look to see the throne where you should sit
> To float in blood, and at thy wanton head
> The glozing head of thy base minion thrown.
> EDWARD. I cannot brook these haughty menaces:
> Am I a king and must be overrul'd?
> Brother, display my ensigns in the field;
> I'll bandy with the barons and the earls,
> And either live or die with Gaveston.
> (ACT I, SCENE 1)

Upon his return to Edward, Gaveston receives various titles, and even the king's brother and most faithful supporter, Edmund, Earl of Kent, finds the extravagance too much. Gaveston is made "Lord High Chamberlain, / Chief Secretary to the state and me, / Earl of Cornwall, King and Lord of Man." Edmund frets because such entitlements seem sure to further anger the barons and earls, who already resent Gaveston's reappearance in their midst.

If Edward's chief failing is to put too much protective faith in his office as king, Gaveston's chief failing is to suffer his lover's delusions, placing himself above church and state and rapidly becoming insufferable. When he imprisons the Bishop of Coventry—who had once advised Edward's father to exile Gaveston—in the Tower of London, the earls and barons are appalled at this turn of events, realizing that if Gaveston will not spare the church, he will not spare them either. Though receiving the news of his entitlements grimly, they are cowed to silence by the king's position—at least until the arrival of the Bishop of Canterbury:

> LANCASTER. My lord, will you take arms against the king?
> CANTERBURY. What need I? God himself is up in arms
> When violence is offered to the church.
> (ACT I, SCENE 2)

And at last, with God joining the barons and earls against Edward and Gaveston's love, there arrives Edward's wife, Queen Isabella, herself French royalty and mother of Prince Edward, heir to the realm. When Lord Mortimer the Younger asks where she is off to, she replies:

> ISABELLA. Unto the forest, gentle Mortimer,
> To live in grief and baleful discontent;
> For now my lord the king regards me not,
> But dotes upon the love of Gaveston.
> He claps his cheeks and hangs about his neck,
> Smiles in his face and whispers in his ears;
> And when I come, he frowns, as who should say,
> "Go whither thou wilt, seeing I have Gaveston."
> (ACT I, SCENE 2)

Mortimer, leader of the burgeoning insurrection against the king, tells her to return to the castle, that they will rid her home of Gaveston's menace, but Isabella demurs:

> ISABELLA. Then let him stay; for rather than my lord
> Shall be oppress'd by civil mutinies,
> I will endure a melancholy life,
> And let him frolic with his minion.   (ACT I, SCENE 2)

The Bishop of Canterbury weighs in, and they agree to see if they can effectively make the king understand the threat Gaveston's continued presence poses to his kingdom, and so bring about the man's banishment. Mortimer also hints at his allegiance to the queen, whom he will take as his lover before Edward's reign is ended.

The nobles and the Bishop of Canterbury come before Edward and tell him they are resolved to see Gaveston exiled from the realm. Edward is angry, but promises to offer them higher positions if they will but leave him in peace "[t]o frolic with my dearest Gaveston" (Act I, Scene 4). They refuse, and Edward realizes he is cornered. He agrees to the banishment, saying of the order, "Instead of ink I'll write it with my tears" (Act I, Scene 4).

> EDWARD. How fast they run to banish him I love;
> They would not stir, were it to do me good.
> Why should a king be subject to a priest?
> Proud Rome, that hatchest such imperial grooms,
> For these, thy superstitious taper lights
> Wherewith thy antichristian churches blaze,
> I'll fire thy crazèd buildings, and enforce
> The papal towers to kiss the lowly ground;
> With slaughtered priests make the Tiber's channel swell,
> And banks rais'd higher with their sepulchres.

As for the peers that back the clergy thus,
If I be king, not one of them shall live.
(ACT I, SCENE 4)

Gaveston arrives and Edward tells him that the rumors he hears are true: He is to be banished. Edward makes Gaveston Governor of Ireland and promises to love him faithfully—and to exact revenge on their enemies. Isabella arrives, interrupting their good-byes, and the three queens have at it:

ISABELLA. Whither goes my lord?
EDWARD. Fawn not on me, French strumpet; get thee gone.
ISABELLA. On whom but on my husband should I fawn?
GAVESTON. On Mortimer; with whom, ungentle queen—
I say no more: judge you the rest, my lord.

Edward is perhaps unwilling to believe Gaveston's insinuation, though he does find the queen "too familiar with that Mortimer," the man he blames for Gaveston's second banishment. He tells the queen that he will not suffer alone, that until he is reunited with Gaveston, he will not consent to see her. At this, the queen is distraught. She cannot have Edward with Gaveston; she cannot have him without Gaveston. She turns, angrily and in bitter regret of the day she ever married, to the barons and earls and begs them to plead for Gaveston's reinstatement at court.

The nobles are baffled, but they consent and Isabella returns to Edward with the news that Gaveston is to be brought back. Overjoyed, he allows his love for Gaveston to spill over onto Isabella and what he recognizes, even from his vale of self-obsession, as her selfless act. But alas, such perceptive capabilities are short-lived, and all his thoughts return to Gaveston, overwhelming even matters of state, to the nobles' frustration. The King of France invades Normandy, at that time under England's control, but feckless Edward cares not.

Gaveston's return, however, facilitates not happiness within the court but even greater discord. Gaveston is unable to learn the game of politics, and his vengeful ways cause the king and his nobles to be at odds again. Isabella, ignored once more, surrenders all hope of compromise. She finds the attention she craves with Mortimer—as Edward disdainfully comes to acknowledge—and resolves to see Gaveston slain.

And so begin the bloodbath and epic of treachery that are the resolution of *Edward the Second.* Gaveston is ambushed, his head cut off by the Earl of Pembroke, one of Mortimer's stooges. Edward is imprisoned soon after, his all-but-pitch-dark cell the septic tank for the castle; he stands knee-deep in excrement. The malevolent assassin Lightborn arrives, takes a hot spit from the fire and impales Edward up the arse, killing him. And Lightborn, for his troubles, is stabbed by one of Mortimer's henchmen who assisted in the murder. The assassin's body pitched into the moat, Edward's corpse is carried up to Mortimer, the man who would be king:

> MORTIMER. The prince I rule, the queen I do command,
> And with a lowly congé to the ground
> The proudest lords salute me as I pass.
> I seal, I cancel, I do what I will;
> Fear'd am I, more than lov'd: let me be fear'd,
> And when I frown, make all the court look pale.
> (ACT V, SCENE 4)

Yet pride goeth before a fall, and Mortimer's power trip causes him to go too far: In Prince Edward's presence, he orders the slaughter of the boy's uncle, Edmund. Mortimer is supposed to be Edward the Third's protector, and as the child watches his uncle dragged away to be beheaded, he wonders, "What safety may I look for at his hands / If that my uncle shall be murdered thus?" It is a moment of revelation for the young prince, one that seals the end of the play. When informed of his father's death, Edward the Third turns on Mortimer as a self-serving traitor, ordering that he be executed. Recognizing the relationship between Mortimer and his mother, he orders her locked away, to stand trial for treason in the murder of her husband, his father, King Edward the Second.

The new king is brought Mortimer's head, and when his father's hearse arrives, he places it firmly upon the coffin.

FIVE QUESTIONS

1. Why does Edward love Gaveston?

2. If Edward had maintained some interest in the Queen, would she have turned against him?

3. What is power?

4. What is the moral of *Edward the Second*?

5. What did Christopher Marlowe, an atheistic homosexual, hope to gain by writing this play as he did and when he did?

Francis Bacon

Essays

A principal fruit of friendship is the ease and discharge of the fulness and swellings of the heart, which passions of all kinds do cause and induce . . . A man cannot speak to his son but as a father; to his wife but as a husband; to his enemy but upon terms: whereas a friend may speak as the case requires, and not as it sorteth with the person.

—"ON FRIENDSHIP"

As was expected of ambitious men of his period—educated at Trinity College, Cambridge, he was an attorney and intermittent court favorite—Francis Bacon married, but the marriage came late in his life, when he was forty-five, and he died childless. He condemns homosexuality in many of his writings. Yet in others he urges an appreciation of same-gender love, albeit never explicitly. The most adventurous of these is the essay "On Beauty"

Born in 1561, Bacon was thirty-two when his mother wrote to his brother Anthony complaining that Francis was keeping that "bloody Percy . . . as a coach companion and bed companion." The phrase "bed companion" is not necessarily the loaded charge here; "coach companion" is. The latter phrase was used to signify a sexual relationship, because coaches afforded the privacy sought for sex—as Flaubert's *Madame Bovary* would most vividly demonstrate centuries hence. Starting shortly after his death, biographers referred to Bacon as a "pederast," a disparaging term then as now, often used to denote homosexuals in general and not just the lovers of little boys.

Bacon's sexual proclivities did not earn him his place in history, however. Through his *Essays* in particular, and other works in general, he forced upon his culture a new philosophy that, while redolent of Greek and Roman thought, steered away from Aristotle's deductive reasoning toward what we would come to understand as true science and experimentation. He insisted upon the facts of any matter being known or experientially discovered, and would argue against truth being derived from authority—a dangerous position at a time when church and king held the greatest influence.

He made a pitch for a utopia in one of his writings, *New Atlantis,* although he declared it would be "without the touch" of "masculine love" (another Renaissance euphemism for homosexuality), so that it is arguable how utopian Bacon might have found it, in the long run, had he lived there.

Bacon died as the result of an experiment: He caught cold while stuffing the carcass of a chicken with snow and ice to see if it would be better preserved. It was, he wasn't. The cold turned into pneumonia and killed him, at the age of sixty-five.

His *Essays* provide a quick-read testament to the diversity and excellence of the human mind and spirit.

Marquis de Sade

The 120 Days of Sodom

TRANSLATED BY AUSTRYN WAINHOUSE
AND RICHARD SEAVER

At the first of these gatherings, the one exclusively given over to the pleasures of sodomy, only men were present; there would always be at hand sixteen young men, ranging in age from twenty to thirty, whose immense faculties permitted our four heroes, in feminine guise, to taste the most agreeable delights. The youths were selected solely on the basis of the size of their member, and it almost became necessary that this superb limb be of such magnificence that it could never have penetrated any woman . . . But simultaneously, to sample every pleasure, to these sixteen husbands was joined the same quantity of boys, much younger, whose purpose was to assume the office of women. These lads were from twelve to eighteen years old.

—"INTRODUCTION"

Born in Paris is 1740, the Comte Donatien-Alphonse-François de Sade was sentenced to death at the age of thirty-two as a "sodomite," but the sentence was lifted four years later. An anarchist of pleasure, he supported the Republic during the French Revolution, but his nobility made his efforts suspect by the new government. His published works—*The 120 Days of Sodom* was not among them—were denounced for immorality. Sade was imprisoned in 1801—one of several incarcerations—and died in a Charenton madhouse in 1814.

In 1782, during a stay in the Bastille, Sade wrote *The 120 Days of Sodom* on thin strips of paper twelve centimeters wide and pasted them together to form a scroll twelve meters long. He began writing on October 22 and stopped on November 28. Seven years later, when the Bastille was stormed, Sade thought *The 120 Days of Sodom* lost, along with other manuscripts in his room at the time. For the rest of his life, the work existed only as a memory he would try to re-create in later, published books, such as *Justine*.

But the scroll of *The 120 Days of Sodom* survived. It was found and preserved by a French family—unbeknownst to Sade, even at his death—who sold it to a German collector. The book was published at last in 1904.

The 120 Days of Sodom is still an incomplete text. Yet what there is of it establishes the work not only as the bedrock receptacle for Sade's thought but as an unsurpassable work of sexual excess.

Like most good works of sexual art, it has at its heart a hatred of restraint forced upon nature by man. Sade despised religion and the societal repression that sprang from it. He was an unapologetic libertine at a time when sexual freedom was not allowed; hence his anger, hence his suffering.

The 120 Days of Sodom, then, like many of the best queer works, bursts forth from a bed of repression. In places, it is sexy, stomach-churning and brutal in the way it reveals human potential for sex-as-exploitation; in others, it is simply redundant, tired and jaded.

William Beckford

Vathek

The two brothers had mutually engaged their children to each other; and Nouronihar loved her cousin, more than her own beautiful eyes. Both had the same tastes and amusements; the same long, languishing looks; the same tresses; the same fair complexions; and, when Gulchenrouz appeared in the dress of his cousin, he seemed to be more feminine than even herself.

Read on its own, *Vathek* is an *Arabian Nights*–influenced morality tale about the dangers of excess and self-indulgence. Read with an understanding of the author's life and background, it is a gender-bending novel of sexual justification and happiness.

Beckford was born to a wealthy and powerful family in London. Educated at home by a series of tutors, he acquired an appreciation for then-fashionable Eastern lore.

As he matured and his interest in all things oriental increased, so did his desire for young men. His first significant emotional attachment, occurring when he was twenty, was to a thirteen-year-old cousin named William Courtenay, a boy everyone in the family called "Kitty." The mutual relationship continued through Courtenay's teens and into Beckford's mid-twenties, fueled by passionate letters that would ultimately prove the pair's undoing.

When Beckford was twenty-four, the letters fell into the hands of Courtenay's powerful and conservative uncle, who started a rumor that he had caught the young men *in flagrante delicto*. The effect was predictable: Beckford's reputation and standing in English society were ruined.

Beckford was something of a prodigy. He wrote his first novel at the age of seventeen and *Vathek* at twenty-one. It poured out of him after a party; by his own account, he completed it in a feverish couple of days. A final, revised text and a translation appeared when Beckford was twenty-six. He had planned a separate series of perspective narratives—similar to what Sade may have attempted with his four narrators in *The 120 Days of Sodom*, although Beckford would certainly have showed more restraint—but these never came to fruition. *Vathek* remains the achievement of his life.

It is the story of a prince, Vathek, in search of power, and willing to make any sacrifice to realize it. The extremes to which he will go—aided by an overbearing mother, probably similar in some respects to Beckford's own—and his love for the willowy Nouronihar, interchangeable in appearance and persona with her male cousin, Gulchenrouz, is the meat of the story, admittedly slender on plot but fat on fabulousness and with an intriguing moral. For while Vathek and Nouronihar are lost to a life without hope, the innocent Gulchenrouz—arguably Vathek's lover, Courtenay, preserved in the text, with Nouronihar his socially acceptable representation—lives to "[pass] whole ages in undisturbed tranquillity, and in the pure happiness of childhood."

Think of it: Courtenay lives happily ever after. And the female doppelgänger society demanded Beckford create for him is banished to (in essence) hell, along with Beckford, the man who failed to stand up for his right to love. Here is a plea, basically, for the chance to live life happily and innocently—free from an awareness of society's judgment.

Sadly, that life would not be Beckford's. While not suffering as hard a fate as Vathek's, Beckford would perhaps never know again the love he had had with Courtenay. *Vathek* proved eerily predictive in its resolution.

Lord Byron

Poetry

Ours too the glance none saw beside;
  The smile none else might understand;
The whispered thoughts of hearts allied,
  The pressure of the thrilling hand;
  The kiss, so guiltless and refined,
    That Love each warmer wish forbore;
Those eyes proclaimed so pure a mind,
  Ev'n Passion blushed to plead for more.
—"TO THRYZA," LINES 29–36[1]

Like Francis Bacon before him, Lord George Gordon Byron was educated at Trinity College, Cambridge. He was hugely affected by the books he read, and his work shows it. Among his influences were Virgil—we have mentioned this homoerotic translation of the Nisus and Euryalus episode—and Beckford, whose *Vathek* personally and creatively chilled even as it stirred Byron's heart. Byron even translated one of Catullus' gayer poems, offered originally by that poet to a lad named Juventius—only Byron readdressed his "To Ellen" for propriety's sake.

---

[1] "Thryza" is believed to have been John Edleston, a choirboy college chum of Byron's, who died young.

Byron lived in a time when homosexuality in England was met with harsh penalties: Execution was a possibility, and scourgings were not infrequent. His discretion was less a matter of cowardice than one of pure survival.

Born in London in 1788, Byron was Scottish by descent, and was born lame. His first published collection of poems, *Hours of Idleness*, appeared when he was nineteen. The next year Byron embarked on his grand tour, visiting Greece and the Aegean along with Spain, Malta and Albania. Letters coded in Latin (after Petronius) to his circle of friends indicate that he indulged his capacity for boy love in Greece, taking up with lads at either end of the spectrum: the girlish Eustathius Giorgiu and the manly Nicolo Giraud. The latter Byron made his heir upon returning to England.

The first edition of the poem that was to make Byron an immediate literary celebrity, *Childe Harold's Pilgrimage*, was published when he was twenty-four. With its veiled homoerotic episodes, its success made Byron London's darling or demon—depending on one's perspective—and offered him opportunities for affairs with fashionable women. He had a long-running liaison with Lady Caroline Lamb, who arrived for their romps dressed as a pageboy and to whom he confided some of his queer yearnings. He would make this mistake again; in matters of passion, Byron remained something of a bumbler, unable to grasp the virtue of discretion.

He would have a disastrous, incestuous affair with his married half-sister, and then wed the stiff-necked heiress Anne Isabelle Milbanke in an effort to escape that familial involvement. Anne Isabelle sought a separation after a year, finding Byron's defense of Greek pederasty incomprehensible, though she knew of or suspected his inclinations. When they separated—and Byron's celebrity made the event newsworthy—she freely discussed his queer desires and his incestuous affair. The result: Byron fled England for Italy, where he wrote *Don Juan* and an autobiography that his family destroyed upon his death.

In 1823 Byron returned to Greece, where he fell in love with Lukas, a fifteen-year-old boy whose passion shapes many of Byron's last verses. Lukas apparently did not love Byron in return but merely exploited him for money and an easy life. Byron died a year later of a fever. His body was returned to England for interment.

Nikolai Gogol

Dead Souls

TRANSLATED BY RICHARD PEVEAR
AND LARISSA VOLOKHONSKY

"You don't want any of the female sex?"

"No, thank you."

"I wouldn't ask much. One little rouble apiece,
for the sake of acquaintance."

"No, I have no need of the female sex."

"Well, if you have no need, there's nothing to talk
about. Taste knows no rules: one man loves the parson,
another the parsoness, as the proverb says."

—CHAPTER 5

Nikolai Vasilievich Gogol-Yanovsky was born on April 1, 1809, in
Ukraine. His father was the country lord of over two hundred
serfs—or souls, as they were known, though in truth they belonged
to Gogol's mother—and a minor playwright. Gogol's mother was a
religious daimon who argued for hellfire and punishment over the
power of Christ's redemption. Gogol's life would be fixed between
the two.

Gogol's much-loved younger brother, Ivan, died when Gogol
was ten. Gogol spent his teen years in an all-male boarding school,

where he developed a penchant for straight boys unable to respond to his amorous advances.

He made his name with a series of short fictions about life in Mother Russia's rural provinces. Many of his writings boast male heroes whose desire for a woman leads them toward danger, if not death. Gogol, however, was at heart a satirist, a comic writer; these tales were less grim than fantastic, and were always graced by Gogol's incredible talent for imagery. He was famous stylistically for mixing the animate and the inanimate in ways that are startlingly vivid and immediate to the reader.

Today Gogol is known both for his stories and for his play *The Inspector General*, but perhaps best of all for his "novel," *Dead Souls*. (Gogol himself always referred to *Dead Souls* as a poem.) This story of a man, Chichikov, who comes to a Russian backwater and sets about buying up the souls of the recently deceased serfs was, as with much of Gogol's work, firmly rooted in the corruption that was the Russian bureaucracy.

At the time, landowners were taxed, and their wealth measured by the number of souls their land could support. But the census was infrequently taken, and in the meanwhile, many of the souls could die, though the landowner would still have to pay tax on them until the next census. When a law was passed that no farm with less than fifty souls could operate a still and make vodka— which was in turn sold for income—a distant relative of Gogol's, whose property fed only thirty souls, swapped vodka for the dead souls registry of his neighbors and therefore maintained his distillery.

Although his tale is rooted in fact, Gogol skews it to increase its potential for humor, as well as for reflective social commentary. But it would be a mistake to label Gogol as a social liberal. When *Dead Souls* led readers and critics to praise him as such, he struck back viciously, writing essays that defended slavery and classist social structures, decrying political change as an offense against Christianity, then the state religion.

In January 1852, unable to bear the guilt over his homosexuality any longer, Gogol confessed to a priest, who told him to abstain from food and sleep in order to purge himself of his "inner filth." A month later, Gogol, wasted from starvation, driven mad by sleep deprivation and further weakened by doctors who bled him with leeches, finally shed the skin of his sexual sin by shedding the flesh of his body. He died on February 21.

"Civil Disobedience"

If a thousand men were not to pay their tax-bills this year, that would not be a violent and bloody measure, as it would be to pay them, and enable the State to commit violence and shed innocent blood. This is, in fact, the definition of a peaceable revolution, if any such is possible. If the tax-gatherer, or any other public officer, asks me, as one has done, "But what shall I do?" my answer is, "If you really wish to do anything, resign your office." When the subject has refused allegiance, and the officer has resigned his office, then the revolution is accomplished. But even suppose blood should flow. Is there not a sort of blood shed when the conscience is wounded? Through the wound a man's real manhood and immortality flow out, and he bleeds to an everlasting death. I see this blood flowing now.

Henry David Thoreau was born in Concord, Massachusetts, on July 12, 1817. His graduation from Harvard, in 1837, was delayed by time taken off to earn money for school and by his first serious attack of tuberculosis. The disease would eventually kill him on May 6, 1862, as it had killed his brother and father before him.

After Harvard, Thoreau returned home to teach and lecture, taking over the Concord Academy, where he had been educated as a boy. In 1841, however, he would close the school to make lead pencils with his father.

In 1839 Thoreau stumbled across his life's work, literally: He made the voyage he would describe ten years later in *A Week on the Concord and Merrimack Rivers*. In this journey he found the seed for his calling, as a writer who commented on the human condition through observations of nature. Soon after these travels, he began regularly publishing poems and essays in the literary magazine *The Dial*.

Thoreau never married. In 1840 he proposed to Ellen Sewall, but she refused him. He lived with philosopher Ralph Waldo Emerson in 1841, 1843 and 1847, working as a handyman, and the nature of their relationship—couched in the hyperbolic romantic sensibility of the day, as evidenced in their letters—is hard to divine. What is not hard to divine is Thoreau's love for the male form, either through his rapturous longing for Alek Therien, the woodcutter of Walden Pond, or the love poems he wrote to eleven-year-old Edward Sewall, Ellen's brother!

In 1845 he built himself a cabin in the woods by Walden Pond (on Emerson's property), and lived there for two years. There he would write both *A Week on the Concord and Merrimack Rivers,* and *Walden, or Life in the Woods,* the latter published in 1854. During his time at Walden Pond, Thoreau maintained an active social life in Concord.

After leaving his cabin, he supported himself with a variety of jobs, including fence building, whitewashing, gardening and surveying. He visited Maine in 1846, 1853 and 1857, and his notes from those travels would be collected and published two years after his death as *The Maine Woods*. His 1850 trip to Canada yielded *A Yankee in Canada*, published in 1866. Selections of his poetry would be published too, as well as edited collections of his letters and portions of his thirty-volume journal. But his essay "Civil Disobedience," first published in 1849 as "Resistance to Civil Government," would be his best-known work after *Walden* and perhaps the work closest to his soul. It was the product of a night he spent in jail in 1846 for his repeated refusal to pay a poll tax to a government that supported slavery and the Mexican War.

Later, Thoreau would assist the Underground Railroad and concern himself with the miserable treatment of Native Americans at the hand of the intruding Union government. But the limits of peaceable opposition would be tested for Thoreau when he met abolitionist John Brown in 1857. Following the man's bloody raid on Harpers Ferry, West Virginia, Thoreau delivered a plea in Brown's defense, saying that although every common use of violence is unjust, Brown's brutal strike toward freedom for all regardless of skin color was not. Thoreau saw Brown's action as a just use of violence, albeit perhaps the only one. Although in conflict with much of his writing—with much of "Civil Disobedience"—this endorsement was in keeping with Thoreau's principal concern: the moral action of the individual against an immoral state or nation.

Thoreau saw his actions, his words, himself, as something of a "chanticleer," a cock crowing to wake up the country to its moral failings.

This American government—what is it but a tradition, though a recent one, endeavoring to transmit itself unimpaired to posterity, but each instant losing some of its integrity? It has not the vitality and force of a single living man; for a single man can bend it to his will . . . But it is not the less necessary for this; for the people must have some complicated machinery or other, and hear its din, to satisfy that idea of government which they have. Governments show thus how successfully men can be imposed upon, even impose on themselves, for their own advantage. It is excellent, we must all allow. Yet this government never of itself furthered any enterprise, but by the

alacrity with which it got out of his way. It does not keep
the country free. It does not settle the West. It does not
educate. The character of the American people has done
all that has been accomplished, and it would have done
somewhat more, if the government had not sometimes got
in its way.

Having "heartily" accepted the motto "That government is best
which governs least" and surpassed it with another, "That government is best which governs not at all," in the opening paragraph of
"Civil Disobedience," Thoreau leads us from perplexity into the
clarity of his second paragraph (reprinted immediately above) and
his first rousing, singular point: The government does not exist in
and of itself, but its people let it. In a sense, this is true of all
governments. It is especially true of American democracy.

Thoreau moves on to make the first of two thesis statements
that form the heart of his concerns, saying, as a citizen of the
republic, ". . . I ask for, not at once no-government, but at once a
better government. Let every man make known what kind of government would command his respect, and that will be one step
toward obtaining it."

Thoreau deplores the fact that he must subjugate the actions of
his conscience as a countryman to the actions of a representative in
Congress, a servitude he deems solely beneficial to the gnashing
gears of government. He would have all citizens vote on all matters
not immediately pressing, hoping for a government decided not by
majority rule but by conscience.

To Thoreau, the government is less concerned with the head
and heart of man—never mind the soul—than it is with a man's
body, which it may use for cannon fodder:

Visit the Navy-Yard, and behold a marine, such a man as
an American government can make, or such as it can make
a man with its black arts,—a mere shadow and reminis-

cence of humanity, a man laid out alive and standing, and already, as one may say, buried under arms with funeral accompaniments . . . The mass of men serve the state thus, not as men mainly, but as machines, with their bodies.

Thoreau claims that these men become as wooden soldiers, handing over their morals to stand by the government's judgment, surrendering all of their own conscience.

But Thoreau is on the way to his second thesis statement, asking, "How does it become a man to behave toward this American government to-day?" Before the reader might have a chance to reply, Thoreau leaps in, saying, "I answer, that he cannot without disgrace be associated with it. I cannot for an instant recognize that political organization as my government which is the slave's government also."

Thoreau is onto something. In order for us to abide with ourselves as good Americans, we must be able first to convince ourselves of our government's ability to fulfill a position of moral certitude that the people, via their representatives, bring to it.

Of course, even as this is perhaps Thoreau's best argument, it is also his weakest. Over a hundred years later, we are jaded enough to understand that, as a rule, people do not vote for their representatives out of a sense of conscience but, rather, for what those representatives will procure for them: fat government contracts that mean jobs, tax cuts that will put pennies in their purses. And despite the American government's being the best government in the world by virtue of the opportunities it provides for redress, the protection of minority interests is a frail, tentative thing, uncertain at best.

We have, a century past Thoreau, grown accustomed to thinking of the American government as something of a behemoth over which we have no direct control. And so we sit passively by as thirty million tax dollars go to provide free fodder for the scandal sheets, as the military spends exorbitant amounts on cheap materials and as queers are continually denied equal access to the benefits of an American society they help create, not only through their public tax dollars but through their private investments in the economy.

In the 1980s Larry Kramer, author of the drama *The Normal Heart* and a cunningly wicked tome on decadent gay life in the '70s, *Faggots,* was able to mobilize a group of gays and lesbians and their friends into ACT UP, a grassroots effort at civil disobedience that is now recognized as the chief reason the FDA at last sped up the release of experimental drugs for the fight against AIDS. Along the way, some shocking pieces of performance art were created, and the queer community, such as it is, was polarized between those who found ACT UP's work deplorable and those who found it laudable, even if they didn't always agree with the way the group went about it.

Regardless, it is undeniable that ACT UP's efforts worked—and that, for a brief moment, a minority sought to rise up and take direct control of its government's moral sympathies.

But how often is the government ever directed by morality? Thoreau moves on to discuss how government manages to support unjust causes—for his argument, slavery—and how many people are apt to talk about their opposition to injustice but do little or nothing to follow through on their concern. He despairs that, by the time the people are able to vote to right a wrong, the wrong really no longer exists, that the vote in such cases is but a token exercise. He addresses the gregarious shell of character—the "Odd Fellow"—that has come to represent the average American, and elaborates further on the determination of individual responsibility and the choices men are faced with, between mere words and deeds. He asks, "How can a man be satisfied to entertain an opinion merely, and enjoy it?" Holding an opinion as to whether we have been rightly or wrongly treated is immaterial; it is in redressing our wrongs—in action—that we find our satisfaction:

Action from principle, the perception and the performance of right, changes things and relations; it is essentially revolutionary, and does not consist wholly with anything which was. It not only divides states and churches, it
divides families; ay, it divides the individual, separating the
diabolical in him from the divine.

Unjust laws exist: shall we be content to obey them, or
shall we endeavor to amend them, and obey them until we
have succeeded or shall we transgress them at once? Men
generally, under a government such as this, think that they
ought to wait until they have persuaded the majority to
alter them. They think that, if they should resist, the remedy would be worse than the evil. But it is the fault of the
government itself that the remedy is worse than the evil. It
makes it worse. Why is it not more apt to anticipate and
provide for reform? Why does it not cherish its wise minority? Why does it cry and resist before it is hurt? Why
does it not encourage its citizens to be on the alert to point
out its faults, and do better than it would have them? Why
does it always crucify Christ, and excommunicate Coper-
nicus and Luther, and pronounce Washington and Franklin rebels?

Masterfully, by evoking Franklin and Washington as last in a line of
those that governments have historically sinned against, Thoreau is
able to bring home his point that American government is a historical monolith, a beast whose instinct for self-preservation out-
weighs its desire to progress toward the moral good. Yet Thoreau is
not some pansy idealist; having already scorned those who talk but
do nothing, he recognizes that some of these injustices the government perpetuates only against itself in the name of self-preservation, a part of the "necessary friction of government." This, Thoreau argues, isn't worth our concern: It is the idiot child playing

with himself in the corner of the room. We should choose our battles wisely, choose them purposefully, for "if it is of such a nature that it requires you to be the agent of injustice to another, then, I say, break the law."

One of man's greatest weapons against his government is financial. Thoreau sets forth the proposal that if we do not agree with the government—if it will spend our money on bullets and smears and oppression—we should not support it, we should refuse to pay our taxes or any portion thereof slated to fund what we have found intolerable. He goes on to set forth the basic premise of grassroots political activism—nonviolent resistance—and the consequences of its alternative, passive acceptance (as quoted above, at the opening of this section).

Thoreau argues for the right of the individual to retain his individual authority in the face of the monolith that is government, to select and define his communities according to their potential for justice. He describes his personal attempts toward this end, explaining his own willing failure to pay a poll tax to the (unjust) State and the incarceration that resulted, saying of his imprisonment, "As they could not reach me, they had resolved to punish my body; just as boys, if they cannot come at some person against whom they have some spite, will abuse his dog." Our government, then, is a mean-spirited, puerile bully—in the nineteenth century and now. (Thoreau was released from jail when someone paid his poll tax for him, an action that, predictably, angered rather than pleased him.)

Thoreau's argument at this point is that government may dictate the realm of the physical man but not the realm of man's spirit, his conscience, his morals: We must render unto Caesar what is Caesar's and unto God what is God's. Yet upon his release from prison, Thoreau finds himself different, separated from his friends in a manner previously unknown to him. Having crossed the line from inaction to action—having been forced to cross it, at the rough hands of the State—Thoreau finds himself, admittedly harshly, saying:

> I saw to what extent the people among whom I lived could be trusted as good neighbors and friends; that their friendship was for summer weather only; that they did not greatly propose to do right . . . that in their sacrifices to humanity they ran no risks, not even to their property; that after all they were not so noble but they treated the thief as he had treated them, and hoped, by a certain outward observance and a few prayers, and by walking in a particular straight though useless path from time to time, to save their souls.

Thoreau wants it made clear that he supports worthy taxes, such as those for the care of roads and schools. He admonishes that "the dollar is innocent." He muses over the base nature of man, and reflects on his own desire to live in a community rather than in self-imposed isolation, but is brought back to the diversity of perspective such a community naturally disgorges and the inevitable governmental shadow of the majority will and the minority concern. In closing, following a lament that the government apes Christian law but will not live it, Thoreau declares:

> There will never be a really free and enlightened State until the State comes to recognize the individual as a higher and independent power, from which all its own power and authority are derived, and treats him accordingly. I please myself with imagining a State at last which can afford to be just to all men, and to treat the individual with respect as a neighbor; which even would not think it inconsistent with its own repose if a few were to live aloof from it, not meddling with it, nor embraced by it, who fulfilled all the duties of neighbors and fellow-men. A State which bore

this kind of fruit, and suffered it to drop off as fast as it ripened, would prepare the way for a still more perfect and glorious State, which also I have imagined, but not anywhere seen.

While this reverie of utopia may be a fine place to end his essay, it does not serve as a closing consideration for ours. More fitting is Thoreau's challenge a few paragraphs earlier, where he claims:

> They who know of no purer sources to truth, who have traced up its stream no higher, stand, and wisely stand, by the Bible and the Constitution, and drink at it there with reverence and humility; but they who behold where it comes trickling into this lake or that pool, gird up their loins once more, and continue their pilgrimage toward its fountainhead.

Thoreau, with his sensitivity to what it means to be an outsider, ostracized by the mainstream community because of something he feels to be a natural part of him (in this case, his belief), in "Civil Disobedience" aptly provides queers with a boilerplate for resistance and the peaceable pursuit of equality. The tragedy (and success) of ACT UP was that its focus was so narrow it shut down when people stopped dying in droves. The tragedy (and success) of the gay community is that while political promises have been kept, they've provided little real change, their true purpose being not our equal standing in society but to lull us to sleep. "Civil Disobedience" exists as a queer manifesto, readily apprehended, if we but waken to the chanticleer.

FIVE QUESTIONS

1. Do we tend to dismiss Thoreau politically because he makes us uncomfortable? Why does he make us uncomfortable, and why is our response to dismiss him?

2. Which is greater, the individual's obligation to the self or the individual's obligation to the community in which he lives?

3. Suppose we were to convert every thoughtless action (things we do by rote, paying taxes, etc.) into thoughtful action. How would our lives change, and why? Do we live our lives thoughtfully, and if not, why not?

4. Is it important to be a good person? What is a good person?

5. Is it the great failure of American liberal politics that it acts from some naive view that the good will win out, denying its proponents the activism that fuels more conservative factions?

Herman Melville

Moby-Dick

Squeeze! Squeeze! Squeeze! all the morning long; I squeezed that sperm till I myself almost melted into it; I squeezed that sperm till a strange sort of insanity came over me; and I found myself unwittingly squeezing my co-laborers' hands in it, mistaking their hands for the gentle globules. Such an abounding, affectionate, friendly, loving feeling did this affectation beget; that at last I was continually squeezing their hands, and looking up into their eyes sentimentally; as much to say,—Oh! my dear fellow beings, why should we longer cherish any social acerbities, or know the slightest ill-humor or envy? Come; let us squeeze hands all round; nay, let us all squeeze ourselves into each other; let us squeeze ourselves universally into the very milk and sperm of kindness.

—CHAPTER 94

From the above passage it is quickly apparent that a reading of America's classic through queer eyes lends itself to a far richer interpretive experience.

Herman Melville was born in New York City in 1819. His family had money and was well regarded in society, but by 1830 his father had been rendered bankrupt and mad. The resulting impoverishment launched the young gentleman Melville upon a seafaring career for which his life in New York society had ill prepared him. Melville also carried with him the fractured sensibilities of his family: inherited legacies, the onus of secrecy (as a result of his father's madness) and the painful, swift loss of position in society. All these influences reflected themselves in his work.

Melville was best known in his lifetime for his exotic narratives, *Typee* and *Omoo*. Yet his place in history has been secured not by these but by *Moby-Dick,* the story of Captain Ahab's pursuit of the great white whale, of Ishmael and Queequeg, and of the first mate, Starbuck.

Moby-Dick is a great novel not because it has suffered endless harangues of literary criticism and psychological analysis, where this theorist read into it one thing and that theorist then contradicted him, but because it has everything. It is a novel of God, reconstructed family, love, slavish devotion to work; of purpose, patriarchal subversion and domination, life's resonance.

The book is redolent with Melville's gay sensibility, much of it in the relationship of Ishmael and Queequeg, who meet in Chapter 3, sleep together and are joined to the story's very end. Although Melville married in 1847 and sired children, his works reveal an almost shockingly queer tack, and this, combined with his passionate letters written to other men, most notably Nathaniel Hawthorne, has led history to try to reconcile his public heterosexual life with a private homosexual one.

All in all, Melville's life was one of much bitterness. *Moby-Dick* was savaged upon publication, and it wouldn't be until thirty years after the author's death, in 1891, that his star would begin to rise in American literature. In part, this has been due to the strong, sympathetic gay following he earned: E. M. Forster, Hart Crane and Matthew Stadler are but a few of the notable writers who have come to acclaim Melville's work—and in Stadler's case, *Moby-Dick* in particular—as wholly remarkable and, even better, wholly readable.

It is a beautiful book to sink into, the wondrous queer heart of American literature.

Thomas Hughes

Tom Brown's Schooldays

The fact was that Tom's heart had already smitten him for not asking his "fidus Achates"[2] to the feast, although only an extempore affair; and though prudence and the desire to get Martin and Arthur together alone at first had overcome his scruples, he was now heartily glad to open the door, broach another bottle of beer, and hand over the old ham-knuckle to the searching of his old friend's pocket knife.

—PART II, CHAPTER 3, "THE SUPPER"

Thomas Hughes was born in Uffington, Berkshire, in 1822 and was educated at Rugby (the experience that shaped *Tom Brown's Schooldays)* and Oriel College, Oxford. He married and fathered a family. He had a vested interest in both the working class—founding the Working Men's College and serving as its president from 1872 to 1883—and in utopian communities, one of which he actually set-

[2] Meaning "faithful friend," derived from a line in Virgil's *The Aeneid*.

tled in Rugby, Tennessee. (He was able to visit it only once, though, in 1880.) He was a liberal, a Christian socialist and a member of Parliament whose other publications included *The Manliness of Christ.*

He was *so* not gay.

Why, then, is his work included in *The Gay Canon*?

Because *Tom Brown's Schooldays,* published in 1857, would prove to be one of the more influential texts for emerging gay writers, or writers with a gay sensibility. Its moral compass is the near-Victorian Thomas Arnold, who infected the British public school system with the idea that Christian moral instruction and religious study were a necessary part of education. This infection would begin to be cured only after a bitchy lancing by the homosexual Lytton Strachey in *Eminent Victorians.*

While sexless, *Tom Brown's Schooldays* creates a virtual dream world of male seclusion, where boys live in fractious harmony with other boys reading Virgil, the grown men around them their ideal, with nary a thought given to women—certainly they serve no sexual utility. Hughes's nascent "muscular Christianity," censoring its own sexuality, provided a breeding ground for homoaffectionalism and, by extension, homosexuality.

This was fertile soil, and it would be tapped by Evelyn Waugh in *Brideshead Revisited* and William Maxwell in *The Folded Leaf.* More important, it would continue to feed the tantalizing image of the British public school system as an isolated male bastion of wealth and privilege, eroticized fraternization and pederastic buggery.

Tom Brown's Schooldays is rife with same-gender love that sweetly sets the heart to swooning, even as it remains, perversely, a children's text, a boy's novel.

Arthur Rimbaud

Complete Works

TRANSLATED BY PAUL SCHMIDT

Soldiers' cocks are a black burlesque;
They rape my heart with what they say.
—"THE STOLEN HEART," FROM VERSE 2

Born on October 20, 1854, Jean-Nicolas-Arthur Rimbaud was the son of an army captain and his strict, disciplinarian wife. The boy was precocious, writing first in Latin, then in French, his native language. At the age of sixteen he ran away from his family home in northern France to Paris. While there, he may have had his first sexual experience—possibly a rape—at the hands of soldiers in their barracks. The poem "The Stolen Heart" is thought to refer to this initiation.

Rimbaud eventually returned home, only to be invited back to Paris by the most renowned poet of the time, Paul Verlaine. Rimbaud had sent the poet, ten years his senior, his verses. Upon the boy's arrival in Paris, the two fell into a wild, passionate love affair, despite Verlaine's marriage. For a year and a half they cavorted in bars, salons and Paris cafés, traveling to Brussels and London together. They referenced each other in their work and even wrote poetry together, such as the memorable sonnet "To the

Asshole," which opens with the lines "Dark, puckered hole: a purple carnation / That trembles, nestled among the moss (still wet/ With love) covering the gentle curvation / of the white ass . . ."

It was during their trip to Brussels in 1873 that the affair, so long fed on alcohol and high-strung art, began to unravel: Rimbaud and Verlaine quarreled, Rimbaud threatened to end their affair, and Verlaine in response shot the boy poet in the wrist. Unable to cut Verlaine loose from his side, Rimbaud staged a scene in the street, never dreaming that charges of sodomy would be leveled against Verlaine as a result. The elder poet was sentenced to two years' hard labor. Verlaine's wife left him, and Rimbaud abandoned poetry, ignoring even the notoriety that the still-devoted Verlaine's publication of Rimbaud's *The Illuminations* earned him in 1886.

Rimbaud traveled, enlisting in the Dutch army in 1876, serving as an Egyptian coffee buyer in 1880; by 1887 he was selling guns. In April 1891 he was troubled by an infection in his leg. He traveled back to France, where his leg was amputated, but to no avail: Rimbaud died on November 10.

Roderick Hudson

Mrs. Hudson fixed her eyes upon the floor in silence. There was not a trace in Roderick's face or in his voice of the bitterness of his emotion of the day before and not a hint of his having the lightest weight upon his conscience. He looked at Rowland with his frank and radiant eye as if there had never been a difference of opinion between them; as if each had ever been for both, unalterably, and both for each.

—CHAPTER 21

Scots-Irish-American Henry James was born in New York on April 15, 1843, and known as "Henry James, Junior" until he was forty-one years old and his father died. The elder James was a well-known theological writer and lecturer, and friend to Ralph Waldo Emerson. This friendship perhaps made its most vivid impression on James's brother, William, whose *Variety of Religious Experience* remains a classic attempt to examine the timeless human desire to believe.

James and his family spent his youthful years tossing between New England and Europe. His family returned to the American Northeast shortly before the outbreak of the Civil War. Henry studied law at Harvard, but not well, and in 1865 began to publish short stories and pieces of literary criticism in distinguished periodicals such as *The Nation* and *Atlantic Monthly*. His potential was quickly acknowledged, and after an abortive European sojourn in 1870—his money ran out—he returned to America and secured a job as Paris correspondent for the *New York Tribune*. In 1875 he again set sail for the Continent, where he met, among others, the writers Turgenev and Flaubert.

His future work would resolve itself somewhat neatly into three distinct periods. The first concerned itself with the impact of America's burgeoning wealth and power upon the old façades of European society, and produced such novels as 1875's *Roderick Hudson*, 1877's *The American*, 1879's *Daisy Miller*, 1880's *Washington Square*, 1881's *Portrait of a Lady*, 1886's *The Princess Casamassima*—almost a bookend to this period, with its return to the titled concerns of *Roderick Hudson*—and *The Bostonians*, published the same year.

The second period found root in James's one willful attempt to shape his life: his decision to live in England. He moved there in 1876, residing in London until 1897, then at Lamb House in Rye, where he lived out the rest of his days. The novels of his second period include 1890's *The Tragic Muse*, 1897's *The Spoils of Poynton* and *What Maisie Knew* and 1889's *The Awkward Age*.

Thereafter, in the last round, James would attempt to reconcile American and English differences in his writing, producing *The Wings of the Dove* in 1902, *The Ambassadors* in 1903—a conscientious reworking of *Roderick Hudson*—and *The Golden Bowl* in 1904.

His attempts at playwriting were not successful. His short stories, however—most notably "The Turn of the Screw" and "The Pupil"—earned him acclaim, and also displayed a muted homoeroticism. In addition, James published critical studies such as *French Poets and Novelists;* a book on the craft of writing, *The Art of the Novel;* a collection of essays and lectures; and a series of memoirs, the last of which was unfinished at his death, by a stroke, in 1916. In 1915, disconcerted by America's failure to join in the war effort, he became a British citizen and shortly before his death was awarded the Order of Merit.

He never married. Oscar Wilde's trial horrified him, as did Wilde's flamboyance. He refused to sign the petition circulated for Wilde's pardon, probably because he feared similar prosecution. The English novelist Hugh Walpole reportedly propositioned James, only to have a trembling "I can't! I can't!" as a response—but this tells us little.

Roderick Hudson tells us more. Written in the manner of a serial that keeps us desperately turning the pages, *Roderick Hudson* is a novel of sublimated desire, and in many ways it probably serves as an accurate chronicle of James's emotional life at the time of its writing. It lacks the restraint the Master increasingly brought to his later works. *The Ambassadors*, as earlier stated, echoes *Roderick Hudson*'s theme, yet provides safe distance between its two male protagonists by separating them, chronologically, by more than a generation. (Roderick Hudson and Rowland Mallet are contemporaries.) This effect, however, rather than desexualizing *The Ambassadors*, manages to evoke a disturbingly pseudopederastic response in the reader. *Roderick Hudson* is a more primitive, more emotive work, mapping the adventures of the masculine heart in love.

Rowland Mallet had made his arrangements to sail for Europe on the first of September, and having in the interval a fortnight to spare, he determined to spend it with his cousin Cecilia, the widow of a nephew of his father. He was urged by the reflection that an affectionate farewell might help to exonerate him from the charge of neglect frequently preferred by this lady. It was not that the young man disliked her; on the contrary he regarded her with a tender admiration, and he had not forgotten how when his cousin brought her home on her marriage he seemed to feel the upward sweep of the empty bough from which the golden fruit had been plucked, and then and there accepted the prospect of bachelorhood. (CHAPTER 1)

So opens *Roderick Hudson*. Mallet is no longer open to marriage to Cecilia. Though she is widowed, in the eight years since her marriage to his now-deceased cousin, "that fancy had died a natural death." Still, he enjoys her company, despite the fact that she is not very wealthy and therefore lives in Northampton, Massachusetts, as opposed to Boston.

Mallet himself, however, is not without his own problems: Though wealthy through his parents' success, he lacks any ambition, or rather, his ambition has no focus. A mixture of Dutch and Puritan stock, he is stout and yellow-haired, with red checks; his early education was that of a poor boy, his father wanting him to grow up without pretensions. He served in the Civil War. "[H]e was an awkward mixture of moral and aesthetic curiosity, and yet he would have made an ineffective reformer and an indifferent artist" (Chapter 1). He smokes cigars, is given to fits of melancholy and is, simply, an idler, waiting for something to come along, intrude upon his life and provide it with purpose and meaning.

Which it does, in the form of a vision in Cecilia's garden, a bronze statue given to her by a local sculptor. Showing a naked boy drinking from a gourd, it is perfectly made, and on the base is scrawled the Greek word for "thirst."

The name of the artist is Roderick Hudson.

Mallet's curiosity is piqued by this beautiful statue. He queries his cousin about the artist, only to find that Hudson is a law student from Virginia, twenty-three or twenty-four to Mallet's newly minted thirty. After Cecilia had admired the figure in clay, Hudson forced the bronze on her on her birthday. Mallet is quite taken by the idea of the young law student who would be a sculptor, who has found happiness and fulfillment in an aspect of his life—a feat Rowland has yet to manage.

In the evening, as he was smoking his cigar on the veran-
dah, a light quick step pressed the gravel of the garden
path, and in a moment a young man made his bow to
Cecilia. It was rather a nod than a bow, and indicated
either that he was an old friend or that he was scantily
versed in the usual social forms. Cecilia, who was sitting
near the steps, pointed to a neighbouring chair, but the
young man seated himself abruptly on a step at her feet
and began to fan himself vigorously with his hat, breaking
out into a lively objurgation upon the hot weather. "I'm
dripping wet!" he said, without ceremony.

"You walk too fast," said Cecilia. "You do everything
too fast."

"I know it, I know it!" he cried, passing his hand
through his abundant dark hair and making it stand out in
a picturesque shock. "I can't be slow if I try. There's something inside of me that drives me. A restless fiend!"

Cecilia gave a light laugh, and Rowland leaned forward in his hammock . . . When he raised himself she
pushed him back and said that the baby must finish its
nap. "But I want to see the gentleman with the fiend inside
of him," said Rowland. (CHAPTER 2)

Rowland does not see the visitor for a while, contenting himself with listening to the fellow's voice, "a soft and not altogether
masculine organ." At last Cecilia introduces the two men, noting
Rowland's pleasure at Roderick's statue:

Hudson smiled and started. "A connoisseur?" he cried,
laughing. "He is the first I have ever seen! Let me see what
they look like"; and he drew Rowland nearer to the light.
"Have they all such good heads as that? I should like to
model yours." (CHAPTER 2)

Rowland appraises Roderick as a "tall slender young fellow, with a singularly mobile and intelligent face . . . in a short time he perceived it was remarkably handsome. The features were admirably chiseled and finished, and a frank smile played over them as gracefully as a breeze among flowers" (Chapter 2). Roderick is as thin as Rowland is stout, as dark as he is fair, as overburdened with drive and potential as Rowland is without them. Rowland quickly invites the boy artist to Europe to bolster his artistic endeavors, offering to pay the cost of the journey against his advance purchase of Roderick's forthcoming statuary. It is settled, and the two men plan to be off as soon as Rowland has met Roderick's family: Hudson's protective mother, who has lost her only other son to the Civil War, and Miss Mary Garland, a distant cousin looking after Mrs. Hudson.

Just before they are to leave, Mallet and Hudson go for a walk on a Sunday afternoon:

The young men walked away at a steady pace, over hill and dale, through woods and fields, and at last found themselves on a grassy elevation studded with mossy rocks and red cedars. Just beneath them, in a great shining curve, flowed the generous Connecticut. They flung themselves on the grass and tossed stones into the river; they talked like old friends. Rowland lit a cigar and Roderick refused one with a grimace of extravagant disgust. He thought them vile things; he didn't see how decent people could tolerate them. Rowland was amused—he wondered what it was that made this ill-mannered speech seem perfectly inoffensive on Roderick's lips. He belonged to the race of mortals, to be pitied or envied according as we view the matter, who are not held to a strict account for their aggressions. Looking at him, as he lay stretched in the shade, Rowland vaguely likened him to some beautiful, supple,

restless, bright-eyed animal, whose motions should have
no deeper warrant than the tremulous delicacy of its structure and seem graceful even when they were most inconve-
nient . . . He sat up beside his companion and looked
away at the far-spreading view. It seemed to him beautiful,
and suddenly a strange feeling of prospective regret took
possession of him. Something seemed to tell him that
later, in a foreign land, he should remember it with longing and regret.   (CHAPTER 2)

This is the beginning of the romantic idyll the two men will share,
even as women intrude upon their exclusive preserve.

Rowland finds Mary Garland's simple, kind intelligence intriguing, but before he can assess her marriageability, a man closer
to her moves in and impulsively offers her his hand: Roderick Hudson. (It should be noted that, throughout, James uses similar language to describe Miss Garland's relationship with the two men and
the two men's relationship with each other—most noticeably, the
loaded term "companion.") As Hudson and Mallet are about to
depart for Europe, Hudson and Miss Garland announce their engagement, to Rowland's muted cheer.

In Europe, things go well at first. Before settling down in
Rome, the two men discuss art in Paris and Venice. Roderick takes
quickly, and with exhaustive happiness, to the idea of life lived as an
artist would live it. This is not without its moments of dramatic,
melancholic fits, as in Venice when Hudson frets that his devotion
to sculpture has all been a mistake, that painting is the thing, and
despairs his wasted effort until:

Then one morning the two men had themselves rowed out
to Torcello, and Roderick lay back for a couple of hours
watching a brown-breasted gondolier making superb muscular movements, in high relief, against the sky of the
Adriatic, and at the end jerked himself up with a violence

that nearly swamped the gondola, and declared that the only thing worth living for was to make a colossal bronze and set it aloft in the light of the public square.
(CHAPTER 5)

But if Roderick's artistic sensibility lends him a bisexual appreciation of beauty, he is rendered speechless when, shortly after arriving in Rome, he encounters Christina Light, a beautiful, utterly bored young girl, parading about with a fabulous poodle, her mother and a sort of withered, passionate butler in tow. That Hudson and Light will eventually meet again is certain. In the interim, the full effects of Rome's cultural indulgences are felt by the young artist. Hudson's newly liberated talent produces spectacular sculptures of Adam and Eve, which earn him respect in Rome, and celebrity as a promising young artist.

Mallet and Hudson develop a small cluster of artistic friends: a quiet painter of great talent, a noisy popular sculptor of little skill and an indulgent patroness. Yet Hudson's newfound freedom is shackled, somewhat, by Mallet's constant presence, and so at last comes the first gentle rift, in a discussion of the two men's summer travel plans:

"Try it!" said Rowland.

"Well, then, I think my journey will do me more good if I take it alone. I needn't say I prefer your society to that of any man living. For the last six months it has been a fund of comfort. But I have a perpetual feeling that you are expecting something of me, that you are measuring my doings by a terrifically high standard. You are watching me; I don't want to be watched! I want to go my own way; to work when I choose and to loaf when I choose. It is not that we are not friends. It is simply that I want a taste of perfect freedom. Therefore I say let us separate."
(CHAPTER 7)

Rowland of course agrees, but there is in this passage an echo of that moment, particularly in any romantic friendship between a heterosexual and a homosexual, where the idyll comes to an end, mutual goals no longer conveniently express themselves, and the couple go their separate ways. Often it is this moment that separates the homoaffectional moment from the homosexual one, and it is this sentiment we find reflected in *Roderick Hudson*. Hudson has tasted life as an artist and found it good; he has also found himself at the limits of his romantic friendship with Mallet.

Hudson sinks into a summer of decadence, physical indulgence and emotional laxity. Mallet tries to save him from all of this, only to see the female physical ideal of beauty, spied earlier in Miss Light, reenter their lives. She will ultimately shatter every hold Mallet has over Hudson, bringing the men's European adventure to disastrous ruin.

As Roderick's flirtation with the coy Christina Light intensifies, so do Rowland's thoughts of Miss Garland. Yet while Roderick's obsession indulges itself in the physical, Rowland's is more pensively moral, a reaction to Hudson's poor treatment of Miss Garland. Rowland's feeling for her lacks the visceral attraction he felt for Hudson and seems born of propriety, a propriety that Roderick runs from. Instead, Hudson pursues an ideal that for him becomes an utterly destructive immersion in the power of overwhelming passion. (Mary Garland's sympathetic presence, however, saves the novel from any misogynistic overtones; she is as selfless as Christina Light is selfish.)

To the gay reader, *Roderick Hudson* remains a love story, charting the intense relationship of two men who somehow seem to complete each other, at least in the beginning. Even at the end, Rowland finds himself thinking that "there was no possible music in the universe so sweet as the sound of Roderick's voice" (Chapter 26). When all is said and done, with the cast of characters for the most part returned to Northampton, the relationship of Rowland and Mary resolves itself not in marriage but in a kind of companionability, evocative of the friendships many gay men and lesbians have come to know throughout the years.

FIVE QUESTIONS

1. Is *Roderick Hudson* a gay novel? Why or why not?

2. Are Mallet and Hudson lovers? If no, why? If yes, why?

3. Does James give his characters names that point as clues to their usefulness in the novel as a whole, or do they serve some other representative function? As an example: Is it a coincidence that Rowland's last name is Mallet, the same as the tool a sculptor uses to bring out the statue hidden within a block of marble? What about Roderick Hudson? What about Christina Light? What about Mary Garland?

4. What is the moral of *Roderick Hudson*?

5. How do Mary Garland and Christina Light represent women in *Roderick Hudson*? Is Hudson's or Mallet's attitude toward women at all misogynistic? Why or why not? If it is misogynistic, is it implicitly so, or is this expressed in a direct way?

Walt Whitman

Leaves of Grass

READING:
Song of Myself

This moment yearning and thoughtful sitting alone,
It seems to me there are other men in other lands yearning and thoughtful,
It seems to me I can look over and behold them
in Germany, Italy, France, Spain,
Or far, far away, in China, or in Russia or Japan, talking other dialects,
And it seems to me if I could know those men I should become attached to
them as I do to men in my own lands,
O I know we should be brethren and lovers,
I know I should be happy with them.

—FROM *CALAMUS (LEAVES OF GRASS,* BOOK V)

Walt Whitman was born in West Hills, Long Island, in 1819. His father, a Quaker carpenter, was philosophically radical (what we would term "hippie leftist"). From 1823 on, Whitman was raised in Brooklyn. He found work as an assistant in a doctor's office, then a lawyer's, and finally in a printer's shop. Eventually he left that job to travel, teaching in American country schools. Whitman returned to the print trade as a profession, however. In 1846 he became editor of the *Brooklyn Eagle*, but that job—and similar jobs that followed—would last only a short while.

Whitman's early work reveals a penchant for moral reform and the virtues of temperance, most fully expressed in an otherwise unremarkable novel, *Franklin Evans* (1842). A year before, Whitman had published a short story with similar concerns—and a queer twist. First entitled "The Child's Champion" and later "The Child and the Profligate," the story deals with Charles, a twelve-year-old boy dragged into a tavern and almost forced to drink by the pub's revelers. Imbibing would break the temperance oath he has sworn to his mother, but she needn't worry—the boy is saved by Lankton, a wealthy if dissipated man who places Charles in the heart of his bed, their union blessed by a hovering angel. Later, Whitman would show signs of the self-censoring revisionist tendencies that mar so many editions of *Leaves of Grass,* placing Charles and Lankton in double beds and changing phrases that dealt with the relationship of the man and the boy—for example, "close knit love" to "friendship." Yet this work, in either version, also hints at another lifelong aspect of Whitman's work, a near pederastic (uh, artistic) appreciation for boyflesh. Further still, it succeeds in doing something wonderfully perverse by coupling the virtue of temperance with the actions of homosexuality. How moral!

In 1848 Whitman left New York for New Orleans, trying to get a job with his brothers on the New Orleans newspaper *Crescent,* but the attempt failed. He returned to Brooklyn to work as a journalist until 1854. Nevertheless, the journey had a great impact on his work, and his heart.

In one of his New Orleans poems, "Once I Pass'd Through a Populous City," he wrote, "[O]f all that city, I remember only the man who wandered with me, there, for love of me." Whitman betrayed that memory by heterosexualizing the verse before publication. There are other Louisiana echoes, notably in "Live Oak with Moss," whose souvenir "makes me think of manly love."

It was on this trip that Whitman is thought to have put forth a claim to have sired six children and to be a grandfather—a spurious claim, otherwise unproven, that insecure heterosexual Whitman "scholars" nevertheless leap to when feeling faint about Uncle Walt's penchant for laddies. Coy as a pop star, Whitman deliberately misled people, indicating the discomfort he felt over his own sexual nature and desires, especially when tied to public acclaim.

In 1855, Whitman published the first edition of *Leaves of Grass*, a slender book of 95 pages whose rhythms provide a vehicle for emotional, spiritual and social freedom. By the time he published the last edition of *Leaves of Grass*, it had swelled to 440 pages, and with a book of prose called *Specimen Days and Collect*, it would form his primary body of literary work.

When one of his brothers was wounded in the Civil War, Whitman was called to tend him, becoming a volunteer nurse in the Northern army. What he saw and experienced in that time took its emotional, intellectual and physical toll, weakening and wearying him with an unending pageantry of waste:

Thus in silence in dreams' projections,
Returning, resuming, I thread my way through the
    hospitals,
The hurt and wounded I pacify with soothing hand,
I sit by the restless all the dark night, some are so
    young,
Some suffer so much, I recall the experience sweet and sad,
(Many a soldier's loving arms about this neck have
    cross'd and rested,
Many a soldier's kiss dwells on these bearded lips.)
—"THE WOUND DRESSER," VERSE 4

In 1865 he accepted a government clerkship from Secretary Harlan, but when the Secretary read *Leaves of Grass*, he fired Whitman for writing "an indecent book." Whitman immediately found another, similar post with a more sympathetic overseer, remaining in Washington until 1873, when he was stricken with paralysis. He then left for Camden, New Jersey, where he had ancestral roots. He remained there until his death in 1891, and would have lived these last years in utter poverty but for the financial support he received from American and European admirers.

Whitman's talent was as vast as the American prairie and as majestic as the Rockies. Everything he encountered in his life fed his poetical output—the lover he walked with in New Orleans, the dying drummer boys on the battlefields. This was especially true of the common American lives that were part and parcel of the experience of living. Whitman desperately loved them. Hoping to answer Emerson's call for a national poet, he gathered up their experiences within himself, only to pour them back out again in tumbling, uncontainable whitewater poems such as *Song of Myself*:

> I celebrate myself, and sing myself,
> And what I assume you shall assume,
> For every atom belonging to me as good belongs to you.
> (*SONG OF MYSELF*, CHAPTER 1)

These opening lines not only bring us into the heart of Whitman's voice with rapid surety but also serve as a kind of thesis statement for the whole of the work.

Song of Myself is a vigorously sexy poem, embracing sexuality as a positive part of life:

> I mind how once we lay such a transparent summer
>   morning,
> How you settled your head athwart my hips and gently
>   turn'd over upon me,
> And parted the shirt from my bosom-bone, and plunged
>   your tongue to my bare-stript heart,

And reach'd till you felt my beard, and reach'd till you
    held my feet.
(CHAPTER 5)

Whitman goes on to say, "And that all the men ever born are also
my brothers, and the women my sisters and lovers" (Chapter 5). As
this follows a homoerotic reference a mere verse before—"As the
hugging and loving bed-fellow sleeps at my side through the night,
and withdraws at the peep of the day with stealthy tread" (Chapter
13)—the reader is keenly aware that this is less an endorsement of
heterosexuality than an acknowledgment of its biological primacy.
Heterosexuality is part of the procreative demand Whitman addresses earlier:

Urge and urge and urge,
Always the procreant urge of the world.
Out of the dimness opposite equals advance, always
    substance and increase, always sex,
Always a knit of identity, always a breed of life.
(CHAPTER 3)

As for the leaves of grass that give the book its title, Whitman
writes:

And now it seems to me the beautiful uncut hair of
    graves

Tenderly will I use you curling grass,
It may be you transpire from the breasts of young men,
It may be if I had known them I would have loved
    them,
It may be you are from old people, or from offspring
    taken soon out of their mothers' laps.

What do you think has become of the young and old
    men?
And what do you think has become of the women and
    children?

They are alive and well somewhere,
The smallest sprout shows that there is really no death,
And if ever there was it led forward life, and does not
    wait at the end to arrest it,
And ceas'd the moment life appeared.
(CHAPTER 6)

Here Whitman begins to make clearer one of the greater spiritual movements in his poem: addressing man's needless fear of death. Tying it into his central theme, stated at the outset of *Song of Myself*, of the inescapable and permanent collective cycle of life, Whitman here turns—without seeking to establish his own religion—toward the concern of all religions: what happens after death.

All religions are born, basically, from man's desire to make sense of the world around him, and in particular, to make peace with the notion of death. Christianity, as we've discussed, was an apocalyptic faith, created by people who believed (as Jesus did when he preached) that the end of the world was imminent. The Egyptians, the Jews, the Muslims, all created elaborate rituals around the moment of death to soften it, render it full of meaning. Whitman seeks to strip away all that, saying in effect that the meaning of death is life itself—the new life that comes from the old. Far from the comforting notion that the "afterlife" is what we knew on earth replicated in an affluent realm of clouds and harps, Whitman's comfort in death comes from the surrender into sleep and from the subsuming of the individual's life into the life all around him, living on, immortal. There is no ego, but there is life—joyous life—ever after.

Whitman's poem does much to hold the reader. No sooner has

he rhapsodized about man being "lucky to die" (7:1) than he gives
us vivid portraits of moments stolen from life and death:

The little one sleeps in its cradle,
I lift the gauze and look a long time, and silently brush
    away flies with my hand.

The suicide sprawls on the bloody floor of the bedroom,
I witness the corpse with its dabbled hair, I note where
    the pistol has fallen.

(CHAPTER 8)

Whitman, in *Song of Myself*, isn't constrained by time and
space. He is free to see all there is of life by virtue of his being *part*
of all there is of life. He is joined to it by the unfettered nature of
his spirit, his imagination, his soul's barbaric yawp. And in Chapter
11 this takes on a beautifully sublimated homoerotic undertone as
the spirit of Whitman slides beneath the skin of a lonely twenty-
eight-year-old woman watching twenty-eight young men frolicking
naked in a river, and travels with her in shared reverie, past the
men, to stroke their wet bodies.

Throughout, Whitman also pointedly addresses the problems
of slavery and its aftereffects, keenly noting the equality of humanity unbound by color. Indeed, after a spinning recitative on the
diversity of human existence—some of it steeped in a certain
homoaffectionalism—he claims that:

These are really the thoughts of all men in all ages and
    lands, they are not original with me.
If they are not yours as much as mine they are nothing,
    or next to nothing,
If they are not the riddle and the untying of the riddle
    they are nothing,

If they are not just as close as they are distant they are
    nothing.

This is the grass that grows wherever the land is and the
    water is,
This the common air that bathes the globe.
(CHAPTER 17)

Having struck at the universality of his doctrine—pleading its case,
as it were, on the altar of common sense—Whitman goes on to
refine it still further, in the process placing women as equals of
men, until, in Chapter 24, we return to the specific nature of the
poet himself, and a vaguely grandiose moment tinged with horror:

Walt Whitman, a kosmos, of Manhattan the son,
Turbulent, fleshy, sensual, eating, drinking and breeding,
No sentimentalist, no stander above men and women or
    apart from them,
No more modest than immodest.

Whoever degrades another degrades me,
And whatever is done or said returns at last to me.
Through me many long dumb voices,
Voices of the interminable generations of prisoners and
    slaves,
Voices of the diseas'd and despairing and of thieves and
    dwarfs,
Voices of cycles of preparation and accretion,
And of the threads that connect the stars, and of wombs
    and of the father-stuff,
And of the rights of them the others are down upon,
Of the deform'd, trivial, flat, foolish, despised,
Fog in the air, beetles rolling balls of dung.

Through me forbidden voices,
Voices of sexes and lusts, voices veil'd and I remove the
    veil,
Voices indecent by me clarified and transfigur'd.
(CHAPTER 24)

Whitman's rapturous song, boldly coming face to face with what it means to be part of all that ever has been, of all that is, of all that ever will be, is nothing less than a stunning act of absolution, purging the world of sin and guilt.

Whitman continues his exploration of his world and vision, never letting us escape for a moment from our inclusion within the work—we are, after all, part of him, and he part of us, even as we read the poem. For the gay reader, the verse provides moment after moment of homoerotic glory, in the hoped-for "Camerado;" the loved boys, the naked assessment of the beauty of men, and at last the point of conclusion, the moment of clarity, where experiences are gathered and meaning shaped.

For Whitman, this is a leveling of the playing field. It is nothing less than the gay Emancipation Proclamation, the difference being that here we declare our freedom and equality, there is no one who need give it to us; it already exists—it has existed all along—for our taking:

I have said that the soul is not more than the body,
And I have said that the body is not more than the soul,
And nothing, not God, is greater to one than oneself
    is . . .
And I say to any man or woman, Let your soul stand
    cool and composed before a million universes.

And I say to mankind, Be not curious about God,
For I who am curious about each am not curious about
    God.

(No array of terms can say how much I am at peace
    about God and about death.)
I hear and behold God in every object, yet understand
    God not in the least,
Nor do I understand who there can be more wonderful
    than myself.

Why should I wish to see God better than this day?
I see something of God each hour of the twenty-four,
    and each moment then,
In the faces of men and women I see God, and in my
    own face in the glass,
I find letters from God dropt in the street, and every
    one is sign'd by God's name,
And I leave them where they are, for I know that
    wheresoe'er I go
Others will punctually come for ever and ever.
(CHAPTER 48, EDITED)

Whitman reviews his thoughts on death, this reincarnation of
the present ever, saying:

Do you see O my brothers and sisters?
It is not chaos or death—it is form, union, plan—it is
    eternal life—it is Happiness. (CHAPTER 50)

Whitman's closing lines are among the most famous in American
literature:

Do I contradict myself?
Very well then I contradict myself.
(I am large, I contain multitudes.)
(CHAPTER 51)

Whitman contains in himself all those who have ever been, and the seed for all those who ever shall be, and so, too, their conflicts and agreements. How? If we've not joined him yet, Whitman seduces us with the simplicity of his closing argument. It is an elegant rephrasing of the child's explanation of the circle of life: The grass nourishes the cow that nourishes the man that (when buried) nourishes the grass. It is, of course, man's unavoidable fate to join this circle and, in so doing, to join Whitman, who has joined before us, and to stretch ourselves out beside him in immortality, skin, bone and heart of those who come after:

> I too am not a bit tamed, I too am untranslatable,
> I sound my barbaric yawp over the roofs of the world.
> I depart as air, I shake my white locks at the runaway
>   sun,
> I effuse my flesh in eddies, and drift in lacy jags.
>
> I bequeath myself to the dirt to grow from the grass I
>   love,
> If you want me again look for me under your boot-
>   soles.
>
> You will hardly know who I am or what I mean
> But I shall be good health to you nevertheless,
> And filter and fibre your blood.
>
> Failing to fetch me at first keep encouraged,
> Missing me one place search another,
> I stop somewhere waiting for you.
> (CHAPTER 51)

FIVE QUESTIONS

1. Whitman and Virgil both set out to provide poetry that would define their nation. How well did they succeed? As poets, how are they similar, how are they different? Is America still waiting for its *Aeneid*?

2. Is sexual conservatism a part of proper morality?

3. What is Whitman's agenda in *Song of Myself,* and how well does he realize it?

4. What does it say about Whitman and America that, well over a century later, Americans are still wrestling with the issues he attempted to absolve us of?

5. Is Whitman's reconciliation of life and death comforting to you? Why or why not?

Selected Poems

EDITED BY AIDAN DAY

W hat time mine own [spirit] might also flee,
As link'd with thine in love and fate,
And, hovering o'er the dolorous strait
To the other shore, involved in thee,

Arrive at last the blessed goal,
And He that died in Holy Land
Would reach us out the shining hand,
And take us as a single soul.
—*IN MEMORIAM*, LXXXIV, VERSES 10 AND 11

Alfred Tennyson became the first Lord Tennyson in 1883, when but nine years of life were left to him. Still, the title is firmly attached to his name in our memory.

Born on August 6, 1809, in Somersby, England, he was the son of an Anglican minister. Tennyson was a poetic Mozart, writing his first verse at age five and his first full-fledged poem by age eight. When he had just turned eighteen, he published a book of minor poetry with his brothers, Frederick and Charles. Like Bacon and Byron before him, Tennyson was a Trinity College (Cambridge) man, as well as a member of its literary society, The Apostles. Tennyson published increasingly popular volumes of poetry in 1830, 1832 and 1842, but it wasn't until 1850 that the poet and his life seemed to fall into step.

The previous two decades were filled with trouble. Tennyson endured the death of his father in 1831; in 1833 his beloved friend Arthur H. Hallam died in Vienna; his poetry was critically dismissed as too sentimental; his relationships with women led nowhere. In 1843 he bottomed out, entering a mental hospital to recover from a nervous collapse.

But in 1845 he was granted a permanent government stipend that enabled him to write full-time, and when William Wordsworth died in 1850, Queen Victoria appointed Tennyson to succeed him as Poet Laureate. That same year he married, remaining a homebody, with his wife and their two children, until he caught the flu and died on October 6, 1892.

As with Melville, here is an example of a writer whose outward life is wholly heterosexual yet whose inward life, as mirrored in his poetry, is homosexual, at least in sympathy. While homoaffectionalism imbues much of Tennyson's output with a sort of heady amorousness, it is with *In Memoriam*, the poem he wrote for his Apostle chum Hallam—and through which he earned the position of Poet Laureate—that this desire finds full voice.

Not simply a lament, *In Memoriam* is a richly complex study of love and friendship, gender and death. Prefiguring Whitman's work in his *Calamus* and *Song of Myself*, the poem is the desperate effort of a lover to make sense of the untimely death of his beloved. He is forced to reconcile his passion in the tenuous unease with which man naturally responds when confronting death. At times he unconvincingly cloaks his love behind an imagined recasting of the narrator as woman.

The poem dizzyingly travels such surrealisms as astral projection, where the lover's soul plays about the prow of the boat bearing back the body of his beloved (XII), and then rapidly re-anchors itself in the mundane, tender truth that holidays, with their repeated rituals, often make the absence of one's beloved shatteringly impossible to bear (XXVIII).

In Memoriam is rich in classical echoes—as is much of Tennyson's other work, most notably "Ulysses" and "To Virgil"—but it is above all a love poem, gorgeously wrought, and in whose lines we find the famous phrase born and repeated: " 'Tis better to have loved and lost / Than never to have loved at all" (XXVII).

Indeed.

Havelock Ellis and John Addington Symonds

Sexual Inversion

I has not, I think, been noted—largely because the evidence was insufficiently clear—that among religious or moral leaders, and other persons with strong ethical instincts, there is a tendency towards the more elevated forms of homosexual feeling. This may be traced not only in some of the great moral teachers of old but also in men and women of our own day. It is fairly evident why this should be so. Just as the repressed love of a woman or a man has in normally constituted persons frequently furnished the motive power for an enlarged philanthropic activity, so the person who sees his own sex bathed in sexual glamour brings to his work of human service an ardour wholly unknown to the normally constituted individual; morality to him has become one with love.

—"INTRODUCTION"

Sexual Inversion contains only fragmentary contributions from John Addington Symonds, a British literary man educated at Harrow (as was Byron) and Balliol College, Oxford. Symonds was elected a fellow of Magdalen College when he was twenty-two and appears to have been pals with virtually every other notable writerly faggot alive at the time, including poet and utopian Edward Carpenter, Walt Whitman and Oscar Wilde's boy-toy, Lord Alfred Douglas. Symonds pursued Whitman with such fervor it unnerved the old poet, who found the youngster's unabashed gratitude at the homoeroticism of Whitman's work in sharp contrast to Whitman's own more circumspect attitude.

But Symonds may perhaps be excused: Having fed himself on the writings of the Greeks and finding his own desire for other men reflected there, how exciting it must have been for him to find that same handsome glimmer in the work of a contemporary. Symonds had little interest, apparently, in living a double life or relegating himself to the position of second-class citizen; if he has literary parallels in the latter twentieth century, it is probably in the writings of Larry Kramer and Michelangelo Signorile, whose abrasive yet persistently gruff demeanor and increasingly high-strung bleating, respectively, inspire in contemporary readers feelings of admiration and disavowal.

Symonds intermittently fell in step with his society's expectations, most notably by getting married in 1864 and fathering four children. But five years prior to his marriage, when he was nineteen, his scandalous affair with the headmaster of Harrow resulted in the loss of that man's position. Never physically very strong, Symonds was diagnosed with tuberculosis a year after his marriage, and he had a mental breakdown when he was twenty-eight, during which he seriously contemplated suicide. He died ten months into the work on *Sexual Inversion,* at the age of fifty-three.

Symonds' activism, in two essays that form the appendix to *Sexual Inversion,* "A Problem in Greek Ethics" and "A Problem in Modern Ethics," sparked in the married Havelock Ellis the idea of a book that, with Baconian clarity, would treat homosexuality free of the colorings of religion or society, as a natural phenomenon to be acknowledged and accepted. Ellis makes an attempt to claim in his preface that his book is merely a recitation of observations and case studies, but this is a thin veil; *Sexual Inversion* indeed argues that homosexuality is a natural part of life and, as such, should not be criminalized.

Reading the book today, we are surprised to find how dead-on Ellis was in many of his conclusions. Without the benefit of genetic research, he intuited homosexuality as biologically predisposed in some, and he concerns himself as much with women as with men in considering same-sex desire, yet another achievement in a time when the only lesbians were natives of Lesbos. While others—Kraft-Ebbing, for example—had studied homosexuality and drawn various positive and negative conclusions, Ellis and Symonds' work is a clear leap ahead in that it brings together all the thought of the period, engages it and then makes a run toward the enlightenment at least a century away, forming something new, impressive and important.

Because of this synthesis, and because nearly everyone read it at the time of its publication and for years thereafter, *Sexual Inversion* was a work of great influence, and its resonance is still felt today. It contains within its pages everything that is the genesis of modern homosexual thought, a remarkable accomplishment.

Sadly, Symonds' literary executor, Horatio Brown, was not so forward-thinking. Horrified by the frankness of the text of *Sexual Inversion,* he withdrew permission after first publication for Ellis to cite Symonds, who became simply "Z" in future editions, and Symonds' notoriety—and his writings on ethics—were driven underground. *Sexual Inversion* eventually came to serve as Part Two in Ellis' collected *Studies in the Psychology of Sex.*

Complete Works

READING:

The Picture of Dorian Gray

Dorian's arms fell to his side. Paralysed with terror, he did not know what to do. Suddenly, a wild hope flashed across his brain. "Stop," he cried. "How long ago is it since your sister died? Quick, tell me!"

"Eighteen years," said the man. "Why do you ask me? What do years matter?"

"Eighteen years," laughed Dorian Gray, with a touch of triumph in his voice. "Eighteen years! Set me under the lamp and look at my face!"

James Vane hesitated for a moment, not understanding what was meant. Then he seized Dorian Gray and dragged him from the archway.

Dim and wavering as was the wind-blown light, yet it served to show him the hideous error, as it seemed, into which he had fallen, for the face of the man he had sought to kill had all the bloom of boyhood, all the unstained purity of youth. He seemed little older than a lad of twenty summers, hardly older,

if older indeed at all, than his sister had been when
they had parted so many years ago. It was obvious that
this was not the man who had destroyed her life.
    —*THE PICTURE OF DORIAN GRAY,* CHAPTER 16

Oscar Fingall O'Flahertie Wills Wilde was born in Dublin in 1854.
His father was Sir William Wilde, his mother Lady Jane Francesca
Wilde, and between the ages of nine and sixteen he attended the
Portora Royal School in Enniskillen. He studied later at Trinity
College, Dublin, and Magdalen College, Oxford. He was, in his
clothing, a dandy, in his philosophy, an aesthete; he despised conventional morality and cultivated an ambiguous sexuality. When he
was twenty-four, he won the Newdigate Prize for his poem "Ra-
venna," a pastiche of memory and history, and three years later, he
published his first book of poetry under the title *Poems.*

A year later, in 1882, he went on a lecture tour of the United
States, and when a customs official asked if he had anything to
declare, he responded, "Only my genius." The tour was, for the
most part, a success, and it allowed Wilde to meet notable American artists, including James Abbott MacNeill Whistler.

In 1884 he married Constance Lloyd, and she bore him two
sons, for whom he wrote the classic children's fantasies collected in
The Happy Prince and Other Tales (1888). In 1886 he met Robbie
Ross, a young Canadian who would be Wilde's lifelong friend and,
at the last, his literary executor.

In 1890 Wilde published *The Picture of Dorian Gray* as a serial
in *Lippincott's Monthly Magazine,* a story inspired by his affair with
the poet John Gray. *The House of Pomegranates* and *Lord Arthur
Saville's Crime and Other Stories* followed in 1891. That year would
also see publication of *The Picture of Dorian Gray* in book form,
expanded and revised, as well as a political tract, "The Soul of Man
Under Socialism," a sort of witty regurgitation of Rousseau.

Wilde also debuted his second play, *The Duchess of Padua,* a verse tragedy, in 1891, but it failed to satisfy his theatrical ambitions. That would have to wait until 1892, when he brought out *Lady Windemere's Fan,* followed in rapid succession by *A Woman of No Importance* in 1893 and Lord Alfred Douglas' translation of *Salomé*—from Wilde's original French—in 1894. *An Ideal Husband* and *The Importance of Being Earnest* hit the boards in 1895 and secured Wilde's reputation as a brilliant, clever dramatist.

Some might say too clever. In a time of passionate secrecy, Wilde's sexual appetite for lads was common knowledge. When the Marquis of Queensberry, father of one of Wilde's treasures—the selfsame Lord Alfred Douglas who had translated Wilde's work—left a note at Wilde's club, "To Oscar Wilde posing as a Somdomite," the playwright, poet, essayist and writer of fiction took it to mean Queensberry was calling him a ponce (fag) and sodomite (BIG FAG) and sued for libel.

You don't sue for libel when the libel is the truth.

Wilde lost his case and was in turn tried and convicted for his sexuality. He could have fled to the Continent—the judge even delayed Wilde's arrest that he might do so—but Wilde didn't, less from bravery and moral courage than from a desire to preserve his place in British society. He was imprisoned in Reading Gaol and wrote the mournful *Ballad of Reading Gaol,* published in 1898, a year after his release. When he received his freedom, and was spurned by the society he had suffered for, Wilde traveled to France under the name of "Sebastian Melmoth," the despised martyr in *Melmoth the Wanderer,* a superb book of horrors written by Wilde's Irish great-uncle, Charles Maturin.

Three years after his release from jail, Wilde was dead. The softness of his constitution was no match for the hard punishment English society meted out to sexual deviants at that time. *De Profundis,* his bitter, recriminatory letter to Lord Alfred, wherein Wilde compares his sufferings to those of Jesus of Nazareth, was published posthumously in 1905.

Also published posthumously was Wilde's expansion of an article published in 1889, "The Portrait of Mr. W. H.," in which he identifies the young man desired in Shakespeare's sonnets as a boy thespian named Willie Hughes, and proposes that Shakespeare was in love with the teen. More to the point, this novelette—the original essay wrapped in pieces of deliberative fiction—reveals the power of Shakespeare's sonnets, present in many great works of literary art: their ability to give the reader a reflection of himself, to give him a glimpse of what it is he desires to see.

In truth, Shakespeare's homosexual characters (that he included any at all was admittedly a breakthrough, one that Marlowe's work facilitated, surely) were hardly role models. They lacked the humanity with which Marlowe endowed his creations. Regarding Shakespeare's "gay" sonnets, it's worthwhile to remember that, as an author who wrote for the stage and was accustomed to speaking in voices, it is entirely—even overwhelmingly—plausible to see those sonnets as yet another character tried on by Shakespeare: that of a woman in love. (Unlike Marlowe's, Shakespeare's personal life was quiet, barring the impact of a lengthy leave of absence from his wife and children for a writer's sojourn in London. We know so little about him personally in great part because so little happened to him, outside of his work.)

The Picture of Dorian Gray has a less lofty agenda than "The Portrait of Mr. W. H.": It is simply a well-told story, a moral fable in the guise of a horror novel.

> "Two months ago I went to a crush at Lady Brandon's . . . Well, after I had been in the room about ten minutes, talking to huge over-dressed dowagers and tedious Academicians, I suddenly became conscious that someone was looking at me. I turned half-way round, and saw Dorian Gray for the first time. When our eyes met, I felt that I was growing pale. A curious sensation of terror came over me. I knew that I had come face to face with some one whose

mere personality was so fascinating that, if I allowed it to do so, it would absorb my whole nature, my whole soul, my very art itself . . . Suddenly I found myself face to face with the young man whose personality had so strangely stirred me. We were quite close, almost touching. Our eyes met again. It was reckless of me, but I asked Lady Brandon to introduce me to him. Perhaps it was not so reckless after all. It was simply inevitable. We would have spoken to each other without any introduction. I am sure of that. Dorian told me so afterwards. He, too, felt that we were destined to know each other."

(*THE PICTURE OF DORIAN GRAY,* CHAPTER 1)

Thus the noted painter Basil Hallward fills in Lord Henry Wotton—conceivably a doppelgänger for Wilde, as he gets the best bon mots—on the boy he met at a party and whose portrait he has agreed to paint. There follows a brief discussion on the nature of friendship, based on the relationship between Hallward and Lord Henry. At one point Hallward chimes in with:

"But according to your category I must be merely an acquaintance."

"My dear old Basil, you are much more than an acquaintance."

"And much less than a friend. A sort of brother, I suppose?"

"Oh, brothers! I don't care for brothers. My elder brother won't die, and my younger brothers seem never to do anything else."

Perhaps they are sisters, then.

Regardless, Lord Henry—Harry—charms Hallward into letting him meet Dorian Gray. While Basil works on the chap's portrait,

Lord Henry talks to Dorian of sin, corruption and the true evil that is self-denial:

> "The only way to get rid of a temptation is to yield to it. Resist it, and your soul grows sick with longing for the things it has forbidden to itself, with desire for what its monstrous laws have made monstrous and unlawful. It has been said that the great events of the world take place in the brain. It is in the brain, and the brain only, that the great sins of the world take place also. You, Mr. Gray, you yourself, with your rose-red youth and your rose-white boyhood, you have had passions that have made you afraid, thoughts that have filled you with terror, day-dreams and sleeping dreams whose mere memory might stain your cheek with shame—"   (CHAPTER 1)

Gray calls out, "Stop!" Until this moment, Gray has been painted as an innocent, a naive boy with no sense of the hard world and its dangers. Lord Henry—a wealthy, upper-class man of the realm and an indulger in the sordid—will change all that, and in so doing mar what Basil has loved most in Dorian Gray, his purity.

Not before Basil has finished the portrait, however. And not before Gray, exhorted by Harry on the horrid temporal frailty of youth and the need for "a new Hedonism" born only of youth, can see the picture and, with Harry's words still swirling in his head, say:

> "How sad it is! I shall grow old, and horrible, and dread-ful. But this picture will remain always young. It will never be older than this particular day of June . . . If it were only the other way! If it were I who was to be always young, and the picture that was to grow old! For that—for that—I would give everything! Yes, there is nothing in the

whole world I would not give! I would give my soul for
that!"   (CHAPTER 2)

And that is it. A moment in a studio, nothing more.

We learn more of Dorian Gray's background. He is a noted
lord's grandson. His father was killed in a duel engineered by Dorian's famed grandfather, whose daughter—Dorian's mother—survived her husband by only a few months; she died within the first
year of Dorian's life. So the young man has money and a position
in society that allows him to move through a circle of parties. His
friendship with Harry grows, even as his relationship with Basil
weakens, though Basil drops off the portrait, which Dorian keeps in
his room.

Dorian, taking up Harry's challenge of a new Hedonism, explores the seamier parts of London. On one these forays, he comes
across the ironically named Royal Theatre, a cheap company that is
putting on a series of miserably staged Shakespearean plays. But it
is there that Dorian first sees the actress Sibyl Vane, there that he
becomes enthralled by her. Every night thereafter, he goes to watch
her perform until, at last, they become engaged. The very next
morning Dorian tells Harry and Basil, and invites them to see her
act.

That evening she is, quite simply, terrible. Dorian is embar-
rassed and ashamed. He had fallen in love with Sibyl's talent, with
the idea that he would be able to bed Juliet and a host of other
Shakespearean lovers. But Sibyl had lived only for the theater until
he came along, and when he proposed to her, she found something
more to live for—and her acting ability vanished. She was Juliet no
more, only Sibyl, as she explains to Dorian when he goes backstage
to confront her, to ask what happened. Her candor does not serve
her well:

Then he leaped up, and went to the door. "Yes," he cried,
"you have killed my love. You used to stir my imagination.

Now you don't even stir my curiosity. You simply produce no effect. I loved you because you were marvelous, because you had genius and intellect, because you realized the dreams of great poets and gave shape and substance to the shadows of art. You have thrown it all away. You are shallow and stupid. My God! how mad I was to love you! What a fool I have been! You are nothing to me now. I will never see you again. I will never think of you. I will never mention your name. You don't know what you were to me, once. Why, once . . . Oh, I can't bear to think of it! I wish I had never laid eyes upon you! You have spoiled the romance of my life. How little you can know of love, if you say it mars your art! Without your art you are nothing. I would have made you famous, splendid, magnificent. The world would have worshipped you, and you would have borne my name. What are you now? A third rate actress with a pretty face." (CHAPTER 7)

When Dorian leaves her, she is in tears. Returning to his quarters after walking the streets all night, he glances at his portrait and notices, that "[t]he expression looked different. One would have said that there was a touch of cruelty in the mouth. It was certainly strange" (Chapter 7).

Hours later, after he has (to his credit) written her a letter of apology, he learns that Sibyl Vane is dead, that she drank poison after she and Dorian parted. There is an inquest. Gray stays clear of it. Nobody at the theater ever knew his name and Sibyl referred to him only as "Prince Charming." But Sibyl's brother, Jim, a roughneck sailor, remembers seeing Gray's face and vows revenge.

The rest is the descent into the maelstrom. Gray goes further and further beyond the pale. As the years pass, he develops a penchant for opium dens and other sordid hangouts. He has surpassed any sense of libertine freedom Harry might have envisioned. Although troubles loom in his path—Basil wants to show the painting, and Jim Vane runs into him in an opium den—Gray manages to slip through life with only the portrait, which he has secured in an upstairs room and draped with a purple cloth, bearing witness to his hideous sins. It has continued to age as naturally—and rapidly—as would a man who leads a life of dissipation. Gray's influence shifts darkly in temperament but continues to be felt in society. For a time Gray cultivates favorites among society's notable and handsome young men, who ape him in dress and share with him his wharfside slumming. Their parents and others, however, begin to shun Gray, sensing the amorality bubbling beneath the boyish veneer.

It cannot go on forever. Gray is plagued not so much by inner conscience as by the physical reminder of all he has done wrong in his life: the portrait Basil Hallward painted of him as an innocent— the vision for which he sold his soul:

> Ah! in what monstrous moment of pride and passion had he prayed that the portrait should bear the burden of all his days, and he keep the unsullied splendour of eternal youth! All his failure had been due to that. Better for him that each sin of his life had brought its sure, swift penalty along with it. There was purification in punishment. Not "Forgive us our sins," but "Smite us for our iniquities," should be the prayer of a man to a most just God . . .
>
> It was the living death of his own soul that troubled him. Basil had painted the portrait that had marred his life. He could not forgive him that. It was the portrait that had done everything . . .
>
> A new life! That was what he wanted. That was what he was waiting for.   (CHAPTER 20)

Dorian Gray's ultimate sin, the failing that leads to his downfall moments after the above passage, seems to be his chronic inability to accept responsibility. Everybody is to blame but him; despite the corrupt façade of the portrait, Gray believes in his heart that he is still an innocent, that the purity he knew when he originally sat for Basil waits only for his reclamation.

The Picture of Dorian Gray teaches a curious lesson, written by a man whose life was brought low when he failed to own up to the truth of his sexuality, preferring to treat that truth as a slur and to risk cutting short a brilliant, wickedly clever career. Oscar Wilde and Dorian Gray shared a naive shortsightedness—in Gray's case, perhaps the last of his charms, the worst of his evils.

FIVE QUESTIONS

1. Is redemption possible for Dorian Gray at the end? If he had accepted responsibility for his actions, could he have begun to take back his soul via a series of good deeds and a life nobly lived, until the exterior of the painting matched the exterior of its subject once again?

2. Does Gray's life prove or disprove Lord Henry's theories on sin and a new Hedonism? What is sin?

3. Is homosexuality among Gray's "sins"—would Harry consider it as such? Does Gray ever take either Harry or Basil as his lovers? Do the older men want that from him, or is their love purely paternal, perhaps Platonic?

4. What is the most painful moment in *The Picture of Dorian Gray*? When, for the reader, does the future loom horribly clear?

5. Gray, in his last despair, sees that there is "purification in punishment." Earlier, Harry says, "The body sins once, and has done with its sin, for action is a mode of purification." Who's right?

A. E. Housman

Collected Poems

> . . . I, a stranger and afraid
> In a world I never made.
> —*LAST POEMS,* NO. 12 (EXCERPT)

A friend memorized portions of *A Shropshire Lad* (source of "When I Was One-and-twenty" and "To an Athlete Dying Young," among others) and recited them to the imprisoned Oscar Wilde. While there is coded homosexual material in the two volumes of Housman's poems published in his lifetime (including the full poem, from which the above excerpt is taken, a rant against society's desire to bend the individual to the will of the majority), his more explicit poems were published after his death, under the watchful eye of his gay younger brother, Laurence. They were released in two collections: *More Poems* and *Additional Poems.* Laurence furthered our knowledge of the poet by crafting an essay, "A. E. Housman's 'De Amicitia,' " which he gave to the British Museum in 1942 on condition that it not be published until 1967. By that time Laurence Housman was eight years dead, but his words did much to illuminate the portrait of his brother and more clearly reveal the interaction between the poet's art and life.

Born in 1859 in Fockbury, Worcestershire, Alfred Edward Housman won a scholarship to St. John's College, Oxford, when he was eighteen. There he met Moses Jackson, a classmate, a straight boy, who was to be the unrequited love of Housman's life and the fuel for much of his verse. Bedeviled by his homosexual desire, intellectually stubborn, trying to deal with his father's illness and simultaneous bankruptcy, Housman bombed out of his final exams and had to leave St. John's for a position at the Patent Office. His pain was eased by the fact that Moses Jackson was already working there, in a better post. For three years Jackson, Housman and Jackson's younger brother, Adalbert, with whom Housman may well have had an affair, lived together in London.

In 1885, however, Moses Jackson and Housman had a falling out. Housman disappeared for a week, and when he returned, he moved out. Housman would live by himself until his death. Jackson and Housman kept up the pretense of a friendship, though Jackson moved to India in 1887, returning only in 1889 to marry—an occasion Housman was not aware of until Jackson had again left the country, new wife in tow. Housman and Adalbert, however, kept in touch until Adalbert died suddenly of typhoid in 1892. In Housman's later years, the only photos in his house were of the brothers he loved, two portraits hanging over the fireplace.

Housman continued his studies and became a distinguished classical scholar, appointed professor of Latin at University College, London, in 1892 and professor of Latin at Cambridge in 1911. He died in 1936.

Samuel Butler

The Way of
All Flesh

It happened that some years previously, a swarm of
bees had taken up their abode in the roof of the house
under the slates, and had multiplied so that the drawing-room was a good deal frequented by these bees
during the summer, when the windows were open. The
drawing-room paper was of a pattern which consisted
of bunches of red and white roses, and I saw several
bees at different times fly up to these bunches and try
them, under the impression that they were real flowers;
having tried one bunch, they tried the next, and the
next, and the next, till they reached the one that was
nearest the ceiling, then they went down bunch by
bunch as they had ascended, till they were stopped by
the back of the sofa; on this they ascended bunch by
bunch to the ceiling again; and so on, and so on till I
was tired of watching them. As I thought of the family
prayers being repeated night and morning, week by
week, month by month, and year by year, I could not
help thinking how like it was to the way in which the
bees went up the wall and down the wall, bunch by

bunch, without ever suspecting that so many of the
associated ideas could be present, and yet the main
idea be wanting helplessly, and for ever.

—CHAPTER 23

Saucily titled, *The Way of All Flesh* is a wicked reading experience, phenomenally funny and almost devastatingly smart. It is Samuel Butler's thinly veiled autobiographical novel, a sprawling generational saga of social satire, personal ridicule and latent homosexuality. The Bloomsbury crowd adored it, and E. M. Forster fell under its influence. As we read *The Way of All Flesh*, it's easy to see why. It's a remarkable book whose entertaining satire is wrapped around a core of unimpeachable truth: that society's morals are a fraud, and most organized religion is concerned less with inspiring faith than with controlling behavior. *The Way of All Flesh* may or may not have been an attack on Victorian society; at the time of its publication, however, it sure read like one, and proved to be just the tonic the culture needed.

Born on December 4, 1835, Samuel Butler was descended from Anglican clergy and followed their example at Shrewsbury and St. John's College, Cambridge. But he began to have doubts about being ordained, and after earning his degree in 1858, he worked for two years among the London poor. In 1860 he left England for New Zealand, where he raised sheep and wrote for regional newspapers.

He didn't return to England until four years later, and then it was to study art. (One of Butler's paintings, *Mr. Heatherly's Holiday*, hangs in the Tate Gallery, London.) He also loved music and wrote several pieces; he proved himself adept at literary translations, including *The Iliad* and *The Odyssey*. But it was his original fiction—novels of social commentary such as *Erewhon*, most notably, and its sequel, *Erewhon Revisited*—that enabled him to make his mark.

He never married but had several intense relationships with

men. One of these, Charles Paine Pauli, he met in New Zealand and brought back to London, where Butler supported the man for thirty years, until Pauli died. Upon Pauli's death, it was learned that the trickster had been supported by two other men during those thirty years, had amassed a fortune and had left Butler out of his will.

Butler also loved a Swiss boy, Hans Faesch, who died young, prompting Butler to write a poem ("In Memoriam H.R.F."—shades of Tennyson!) and roam about with a snipping of the lad's hair in a locket. Throughout the dramas of Butler's personal life, Henry Festing Jones was Butler's companion. His eventual biographer, Jones was there, along with Butler's devoted servant, Alfred Catie, when Butler went the way of all flesh, at the age of sixty-seven, after a prolonged illness. A year later, the novel that would spark the antiestablishment sarcasm of subsequent generations was published—happily for us who have the chance to read it.

Mikhail Kuzmin

Selected Prose and Poetry

TRANSLATED BY MICHAEL GREEN

Circling a glade, they continued to follow the same path, and the laughter of children playing ball came to them remotely.

"Tomorrow I'm supposed to be going to Bari, but I could stay; it depends on you: if your answer is no, send me a note saying 'go'; if it's yes, then write, 'stay.' "

"What do you mean, 'no' or 'yes'?" asked Vanya.

"Would you like me to spell it out for you?"

"No, don't, I understand; but is this really necessary?"

"It has become unavoidable. I'll wait until one o'clock."

"I'll give you my answer, one way or the other."

"Just one more little effort and you'll grow wings. I can see them already."

"Perhaps—but the growing can be very painful," said Vanya with a wry grin.

—*WINGS*

The above scene appears toward the end of Mikhail Kuzmin's groundbreaking Russian novel, *Wings*, and it begs the question pivotal in any relationship: Dare we take this to the next level? This is an especially tender concern in gay relationships, where, as practically the entire Anglo-American nineteenth century attests via works such as *Tom Brown's Schooldays* and Walt Whitman's poetry, there can be a dividing line (often self-deluding) between homo-affectionalism and homosexuality.

At some point the homosexual relationship has to cross that line if it's to be realized—if it's to take flight.

Mikhail Alekseyevich Kuzmin was born either in 1875—this is the date given on his tombstone—or 1872. His first love was music, and he studied it for several years, at the same time discovering a talent for languages in his studies of Italian and German. He would go on to learn English, French, Greek and Latin, and would, in his lifetime, produce many notable translations into Russian, including the poetry of Byron.

Kuzmin was led to these pursuits through his friendship with the queer Georgy Vasilevich Chicherin, who would later become the first important Soviet diplomat. Chicherin also introduced Kuzmin to an influential clique known as the World of Art in 1904; the circle included dance notables Sergei Diaghilev and Vaslav Nijinsky. Kuzmin was drawn to their theatricality and their frequently foppish attire—and in their company he could feel comfortable being an openly gay man.

Around the time *Wings* was published, in 1906, Kuzmin began attending the poet Vyacheslav Ivanov's literary salon, held in Ivanov's apartment, nicknamed "The Tower." Eventually Kuzmin moved in, but the two poets' works were so disparate in nature that it is unlikely they had any real influence upon each other. It would be wrong to assume that there was also a sexual component to their relationship—Ivanov at the time was on his second marriage, to

Lydia Zinovoeva-Annibal—although it's worth noting that she was the author of the first work in Russian to deal openly with lesbianism, "Thirty-three Freaks."

Kuzmin's poetry (in particular his "Alexandrian Songs"; his interest in music led him to verse) first earned him literary attention, but it was *Wings* that confirmed his talent. As with other Western gay novels that preceded it, *Wings* is grounded in the philosophy and lore of ancient Greece and Rome. It is a remarkably intimate novel, small in scope yet vast in impact, and quickly lures the reader into the dawning sexual awareness of its protagonist, Vanya. Unlike later American novels that bear similar echoes—most notably James Baldwin's *Giovanni's Room*—it steers away from the grim. Perhaps it was the insular, supportive nature of Kuzmin's coterie that allowed him to avoid what seemed to be the prerequisite unhappiness of most American and European gay-themed novels.

Certainly, his personal life was far from idyllic. In 1910 he met the bisexual poet Vsevolod Knyazev, and the two men became lovers. But Knyazev committed suicide in 1913, by which time he had already begun to drift away from Kuzmin. (Around this time Kuzmin and Ivanov also had a falling out, and Kuzmin left "The Tower.") It was not long, though, before Kuzmin met another poet, Yury Yurkun, and the two began a relationship that would last until Kuzmin's death from pneumonia in 1936. The two men—such good boys—lived with Yurkun's mother, and for a while were even joined by Yurkun's wife!

As his contemporary William Butler Yeats would find profitable, Kuzmin dabbled in mysticism, hanging out with a metaphysical crowd known collectively as the Acmeists. It never really took. He would look to Anna Ahkmatova, whom he met through this gang, as "my wonderful teacher"—or so he inscribed her first book of verse, to which Kuzmin wrote a foreword. But the two would also have a falling out, and later she would ridicule him in "A Poem Without a Hero" and paint a bitter picture of him in her memoirs.

In the new Communist regime, Kuzmin enjoyed seven years of popularity, from 1917 to 1924. He sat on the Praesidium of the Association of Artists in Petrograd, founded a literary journal and published volumes of poetry and chapters of prose. He worked as a translator under Maksim Gorky, but eventually his connections were no match for the distaste conservatives in the people's government felt for homosexuality and the homoeroticism—romanticized or not—present in Kuzmin's work. His journal was shut down. He fell from political favor but not public appeal, and at his last public reading, in 1928, he was showered with flowers as a token of his readers' love and admiration. His death in 1936 spared him Stalin's bullet. Yurkun was not so lucky: In 1938 he was arrested and shot.

Thomas Mann

Stories of
Three Decades

READING:

Death in Venice

TRANSLATION BY H. T. LOWE-PORTER

H e felt the rapture of his blood, the poignant pleasure, and realized that it was for Tadzio's sake the leavetaking had been so hard.

—*DEATH IN VENICE*

Thomas Mann was born into money in 1875, his family a collection of wealthy merchants and senators in Lübeck, Germany. His mother, a talented musician, was of mixed German and Portuguese West Indian blood. This conflict of fiscal conservatism and artistic liberalism, of stoic German and emotive Indian, influenced by Schopenhauer's popular perspective of art as the self-denial of the will and the end product of decay, would form Mann's basic approach to his own work, where conflicted desires were often caught in a downward spiral of morality.

Following a dilettante's attempt at college—he failed two of the six years required—Mann left school at the age of nineteen to settle with his mother in Munich. Soon after, he left her to live with his brother in Italy. There he produced the first significant achievement in a remarkable body of work, *Buddenbrooks,* published in 1901, when Mann was but twenty-five. It was a family saga much like his own, with business acumen decaying, only to be replaced over generations by artistic sensibilities.

When he returned to Munich, he was a revered German novelist. He read manuscripts for *Simplicissimus,* a magazine of literary satire that published many of Mann's early short stories, among them the homoerotic novellas *Tonio Kröger* (1903; itself an echo of homoaffectionalist Johann Wolfgang von Goethe's tragically sexy *The Sorrow of Young Werther*) and *Death in Venice* (1912). The latter work was the result of a 1911 holiday Mann took in Venice, where he fell under the sway of a handsome fourteen-year-old Polish boy he would never meet.

Throughout his life, Mann would display a weakness for good-looking young men. His relationship with Paul Ehrenburg lasted from 1899 to 1903. In 1927 the fifty-two-year-old Mann began a relationship with sixteen-year-old Klaus Heuser, which also lasted several years.

Shortly after his relationship with Ehrenburg ended, in 1905, Mann married Katja Pringsheim. They had six children, three sons and three daughters, several of them sharing aspects of Mann's talent and homosexuality. His daughter Erika was an actress who married W. H. Auden for his British citizenship; she would serve as Mann's literary executor after his death. Mann's eldest son, Klaus, was openly gay and wrote novels, plays, essays and short stories about bohemian Germany between the wars. His openness about his sexuality led him into conflicts with his father, who kept his desires for men closely guarded and did not consider the adventures of his heart along boyish lines to be of public concern.

World War I would separate Thomas Mann from his brother, writer Heinrich Mann. (Heinrich's novel *Professor Unrat* would become the basis for Marlene Dietrich's star turn in *The Blue Angel*.) Thomas believed fervently in German patriotism but distrusted all political ideologies, a perspective perhaps impossible to reconcile for readers after World War II, for whom that war's battles and media have seared together the two concepts.

Mann first produced an outline of his hopes for Germany in a 1922 speech, "On the German Republic," calling for a Whitmanesque democracy where the "spiritual love of comrades" was not usurped for conservative, nationalistic purposes but, instead, used to establish a new Germany along those manly lines as innocent, as primal, as "the queerly sympathetic response one feels upon touching with one's own hand the naked flesh of the body." However, Mann's worst dreams came true, and he would later watch the perversion of his ideal in the development of the butch Nazi aesthetic.

He would better articulate his political concerns in the 1924 novel *The Magic Mountain,* an allegory about the evils of fascism. Winning Mann the Nobel Prize for Literature in 1929, it offered up queer concerns in its pages. That same year, Mann campaigned against the Nazis, and in 1930 he tackled Italian fascism in the novella *Mario and the Magician,* a work darkened by a fatal homoeroticism.

In 1933 Mann abandoned Germany for Switzerland. Three years later, on Freud's eightieth birthday, he delivered an address in honor of his friend. From his time spent with Freud, and from the two men's shared affection for the Jewish patriarchal hero Joseph, would come Mann's tetralogy, *Joseph and His Brothers,* which he did not finish writing until 1943. Shortly after delivering his speech in honor of Freud, Mann decamped for the safe distance of America.

In 1939 he published *Lotte in Weimar,* a novel about Goethe in love. Mann's speeches against Hitler—broadcast in Germany—were collected and published there in 1945. Two years later, in 1947, he went back to Europe, the only returning refugee to be honored with celebrations of his life and work in both East and West Germany. That same year, Mann published *Doktor Faustus,* reworking the medieval legend, recasting the concerns of art and politics against the destruction of his beloved Germany, and concerning in part the homosexual relationship of its protagonist. Mann died in 1955 before he could finish his last work, *Confessions of the Confidence Trickster Felix Krull,* although Part One was completed and published in 1954, revealing a deft, comic talent in the pared-down prose, so different from the thick sentences of his larger works, his *Bildungsromane,* or novels of education.

> He was brought back to reality by the sight of a man standing in the portico, above the two apocalyptic beasts that guarded the staircase, and something not quite usual in this man's appearance gave his thoughts a fresh turn. *(Death in Venice)*

Aschenbach, when he sees this man, is looking on a graveyard that is thick with Greek crosses and engraved, pat Christian phrases of grief, heavy with mysticism; he has lost himself in their contemplation. What is unusual about the stranger's appearance is that he is thin, so thin as to resemble a skeleton, even to his lips "seeming to curl back" and complete the effect of a death's head, with "colourless eyes" and a "little turned-up nose." A redhead, the man has white, ghostly pale skin. *Death in Venice* begins as it ends, in death, in the contemplation of a Munich graveyard and in Aschenbach's illusory meeting with his future, the end of life in the form of a stranger.

Death in Venice has much in common with *Roderick Hudson.*

Like Hudson, Aschenbach encounters his artistic ideal and it leads him to ruin, but *Death in Venice* takes as its protagonist not a young man at the start of his career but an older man in his work's twilight. Widowed, his daughter grown, Gustav von Aschenbach is a man adrift in society, having reaped his fame in earlier years with rich novels and brilliant writings on "the theme of Mind and Art." His primary literary innovation was a hero who embodied " '[t]he conception of an intelligent and virginal manliness, which clenches its teeth and stands in modest defiance of the swords and spears that pierce its side.' " But having realized all this, Aschenbach finds himself at loose ends until the stare of the stranger he encounters in the graveyard inspires him—as if by a "seizure"—to travel in search of "a fresh scene, without associations, which should yet be not too out of the way . . ."

His first choice is an Adriatic island, but that falls apart, as "an inner impulse made him wretched, urging him on he knew not whither; he racked his brains, he looked up boats, then all at once his goal stood plain before his eyes. But of course! When one wanted to arrive overnight at the incomparable, the fabulous, the like-nothing-else-in-the-world, where was it one went?"

Ten days later, Aschenbach has arranged to leave the island and is on board a ship heading for Venice.

Mann goes to great lengths to make it clear that Aschenbach is the subject of forces beyond his control, first the "seizure" of the desire to travel and then the "inner impulse" that drives him not toward his conscious choice but toward Venice. The events of *Death in Venice* are not happenstance or coincidence, they are fate and destiny.

Aboard the boat, Aschenbach notes a group of boisterous youths. One, however, crows louder than all the rest and is revealed, as Aschenbach considers him, to be not a youth at all but an old man, or, given the illusion the aged fop pursues, a young-old man.

His face is wrinkled, but his cheeks have been rouged red, his thick brown hair is a wig. His neck is thin and tough, his mustache and goatee are dyed. When he smiles—grimaces—he reveals a set of cheap, yellowed false teeth. His hands are be-ringed, but they are the hands of an old man.

Aschenbach is horrified to recognize the aging pretender in the midst of the boys. He doesn't understand their tolerance of the man's caricature of their vitality. The revulsion Aschenbach feels toward the old queen is visceral, and strikes deep. Moving to the other side of the ship, he sinks down into a deck chair and drowses, the old queen appearing to him in a half-horror. He awakens, is summoned to lunch and afterward again spies the old queen.

By this time the young-old man is drunk. He's staggering, leering, a skin-crawling exaggeration of the ridiculous pretense he exhibited earlier.

In the slipping of the young-old man from sobriety into drunkenness, and its accompanying lechery, Aschenbach senses life melting from reality toward the grotesque.

It is with this concern—this self-reflective horror, vivid in the old man's desperate pursuit of youth—that Aschenbach turns and sees at last his tormented destination, the glittering island city of Venice. But he does not escape the boat without an obsequious farewell from the drunken aged fop. After a tussle with an unlicensed gondolier, Aschenbach arrives at the Hôtel des Bains, where, having settled, he goes for tea.

At a wicker table next to him sits a governess and her charges: three young girls, between the ages of fifteen and seventeen, "and a long-haired boy of about fourteen."

The great writer is immediately struck by the boy's "perfect beauty. His face recalled the noblest moment of Greek sculpture— pale, with a sweet reserve, with clustering honey-coloured ringlets, the brow and nose descending in one line, the winning mouth, the expression of pure and godlike serenity." Paired with this physical beauty is an innate charm that appears to Aschenbach more complete, more self-satisfied than anything he has hitherto encountered or imagined.

To Aschenbach, the boy is obviously the product of an indulgent childhood. His curly hair has never been cut. He's costumed in an English sailor's suit, with a drooping red breast knot that gives him "a spoilt, exquisite air." While his sisters' poise is stiff and calculated, the boy sits relaxed, almost careless. He might be frail physically: His skin is "ivory-white." However, given the child's other emblems of a soft life, Aschenbach is more inclined to deem the boy's pallor the color of his pampering, proof of his ability to command a possessive, sheltering love in those around him.

> For in almost every artist's nature is inborn a wanton and treacherous proneness to side with the beauty that breaks hearts, to single out aristocratic pretensions and pay them homage.

From that moment on, the boy—whose name is later revealed to be Tadzio—becomes the center of Aschenbach's stay in Venice.

Superbly, Mann straddles the line between sexual and artistic obsession. Is Tadzio simply the embodiment, to an aging artist, of his life's work, the new hero that brings its creator so much fame? Does Aschenbach dream of possessing the boy physically? Following Aschenbach's attempt to render his attraction to Tadzio comprehensible via Plato's *Phaedrus*, the aging author has a dream revealing the passion simmering beneath the reason: He hears voices calling out for "the stranger god," and from a rocky woodland pours forth a frenzied crowd of men and animals, their impassioned stumblings something of a rutting dance. The men are horned and beat drums as they dance. There are women too, banging tambourines, screaming and slashing the skin of the night with torches. With living serpents belting their waists, they squeeze and tear at their breasts. "(T)roops of beardless youths" appear, carrying spears wrapped with woven bands of flowers, and join the mad revel.

And one and all the mad rout yelled that cry, composed of
soft consonants with a long-drawn *u*-sound at the end, so
sweet and wild it was together, and like nothing ever heard
before! . . . His heart throbbed to the drums, his brain
reeled, blind rage seized him, a whirling lust, he craved
with all his soul to join the ring that formed about the
obscene symbol of the godhead, which they were unveiling
and elevating, monstrous and wooden, while from full
throats they yelled their rallying cry . . . But now the
dreamer was in them and of them, the stranger god was
his own.

The "*u*-sound" Mann refers to is an echo of Aschenbach's piecing
together of the boy's name while eavesdropping. Here, while a bac-
chanal delivers itself around the rallying cry of the name of a beautiful fourteen-year-old boy, Aschenbach surrenders himself to the
massive priapus—a vast wooden cock—thrust upward before him.

So much for art.

Venice sours. Although news is suppressed, it appears a plague
is infesting the filthy canals that vein the city. Aschenbach attempts
to leave but finds he cannot, drawn back inexorably, almost against
his will, to the Hôtel des Bains by Tadzio's constant presence. "Like
any lover, he desired to please," leading him to make "frequent
visits to the hotel barber," who restores Aschenbach's gray hair to a
color "as black as in the days of his youth."

Aschenbach is unable to stop the barber in his cosmetic casting. And so the aged, respected writer watches in the mirror as his
eyebrows are plucked and colored, his eyes made more dramatic by
the application of liner, his cheeks made red with rouge, his mouth
turned carmine with lipstick. A cream spread over his face hides the
lines in his skin, and at last in the mirror, Aschenbach sees himself
as a young man.

A young-old man.

Aschenbach becomes, then, the berouged nightmare he had

spied on the boat that brought him to Venice, his hatred of the old queen revealed as nothing but self-loathing, a fearsome premonition. Rendered helpless, as he now is, unable to control his own dignity or heart, what is left for Aschenbach but days spent prettily dressed, watching a fourteen-year-old boy he has never spoken to cavort in a bathing suit on the hotel beach?

What, indeed.

FIVE QUESTIONS

1. What kills Aschenbach?

2. What is Tadzio's response to Aschenbach?

3. Does Aschenbach's interest in Tadzio seem to be more sexual than artistic or more artistic than sexual—and why? Is it possible, realistically, to separate physical from aesthetic desire?

4. Aschenbach was happily married (so far as we know) for years and has a grown daughter at the time of *Death in Venice*. Still, given the events of the narrative, is he gay? Is Tadzio gay? What, really, does it mean "to be gay"?

5. Does *Death in Venice* try to teach us anything? Does it hold a moral, and if so, what is it?

E. M. Forster

Maurice

But as he returned to his bed a little noise sounded, a noise so intimate that it might have arisen inside his own body. He seemed to crackle and burn and saw the ladder's top quivering against the midnight air. The head and shoulders of a man rose up, paused, a gun was leant against the window sill very carefully, and someone he scarcely knew moved towards him and knelt beside him and whispered, "Sir, was you calling out for me? . . . Sir, I know . . . I know," and touched him.

—CHAPTER 37

Edward Morgan Forster's architect father would die within a year of his son's birth, which took place in London on January 1, 1879, and the boy would be raised in the company of women. The young man's sexuality would make itself known to him even as Oscar Wilde was being sent to Reading Gaol, and the resulting heightened societal repression would make it impossible for Forster to publish openly about homosexuality in his lifetime.

Maurice, written in 1913 and 1914, sprang in its first form from a visit Forster made to the home of Edward Carpenter, a sort of British Walt Whitman. Carpenter was less of a poet than Whitman, though he did better at conceiving a well-lived and unapologetic homosexual life through various works such as *Towards Democracy.* Carpenter lived with his lover, George Merrill. In his terminal note to *Maurice,* Forster writes that the presence of the two men "combined to make a profound impression on me and to touch a creative spring." He notes further that "George Merrill also touched my backside—gently and just above the buttocks. I believe he touched most people's." Still, the touch was not just a touch, for Carpenter's home, a place of freed and dignified queer life, ignited a creative spark in Forster that is the whole story of *Maurice*—characters, happy ending and all.

Much of the novel is drawn from Forster's own life, though apart from their sexuality, Maurice and Forster have little in common. Still, their erotic episodes echo: Like Maurice, Forster enjoyed—or suffered through, depending upon how you look at it—a Platonic relationship with a fellow student while at Cambridge. Maurice and Forster also found their sexual desires fulfilled by members of the lower class.

In Forster's case, this further specialized itself in an attraction to foreigners. Forster was thirty-nine before he first found a fulfilling gay relationship in the person of Mohammed el Adl, an Egyptian tram conductor. The relationship was cut short by the man's early death in 1922. In 1930 Forster's next and last relationship began, with a handsome and smart police officer named Bob Buckingham. Their relationship would endure until Forster's death, despite Bob's marriage in 1932.

Indeed, Forster died in the Buckinghams' home, at Coventry, in 1970. A year later, *Maurice* was published, and the year after that, a collection of mostly gay short fictions, *The Life to Come.*

While Forster wrote many fine novels through which a homosexual sensibility may be traced—including *A Room with a View* and *A Passage to India,* the latter title lifted from a Whitman poem—it is *Maurice* that remains the heart of his work. It is certainly the most open expression of his heart's desires. Packed with portraits of other notable queers as active characters—Risley, the clever Trinity undergraduate, was based on Lytton Strachey, for example—it was dedicated "to a happier year." In his terminal note, Forster makes it clear that the year he hoped for was one when homosexuality would no longer be a crime; it was a year he never knew.

Of Human Bondage

He thought of his desire to make a design, intricate and beautiful, out of the myriad, meaningless facts of life: had he not also seen that the simplest pattern, that in which a man was born, worked, married, had children, and died, was likewise the most perfect? It might be that to surrender to happiness was to accept defeat, but it was a defeat better than many victories.

—CHAPTER 122

William Somerset Maugham avoided both homosexual themes and homosexual characters in his literary efforts. The queer American novelist Glenway Wescott—whose published journals, *Continual Lessons,* make for remarkable reading on gay life in the early and middle parts of the twentieth century—suspected that it was because "Willie's generation lived in mortal terror of the Oscar Wilde trial."

Perhaps that is so. Maugham was born in 1874. His career spanned sixty-five years, and though he longed for literary greatness, by his own admission he was "in the very first row of the second-rate." He was a doctor before he was a novelist and was periodically employed by the British government as a secret agent. He produced nineteen novels, six short story collections, eight nonfiction volumes, thirty-one plays and four legitimately autobiographical works. *Of Human Bondage* is also an autobiographical work, but one cobbled together in the guise of fiction—and his most successful and enduring novel.

Of Human Bondage is, ultimately, a story of sexual obsession and choices. Its protagonist, Philip Carey, is set apart from others by a clubfoot, a representation of Maugham's own separating characteristic, a noticeable (and lifelong) stammer. Throughout, the book is linked to episodes in Maugham's life; in fact, at times it seems packed with incidents—included simply because they happened—but despite its bulk, the novel still manages to move at a brisk pace.

The book is also a *Bildungsroman*, one in which Philip Carey is rendered deftly human by his apparent lack of wit and occasional self-obsessive bitchiness. We are drawn into his story not in spite of but because of his imperfections.

Philip plows through a series of women, but for the most part the relationships end with his initial feelings of infatuation or attraction souring into awkwardness and revulsion. In her introduction to the Bantam Classics edition of the novel, Jane Smiley suggests that the roots of this repeated response "are to be found in his creator's discreet but lifelong homosexuality."

Maybe. Philip finally does choose the stodgy security of marriage to the likable Sally over his affair with the combustible, sexually shameless Mildred. Full as the latter relationship is with episodes of betrayal and humiliation, it is also powerful and passionate, an entrance into the world of feeling, just as Athelney is the world of self-justifying bloodless practicality.

This is perhaps too harsh a reading, but it is easy to draw from it the classic homosexual dilemma that has haunted much of Western culture: the society-blessed life of the fraud heterosexual or the spirited, passionate life of the outlaw homosexual.

In his own life, Maugham trod a middle road. He fathered a daughter in 1915 and married her mother, Syrie Wellcome, in 1916. They rarely lived together and divorced in 1927. For Maugham, the relationship that would endure was with Gerald Haxton, a young American he met in 1914 and with whom he shared a life until Haxton's death in 1944. They lived in the South of France for much of that time, but Haxton would die in America, where they resided after 1940. Maugham, then alone, returned to the Riviera in 1946. He died in 1965.

Gerard Manley Hopkins

Poems and Prose

There! and your sweetest sendings, ah divine . . .
Breathing bloom of a chastity in mansexfine.

When limber liquid youth, that to all I teach
Yields tender as a pushed peach . . . !
—"THE BUGLER'S FIRST COMMUNION,"
VERSES 4 AND 6 (EXCERPTS)

Born in 1844 at Stratford, London, Gerard Manley Hopkins was the
son of a prosperous marine insurance salesman, who, in the year
before Gerard's birth, published a volume of verse. The boy's
mother was a devout member of the Church of England.

Hopkins was the oldest of eight children, educated at Highgate
School (where he won the poetry prize in 1860) and Balliol College,
Oxford, where he studied under Benjamin Jowett, one of the foremost translators of Plato, and Walter Pater, destined to become a
modern aesthete. But it was the fervor and self-denial of the Jesuits
that would fill Hopkins' life—or keep its emptiness secure. The
Church of England was in a state of upheaval at the time, which
allowed Hopkins to discover the Catholic Church; he converted at
the age of twenty-two. Two years later, he became a Jesuit and
burned all his early poems (or so he thought—four survived the

purge). For a while he "resolved to write no more," but he eventually found a way, through philosophical exercise, to submit himself again to the poetical flow that, in its rousing use of language, spiritually heightened imagery and blatant energized sensuality, seemed to be the outlet for all that Hopkins denied himself: his passion for masculine beauty and emotional freedom.

It has been said that he had a crush on a religiously foppish, emotionally immature lad three years his junior by the name of Digby Mackworth Dolben, whom he met at Oxford. Digby, though, drowned at the age of nineteen. Regardless of the nature of Hopkins' feelings for the boy, this loss would forever temper his willingness to extend himself emotionally in his friendships.

Hopkins lived the rest of his life teaching, serving various communities—London, Oxford, Liverpool, Glasgow—as a Jesuit priest and writing some of the most striking poetry of the Victorian Age. His poems, however, were not published until 1918, by which time Hopkins had been dead for almost thirty years.

In 1885 he accepted a position as professor of classics at University College, Dublin, but his physical and nervous failings, which had begun to show themselves in 1874, would there overtake him: he died on June 8, 1889, at forty-five, of typhoid fever, complicated by peritonitis. His parents were with him. The last words of the man who once wrote "I am a eunuch, but it is for the kingdom of heaven's sake" were "I am so happy, so happy."

His poetic legacy would echo that sentiment, revealing an original approach to religion and desire that would fly in the face of Victorian repression to breathe life into that most poetic of sentiments: amorous holy yearning.

Eminent Victorians

Doubtless it was important to teach boys something more than the bleak rigidities of the ancient tongues; but how much more important to instill into them the elements of character and the principles of conduct! . . . And he was constantly impressing these sentiments upon his pupils. "What I have often said before," he told them, "I repeat now: what we must look for here is, first, religious and moral principle; secondly, gentlemanly conduct; thirdly, intellectual ability."

—"DR. ARNOLD"

Dr. Arnold is recognizable to us as the patron saint of *Tom Brown's Schooldays,* and it is against him that Lytton Strachey rails, creating with words a Dorian Gray–esque portrait, stripping away the soft veil of lore and legend that so informed Thomas Hughes's work. But what did Arnold do that, for Strachey, was so terrible? He subverted the educational goals of the day, creating a cultural experience instead of an intellectual one, and for intellectuals like Strachey, this meant a world upended, where the good-looking and well-dressed ruled the day and fed a society favoring gloss over substance.

Giles Lytton Strachey was born on March 1, 1880, the son of British soldier and Indian civil engineer Richard Strachey. His mother, Jane Maria Grant, was thirty years younger than Richard, and Lytton was closest to her, although he was but one of a brood of thirteen.

Lytton was educated at Trinity College, Cambridge—must every gay writer go there?—and he began his literary career as a book reviewer. He was a conscientious objector during World War I and formed part of the core Bloomsbury Group, a coterie of British intellectuals that included Virginia Woolf and the woman with whom Lytton's life would be forever linked, painter Dora Carrington. (Perhaps the St. Joan of fag hags, she killed herself after he died from cancer in 1932—she was always hopelessly in love with him, though she knew full well he was queer.)

Strachey made his claim to fame with the publication in 1918 of *Eminent Victorians,* where the skills he sharpened as chief bitch of the Bloomsbury Group found ready public acceptance. Prior to *Eminent Victorians,* biographies tended to shape and develop the legend of a public notable. Strachey went in the opposite direction, writing scathingly honest biographies of some heroes from the then-passing Victorian Age. He shattered the pedestals people had so eagerly constructed for Cardinal Manning, Florence Nightingale, General Gordon and, of course, Dr. Arnold, leaving their personas in heaps among the rubble.

In a way, we have Strachey to thank for modern tell-all biographers such as Kitty Kelley, yet it is probably, perversely, the combined efforts of Strachey and his nemesis Dr. Arnold that have led to a culture where we are not only eager to see our heroes debunked but revel in it.

Eminent Victorians is a primer on how to write a biography. Strachey's crisp, sharply humorous essays remain provocative. Dated as they may be by their fixation on a particular subject, we nevertheless leave the essay on Dr. Arnold wondering just what it is we currently value in education—not only our children's but our own as well—even as his essay on Florence Nightingale uncomfortably recalls the rush to canonize the veneer of Mother Teresa, despite the complicated darkness roiling beneath the surface.

Collected Poems

L et my inscription be this soldier's-disc . . .
Wear it, sweet friend. Inscribe no date or deed.
But may thy heart-beat kiss it, night and day.
—"TO MY FRIEND," VERSE 3 (PARTIAL)

At the outset of World War I, the beautiful, mad English poet Rupert Brooke died, and his poems, most notably "1914," were touted by Winston Churchill, an acquaintance of Brooke's, as emblematic of all the youthful poetic hope of England.

Gay men in particular proved vulnerable to Brooke's physical charms. These men were encouraged by Brooke's hypersentimental verse, as well as a raunchy letter written by him, and eventually published, that vividly describes a messy night of sex with a fellow student. But Brooke, alas, wasn't gay. His romantic and erotic obsession for most of his life was a woman named Noelle Olivier. As for Brooke the soldier, Churchill had to do some PR work to make the image fit. Brooke's life barely scraped the true horrors of war: he died in 1915 of blood poisoning while on a military boat off the shores of Greece, and never really saw action.

It would take Wilfred Edward Salter Owen, who fought in the trenches, was wounded and then sent back to the front lines, only to die a week before the 1918 peace accord, to give full voice to the youthful waste of that war.

Owen was a Shropshire lad, born in 1893. His father worked on the railway, and although Owen, educated at the Birkenhead School and at Shrewsbury Technical School, had hoped to finish his studies at London University, money proved too tight. He went off to work for eighteen months with an Oxfordshire minister, but an increasingly developed social conscience split him away from the church in 1913. Later that year, Owen went off to teach English in France at the Berlitz School. He left that school to tutor two Catholic boys and was with them in the Pyrénées when war was declared. Immediately he sailed back to England and enlisted; he was assigned to the Artists' Rifles.

The pointless slaughter of male beauty in war seems to have appalled him, and in his revulsion he found purpose and direction, two things his life had long lacked. He wanted to be a poet, but wasn't quite sure how to go about it, though he prophetically noted a young poet's apparently necessary obsession with death. Remarkably, much of Owen's poetry seems determined to do the reverse: uncover the life within death, reviving the dead to vibrancy through memory and frozen slices of verse.

In June 1917, suffering from a concussion and trench fever, Owen was sent to recuperate near Edinburgh. While there he met Siegfried Sassoon, the bisexual poet, and the introduction proved a fruitful turning point in Owen's creative life. Not only did Sassoon work with him on his poetry, but he introduced the twenty-four-year-old Owen to the denizens of London's gay literary circles, including C. K. Scott-Moncrieff, the translator of Marcel Proust's *In Search of Lost Time*. Owen's poetry is rich with a homoerotic and homoaffectional sensitivity to the men he encountered on the battlefields (perhaps best observed in the horrifically sexy "Arms and the Boy") and in life (the altar boy whose brown hand he kisses instead of the offered silver crucifix in "Maundy Thursday," an act clearly setting him apart from the men and women who precede him to the metal).

Around September 1, Owen returned to France for active service, hoping somehow to use his position at the front to dramatize his antiwar position. He was a good soldier, caring for the well-being of the men around him. A month after his return, he was awarded the Military Cross; a month after that, he was dead.

Owen was killed trying to get his men across the Sambre Canal. His parents found out their son had died just as the bells began to toll for the signing of the Armistice. Only four of Owen's poems were published in his lifetime, but since his death his work has gained a respect eclipsing that accorded the lesser war poets: Sassoon and, yes, even Brooke, remembered now more as a romantic than as a soldier.

Marcel Proust

In Search of
Lost Time

TRANSLATED BY C. K. SCOTT-MONCRIEFF
AND TERENCE KILMARTIN AND REVISED
BY D. J. ENRIGHT

At this moment I noticed that there was a small oval window opening from the room onto the corridor and that the curtain had not been drawn across it; stealthily in the darkness I crept as far as this window and there in the room, chained to a bed like Prometheus to his rock, receiving the blows that Maurice rained upon him with a whip which was in fact studded with nails, I saw, with blood already flowing from him and covered with bruises which proved that the chastisement was not taking place for the first time—I saw before me M. de Charlus.

—*TIME REGAINED*

Marcel Proust was born in Auteuil, Paris, in 1871. He was sickly all his life, a semi-invalid cared for by his mother until she died, when he was thirty-four years old. Something of a social butterfly until then, upon her death he cocooned himself in a cork-lined room that kept out sound and whose air was perpetually thick with vapors designed to prevent the asthma he first experienced in 1880. Three years after that attack, he'd lock himself in the bathroom to jack off for the first time. When he was eighteen, he did a year's military service at Orléans. He took a degree in law in 1893; and two years later, another one in philosophy at the Sorbonne.

He was very much a product of his day and wholly, immediately enmeshed in it. The opening of the section of *In Search of Lost Time* published in 1921, *Sodom and Gomorrah,* is a discourse on homosexuality refuting many of the more liberal claims made in 1920 by fellow Frenchman André Gide in *Corydon.*

Proust probably never came happily to terms with his own sexuality. He had many Platonic relationships with men who were his peers, some of which may have become sexual. Otherwise, the socialite Proust found his partners mostly in the lower classes—the most important of these being his chauffeur, Alfred Agostinelli, whom he met in 1907.

Before embarking in search of lost time in 1909, Proust attempted another autobiographical work, *Jean Santeuil,* which he began in 1895 and worked on for four years, but it never satisfied him and was eventually abandoned.

In Search of Lost Time is voyeuristic. It is sexually fluid, redolent of homosexual undertones that approach a modern camp sensibility. The work can be emotionally moving, disturbingly erotic and suddenly comic—all within pages. But the work itself hangs together under the conceit of time as a function of memory—that is to say, abstracted time laid over the sustained, predictable progression of time as we know it in the physical world. Among other French philosophers, Proust was influenced by the greatly underrated Henri Bergson, who wrote extensively on the subconscious. (His theory, expressed in *Creative Evolution,* that there is a moral or spiritual development in nature corresponding to physical evolution, is remarkably compelling.) *In Search of Lost Time* is a novel of the way a life is built and then continually reassembled via memory, a novel loosely cobbled together from impressions into one stunning, at times overpowering mosaic that is the whole of our existence.

André Gide

Corydon

TRANSLATED BY RICHARD HOWARD

"Then what are you complaining about?"

"About hypocrisy. About lies. About misrepresentation. About that smuggler's behavior to which you drive the uranist."[3]

"Then you'd like to go back to the old Greek ways?"

"If it pleased the gods! . . . and for the good of the state."

—DIALOGUE FOUR

André-Paul-Guillaume Gide was born in Paris in 1869. His father, a professor of law at the Sorbonne, died when Gide was eleven, leaving him in the hands of a crowd of conservative women: his mother, aunts, maids and cousins. Their repressive moral values would form the center of Gide's lifelong societal rebellion.

Gide claims in his autobiography that he turned to writing to "give form to a confused inner agitation," to make sense of his life.

---

[3] Homosexual.

He was forever a work-in-progress, consistently open to change and evolving philosophically as he traveled life's course. He would produce over fifty volumes, many of them centering around man's moral conflict with an immoral status quo.

At the age of twenty-four Gide and the artist Paul A. Laurens went to North Africa. The trip would prove revelatory for Gide: He had his first homosexual experience there with an Arab boy named Ali, tapping into the whole of his romantic and sexual ardor, hitherto repressed. Two years later, he returned to North Africa to meet up with Oscar Wilde and Lord Alfred Douglas. More Arab boys were buggered by Gide, and it seems that his sexual preferences were all but confirmed. (A later liaison with Elisabeth Van Rysselberghe would result, in 1923, in the birth of a daughter, Catherine, Gide's only offspring.)

That May his mother died, and that October he married his cousin, Madeleine Rondeaux. He idealized her, however, writing her into several of his books (including *The Immoralist,* as Marceline). He never consummated their marriage, out of a fear of tarnishing his image of her. For the most part, she accepted his terms, though at times she did rebel: In 1916, while Gide was off in Switzerland having perhaps the most meaningful love affair of his life with a lad named Marc Allégret, his wife was at home burning all of Gide's letters to her. Her act horrified him when he learned of it upon returning to Paris, after the end of his relationship with Allégret; it shattered his image of her, for he felt the letters contained some of his finest writing. From this hornet's nest would come his 1926 novel *The Counterfeiters,* wherein the relationship between Édouard and Olivier recasts Gide's own relationship with Allégret.

Roughly a year prior to *The Counterfeiters,* Gide published a series of "Platonic" dialogues in *Corydon,* which had already seen several privately printed incarnations, in 1907, 1911 and 1920. But *Corydon* was publicly issued only after Gide had had the opportunity to read Freud, and find in the popular author supportive sympathies. At one point Gide hoped to prevail upon James Strachey,

Lytton's brother and Freud's translator, to secure an introduction by Freud. It did not happen—the request was not made—but *Corydon* dovetailed with Freud's ideas in recognizing homosexuality as a manifestation of the spirit and not simply the genitals.

Corydon makes several arguments in its four dialogues, between a first-person narrator—not Gide, but a typically bigoted boor—and Dr. Corydon, who is hard at work on a book entitled *The Defense of Pederasty*. The first dialogue is introductory; the second addresses the occurrences of homosexuality in nature, seeking to establish it as wholly natural through example and precedent, heavily citing Darwin. The third dialogue tackles homosexuality's alliance with art, arguing that the times when it was embraced by society rather than reviled were times of artistic change and growth. (Perplexingly, among those Gide calls upon to illustrate this point is the queen of self-loathing, Michelangelo.) The final dialogue makes other historical points, referring to Sparta's Army of Lovers, classical arguments on virtue, and the sexual compatibility of young men (adolescents) and older men (mentors) in ancient Greece and Rome.

The publication of *Corydon*—although it angered, appalled and inspired his circle of gay literary chums—did not finish Gide's career. While he refused a nomination to the French Academy after its publication, in 1947 he accepted an honorary doctorate from Oxford University, the same year he was awarded the Nobel Prize for Literature. He died in 1951.

Five Novels

READING:

Prancing Nigger

Delegates of the agricultural guilds bearing banners, making for the Cathedral square (the pilgrims' starting point), were advancing along the avenue amidst applause: fruit-growers, rubber-growers, sugar-growers, opium-growers, all doubtless wishful of placating Nature that redoubtable goddess by showing a little honour to the church. "Oh Lord, not as Sodom," she murmured, deciphering a text attached to the windscreen of a luxurious automobile.

—*PRANCING NIGGER,* CHAPTER 14

Arthur Annesley Ronald Firbank was born in London in 1886, the son of a noted railway executive and a member of Parliament, Sir Thomas Firbank. His mother, Lady Firbank, was the daughter of an Irish clergyman; she and Sir Thomas became famous collectors of rare prints and porcelain. His mother was supportive of her son, providing shelter from a world he often found hard and cold, and he outlived her by only two years. Firbank's sense of himself as an outsider to the world, despite being to the manor born, perhaps helped him develop a sympathetic sensitivity to those on the fringes of society—queers, women, people of color.

Firbank was educated at Uppingham, and later at Trinity Hall, Cambridge, where in 1907 he converted to Roman Catholicism, not from the profound belief Evelyn Waugh would later embrace but simply because it best offered religion as theater—and served the added purpose of further estranging himself from mainstream British society. He dropped out of college in 1909, traveling to Spain, the Middle East, North Africa and Italy, where he thought about becoming a priest but was refused. This rejection, in part, fueled his desire to base some of his most perverse characters in the belly of the Catholic hierarchy and mythology. He would be spared military service as a result of a bout of sunstroke suffered as a child, rendering him frail throughout his life. Although he had friends, he chose a solitary life, becoming a sort of London curio, regularly spotted alone at the theater. He was painfully reticent, his first words in conversation seeming to cause him actual pain. He was known for a light appetite, once consuming only a pea at a dinner party. His laugh, however, was startlingly unfettered.

He clung to eccentricity, keeping a set number of objects about him that constituted his life as he moved about. These included a bronze bull, a pencil portrait of himself, a small patinated Egyptian bronze, elaborate inkpots, a vast tortoiseshell crucifix and a palm tree that he hired a gardener to water twice a day. When he went to Portugal, he had to stay in the Palace at Cintra, where William Beckford had lived. He wrote everything on blue postcards, but his handwriting was so large that they each could hold only about ten words.

He published two short stories in 1905, but his career began in earnest with the publication of the novel *Vainglory* in 1915, followed quickly by *Valmouth* (1919) and *Prancing Nigger* (1924), a story inspired by a visit to Haiti. (Carl Van Vechten, the noted proponent of African-American equality and chum of Gertrude Stein, gave Firbank the title.) Firbank wrote plays as well, but they proved less successful, and less enduring, than his novels.

Ronald Firbank died of collapsed lungs on May 21, 1926, in Rome, at the age of thirty-nine, just as *Concerning the Eccentricities of Cardinal Pirelli* was published. There were those who said his death was hastened by alcoholism; others, that his lifelong frailty simply caught up with him. During his lifetime his work had a small, devoted following—with the exception of *Prancing Nigger*, which sold well in the United States. Since then he has come to influence many writers, most notably the genius that is Patrick Gale.

> In what way, she reflected, would the family gain by *entering Society*, and how did one enter it at all? There would be a gathering, doubtless, of the elect (probably armed), since the best Society is exclusive and difficult to enter. And then? Did one burrow? or charge? She had sometimes heard it said that people "pushed" . . . and closing her eyes, Miss Miami Mouth sought to picture her parents, assisted by her small sister, Edna, and her brother, Charlie, forcing their way, perspiring but triumphant, into the highest social circles of the city of Cuna-Cuna.
>
> (CHAPTER 1)

When Van Vechten suggested the title *Prancing Nigger* for Firbank's slender new novel, he did so seeking to shock. The book as a whole is intended simply as an outrage, a skewering of the pretensions attached to the very idea of "entering Society" and of the inherent buffoonery such elitism invites.

Miss Miami Mouth is happy in Mediavilla, happy wearing her grass skirts and keeping company with her boyfriend, Bamboo. Her mother, however, harbors grandiose notions that she attempts to hide beneath her apparent selflessness. She is bored, and as her pearl wedding anniversary draws nigh, she longs to announce that the Mouths will be leaving the remote and primitive small town of Mediavilla to provide a better education for their daughters in the city of Cuna-Cuna. (Little thought, apparently, is given to the future of Charlie, their son.)

Mr. Mouth, the "Prancing Nigger" of the title, is less inclined to uproot his life and that of his children to satisfy his wife's plan. Mrs. Mouth, thinking he's reluctant to leave his church, suggests that there are other churches in Cuna-Cuna.

Mr. Mouth is still less than eager, referring to Cuna-Cuna as that "modern Sodom" he has asked her never to mention by name in his presence. But Mrs. Mouth retorts that the devil as readily visits a small town as he does a city—a statement to which Mr. Mouth can only acquiesce with "Sh'o nuff."

Mrs. Mouth will not be persuaded from her course. She recounts the latest township horrors, and at last breaks down, admitting her passion for a " 'Villa with a watercloset,' " to which Mr. Mouth cries out, "De Lord hab pity on dese vanities an' innovations!" (Chapter 2). Mrs. Mouth then launches into her litany of concerns—their lack of intelligent neighbors, their children's welfare, and so forth—until, bit by bit, she wears down her husband. He, however, slips away without promising anything. At this point Mrs. Mouth sees Miami, naked, her grass skirt thrown away, teaching the cat to dance by the music of their gramophone. Mrs. Mouth mutters, " 'Fie, fie, my lass. Why you be so Indian?' "

At the Mouth's Pearl Wedding Feast, Mrs. Mouth continues to put forth her children's education as the reason for their move. The rumor that they will be leaving slowly gathers steam as more and more people believe it. Eventually, even Mr. Mouth must surrender to what has become common knowledge. Despite their parents' admonition against the new trend of " 'close dancing,' " the young men and women dance chest-to-chest, "while even a pair of majestic matrons, Mrs. Friendship and Mrs. Mother, went whirling away (together) into the brave summer dusk" (Chapter 4).

Bamboo spirits Miami Mouth away from the dance, and they walk along the road, passing two young men, holding hands, who salute them quietly.

Clearly, Mediavilla isn't a bad place: Mr. Mouth, his daughter Miami, her brother, Charlie (who chases butterflies all day with his net), and Bamboo are all quite happy with the life the town offers them, a life that seems less provincial than simple.

Upon their arrival in Cuna-Cuna, the Mouths install themselves in the Grand Savannah Hotel. From its balcony, they view the handsome men and beautiful women of the city, even as they chafe against their formal clothing. Edna, Mrs. Mouth's other daughter, becomes overwhelmed with the glory of the city, with its life and promise:

> "Oh, Jesus honey!" Edna cooed, scratching herself in an ecstasy of delight.
>
> "Fo' shame, Chile, to act so unladylike; if any gen'leman look up he t'ink you make a wicked sign," Mrs. Mouth cautioned, stepping out on the balcony from the sitting room behind.   (CHAPTER 6)

Mr. Mouth, however, is finding the place to be everything he feared. He searches for the church, but finds only a prostitute.

The family secures a rental property, the lease to which is held by the "arbitress absolute of Cunan society," the widow Madame Ruiz, who lives in the fabulous Villa Alba with Miss Eurydice Edwards, her, ah, companion. Charlie Mouth arrives, with nothing to declare upon entering the city but his butterflies, and finds the city market simply a larger version of Mediavilla's. There he finds his mother, who takes one look at him and promises to buy him an "Eton colleh" as soon as possible.

Mrs. Mouth, her head swimming with the luxuries available in the city, still dreams of her children's pending education at the university, even as she waits for Madame Ruiz to invite her to an upcoming cotillion. She had hoped another Mediavilla expatriate would be able to help her secure the invitation, but the woman has turned out to be a dancer in a bar, to Mrs. Mouth's chagrin, for now the woman is of no use to her. So Edna is sent with an armful of flowers to court Madame Ruiz, finding instead Vittorio Ruiz, Madame's son, who takes the pretty, unspoiled thirteen-year-old girl in his arms.

Charlie, meanwhile, spurns the murmured appreciation of the town's belles and falls in with a group of men, apparently from the University, who hang out in the park and drink rum. One of them has a father who runs a dance hall; another is entering the church; yet another dreams of the stage and claims to know the leading actress of Cuna-Cuna; and a last boy hopes only to be a dress designer to foreign princesses. Charlie is taking his leave of them one evening when an earthquake strikes, shaking up Cuna-Cuna but for the most part sparing the city. The rest of the island is not so fortunate.

This, however, works to Mrs. Mouth's advantage, for a benefit is to be held at the Villa Alba to help earthquake relief efforts in other parts of the island, and Mrs. Mouth sees a perfect opportunity to get herself and her daughters noticed by society.

Firbank's description of Cuna-Cuna society is wickedly vicious and funny, all the more so because he flowers in the heart of it. First, there are the real flowers swathing Villa Alba; then, nestled among them, there are the blooms of society, with Firbank himself described as among those claiming the greatest respect, "a dingy lilac blossom of rarity untold."

The benefit gets under way and, with Mrs. Mouth at its center, quickly reveals itself as a madcap series of misadventures. The have-nots insist on their right to stand as peers with the haves, and Mrs. Mouth metamorphoses from a tiresome social climber to something of a social butterfly who refuses to be cowed by the titles of others. When the Duke of Wellclose wanders off from his duchess, and Mrs. Mouth attempts to seize the empty chair, she will not be denied. White women be damned, Mrs. Mouth's determined reply to the duchess's horrified protestations is "I pay, an' I mean to hab it" (Chapter 12).

Taking advantage of the distraction provided by the scene between Mrs. Mouth and the duchess, Vitti Ruiz readily makes off with Edna, walking her down to the isolated white sands of the beach. The benefit winds down, but the Mouths still wait for Edna's return, performing a postmortem on the evening under the increasingly hostile stares of the servants, who have hopes of getting to bed at some point. At last, at daybreak, the Mouths—less Edna—return home, only to find a letter waiting for them there: Bamboo is dead.

He had taken his boat out to sea to avoid the earthquake, but the boat overturned and the sharks tore at him. Miami Mouth can only sob at the news and at the emptiness of her fatally love-bereft heart. She bemoans Cuna-Cuna—

> City life, what had it done for any of them, after all? Edna nothing else than a harlot (since she had left them there was no other word), and Charlie fast going to pieces, having joined the Promenade of a notorious Bar with its bright particular galaxy of boys.   (CHAPTER 13)

—even as Mrs. Mouth returns from church, with a vision in her head of the marriage of her daughter to Vittorio Ruiz. At suppertime Mr. Mouth and Mrs. Mouth find themselves alone at the table—Miami heartbroken in her room, Edna ensconced on the lap of Vitti Ruiz, Charlie out with the boys. There is nothing left for them but the same conversations that they shared in Mediavilla. There is a hollowness in the familiar strains of their dialogue, inviting echoes of that former home, where the family was together, Miami loved Bamboo, Edna was her mother's favorite chile, and Charlie chased butterflies.

The last chapter of the book takes place on Crucifix day, when the city's Christians wear black briar crosses and a procession moves through the streets. Miami Mouth is in that procession, but she passes the apartment in which Vitti has installed Edna without looking up, and Edna's cries to her are lost in the noise of the parade. Moments before, Vittorio had held her.

> And smiling down on her uplifted face, he asked himself whimsically how long he would love her. She had not the brains, poor child, of course, to keep a man for ever. Heigho. Life indeed was often hard . . . (CHAPTER 14)

FIVE QUESTIONS

1. Is *Prancing Nigger* racist? Why or why not? If it is racist now, was it racist when it was published? How? What makes the difference, and how responsible are we in judging past works by present standards? Is that a good thing to do—or a bad thing? Is it necessary?

2. *Prancing Nigger* is a slender book, but complete. Is it a parable? If so, what is its moral?

3. What is behind Mrs. Mouth's drive to enter society? Is she genuinely concerned about her children's education—or even, at the end, their welfare?

4. We like to think of America as a classless society, of Western civilization in general as increasingly classless, but is this realistic? Does *Prancing Nigger* remain as virtually dead-on target as it was when it was written, in an effort to lampoon the snobs and the wanna-bes that clamor about them?

5. Who is the centerpiece—the heart—of the work? Miami? Charlie? Edna? Mrs. Mouth? Or Mr. Mouth? Why does Mrs. Mouth call Mr. Mouth "Prancing Nigger"?

Jean Cocteau

The White Book

TRANSLATED BY MARGARET CROSLAND

Instead of adopting Rimbaud's gospel, the time of the assassins has come, young people would do better to remember the phrase Love must be re-invented. The world accepts dangerous experiments in the realm of art because it does not take art seriously; but it condemns them in life.

Jean Cocteau was born into a middle-class Parisian family in 1889. His father died when Jean was ten. The boy attended a prestigious school but was an indifferent scholar. While in school, however, he met Pierre Dargelos, a classmate who epitomized nature's masculinity for him, its untamed, brutal yet beautiful heart. Dargelos features prominently in many of Cocteau's works. Dargelos' early death, however, would find itself echoed honestly only in *The White Book*.

Dargelos' death spurred in Cocteau a desire to flee all that he had known, and he ran away to Marseilles, where Rimbaud had died. He spent his time among sailors and whores, feeding the base desire for indulgence that was to charge Cocteau's creative output with a kind of wildfire.

Upon his return to Paris, he immersed himself in the artistic world, at the time vibrantly flourishing in the darkness of theaters and in the yellow light of cafés, galleries and salons. He learned as much from nights spent in the company of aesthetes as he did from hours lost with lovers. Cocteau's mother approved when the actor who played opposite Sarah Bernhardt, Édouard de Max, offered to serve as the boy's artistic guide; he would later finance publication of Cocteau's first three books of poetry, starting when Cocteau was twenty.

Among the creative luminaries Cocteau brushed up against were Kuzmin's pals Nijinsky and Diaghilev, the latter ordering Cocteau in 1912 to "astonish me." Cocteau would take the two words as his creed, and they fed a diversity of endeavors from sketches to ballet scenarios, from prose to poetry, from plays to film.

While young, Cocteau had sought out older men; as he matured, his interest turned to young boys. Perhaps the most productive of these liaisons was with Raymond Radiguet, fifteen when he took up with then thirty-year-old Cocteau. It was a case of opposites attracting, Cocteau demanding that Radiguet be wild, Radiguet demanding that Cocteau get serious. Together they produced four celebrated novels. A series of boys followed in the wake of Radiguet's early death in 1923; some of the affairs ended happily, others not.

In 1928, *The White Book* was published anonymously, though certain things—most notably the primary importance of a character named Dargelos—pointed to Cocteau. It is theorized he didn't publish it under his own name because he wanted to protect his mother, still alive at the time. Only late in life did he allow its discreet inclusion as part of his official bibliography—his sole gesture toward recognizing the book as his own.

The White Book is not a happy story. Its queer protagonist comes to terms with his sexuality and embarks on a series of erotic episodes that end, for the most part, unhappily—or in death! At the story's conclusion, he makes a plea for the acceptance of the love of boyflesh as he finds himself rejected by everyone and everything he once hoped would embrace him: his lovers, his society, his God.

Still, *The White Book* is a powerful miniature and a major work. Almost a prose poem in the power of its compact, sexually charged imagery, graced as it is in present editions with Cocteau's erotic line drawings, it manages to stir the groin as it saddens the heart. In sum, it astonishes us—and perhaps that, along with a measure of true feeling, was what Cocteau hoped to achieve. In a sense, *The White Book* is a visceral response—from the cock and heart—to the analytical passion of Gide's *Corydon*.

Cocteau's career was an argument against the overspecialization now encouraged in most universities. He realized—and has been continually acclaimed for—success as an artist, writer and filmmaker. He lived in Paris at a time when it was a hothouse of extraordinary geniuses, and he counted Pablo Picasso, Gertrude Stein, Marcel Proust and Colette among his chums. His relations with Gide, on the other hand, were usually touchy; Cocteau said their predilection for similar lovers brought an edge of jealousy to their friendship. His relationship with Jean Genet was also prickly. He kept trying to cast Genet as Rimbaud to his Verlaine, but Genet would have none of it. Cocteau, however, always stood by Genet, testifying for him in his trials and providing line drawings of sailor-sodomites for his *Querelle of Brest*.

Cocteau was elected to the French Academy in 1955, and died in 1963.

Hart Crane

The Poems

O Walt!—Ascensions of thee hover in me now . . .
Thou bringest tally, and a pact, new bound
Of living brotherhood!
—"CAPE HATTERAS," LINES 159 AND 167–168

Harold Hart Crane was born on July 21, 1899, in Garrettsville, Ohio, but belongs wholly to the twentieth century. He was in many ways the queer embodiment of the notions that defined being a writer to the American imagination in the wake of the Roaring Twenties. Handsome, with a broad forehead and an open face, he was born to average means—he was never formally well-educated—and spun out in a drunken suicide at thirty-two. His life by then had become a war between his ability to write and his capacity for drinking, the latter often accompanied by reckless sexual episodes.

Sadly, the writing lost.

Hart Crane's life was torn apart by his parents. His mother was intelligent and sensitive; his father, a driven businessman. In 1904 they moved from Garrettsville to Warren, Ohio, where Crane became his mother's confidant, the sole ear for her sorrowing, failed artistic ambitions. In 1908 the household cracked apart. Crane's father moved to Chicago, and his mother was deposited in a sanatorium; the boy went to his mother's parents' house in Cleveland. Until he was twenty-six and the house was sold, it was the place Crane would think of as home.

Eventually his family reconciled, Crane's father agreeing to divide his time between Chicago and Cleveland, where Crane's mother resided after leaving the sanatorium. In 1911 Crane's father opened a family-financed candy company and settled in Cleveland with his wife and son. By 1914, however, all the old troubles resurfaced. Crane's mother sought escape in travel and dragged the boy out of school to accompany her. As a result, his grades suffered. But the schooling that mattered to him was what Crane taught himself through voracious reading. He spent his boyhood allowance on copies of Plutarch's *Lives* instead of candy, and found education through dialogues that took place in the belly of the local bookstore. In the course of these dialogues he was introduced to the poetry of Walt Whitman, whose hand he was to memorably clasp at the end of "Cape Hatteras," a portion of *The Bridge* (see the excerpt, above). During this time Crane dabbled in sex, usually with older men. They were only experiments; his great love awaited him.

At the age of seventeen Crane published his first poem in a Greenwich Village magazine. But this success—and others that followed or seemed promised—fell into temporary shambles when, in 1916, his father moved out, his mother sued for divorce, and Crane dropped out of school to work and bring in money. The divorce settlement, however, freed him from any immediate financial concerns and provided for him until the age of twenty-one. Though he could have gone to college, he went to New York.

The boy would be a poet.

Following the divorce and Crane's departure for New York, his mother came to depend upon him for all her worldly love. Crane provided it, though it would smother him and engender a claustrophobic rebellion, some of it in the form of blind drunkenness.

In New York, Crane managed to fall in with Irish poet Padraic Colum, whose wife, Mary, was a friend of Yeats. Under the Colums' tutelage, he studied not only Yeats but Rimbaud, Verlaine and others. He eagerly read new poems by Eliot as they appeared and devoured the serialization of Joyce's *Ulysses*. (Both *The Waste Land* and *Ulysses* would shape Crane's great work, *The Bridge*; Joyce's work fed it structurally, while Crane conceived the poem itself as an "answer" to Eliot's pessimistic work.)

This poetic education was to be interrupted by familial episodes that would tear him away from New York and thrust him back into the unstable mess that was his parents' love affair. He worked briefly for his father, but it ended quickly and disastrously. Afterward he trained at Western Reserve University for work as an advertising copywriter, the only trade he would ever learn.

Around this time Crane began the sequences of poems he called "Voyages," which he wrote for a blond and ruggedly handsome Danish ship's officer named Emil Opffer, a man close in age to Hart. Crane was twenty—and as far as men went, Emil Opffer would prove the love of his life.

During his days in New York, Crane developed an openness about his sexuality, his love for men. He also developed into quite a drunk. The last years of his life were marked by his travels to places where he might attempt to write more and be free of distraction—California, Europe and, at last, a trip to Mexico financed by money he won as a Guggenheim Fellow.

In the course of his European travels, he met up with Harry Crosby in France. The handsome founder of Black Sun Press agreed to publish Crane's poem *The Bridge* when it was complete, and the inspirational gambit worked: Crane returned to New York to finish the poem in 1929.

It was perhaps his last bout of productivity. As Crane failed to write, his life began to fall apart. In July 1932 his father died. The frequency and violence of Crane's drunkenness continued to escalate. He often woke up in jail.

Hart Crane hoped he might find salvation in the genuine love he found with friend Malcom Cowley's wife, Peggy. They were to be married when her divorce came through, and she followed him to Mexico, where he managed to drink much but write little—only a single lyric, "The Broken Tower." They abandoned Mexico, and on April 26, 1933, he and Peggy had a slight falling out over a missed lunch in Havana. After their ship set sail for the States, they spent the evening separately. She sedated herself in her cabin and went to sleep, unable to hear his drunken poundings on the door. The ship's purser confined Crane to his quarters and had the door nailed shut. Crane broke out and again prowled the ship.

It was now the early hours of April 27. He tried to solicit sex from the sailors. He was beaten up, his wallet and ring stolen. At 3:30 A.M. he tried to throw himself overboard. The purser stopped him and again confined Crane to his cabin, forcing him to take a sleeping pill and waiting until Crane was fast asleep before leaving.

In the morning Crane had a huge breakfast with Peggy. She left to get dressed. He started to drink. He drank more. Whisky. Just before noon he stopped by Peggy's room, wearing his pajamas and a light topcoat. He said, "I'm not going to make it, dear. I'm utterly disgraced." She told him he would feel better after he shaved and dressed.

Crane went above deck and stood at the edge of the rail. He took off his coat, folded it neatly and laid it down on the deck.

He flung himself into the sea.

C. P. Cavafy

Complete Poems

TRANSLATED BY RAE DALVEN

And yet the love you wanted, I had it to give you . . .
Our bodies sensed and sought each other;
our blood and our skin understood.
—"ON THE STAIRS," VERSE 2 (EXCERPT)

Constantine P. Cavafy was born in 1863 in Alexandria, Egypt, to a Greek merchant family. His father died in 1872, and he spent the next five years with his mother in England before returning to Alexandria. The British bombardment of that city in 1882, however, drove him to Constantinople, where he had his first sexual experiences with other men and where he stayed until 1885. When he went back to Alexandria in 1889, he took a job as a civil servant, working for the Department of Irrigation. Barring holiday excursions to England, France and Greece now and again, he would live the rest of his life in the city of his birth. In 1922 he retired on money he made in the stock exchange. He died of throat cancer in 1933.

In 1907 Cavafy moved out of the family home to live with one of his brothers in an apartment in the Rue Lepseius, a less than desirable part of town. His brother eventually moved out, and for the rest of his life Cavafy lived alone. He published a few poems in magazines during his lifetime; mostly he made copies privately for his friends. The first collection of his poems was published commercially two years after his death.

Still, the poems he circulated privately earned him a position of eminence in Alexandrian literary circles. He knew such notables as Lawrence Durrell and E. M. Forster. Forster proved very instrumental in getting W. H. Auden, Marguerite Yourcenar and James Merrill to promote Cavafy, the man and the poet, throughout Europe. Cocteau even illustrated a few of Cavafy's poems!

Poetically, Cavafy is primarily concerned with historical presentations of Greece and Alexandria and with the veiled homoeroticism that floats through the everyday life of the circumspect queer. Thus, the poems are able to find the sexual promise in a fleeting glance, and in a sense they serve as early "cruising" poems, where the sexuality is observed or, if participatory, expresses itself via a sudden onrush of desire rather than years of love-lorn devotion.

Cavafy loved men and he loved his country. In wedding the two, he provided rich images of an almost sexually enhanced patriotism. His other, more erotic poems testified to the omnipresence of homosexual desire—in cafés, on stairways—simmering beneath the heterosexual gloss of early-twentieth-century life.

Federico García Lorca

Selected Poems

VARIOUS TRANSLATORS

Not for one moment, Adam of blood, male,
lone man in the sea, beautiful aged Walt Whitman,
. . . the pansies, Walt Whitman, dreamed of you.
—"ODE TO WALT WHITMAN," VERSE 9 (EXCERPT)

Federico García Lorca's life has long been shrouded in mystery. This is partially because of the oppressive government that butchered him, and partially the result of familial homophobia and heterosexual, patriarchal, academic elitism.

Lorca was born on June 5, 1898, in Fuente Vaqueros, a province of Granada. His was a privileged childhood: Lorca's father was a wealthy landowner, and Lorca spent his time studying music, painting and crafting puppets. His study of music continued after 1909, when the family moved to the city of Granada, and his exposure to the Arabic culture there would shape many of his poems. In Granada he would also encounter the Gypsies—hardly Gypsies as we understand the name, since at that time they had lived for four hundred years in the caves of the Sacromonte—and they, too, would have an influence on the poet's work, most noticeably in his *Gypsy Ballads*.

In 1919 Lorca went off to the University of Madrid. U of M boasted the Residencia de Estudiantes, a student dorm opened in 1910 to provide gifted students a chance to casually intermingle and creatively feed off (or inspire) each other. Hormones being what they are, and adolescents what they are, the place was fraught with daring ambition and potential, but it also resembled something of a soap opera. Salvador Dalí, the painter, was there at the same time as Lorca, and Lorca craved him, body and soul. The body would be denied him, and when Lorca later failed to distract himself through a troubled relationship with the young sculptor Emilio Aladrén Perojo, he took off for New York in 1927. He would stay away for three years, feeding off the character of New York as he had Granada earlier, producing singularly superb poems later collected under the title *Poet in New York*.

The Spain Lorca returned to was not the one he had left: It was entering a dark time of political tension and, eventually, bloody unrest. Lorca wrote steadily through the increasing troubles, receiving notoriety for his plays as well as his poetry. Six years after his return, while he was living in Madrid, his country simmered toward Civil War. On July 18, 1936, a few days before the war at last erupted, Lorca, frightened by Madrid's descent into violent madness, returned to the family home in Granada. But he was not to find safety there.

Often when a new and repressive regime seeks to establish itself, the first order of business is to kill all the artists and intellectuals. Franco would prove no different; on August 16, 1936, Lorca was arrested by fascist extremists. A few days later, the man who was arguably Spain's greatest twentieth-century playwright and poet was shot dead—one of the assassins claiming to have fired two extra shots into Lorca's rump because he was a faggot—and buried in a common grave.

Lorca never wrote openly of his homosexuality, barring perhaps a play called *The Public* and the *Ode to Walt Whitman,* privately published in Mexico in a limited edition of fifty copies. Although his works are redolent with a homoerotic sensibility, they are also the work of a moralist who took a dim view of effeminacy and wanton sexual excess.

Christopher Isherwood

The Berlin Stories

"Been seeing any more of your friend Norris?"

"Yes," I said. "Why?"

"Nothing," drawled Fritz, his naughty eyes on my face. "Eventually I'd watch your step, that's all."

"Whatever do you mean?"

"I've been hearing some queer things about him."

"Oh, indeed?"

"Maybe they aren't true. You know how people talk."

"And I know how you listen, Fritz."

—*THE LAST OF MISTER NORRIS,* CHAPTER 4

While the above selection isn't necessarily about homosexual tendencies, it isn't necessarily not about them either, and it is this tone that suffuses Christopher Isherwood's *The Berlin Stories:* a sort of coy humanism that flirts with real life even as it reveals it.

Homosexuals are neither played up to nor repressed in *The Berlin Stories*—two once separate works, *The Last of Mr. Norris* and *Goodbye to Berlin,* later cobbled together for their singular concern. Homosexuals, when they appear, are for the most part dealt with candidly by Isherwood and often share the same fatalistic sensibility as many of the work's heterosexual protagonists. It is a sensibility reflected by Berlin in general between the wars, when the party was one not of celebration—as the Roaring Twenties in the States—but of desperation. And there is the confused yearning of Isherwood's self-based protagonists toward the bravery of men who love men, as well as the foolishness of men in love with women.

Not until 1971, in *Kathleen and Frank,* a biography of his parents, would Isherwood come out, a statement he would reaffirm vociferously five years later in his own autobiography, *Christopher and His Kind.* Prior to this, however, his work had featured increasingly out gay characters, perhaps none more memorable than Quaker Bob Wood in *The World in the Evening.* Wood wants to "march down the street with a banner saying, 'We're queer because we're queer because we're queer,'" but his lover, Charles, a Jew who has changed his name in an effort to assimilate, keeps Bob from fulfilling this fantasy because he "is sick of belonging to these whining, militant minorities."

The more things change, the more they stay the same.

Born on August 20, 1904, in Cheshire and educated at Cambridge (though he failed to get a degree), Isherwood was chums there with W. H. Auden, with whom he had previously attended St. Edmund's preparatory school. Isherwood was perhaps the first writer of his generation to fully embrace the modern gay rights movement, firmly aligning himself with "his kind." He was also deeply spiritual; under the guidance of a Hindu monk, he converted to Vedantism in 1940, a year after he emigrated to America.

Isherwood became an American citizen in 1946, and seven years later fell in love (at the age of forty-nine) with an eighteen-year-old boy, Don Bachardy. The relationship lasted until Isherwood's death, and Bachardy became a noted artist in his own right.

Christopher Isherwood left a legacy of iconic entertainment mixed with as-yet-unmatched political moral standing, devoid of histrionics. His creation of Sally Bowles in an eponymous portion of *Goodbye to Berlin* would give us the musical *Cabaret* and launch the formidable talent that is Liza Minnelli, Judy Garland's spawn, into drag routines everywhere and on a career all her own.

Isherwood's public creations would define the potential of twentieth-century homosexual entertainment; his private life would define the potential of the twentieth-century homosexual spirit.

Jean Genet

Our Lady of the Flowers

TRANSLATED BY BERNARD FRECHTMAN

Fags are the great immoralists.

Jean Genet was born in Paris in 1910. When he was seven months old, his mother gave him up for adoption and the Hospice des Enfants Assistés placed him with foster parents two days later.

As a child, he evidenced religious inclinations, serving as altar boy in the local church. His life, however, was lived creating his own sacraments, products of the time he spent in reformatories and prisons for various crimes in France and abroad, including theft and prostitution, from the age of fifteen. In 1942, while imprisoned in Fresnes, facing a life sentence after ten convictions for theft, he wrote his first novel, *Our Lady of the Flowers*. The first draft of it was taken from him by a guard and burned. Genet started over. He wrote on the rough paper from which prisoners made bags as a part of their work duty. When the book was published in 1943—it would not be translated into English for twenty years—it caused a sensation with its use of the language and religious imagery of his childhood to display an erotic and criminal desire.

In 1946 he published *The Miracle of the Rose,* a fictionalized account with mystical overtones of his journey from boy-bottom to man-top via various incarcerations (nineteen years later came the translation). *Funeral Rites* followed in 1947, and *Querelle of Brest* also appeared that year (a translation arrived in 1966). Genet's cause was taken up by French intellectuals, including Jean-Paul Sartre, whose *Saint Genet* canonized the thief in 1952 (translation 1963), and Jean Cocteau. Their petitions to the French President on Genet's behalf resulted in his full pardon in 1948.

He was their rough darling.

In 1949 he published a novel-cum-memoir, *The Thief's Journal* (translated in 1964). Exploiting the most provocative elements of his fiction, he wrote poetry as well as plays—the latter including *Deathwatch* in 1946; *The Maids* in 1947 (revised in 1954), a play usually performed by women, though Genet meant it for male actors; his whorehouse fantasia, *The Balcony,* in 1956; *The Blacks* in 1958; and the epic Algerian war drama, *The Screens,* in 1961. In the sixties and seventies he used his celebrity to draw media attention to the causes of revolutionary movements in many countries, the most notable examples being the Black Panthers in the United States, the Palestine Liberation Organization and Chairman Mao's Red Guard. His last work, *Prisoner of Love,* published the year of his death, was a political-erotic study in which he admitted that part of his attraction to these rebel causes was sexual, a lustful penchant for black dick and young Arab soldiers. But this was familiar ground for Genet, who admitted thirty-seven years before in *The Thief's Journal* that part of the thrill of homosexuality for him came from its illegality.

Jean Genet died in 1986.

At night I love them, and my love endows them with life
. . . Beneath the sheet, my right hand stops to caress the

absent face, then the whole body, of the outlaw I have chosen for that evening's delight.

Our Lady of the Flowers is a stroke book. It takes place entirely within the imagination of Jean, the prisoner, its images taken from pictures he has clipped from magazines and stuck to the walls. They are the stuff of his fantasies:

> So, with the help of my unknown lovers, I am going to write a story. My heroes are they, pasted on the wall, they and I who am here locked up. As you read on, the characters, and Divine too, and Culafroy, will fall from the wall onto my pages like dead leaves, to fertilize my tale.

A taut suspense underpins *Our Lady of the Flowers*. Jean is awaiting a hearing, at which he faces several possible sentences, ranging from the unthinkable (release) to death (also a release). The fantasies Genet scribbles on the rough brown paper are unrestrained by logic or time. Characters die, then are resurrected. What is constant in Jean's reverie is an unrestrained sexual indulgence, as well as a willingness to embody the most outrageous characters, who ultimately pull together into the singular identity of one man, Jean, the narrator.

Our Lady of the Flowers may well be the reflective harbinger of gay culture's almost sole base concern in the late twentieth century: identity. It is all the more beautiful because Jean slips in and out of character—and degrees of masculinity, perhaps even gender—with a startling, yet wondrous fluidity. "I shall speak to you about Divine," Jean writes, "mixing masculine and feminine as my mood dictates and if, in the course of the tale, I shall have to refer to a woman, I shall manage, I shall find an expedient, a good device, to avoid any confusion."

Though many characters flow consistently through the book's nonnarrative—Culafroy, Darling, Divine and, of course, Our Lady of the Flowers among them—often the book stops suddenly to remind us that we are here for a purpose primarily sexual. Yet as its stories slowly build, page after page, until they threaten to crush us with their density, the work begs the question: How can one separate the sexual from the self?

> The woodcutter's lips came down on the abbé's mouth, where, with a thrust of the tongue more imperious than a royal order, they drove in the butt. The priest was knocked down, bitten, and he expired with love on the soggy moss. After having almost disrobed him, the stranger caressed him, gratefully, almost fondly, thought the abbé. With a heave, he shouldered his game bag, which was weighted down with a wildcat, picked up his gun, and went off whistling a raffish tune.

For Jean, it is not so much the act of sexuality as it is the manipulations of power that form the thrill of the erotic. While the details of the athletic young priest's rape by the handsome woodcutter would have been the focus of any other masturbator's yearning, for Jean they are almost incidental. It is the fact that the rape has happened—that the church has been impaled on the altar of masculinity—that spunks him.

And this is only one of the delicacies of *Our Lady of the Flowers,* a work that has been tortuously overexamined since its publication, feeding graduate theses by the score. It is the product of remarkable intelligence, its occasional literary references serving to remind us that this is not the work of an uneducated convict, however desperately its author might seek to cultivate that illusion. It has offered itself up to reinterpretations that draw us away from the truth that this book was written as a sexual outlet, as a fantastical reverie to help a man in the shadow of sentencing distract himself from his guards and the hell of waiting. It is far less meaningful to look outward, at the "postmodern" library of words this book has spawned, than to look inward and find the captured scribbler lurking behind the words pressed upon every page.

> The world of the living is never too remote from me. I remove it as far as I can with all the means at my disposal . . . I believe in the world of prisons, in its reprehended practices. I accept living there as I would accept, were I dead, living in a cemetery.

This separation from society, from life, is the loom upon which *Our Lady of the Flowers* is woven, Jean's fantasies its skein, and sperm his dye. As Jean spins out his stories, his characters develop increasingly complex relations—love affairs, jealousies, trials of their own—until it is impossible to separate their fictive lives from Jean's memories of his own life, impossible to ferret out the truth from the fantastic.

When the bastard Darling, the queens' butch darling, is arrested for shoplifting, he is taken to Genet's prison. There, Darling is asked his name, and then the names of his parents, which, even though he must lie to deliver the name of his father, he skips through quite readily. He stumbles, however, when asked his occupation, almost blurting out the coy term "barmaid." At last he admits to being unemployed, only to realize that, for himself, being unemployed *is* as much of a job as being a barmaid.

He is stripped and searched. He is told to bend down, and the guard sees in the crack of Darling's ass a black spot:

> The black spot was a rather big lump of dung, which got bigger every day and which Darling had already several times tried to pull away, but he would have had to pull the hairs out with it, or take a hot bath.

Does Genet write of this—and other instances of shit, and of farts, ripe odors and so on—because he seeks to convey honestly his desires, finding his characters' debasement liberating, as he does his confirmation as a thief, as he does his outlaw sexuality? Or is he anticipating a middle-class readership as he writes—these portions becoming his way of lashing out at the bourgeoisie through his dreams, rupturing the connection between artist and audience, no longer thinking of his work solely as an erotic exercise but as something more profound?

It's probably both. In his introduction Jean-Paul Sartre writes, "Before *Our Lady*, Genet was an aesthete; after it, an artist. But at no moment was a decision *made* to achieve this conversion. The decision is *Our Lady*." This book offers us a chance to accompany a prisoner on his erotic exercises as he hopes to ease the pain of waiting for the inevitable, but more than that, we see a consciously artistic imagination awakening to itself and its own power.

Even the language signals this awakening. The rough phrasing of the opening chapters is no match for the evolved lyric that closes *Our Lady of the Flowers*, returning us with force to the confines of Jean's cell, the real world as it is not denied him. He cannot sleep, for the hearing weighs upon him and demands, even before its appointed hour, his attention. He is stabbed by thoughts of hope, and fear, until at last he can address the base question:

> What if I am condemned? I shall don homespun again
> . . . I shall feel myself becoming humble and glorious;
> then, snug under my blankets . . . shall, for the enchant-
> ment of my cell, refashion lovely new lives for Darling,
> Divine, Our Lady and Gabriel.

Under the covers, where our story began.

What is *Our Lady of the Flowers*? An erotic reverie? An exercise in scatological pornography? A meditation on the fluidity of the roles we play? A thief's attempt to steal away from us our very (sexual) identity, to pry loose our concepts of masculinity and femininity?

It is all of these and more, the remarkable witnessing of an adolescent talent as it matures and fastens securely to its place within the world. It is saved—and rendered all but impossible to duplicate—by the relentless coalescing of its concerns into, at last, a whole, as shards of colored glass come together to form the image in a stained-glass window. Starting out almost as a piece of juvenilia, it is, finally, a work of superb artistry, and this is what surprises us. Not that we have been taken in, by the artist posing as a thief, but that we have been overwhelmed.

FIVE QUESTIONS

1. Is there a point in *Our Lady of the Flowers* where the artist begins to assert himself convincingly? If so, where is it? What separates it from the pages that precede (or follow) it?

2. Is *Our Lady of the Flowers* a novel or a memoir? Why?

3. If Genet's writing at times repulses us, what does that tells us about Genet and, more important, about ourselves? Why is extreme effeminacy repellent to some and ideal to others? Why is shit erotic to some and not to others? What is right and what is wrong, and why?

4. How much of *Our Lady of the Flowers* is a pose on the part of the author? All of it? None of it?

5. Using the text as your basis, what is Genet's relationship to God? To religion?

Evelyn Waugh

Brideshead Revisited

And we would leave the golden candlelight of the dining room for the starlight outside and sit on the edge of the fountain, cooling our hands in the water and listening drunkenly to its splash and gurgle over the rocks.

"Ought we to be drunk *every* night?" Sebastian asked one morning.

"Yes, I think so."

"I think so too."

—BOOK I, *"ET IN ARCADIA EGO,"* CHAPTER 4

Evelyn Arthur St. John Waugh was born in Hampstead, London, in 1903. His father, Arthur Waugh, was a minor literary figure in London and eventually served as managing editor for Chapman and Hall, Publishers. Educated at Heath Mount, Lancing, and Hertford College, Oxford, Evelyn Waugh read modern history but invested little effort in his studies, preferring a life of indulgence that included more than a couple of homosexual affairs. As a result, he received only a third-class degree. From 1925 to 1927 he was a schoolmaster, an experience that depressed him so greatly he attempted suicide. With his recovery, however, came his first comic novel, *Decline and Fall,* published in 1928. It turned him into an immediate celebrity—people felt a voyeuristic thrill while reading it, so clear were the comparisons between the author's life and work. (Previously, he had published only one essay and an unacclaimed biography of Dante Gabriel Rossetti.)

He impulsively married Evelyn Gardiner the year that first novel was published. The marriage fell apart the year his second novel, *Vile Bodies,* and first travel book, *Labels,* appeared, in 1930, though the couple remained legally married for a while longer. Waugh spent the next few years traveling; another travel book, *Remote People,* followed in 1931.

But the year 1930 was most notable to Waugh because it was then he became a Roman Catholic; throughout his life he claimed this to be the most important thing ever to happen to him. Restless, he continued to roam the globe, visiting British Guyana, Brazil, Morocco, Abyssinia and various ports in the Mediterranean, until he married Laura Herbert in 1937, a year after his marriage to Gardiner was successfully annulled. Together, Evelyn and Laura Waugh would raise six children.

The newly minted Waugh family settled at Piers Court, Stinchcombe, Gloucestershire. Waugh published in his first year there the farce *Scoop,* about a misassigned foreign correspondent. Before the outbreak of World War II, Waugh was back on the road, traveling to Hungary and Mexico as a junior officer. During the war he continued to publish, bringing out four books, including 1942's *Put Out More Flags* and, at war's end, *Brideshead Revisited.* Both of these works are notable for the fabulous queens Waugh creates within their pages—Ambrose Silk in *Put Out More Flags* and Anthony Blanche in *Brideshead Revisited.*

In 1947 Waugh published *The Loved One,* and in 1950, *Helena.* Time, and perspective on World War II, would give him the ability to create the Sword of Honor trilogy: *Men at Arms* (1952), *Officers and Gentlemen* (1954) and *Unconditional Surrender* (1961). In 1957 he would come almost full circle with *The Ordeal of Gilbert Pinfold*, a thinly veiled, pseudoautobiographical account of a middle-aged writer's on-ship crack-up as a result of drugs and alcohol. He published the first volume of his autobiography, *A Little Learning*, in 1964; he didn't live to complete the rest. He died suddenly in 1966 in Combe Florey, Somerset. His diaries, and then his letters, were published posthumously.

> My cousin Jasper . . . was in his fourth year . . . He called on me formally during my first week and . . . laid down the rules of conduct which I should follow . . . "You'll spend half your second year shaking off the undesirable friends you made in your first . . . Beware of the Anglo-Catholics—they're all sodomites with unpleasant accents." (BOOK I, CHAPTER 1)

Brideshead Revisited is the reverie of thirty-nine-year-old Captain Charles Ryder, returned to the remains of an English country manor during World War II. The surprise at coming across Brideshead after so many years plunges him into memory—and from that memory the novel is built.

Brideshead Revisited is incredibly sweet, incredibly tender. A remarkably thorough book of heartfelt construction, it is a novel of a boy who becomes a man, and of the lovers he takes along the way. It is a novel of friendship, and of marriage, and of England's twilight hours. However sentimental all this may sound, the book is remarkably free of mawkish indulgence.

Charles Ryder meets Sebastian Flyte shortly after arriving at Oxford. Charles has noticed Sebastian almost from the first. It is hard not to, for Sebastian carries a large teddy bear named Aloysius everywhere he goes. The two men do not meet, however, until Flyte pauses to lean in through Ryder's ground-floor windows and vomit. Flyte then staggers off, and another boy makes his apologies;

the next day, Ryder receives a note: "I am very contrite. Aloysius won't speak to me until he sees I am forgiven, so please come to luncheon to-day. Sebastian Flyte" (Book I, Chapter 1).

Charles goes, somewhat tremulous with anticipation, for it is all so foreign and new to him—being at college, meeting men who carry on quite serious conversations with teddy bears and who drive convertibles. A voice, tiny and prudish, bleats in his ear for him to ignore Flyte's invitation, but Charles cannot:

> I was in search of love in those days, and I went full of curiosity and the faint, unrecognized apprehension that here, at last, I should find that low door in the wall, which others, I knew, had found before me, which opened on an enclosed and enchanted garden, which was somewhere, not overlooked by any window, in the heart of that grey city. (BOOK I, CHAPTER 1)

Ryder describes Sebastian as "magically beautiful, with that epicene quality which in extreme youth sings aloud for love and withers at the first cold wind." And it is at this lunch, cowed by others more familiar with Sebastian, that Ryder meets Anthony Blanche—the stammering, fabulous fairy who will proceed to shake up every page of the book on which he appears. Blanche ends their lunch by reciting T. S. Eliot's *The Waste Land* through a megaphone for those walking past Flyte's rooms on their way to the river.

That first meeting of Sebastian and Charles is also the first time Charles sees Brideshead, Flyte's family home. Sebastian's mother lives there, and his older, staid brother returns often. His younger sisters Julia (who appears to Ryder, physically, as Sebastian's near-identical twin) and Cordelia (the good daughter, who will spend her life in relief work) reside there too, along with the nanny who raised them and loyal servants like Wilcox. Flyte's father lives in Paris with his mistress.

If there is any doubt about Sebastian's sexual proclivities, they are never directly addressed. Instead, there are simple allusions, and the increasing realization by the reader that Sebastian's entire family thinks, initially and for a great while thereafter, of Sebastian and Charles as lovers "in the English habit." As for Anthony Blanche, there was an attempt made in his boyhood to fashion him into a proper English gentleman, with two years at Eton, but he escaped to live with his mother in Argentina during World War I. After the war mother and son toured Europe and the Americas, where Anthony romped about beaches, villas and casinos, went in drag to the Buenos Aires Jockey Club to gamble and rubbed up against kindred, albeit more literary souls:

> . . . he dined with Proust and Gide and was on closer terms with Cocteau and Diaghilev; Firbank sent him his novels with fervent inscriptions.   (BOOK 1, CHAPTER 2)

Anthony in his short life has been the cause of at least three feuds and has studied the black arts in Cefalu. In California he cured himself of his drug addictions, and in Vienna, his Oedipus complex!

Blanche reveals to Charles that he has been a school chum of Sebastian's for years, and that people used to refer to Flyte as a "little *bitch*." Blanche serves as a link between Sebastian and another well-to-do English lad who drinks recklessly, Boy Mulcaster. It is Anthony who recognizes Charles as an artist—dangling the prospect of Cocteau before him—and truly, Charles *is* an artist and eventually will carve out a career for himself as such.

In the meantime, Charles is drawn deeper into the web of Sebastian's family. Ryder's own father is distant, and when Charles must return home for his first college summer, Sebastian offers him a way out and Charles seizes it. In the course of visiting Sebastian's father, Lord Marchmain, instead of his own, Charles converses with Cara, Marchmain's mistress, when the two are at last alone. She begins by noting that Charles seems very "fond" of Sebastian, which he quite readily admits, thinking her intent to be innocent.

It isn't. Cara goes on to say that she is familiar with the romantic friendships German and English men have with each other, adding that she thinks it best if those friendships are short-lived.

Charles is dumbfounded. Cara takes advantage of his silence to continue, matter-of-factly:

> "It is a kind of love that comes to children before they know its meaning. In England it comes when you are almost men; I think I like that. It is better to have that kind of love for another boy than for a girl. Alex you see had it for a girl, for his wife. Do you think he loves *me*?"
> (BOOK I, CHAPTER 4)

"Alex" is Lord Marchmain, of course, and moments later, Cara finishes their conversation by saying, quite bluntly, that Sebastian's drinking will ruin him; he cannot handle it. For Charles, it is a phase, the thing to do; for Sebastian, it is his destiny, unless someone intervenes. Apparently, it is also Sebastian's heritage, for Cara lets on that Alex was all but a drunkard when she met him. She wants Charles to know: This will separate them.

She is right, of course. And after the summer, when Charles and Sebastian return to Oxford, everything is different. Their friendship sustains them, even as they both set about fulfilling cousin Jasper's prophecy and cut loose deadweight friends from their first year. Anthony Blanche is gone; Sebastian's letter from him says that "[a]pparently he's taken a flat in Munich—he has formed an attachment to a policeman there" (Book I, Chapter 5).

The idyll of the first year at Oxford is clearly over. There is a drunk-driving incident, for which Boy Mulcaster is responsible but Sebastian takes the fall. As a result of this, and his mother's efforts to control his drinking, he is assigned to the care of Mr. Samgrass, an increasingly horrid toady of a man. At last Sebastian quits Oxford, prompting Charles Ryder to say to a friend:

> "I'm the loneliest man in Oxford. Sebastian Flyte's been sent down." (BOOK I, CHAPTER 5)

His friendship with Sebastian continues, of course. Charles disapproves of Lady Marchmain's attempts to control her son's access to alcohol because, perhaps predictably, they only result in Sebastian's drinking more. At last, when Sebastian wanders off from a hunting party and gets drunk on money given him by Charles, Sebastian's mother turns on Ryder. He feels himself driven out of Brideshead, unable to stay there if it means being complicit in Lady Marchmain's torture of Sebastian. As he drives away, he turns and looks back for a moment, thinking it will be his last view of the house. He feels the place will haunt him, that in leaving Brideshead he is leaving behind a part of himself, and indeed he is:

> A door had shut, the low door in the wall I had sought and found in Oxford; open it now and I should find no enchanted garden. (BOOK I, CHAPTER 6)

Yet Ryder cannot sever himself from the family of Brideshead. Despite distancing marriages—his own, as well as Julia's—and Sebastian's dissipation with a thick German soldier, Ryder is trapped in his orbit around the Marchmains. His prowess and acclaim as an artist increase, as his love for Sebastian remains, flickering, then blazing, incarnate:

> I had not forgotten Sebastian. He was with me daily in Julia; or rather it was Julia I had known in him, in those distant, Arcadian days. (BOOK III, CHAPTER 4)

Eventually Charles and Julia turn to each other, their separate marriages—his to Boy Mulcaster's sister Celia; hers to Rex Mottram, the book's aggravatingly stereotypical American—dissolute if not ended. Julia and Charles smash together around the singular memory of her brother as she loved him, and his lover—as he loved him.

Brideshead Revisited is a great book because it doesn't choose to do too much. It doesn't seek to evolve into a generational saga, spanning centuries. Neither does it restrict itself to a golden period in its protagonist's life. Instead, it concerns itself not simply with friendship but with friendship's effect, those resonances felt throughout our lives in moments when a certain wind carries with it a noise or odor, or someone tilts his or her head a certain way or says something just so. A reverie, it is only about the echoes of words spoken in haste or passion, from hate or love. By confining its concerns so simply, *Brideshead Revisited* is utterly profound in its impact. Because the truth of the matter is that this is what life is made of: memories of our failures and fading happy dreams.

Charles Ryder exults not so much in his brush with privilege during his Oxford days as in the friendships those days brought him, friendships that changed lives. This book, popularly misconstrued as a mere Oxford homage, goes beyond its story of those schoolboy friendships, telling of families cobbled from love instead of blood—certainly the Marchmains are closer to Charles than his own, blood family—and for queer readers, what could be more important? Anthony Blanche and the English habit of Sebastian and Charles are but icing on *Brideshead*'s cake—delicious icing though it is.

FIVE QUESTIONS

1. How do you feel about Charles's relationship with Julia? Is it wonderful—or creepy? If he could be with Sebastian instead, would he?

2. Was Charles's relationship with Sebastian sexual or not? Does it matter?

3. Given the fact that Waugh was an Anglo-Catholic when he wrote the book, what do you make of Jasper's opening comments, and of the presence throughout *Brideshead Revisited* of religion? Is it what you would expect? Keeping close to the text, say why or why not.

4. Is homosexuality a normal part of sexual development, as Cara seems to propose, and if so, is it in its very nature immature, as she would also seem to suggest? Certainly, her theory echoes the pederastic appetites of the Greeks and Romans, doesn't it?

5. Are we ever free of the past?

William Maxwell

The Folded Leaf

There was a screen between Lymie's bed and the door, and for a second he didn't know who it was that had come. He saw Rhinehart first, and then coming up behind him into the room someone else. Lymie was too weak to sit up but he made a slight movement with his hands which Rhinehart saw. He moved to one side so that Spud could get past him and backed out of the room. Spud came and sat on the edge of the bed. His eyes were filled with tears. The tears ran down his cheeks and he made no effort to wipe them away. Neither he nor Lymie spoke. They looked at each other with complete knowledge at last, with full awareness of what they meant to each other and of all that had ever passed between them. After a moment Spud leaned forward slowly and kissed Lymie on the mouth. He had never done this before and he was never moved to do it again.

—CHAPTER 59, "A REFLECTION FROM
THE SKY"

Straight boys don't kiss.

William Maxwell was born in 1908. He was fiction editor of

The New Yorker from 1936 to 1976. His own published fiction includes the novel *So Long, See You Tomorrow,* which garnered him the American Book Award, one in a long line of awards Maxwell has received.

The Folded Leaf was Maxwell's third published novel, and it is, in essence, a love story—or a story of friendship, defined in Platonic or Aristotelian terms. Lymie Peters first meets Spud Latham in swimming class, during a torturous—for Lymie—game of water polo, when they are both naked. (The setting is purely primal.) When some of the boys hold Lymie under and all but drown him, it is Spud who inhibits their cruelty and frees the little nerd. From that moment on, Spud is Lymie's hero and best friend, and the two of them develop an at times edgy co-dependency.

Traditions of homophobia were not so firmly entrenched in the first half of this century as they have become in the second. Poor boys sleeping in one bed side by side, bundling for warmth on cold nights in a poorly heated room was not necessarily a homosexual activity. And indeed, this is what Spud and Lymie do when they are away at college, sharing a room in a boarding house run by a somewhat foppish old antiques collector, who takes special joy in having his house always filled with young men and their boisterous rowdiness. Spud and Lymie sleep together, for comfort and warmth.

The two boys come to define home to each other, the way lovers do, so much so that even after Spud joins a fraternity and finds better lodgings than the cold room he shared with Lymie, he returns and slips into bed beside Lymie, who instinctively tucks his body into that of his friend; their hands meet and clasp.

Even the women who join their lives cannot affect this bond, and they orbit about the pair, a girlfriend in Spud's case and a chum in Lymie's.

In a sense, *The Folded Leaf* takes place in a kind of paradise, where men may love other men in a sense that knows no shame. It is a place where friendships between men are virtually as intimate as those society allows between husband and wife, and as queers know between lovers. Yet every paradise has its forbidden fruit, and Maxwell's is no exception: Eventually the friends must separate and travel the paths fate has spun out for them. Siamese-twin-like as Lymie and Spud are, this separation will not be easy. It will not be without its edge of pain, or sharp knowledge of flowing darkness.

William Maxwell's *The Folded Leaf* is every bit as good as F. Scott Fitzgerald's *This Side of Paradise*—better, even, when it comes to developing a heart-tugging emotional wallop. For by the end of Maxwell's book, we share in the love of the men for each other. *The Folded Leaf* deserves to be considered an American classic, and the best, most nakedly honest novel of friendship in our time.

Tennessee Williams

The Glass Menagerie

AMANDA: I think you've been doing things that you're ashamed of. That's why you act like this. I don't believe that you go every night to the movies. Nobody goes to the movies night after night. Nobody in their right minds goes to the movies as often as you pretend to. People don't go the movies at nearly midnight, and movies don't let out at two a.m. Come in stumbling. Muttering to yourself like a maniac! You get three hours sleep and then go to work. Oh, I can picture the way you're doing down there. Moping, doping, because you're in no condition.

—SCENE 3

Tennessee Williams was born in Columbus, Mississippi, in 1911. His father was a traveling salesman—who had the habit of calling his son "Miss Nancy"—and his mother was a reserved minister's daughter. As a child, Williams was prone to illness, and writing helped alleviate the strains of boredom caused by convalescence.

Williams' college education was spotty. He attended Washington University in St. Louis and the University of Missouri, but it wasn't until he was twenty-seven that he received his degree from the University of Iowa.

He moved to New York and worked menial jobs in Greenwich Village restaurants and movie theaters. Two years after he graduated, however, fortune took notice of him: He received a Rockefeller Fellowship for his first play, *Battle of Angels.* Three years later, MGM signed him for a six-month contract that they later canceled when Williams delivered the autobiographically redolent effort that would become *The Glass Menagerie.*

As a play, *The Glass Menagerie* secured Williams' place in the pantheon of American theater, winning him the 1945 New York Drama Critics' Circle Award. Three years later, *A Streetcar Named Desire* won him the Pulitzer Prize; seven years after that, the Pulitzer would be his again, this time for *Cat on a Hot Tin Roof.* In 1969 the American Academy of Arts and Letters and the National Institute for Arts and Letters each awarded him their Gold Medal for Literature. Williams also published collections of poetry and short fiction, one novel, and a collection of autobiographical essays. He even returned to writing scripts, with what must've been a twinkle of self-satisfaction in his eye. After his death in 1983—from choking on the cap of a medicine bottle—he would become the subject of numerous tell-all biographies from ex-lovers and other intimates.

Williams' sister Rose was institutionalized in the 1930s for accusing her father of sexual abuse; she was later lobotomized. While Laura in *The Glass Menagerie* is an echo of Rose, Tom perhaps is an echo of Williams himself. Reading the play from a gay perspective, Tom suddenly takes on new dimension, his secret life fleshed out. His mother forbids him to read D. H. Lawrence, going so far as to confiscate and return the book he'd checked out from the library. (Lawrence was not without his own self-censored homoerotic passions, some reflected in his work, most notably the suppressed prologue to *Women in Love,* the phallically titled *Aaron's Rod* and the brutal short story "The Prussian Officer.") Tom goes "to the movies" at midnight, falling home at two in the morning. He is the classic example of the private queer who chafes against the society that keeps him closeted—eventually forcing him to run away, to start a new life, one he can call his own. This, of course, is exactly what Tom does. To be sure, *The Glass Menagerie* is Laura's play, and an example of the liberating potential of love, though it is Tom who escapes while Laura remains behind. She is trapped in a society that finds her deficient by nature, relegated to the position of second-class citizen simply because she is different.

The Glass Menagerie, read from our gay experience, becomes a play richer in homosexual meaning than either *Cat on a Hot Tin Roof* or *A Streetcar Named Desire*. It deals not with our ability to exercise amusing, yet ultimately corruptive, capabilities for queer appropriation. Rather, it deploys Williams' stunning capability to create, in the fully fleshed form of Tom, a portrait of the gay soul railing against the chains of society that hold him down. Eventually Tom snaps them, finding—although pursued by memory—a greater life, in a "world lit by lightning."

Paul Bowles

The Sheltering Sky

His cry went on through the final image: the spots of raw, bright blood on the earth. Blood on excrement. The supreme moment, high above the desert, when the two elements, blood and excrement, long kept apart, merge. A black star appears, a point of darkness in the night sky's clarity. Point of darkness and gateway of repose. Reach out, pierce the fine fabric of the sheltering sky, take repose.

—BOOK II, "THE EARTH'S SHARP EDGE,"

CHAPTER 23

Paul Frederick Bowles was born in Queens, New York, on December 30, 1910. His father was a dentist, and stingy with love—passive, rigid and secretive, qualities that would come to inform his son's writing. Bowles had few friends in his boyhood, and writing fantasy tales helped fill that void. As a child, Bowles was particularly fond of a queer uncle. One evening when young Paul was spending the night at his uncle's, he wandered into a room where men were dancing closely together. Bowles's uncle was angry at the naive intrusion, but Bowles himself displayed a calm indifference—an attitude toward sexuality that would mark not only his fiction but his life.

Paul Bowles studied at the University of Virginia, but found the prospect of an academic career less than enthralling. He moved to Paris in 1929 to study music with Aaron Copland, becoming himself a composer and a music critic. In 1938 he married Jane Bowles, whose writing has often been favorably compared with that of Gertrude Stein, but whose lifelong health problems limited her body of work. Like her husband, she explored same-sex love both physically and artistically.

Paul Bowles didn't start writing until after World War II, and his first novel was 1949's *The Sheltering Sky*. In 1952 he established himself as a resident in Tangier—where he had moved with Jane in 1947—that year publishing another novel, *Let It Come Down*. He followed it up with two others, *The Spider House* in 1955 and *Up Above the World* in 1966. He published two collections of short fictions, the highly praised *Pages from Cold Point* in 1968 and *Midnight Mass* in 1981, along with nonfiction, poetry, numerous translations and an autobiography.

Tangier, during Bowles's early years there, was a center of queer literary activity, with Joe Orton, William Burroughs, Allen Ginsberg, Tennessee Williams and Truman Capote, among others, passing through. Tangier was indulgent of divergent sexual appetites, and of the drug use that Western society condemned.

Jane Bowles died in 1973. People moved on to other scenes or hot spots. Paul Bowles remained in Tangier, however, and continues to produce fine work, including superb translations of Sartre.

> Port said, "I had a strange dream yesterday. I've been trying to remember it, and just this minute I did."
>
> "No!" cried Kit with force. "Dreams are so dull! Please!"   (BOOK I, "TEA IN THE SAHARA," CHAPTER 2)

The Sheltering Sky is not an overtly gay novel—the primary male characters, Port and Tunner, never get it on. For all intents and purposes, they and Port's wife, Kit, could be said to be resolute heterosexuals. But there is nothing absolute in *The Sheltering Sky*, and small twinges of uncertainty not only betray Bowles's passivity in response to human sexual diversity but reveal *The Sheltering Sky* as a novel of primal dissolution.

The concern of *The Sheltering Sky* is identity, the pivotal concern of queers in the twentieth century. We are pages into the work before we learn the Christian names of our protagonists and their most basic relationships to each other; it is not until the very end of the book that Port and Kit's last name is revealed; we never do learn Tunner's first name. But this is because Tunner serves as the one constant in the book: When we leave him, he is the same as when we first met him, unchanged by either his experiences in Africa or his time with Kit and Port. He remains, from start to finish, the resolute embodiment of the American masculine ego, forever looking about for a hero, yet self-confident enough in his "astonishingly handsome" good looks to parade about naked, and pursuing romantic attractions with the rough certainty of a cowboy rounding up cattle. All three characters, however, are refugees from New York, sitting on the lip of the vastness of North Africa.

Port's dream, above, forms the start of the novel and, in a way, serves as a prophecy for the remainder of the work.

Port and Kit are a husband and wife who have not been sexually intimate in over a year, yet remain joined to each other in a fashion that makes divorce inconceivable. They are lovers—but not in the physical sense, and for Kit it is much more than this: Port shapes her very sense of self, her credible soul, her identity. Yet both of them pursue extramarital sex, Port with a desert prostitute named Marhnia. As he makes love to the whore, he finds himself imagining Kit is watching them. The thought turns him on.

Tunner, meanwhile, has targeted Kit for his affections. When Port takes an offered ride to Boussif with Eric Lyle, a disturbingly puffy English boy about whom hovers the occasional queer whiff, and Eric's overbearing, chronically ill, paranoid, anti-Semitic photographer mother, he leaves Kit behind because she will not aban-

don Tunner, even though Port wants her to. Tunner is at last alone
with Port's wife.

He has convinced himself she needs him. Knowing that Port
has left, Tunner meets Kit in the hotel dining room, where he
orders champagne:

> "At a thousand francs a bottle!" she remonstrated. "Port
> would have a fit!"
> "Port isn't here," said Tunner.   (BOOK I, CHAPTER 8)

On the train Tunner plies Kit, who hates to travel, with the bottles
of champagne he has brought on board, only to have her wander
off at one stop from their first-class compartment to the fourth-
class carriage. Fourth class is nothing more than a platform with a
few benches on wheels, and it is crammed with people, including
lepers and Muslims, to whom her appearance is a scandal. As she
tries to escape the train, she finds herself on the edge of the platform in the rain, holding on to an iron railing and looking directly
into the face of a man whose nose is missing, leaving only a black
triangle in the middle of his face, and whose lips are white, the
whole effect reminding her of a lion's muzzle. She cannot look
away, and imagines what Port would tell her about her revulsion to
the man's appearance: that she feels repulsed by what she sees—
the emptiness of the man's face—because she is the product of a
materialistic age; that in a nonmaterialistic age it would be the
reverse that is truly repellent: the healthy face, twisted by immorality.

At the next stop Kit returns to Tunner and their compartment.
She dries off, and gets warm, and Tunner dims the lights. He holds
her. She protests, but he soothes her, and she acquiesces, despite the
noise of the train wheels beating the words "not now" inside her
head. He is near, she is warm again, and he does not frighten her.
At last, in one of those nicely put euphemistic train-going-
into-a-tunnel moments:

The rain beat against the window panes.
(BOOK I, CHAPTER 10)

Afterward, when they meet up with Port, her guilt leads her to side with her husband, and they manage to shake Tunner, eventually.

So what of it? Is there any reason for her to feel guilty when she perhaps knows what we know, even if it is never spoken: that her husband has not been sexually faithful to her in their conjugally barren marriage? (To her credit, she is also nagged by guilt at abandoning Tunner.) What defines a marriage? In this age of therapy, problems are talked to death and people are encouraged to establish themselves as the victim rather than accept responsibility for their actions. And yet more marriages fail than ever before, and we as a culture have less of an idea than ever before how to make the traditional marriage—husband, wife, monogamy, forever—work.

Perhaps that's because the traditional marriage is a lie. Gay relationships actually have the opportunity to serve in the vanguard here, forging marriages that are diverse enough to honestly encompass the vagaries of the human heart, conscience and loins in the pursuit of intimacy. Yet for the most part we pursue heterosexual stereotypes, forcing failed models of behavior upon our own hearts, surprised and angry when they fail us as well.

We become bitter toward love, toward the idea of the committed relationship.

If *The Sheltering Sky* is about anything, it is about the committed relationship between Port and Kit. It is about being so much a part of another's life and soul that living without that person, while retaining any semblance of the identity embedded within you as part of that couple, seems impossible. As Port and Kit find, at sunset, overlooking the desert. She knows that he loves sharing the silence with her, the empty, infinite panorama of the sand and the sky. She thinks she waits for the time when she will be moved by it all, as he is:

He had often told her: "It is your only hope," and she was never sure what he meant. Sometimes she thought he meant that it was *his* only hope, that only if she were able to become as he was, could he find his way back to love, since love for Port meant loving her—there was no question of anyone else.   (BOOK I, CHAPTER 10)

Clearly, theirs is not a model relationship. Yet despite his estrangement and her intransigent delicacy, their lack of shared sexual activity, they are committed to each other, and their relationship will last till death do them part.

Who are we? We tie our identities to intangibles such as our nationality, our individuality. Yet without our passport, what establishes our patriotic sensibilities? Kit and Port are Americans, sure, tenuously "hanging onto the outside" (Book I, Chapter 13) of life, but without their passport, would their American identity fragment, dissolve? Without Kit, what is left for Port? Without Port, who is Kit?

   With the exception of Tunner and certain characters who exist on the periphery of our travelers' lives, all the substantial relationships in *The Sheltering Sky* are skewed. Kit and Port are sexually estranged; Eric Lyle and his mother carry their own secrets. The desert sand spills empty before this book's cast of characters, and they bring nothing with which to fill it.

   Sometimes we carry around talismans that reassure us as to who we are. For some, these may be as simple as our door keys, which remind us we have a place to live, a place that offers us something of home. For others, the talismans are overt—a rosary, a photo. Or oblique: work, cigarettes, makeup, a flask, wealth, or some absurd idea of class. In our time, talismans can take on larger, concrete forms as well: Few Americans traveling abroad can resist the baptismal properties of home found in a visit to McDonald's.

We latch on to the idea of a Big Mac and fries because—regardless of how we may feel about them in actuality—they represent America's wondrously insidious capitalistic imperialism, and in the restaurant's pale light and plastic seating, we are reanchored to our sense of identity.

We are reaffirmed.

And Port had said: "Death is always on the way, but the fact that you don't know when it will arrive seems to take away from the finiteness of life. It's that terrible precision that we hate so much. But because we don't know, we get to think of life as an inexhaustible well. Yet everything happens only a certain number of times, and a very small number, really . . . And yet it all seems limitless."
(BOOK I, CHAPTER 13)

Port illustrates his point with frighteningly common examples: How often might we remember a key moment that shaped our lives? How many more times will we see the full moon rise? He presses past the great human skill for denial upon which we hang our lives. We buy calendars every year and fill them up with appointments with the understanding—the vain hope, really—that we'll be there when those moments arrive. We deny the finality of death for the most part, but in the process, what do we lose?

What other choice is there?

Of course, by pinning your identity to any one thing or person, you run the risk of losing it when that thing or person ceases to exist. For queers, this is particularly problematic because in great part we are defined by our oppression: We exist because someone points at us and claims that we are aberrant, separate somehow from the whole, the rest. If bigotry against sexual orientation disappeared tomorrow, what would be our identity? Less specious, perhaps—for even if that miracle did happen, odds are some other prejudice would rise up to take its place—is the question of where we belong as individuals within the gay community, a contemplation inevitably distracted by arguments over whether or not such a thing exists.

The Sheltering Sky pierces us, then, right to the core. Are our talismans—feather boas, leather vests, J. Crew baseball caps—any good to us if they can be so easily co-opted from our queer minority by their straight majority? No. In the bar-culture desert that is sadly so much of gay life in this our end-time, how much do our talismans tie us to anything certain? They don't, really. If the black sky above is filled with moving stars from the pinpoint spotlight bouncing off the disco glitter ball, while the pounding music somehow creates in our hearts a hollow vacuum, does it reassure us to think that everything we have tied ourselves to, everything that we say defines who we are, cannot be washed away in swilled beer, and sperm, and sweat?

We are nothing, then. Nothing of any substance. Nothing of any worth.

Someone once had said to her that the sky hides the night behind it, shelters the person beneath from the horror that lies above. Unblinking, she fixed the solid emptiness, and the anguish began to move in her. At any moment the rip can occur, the edges fly back, and the giant maw will be revealed. (BOOK III, "THE SKY," CHAPTER 30)

FIVE QUESTIONS

1. According to the novel, what is the sheltering sky?
2. Bowles gradually builds upon the imagery of the sky. Take a moment to review the text and trace the development of this imagery. Chart it. Does it mean different things at different times, or is it, like Tunner, a constant? What is the author working toward in

bringing it so much to our attention, even fixing it so blatantly in one regard in the title of the work?

3. Without limiting your definition to an academic sense but, rather, pursuing a common and practical understanding: What makes a culture "alien"?

4. Why do Kit and Port stay together?

5. Is the gay identity meaningful? Why or why not? What is the gay identity?

Yukio Mishima

Confessions of
a Mask

TRANSLATED BY MEREDITH WEATHERBY

During this time the attraction I had formerly
felt only toward older youths had little by little been
extended to include younger boys as well . . . Along
with my natural growth there was developing in me
something like a guardian's love, something akin to
boy-love.

Yukio Mishima was the pen name of Hiraoka Kimitake. He was
born in Tokyo in 1925 and published his first story when he was
just nineteen years old. Like the hero of *Confessions of a Mask,* he
was raised almost exclusively in the company of women, though
kept from his mother for a long time by his grandmother. The cold,
emasculative isolation of his youth led to a hatred of people in
general, who often tormented the effeminate child, and of women
in particular.

Mishima attended Tokyo University before becoming a civil
servant and then embarking on a literary career that was nothing

short of distinguished, nothing less than remarkable. The breadth of his talent knew no apparent limit: Mishima wrote twenty-three novels, along with over ninety short stories, poetry, travel volumes, hundreds of essays and forty plays, including modern Kabuki and Noh drama. (Mishima also sang onstage and starred in and directed films.)

Confessions of a Mask, published in 1949 and translated in 1958, was his first major work and, like Evelyn Waugh's first success, proved a lightly disguised fictionalizing of his own life. In Mishima's case, specifically, it served as a vehicle for the writer to make sense of his passions, coming to terms with his sexuality. From 1965 to 1970, Mishima published the books that would form *The Sea of Fertility,* a reincarnationist tetralogy that attempts to tackle Japan's place in the twentieth century on levels both intimate and epic.

When he was thirty, Mishima resolved to make himself into the icon of masculinity he revered, and he immersed himself in the worlds of weightlifting and boxing; he dressed in hypermasculine attire, including civil and military uniforms, and wore sport shirts opened to show his newly muscled chest. He posed nude for magazines, displaying his realized ideal. In perhaps the most aggressive display of his will to (heterosexual) power, he fucked women and married one, fathering two children by her.

Mishima was wholly obsessed with masculinity, an obsession that took the form of a slavish interest in the chivalrous traditions of Imperial Japan. He believed in the pursuit of destiny, as well as in the possibility of ideal beauty; he believed in the gloriously exalted concept of death in battle. He became an expert in such martial arts as karate and kendo. In 1968 he founded the Shield Society, a group of one hundred handsome young men dedicated to the revival of the samurai code of honor, the Bushido. In short, for two years he created his own homoerotic cadre. His political ideology was extreme right-wing elitism; his aesthetic a more nobly presented (and Japanese) Nazi ideal. He found language effeminate, but as a writer, he couldn't separate himself from it. Mishima sought to reconcile manliness and literature in terms of the "sword and chrysanthemum," respectively. But the softness of words remained a rift in his testosterone-based armor.

On November 25, 1970, in hopes of reinvigorating Japan's flagging sense of nationalism, he attempted to stage a military coup d'état at the headquarters of the Japanese Self-Defense Forces in Ichigaya, Tokyo. He was accompanied by four young men from the Shield Society. The effort ended with the gathered Self-Defense Forces laughing in his face, and in response Mishima then and there committed ritualistic suicide by hara-kiri, slicing his taut belly open with the sharp blade of a sword.

> It was a young man who was coming down toward us, with handsome, ruddy cheeks and shining eyes, wearing a dirty roll of cloth around his head for a sweatband. He came down the slope carrying a yoke of night soil buckets over one shoulder, balancing their heaviness expertly with his footsteps. He was a night-soil man, a ladler of excrement. He was dressed as a laborer.

The never-named narrator of *Confessions of a Mask* is born on January 4, 1925, his hair "blondish for a long time, but they kept putting olive oil on it for a long time until it finally turned black." On his forty-ninth day, he is snatched away from his parents' care by his grandmother. Three days before his fourth birthday, he vomits "something the color of coffee" and falls into a virtual coma as a result of "autointoxication," a chronic illness he will have no choice but to live with. *Confessions of a Mask* is similar to Genet's *Our Lady of the Flowers* in some respects: It is autobiography masquerading as a novel and finds a portion of its sexual thrill in the forbidden, be that pederasty or pain.

Shortly after his first episode of autointoxication, he is pulled to the side of the road as the night-soil man passes, and his small body is racked by its first sexual thrill. Further, he imbues the night-soil man—and other uniformed workers after him—with " 'tragic lives,' " because their lives are harder, rougher than his own and because they work in air tainted by heavy odor—the smell of shit, the sour air of the subway.

Coupled with this awareness is the boy's attraction to a figure in a picture book, a "knight mounted on a white horse, holding a sword aloft." The knight, too, is imbued with a sense of tragedy; in the boy's imagination, he is confronting "Death, or at the very least, some hurtling object of evil power." But this quiet moment of preserved terror—the potential for a man's destruction without the realization of it, for the picture never changes and the story is not continued—holds its own surprise for the child.

The young knight he has been attracted to is not a man but Joan of Arc.

He's a she.

The revelation ruins the book for him. He doesn't read it again.

A last image fills his childhood, providing the other side to the tragic lives earlier described, and as with the night-soil man, he is pulled to the side of the road, this time to avoid being stepped on by passing troops.

The boy is fascinated not just by the beating of the soldiers' shoes against the ground, by their thick, stained uniforms and by their perched rifles, but by their sweat, their smell. The odor intoxicates him, for in it lies the promise of a soldier's destiny, exotic ports of call and violent death.

In the opening pages of his first novel, Mishima is slowly building an argument that sexuality, if not biologically predetermined, is at the very least shaped at an early age. As an apology (in the academic, not the moral sense) for his own erotic predilections, centering as they do around the military and pain and death, it is a well-built, powerful argument, leading to the understanding of a pathology, if not the recognition of it.

There's more, of course. Despite his earlier disgust at Joan of

Arc's sartorial gender-bending, the boy experiences a period in his life when he attempts something similar, albeit briefly. Entranced by a female lounge singer he has seen, he burrows within his mother's closet to emerge wrapped in her kimonos, then avails himself of her powder and baubles, crowing the name of the lounge singer.

He runs into the room where his reunited family—grandmother and mother, plus a maid and a visitor—sit, convinced that they will no longer see a little boy but a fabulous cabaret artist. Convinced, that is, until he sees his mother's face is pale. As their eyes meet, she looks away and he realizes he has shamed her.

The maid grabs him, hustles him off to another room and strips the makeup from his face, the costume from his body.

To the smell of soldiers, and the promise of pain and death, is added shame, yet the boy learns to hide it, finding further thrills in movie goddesses, most notably Cleopatra, and dressing up for his younger sister and brother. And then, at last, comes the final piece of the puzzle:

> Although as a child I read every fairy story I could lay my hands on, I never liked the princesses. I was fond only of the princes. I was all the fonder of princes murdered or princes fated for death. I was completely in love with any youth who was killed.

From the idea of death to its actuality, the child's erotic sensibility is soon complete. He begins to fantasize about his own death. He contrives elaborate scenarios of suspicion and mortality: Is the maid trying to poison his food? And in the war games he plays with other children, he is quick to get shot and die.

As he grows physically, these feelings also increase, and fall into sharper relief. He is drawn to gory stories of adventure and death. One day, while home sick, he receives a revelation from an art book of his father's. It is Guido Reni's painting *St. Sebastian*.

The saint is pinned against a tree. He is naked but for a loin-cloth. His hands are raised high above his head and bound together, his body stretched out against the tree's tough skin.

The narrator guesses that it must be a painting of a Christian martyr. He indulges in a rapturous description of the body of Sebastian as painted by Reni, its athletic youth, vibrant and evocative of Antinous, Hadrian's beloved boy. In retrospect, the narrator will realize that he saw not pain on the martyr's face but some passing "melancholy pleasure." Were it not for the arrows sunk into Sebastian's left armpit and right side, Reni's painting could simply depict a resting Roman athlete. But:

> That day, the instant I looked upon the picture, my entire
> being trembled with some pagan joy. My blood soared up;
> my loins swelled as though in wrath. The monstrous part
> of me that was on the point of bursting awaited my use of
> it with unprecedented ardor, upbraiding me for my igno-
> rance, panting indignantly. My hands, completely uncon-
> sciously, began a motion they had never been taught. I felt
> a secret, radiant something rise swift-footed to the attack
> from inside me. Suddenly it burst forth, bringing with it a
> blinding intoxication.

There are repeated themes within *Confessions of a Mask*—among them pain, the hollow of the armpit, the nearness of death—that join here to provoke the boy's first ejaculation. As he grows older, and the "mask" of expected behavior entrenches itself upon his face, he will fall in love with a boy a few years ahead of him in school, the roughneck Omi, whose armpits are the first to sprout dark hair and whose body is athletic and masculine when most of the other boys still look like children, twigs without gender. After that will come a disastrous attempt to feign a romantic interest in a woman, the sister of a friend. The war that scorches Japan in the protagonist's young adulthood makes its impact felt distantly, as he

is protected through medical disability from serving. Even as it
brings him together with the woman—he is that rarest of all things
in war-torn cities, a young man—it provides quick excuses to keep
them apart. A visit to a whore with a friend ends in disaster too,
although that friend later provides, if derisively, a clue to his own
identity:

> "You promised to lend me a book by Marcel Proust, re-
> member? Is it interesting?"
>
> "I'll say it's interesting. Proust was a *sodomite*"—he
> used the foreign word. "He had affairs with footmen."
>
> "What's a sodomite?" I asked. I realized that by feign-
> ing ignorance I was desperately pawing the air, clutching
> at this little question for support and trying to find some
> clue to their thoughts, some indication that they did not
> suspect my disgrace.

But they do.

At last, for the self there is only honesty, surrender to the fact
that sexual desire is present in the tattooed chests of shirtless boys
in bars and not in the soft bodies of women, however much they
might be loved sentimentally. But the honesty brings with it lies,
and the confessor remains behind his mask, hidden, talking quietly,
feverishly denying, then exulting in his love, his passion, his torment.

Mishima, of course, took the shell of the mask and developed it
into the whole of himself—a carapace of testosterone. *Confessions of
a Mask* separates itself from *Our Lady of the Flowers* in its concern
with the development of desire rather than with just immersion in
it: Never does Genet question what he loves or why. It is enough
that he loves, and indulges his appetites, in anticipation of escape or
obliteration. For Mishima, the stakes—escape or obliteration—are
similar, but escape from the society that surrounds him seems impossible. Unlike Genet, but evincing a sensibility similar to the pre-

trial Wilde's, he is unwilling to sacrifice position and class. The ready identification with the criminal does not overwhelmingly satisfy his lust, as it does Genet's.

For Mishima, being a man—as society defines it—overrides any sexual aberration on his part, so that his eventual response is predictable: to bend society to his will, or die trying.

FIVE QUESTIONS

1. Is *Confessions of a Mask* a plea for the acceptance of the homosexual or merely the acknowledgment that queers exist? How? Why?

2. Mishima retrospectively acknowledges the St. Sebastian painting as Christian with pagan attributes, but then describes the rush of sexual desire that follows as purely pagan. Why?

3. Like Genet, Mishima challenges what we accept as erotic. Compare the obsessions of *Confessions of a Mask* with those of *Our Lady of the Flowers*. Compare your own sexual appetites with the appetites deemed publicly acceptable. Are there differences? Similarities? What? How? Why?

4. Using the text as your basis, what is the role of "intoxication" in *Confessions of a Mask*?

5. What is the position of the homosexual in society, and given such, what is the homosexual's obligation to the society surrounding him, to other homosexuals and to himself?

Marguerite Yourcenar

Memoirs of Hadrian

TRANSLATED BY MARGUERITE YOURCENAR
AND GRACE FRICK

I did not love less; indeed I loved more. But the weight of love, like that of an arm thrown tenderly across a chest, becomes little by little too heavy to bear. Passing interests reappeared: I remember the hard, elegant youth who was with me during a stay in Miletus, but whom I gave up. I remember that evening in Sardis when the poet Strato escorted us from brothel to brothel, and we surrounded ourselves with conquests of doubtful value. This same Strato, who had preferred obscurity in the freedom of Asia taverns to life in my court, was a man of exquisite sensibility, a mocking wit quick to assert the vanity of all that is not pleasure itself, in order perhaps to excuse himself for having sacrificed to it everything else. And there was that night in Smyrna when I forced the beloved one to endure the presence of a courtesan.

Marguerite Yourcenar was the anagrammatical pseudonym of Marguerite Antoinette Jeanne Marie Ghislaine Cleenwerck de Crayencour, born in Brussels on June 8, 1903. Her mother died shortly after her birth, and she was home-schooled, surrounded by money and culture, traveling with her father, Michel, who had been almost fifty when she was born. She was reading Greek authors by the age of eight and privately printed two books of poetry while still a teen. She lived for extended periods in various countries, often as result of wartime exile—World War I exiled her to England; and World War II, to the United States. She wrote novels, poetry, plays and essays. She is best known for her novels, many of them set in the past and seeking to re-create the mindset of the times, as with *Memoirs of Hadrian,* which she first saw published in 1951 and translated in 1954. She also wrote extensively about her religious experiences, most notably in an introduction to a 1958 anthology of American spirituals and in her autobiography, published in 1977.

In 1929 the stock market crash and her half-brother's poor management left her without her mother's inheritance; that same year her father died, penniless as well, though he had married again but two years before. Yet this was also the year that would see her first novel, *Alexis,* published. The story of a man writing his wife and small child a letter explaining why he must leave them to pursue his queer heart's desire is an exercise in refinement, and established a pattern for the rest of Yourcenar's career, during which then scandalous subjects received nonsensationalist treatment. The method was to serve her well; she could support herself as a writer from the proceeds of her work, and in the course of a lifetime she racked up a staggering collection of awards and honors.

She spent the 1930s indulgently, having numerous affairs with women, though lesbians figure only tangentially in her work and her portrayals of women are as a rule less than empowered. She also entangled herself with two men who paid her no attention at all, a frustration that translated itself in a series of prose poems collected as *Fires* in 1935. In 1937, however, Yourcenar met Grace Frick, an American college professor, and her work's hedonistic lament would come to a happy, personal end. Yourcenar and Frick became lovers and coworkers, Grace managing aspects of Yourcenar's career and translating her writing into English with the author's cooperation.

In 1939 Yourcenar was visiting Grace in New York City when war broke out and she was unable to return to Europe. From New York the two moved to Hartford, Connecticut, where Frick found work. In 1942 they spent their first summer on Mount Desert Island, off the coast of Maine. In 1950 they moved there permanently. Yourcenar taught comparative literature at Sarah Lawrence College from 1942 to 1953 and became a U.S. citizen in 1947.

Four years later, *Memoirs of Hadrian* appeared. It was a work she had consigned to the fire countless times as she developed it over the decades. The discipline paid off, however, since it proved a critical and commercial smash hit, firmly establishing her financial security and sparking, with the Prix Femina Vacaresco, a chain reaction of prizes—the Page One Award of the Newspaper Guild of New York (1955) and the Prix Combat (1963) among them.

But these accomplishments would prove hollow. In 1959 Frick was diagnosed with breast cancer. It would kill her at last twenty-one years later, and a few months after that, her lover would ironically be deemed the first woman "immortal" with her January 22, 1981, entrance into the prestigious French Academy. Yourcenar died almost seven years later, at the Maine island home she shared with Grace, on December 17, 1987. The death of an immortal was a fitting final paradox for a woman whose life and work were a series of paradoxical investments of intellectual and emotional capital, sterling talent and hard-metaled craft.

Memoirs of Hadrian is itself something of a meditation on a life lived, and at its end. It is cast in the form of a letter from the emperor Hadrian to his successor, Marcus Aurelius, and its staggering achievement is that it seamlessly, convincingly re-creates the mind of the man who loved the boy Antinous so much that he made him a god. In so doing, the work takes us within the soul of the Roman Empire's last gasp.

Historically thorough, Hadrian's reflections never shy away from honest remembrances, some of them erotic, others tender. But significantly absent here is the pornography lesser writers find themselves seduced by when writing about the Roman world and those who embodied its morals. The result is not simply a literary work but a marvelous accomplishment of time travel, embedding the reader within the emperor's heart and mind. Yourcenar treats us to palace intrigues; the political strains within a ruling nation that work to keep its conquered peoples happy, most noticeably the Jews; loveless marriages; the reasons behind certain political appointments, including that of Hadrian's successor; and the horror that is Antinous' suicide in the muddy waters of a shallow river.

While gay readers will find themselves waiting for Antinous' arrival, it's better not to anticipate Yourcenar's revelations as much as to surrender to them, and in the process realize that love is part of a well-lived life—but not all of it.

Angus Wilson

Hemlock and After

Terence had seen them coming and quickly wedged himself securely in the crowd that was battling for coffee and lemonade. His companion, Sherman Winter, however, advanced eagerly towards them. "Bernard my dear, Heaven!" Sherman's speech had not changed for twenty-five years. "And with such beauty, double Heaven! Don't be cagey, dear, introduce!" When Bernard said, "This is Sherman Winter, Eric. Eric Craddock, Sherman. I only hope you hate each other like poison," Sherman only laughed and said, "Pleased to meet you, I'm sure," in Cockney. To see him like this, thought Bernard, anyone would think he was just another routine, harmless old queen.

—CHAPTER 5, "CAMP FIRE CAMEOS"

Knighted in 1980, Sir Angus Wilson was born Frank Johnstone-Wilson of an English father and a South African mother. He was educated at Westminster School and Merton College, Oxford, joining the staff of the British Museum Library in 1937. He started writing in 1946, when he was thirty-three. His literary reputation gained a foothold with the publication of his first collection of short stories, *The Wrong Set*. More books followed, and in 1952 he produced the first of eight novels, *Hemlock and After*. It was a bestseller, enabling Wilson, after another three years, to resign his position as deputy superintendent of the British Museum reading room to write full-time.

From 1966 to 1978, Wilson served as professor of English literature at the University of East Anglia, and in the course of his lifetime he would hold visiting appointments at fifteen American universities. He was active on the Arts Council of Great Britain and with the Royal Society of Literature. He died in 1991.

Throughout, his literary career would be something of a romp. He refused to be pigeonholed. In addition to his popular fiction, he wrote diverse scholarly treatments of authors such as Dickens, Zola and Kipling; published essays on the craft of writing; and, around the time that he resigned from the British Museum, even tried his hand at playwriting.

His bailiwick, though, was fiction, and Wilson himself stated its singular defining feature as an "open statement of the possibility of homosexual happiness within a conventional framework."

Certainly, *Hemlock and After* was a harbinger of that focus. Although it is not a happy book—it is a bleak, bitchily sarcastic comedy—its homosexual characters are fully realized human beings, replete with failings, wonders and, ultimately, a sort of absolution.

Hemlock and After deals with aging writer Bernard Sand's efforts to open a writers' colony at Vardon Hall, an abandoned mansion the neighboring townsfolk had hoped to turn into a hotel. His wife is a failing, broken creature, for reasons long undetermined, and in the course of the colony's establishment, Sands finds himself in love with a young man, Eric. The tensions among the three, the convoluted ties they develop with the locals—together with the further press of ambition and reality within the colony and its dubious economic and governmental survival—form the skeins of this skillfully unraveling novel. It is an unraveling that ends, as it must, with a horrific emptiness, from which Wilson perfectly manages to salvage just a bit of hope. The neighboring townsfolk each are memorably sketched, perhaps none more so than the gargantuan Mrs. Curry, whose folds of flesh and utterances on love disguise the serpent nursing at her breast.

Clever, funny, poignant and resonant, *Hemlock and After* was but the first salvo from a brilliant pen that recast England in the eyes of her people. It was published fifteen years before homosexuality would be decriminalized in England, giving Wilson the balls that Forster should have had, and in the process earning Wilson the admiration of Forster himself and other queer luminaries such as Auden. It was an honest book at a time when England most needed honesty, and a brave book at a time when cowardice and code were the order of the day.

It is also a helluva fun read, the kind of yarn that rapidly spins itself out, a novel whose swiftly turning pages you hold on to for dear life.

William Inge

Four Plays

BO: Virge. I hate to sound like some pitiable weaklin' of a man, but there's been times the last few months, I been so lonesome, I . . . I jest didn't know what t'do with m'self.

VIRGIL: It's no disgrace to feel that way, Bo.

BO: How 'bout you, Virge? Don't you ever git lonesome, too?

VIRGIL: A long time ago, I gave up romancin' and de- cided I was just gonna take bein' lonesome for granted.

—*BUS STOP,* ACT II

William Motter Inge was born in Independence, Kansas, in 1913. He was educated at the University of Kansas and the George Peabody College, and was a fraternity brother in Sigma Nu. He taught art criticism and wrote about art for the *St. Louis Star-Times* before creating a solid quartet of plays set in his native Midwestern territory. *Come Back, Little Sheba,* in 1950, was his first, followed by *Picnic,* which won him the Pulitzer Prize for Drama in 1953. Then came *Bus Stop* in 1955 and *The Dark at the Top of the Stairs* in 1957, although the latter was actually a revision of a play Inge had written ten years earlier.

Inge often adapted his plays into films, but in 1961 he won the

Academy Award for Best Original Screenplay for *Splendor in the Grass*. Twelve years later, after mounting difficulty controlling his use of alcohol, as well as failed psychoanalysis, Inge committed suicide.

Not a pretty picture, and despite its successes, not a pretty life. Inge was damned by the repressive mentality of the Midwest that spawned him. In his works he rarely created openly gay characters, although the one-acter *The Boy in the Basement, The Disposal,* and Inge's last play, *Where's Daddy?,* did feature such characters, not always in a kindly way. But as Tennessee Williams did with Tom in *The Glass Menagerie,* Inge wrote characters and plays that instead offered important subtleties for the gay reader. This is not to say that the plays are written in code; more to say that the gay reader brings to them an added level of perception the heterosexual reader simply fails to consider. And so, for the gay reader, nuances round out character and certain lines ring truer.

While *Picnic* may be his most famous play, *Come Back, Little Sheba* his most histrionic and *The Dark at the Top of the Stairs* his edgiest, it is *Bus Stop* that perhaps allows Inge to address the central theme of human existence that he never realized for himself: love.

In the introduction to *Bus Stop,* Inge writes, "I meant it only as a composite picture of varying kinds of love, ranging from the innocent to the depraved." And so it is, but in the way it resolves the various stories of five travelers stuck in a diner during a snowstorm, it holds a far greater resonance.

Grace, who runs the diner, doesn't know if Carl—the bus driver with whom she's been carrying on an affair—is married or not, and it isn't until the snowstorm sticks them together for more than the usual twenty-minute layover that they realize they want to know more about each other. Innocent Elma, who works for Grace, is coveted by the heterosexual, pedophilic, drunken Rhodes Scholar Dr. Lyman, who hopes in her innocence to reclaim his own—perhaps the drive behind his criminal lust. He has otherwise been divorced three times. Cherie, a Marilyn Monroe type, is on the run from Bo, a cowboy accompanied by his faithful chum, Virgil. She's a bar singer who's been around, and Bo is—was—a virgin who thinks their night of passion means marriage—and ultimately it does. There's the sheriff, floating about, keeping things moving, a sort of ersatz cupid. And last but not least, the aforementioned Virgil Blessing, who speaks of a woman in his life but clearly loves and is devoted to Bo. When Bo announces that Cherie has agreed to go back with him to the ranch, Virgil abdicates the care of Bo to Cherie. Virgil is left by himself in the diner as it closes after the bus leaves. He refuses Grace's offer to put the sign out for the next bus to stop, pick him up and take him back to Kansas City. Shutting up the diner, she says to him, "Then I'm sorry Mister but you're just left out in the cold."

> VIRGIL *(to himself):* Well . . . that's what happens to some people.

His first name evokes the Roman poet who wrote so stirringly of Corydon's love for Alexis in *Eclogues.* His last name suggests his resignation to Bo's promised union with Cherie. Virgil Blessing's emptiness resonates painfully with Lymie's hard acceptance at the end of Maxwell's *The Folded Leaf.* In both cases, the lover ends up alone because the beloved has moved on, folded seamlessly against the bosom of the society that spawned him. The lover, by virtue of his love, cannot follow.

Virgil's sacrifice of his place in his friend's life, although inspired by his love for that friend, is awkward, for it makes homosexuality seem second best. In an ultimately homophobic society (the society known by Inge, and let's not forget Forster, whose happy-ever-after gay love story had to wait fifty-seven years for publication, until the year after his death), perhaps it is second best. This is the reflection of the lives many of the writers in the Canon knew, the lives of the homosexual outsiders, forever pressing their noses against the windows of houses where former crushes or even lovers live with their wives and children, seeing a happiness they feel will never be theirs, while around them the wind blows bitter cold and it is always, ever night.

James Baldwin

Giovanni's Room

I repent now—for all the good it does—one particular lie among the many lies I've told, lived, and believed. This is the lie which I told to Giovanni, but
never succeeded in making him believe, that I had
never slept with a boy before. I had. I had decided that
I never would again.

—CHAPTER 1

James Arthur Baldwin was born on August 2, 1924, in a poor section of Harlem to an unmarried twenty-year-old woman named
Emma Berdis Jones. His father was a storefront preacher. James,
who grew up taunted by his peers for his small build and effeminacy, sought solace in the church. At the age of fourteen he under-
went a rapturous spiritual conversion and started ministering in
various Harlem evangelical churches. It was also during this time
that he started to write book reviews and essays.

After holding a variety of jobs—elevator operator, railroad
construction worker—Baldwin fled first to nearby Greenwich Village in 1947, then a year later, with forty dollars in his pocket, to
Europe. He lived mainly in Paris from 1948 to 1958, when he returned to the United States as a civil rights activist. Most, if not all,
of his work can be said to contain a strong autobiographical ele-

ment, as Baldwin tried to make sense of what he saw as the black (gay) man's place in the white (straight) man's world, and grappled with such core concerns as religion, racism, love, social conscience and true freedom. For Baldwin, homophobia and racism seemed to spring from the same seed.

He first tasted success with the publication of his novel *Go Tell It on the Mountain* in 1953. A book of essays, *Notes of a Native Son*, followed in 1955, along with a play, *The Amen Corner*. Baldwin then returned to fiction for 1956's *Giovanni's Room* and 1962's *Another Country*, publishing *The Fire Next Time*, a book of vision-ary civil rights essays, in that year, and a play, *Blues for Mister Charlie*, the year thereafter. In 1968 he brought out the novel *Tell Me How Long the Train's Been Gone*. His output during the seven-ties was lesser in quantity and quality: the 1972 play, *The Women at the Well* and the 1979 novel *Just Above My Head*.

He died in Paris on December 1, 1987.

> Now, from this night, this coming morning, no matter how many beds I find myself in between now and my final bed, I shall never be able to have any more of those boyish, zestful affairs . . . People are too various to be treated so lightly. I am too various to be trusted. If this were not so I would not be alone in this house tonight. Hella would not be on the high seas. And Giovanni would not be about to perish, sometime between this night and this morning, on the guillotine. (CHAPTER 1)

Giovanni's Room is David's confession. David, a blond all-American boy, has loved Giovanni, a dark-haired Italian boy, and in the pro-cess estranged himself from his fiancée, Hella. The novel is not a study in race so much as it is a study in class, for David and Giovanni are both white. Joey, David's first male lover while both were still in their teens, may well have been black, though their public displays of camaraderie seem to argue against it, given the ready bigotry of much of America in the first part (and latter part) of the twentieth century, when *Giovanni's Room* takes place. The morning after David and Joey have had sex, David is filled with remorse and the coals of guilt. He does not have breakfast with Joey; he has coffee and leaves early. Joey doesn't stop him.

And after that, David no longer goes to see Joey; Joey no longer goes to see David. When the two boys do meet again at the end of summer, David tells Joey a lie, that he has been busy with a new girlfriend. When school starts, David joins an older, rougher crowd. Together, they pick on Joey, until at last Joey moves away and is lost to David.

What David tells the reader while confessing his sins against Joey is that he has always been, and still is, to the day of this regurgitation of conscience, a coward. Not in the misguided, hypermasculine way in which violent men call peaceniks cowards, but in the honest sense of the word: David shirks what he knows is right, sacrificing everything on the altar of his momentary self-preservation. Of course, the upshot of all this is that, before too long in a life lived this way, there's not much worth preserving.

David's mother died when he was five, and he has been raised by his father and his aunt, Ellen. Ellen and David's father don't get along, however, and there is a fleeting suggestion that his father's drinking and unexplained absences have their root in homosexuality. The thought never occurs to Ellen, though the modern gay reader is not so blind. Sometimes a pause, a verbal stumble where there should be certainty, can speak volumes.

In David's later, growing awareness of himself and his desires and their place in the world, there is an echo of the effects that the Oscar Wilde trial had on gay writers, Henry James most noticeably among them:

> People who believe that they are strong-willed and the masters of their destiny can only continue to believe this by becoming specialists in self-deception. Their decisions

are not really decisions at all—a real decision makes one humble, one knows that it is at the mercy of more things than can be named—but elaborate systems of evasion, of illusion, designed to make themselves and the world appear to be what they and the world are not.   (CHAPTER 1)

David, however, cannot escape his true nature. There are other incidents, including one with another soldier in the army; that soldier is later court-martialed.

So David pitches himself across the ocean, to Paris, in hopes of escaping his desires for other men. But an American fag in Europe is still a fag—and an American coward in Europe is still a coward.

David has been in Paris for two years when he meets Giovanni. This happens when the almost-broke David solicits "an aging, Belgian-born, American-businessman, named Jacques" (Chapter 2), a lonely old queer from whom David knows he can cadge a free meal and a few drinks. Before they're through their first round of drinks at a nice restaurant, David borrows ten thousand francs from Jacques, though this commits him to spending the evening with him. The night's events include drinking heavily at Jacques's favorite bar, a dimly lit dive with a less than respectable clientele and owned by another old queen, Guillaume.

As they push their way through the crowd, they notice a new barman on duty, "insolent and dark and leonine."

This is Giovanni. His first words to David are simply "What will you have?" Jacques, meanwhile, is giggling like a schoolgirl and pitching his voice up into preadolescent range in an effort to seem coquettish and attract the new boy, who pays him no heed. Jacques begins to think Giovanni's straight, saying to David:

> "Anyway, I'm sure he sleeps with girls. They always do, you know."
>
> "I've heard about boys who do that. Nasty little beasts." (CHAPTER 2)

Jacques tries to get David to invite Giovanni for a drink, but David demurs, saying that he's "queer for girls" himself, so that he doesn't spend his money on men.

Jacques is a tad put off by this—after all, David hasn't minded Jacques's outlay of cash—but rises above it, saying that David would be doing him a favor if he asked Giovanni to join them for a drink after work. Jacques says he himself is sure to be refused, whereas David may well succeed—and if there's any confusion as to who is interested in whom, Jacques promises to clear it up, well, straightaway.

And so it is revealed to us that two years in Paris have done nothing to improve David's penchant for a life built upon deceit and lies. The reader is always a silent presence in this confessional narrative; we are seeing the story as David shares it with us. Giovanni, of course, is not privy to the reader's insight.

Over the course of the long night, the two young men lean toward each other, conspiratorially, amorously. This does not go unnoticed by Jacques, who bitterly reminds David that he is too old to play the "confused" role, a piece of advice David smashes aside with the offer of another drink.

David gets drunk. Periodically he thinks of Hella, touring Spain at the moment, and searches for the willpower to leave the bar and find himself a woman, a whore. But there is no turning from "the ferocious excitement which had burst in on me like a storm," and at reverie's end, no escaping the present:

> That was how I met Giovanni. I think we connected the instant we met. And remain connected still, in spite of our later *separation de corps,* despite the fact that Giovanni will be rotting soon in unhallowed ground near Paris.
> (CHAPTER 2)

Giovanni's Room is a remarkable novel of suspense, even as it lets the reader know the outcome from the start. The profundities are equally obvious, but Baldwin so skillfully strips away the layers of David's deceit and Giovanni's sweet guile that we are unable to resist turning the pages, especially toward the end of the book, which rushes toward us with all the fierce velocity of the guillotine blade descending on Giovanni's neck.

After having breakfast with Jacques and Guillaume, David and Giovanni return to Giovanni's room on the edge of Paris. It is small, a former maid's room, and Giovanni works periodically to build the room up, to clear away the decay, to establish it as their home. For broke as he is, and about to be turned out of his hotel, David moves in with Giovanni and their idyll begins. Yet we are aware that Hella—poor, stupid Hella—will return eventually and that David's track record is less than stellar when it comes to dealing with his homosexual conflict. For us, this hangs over Giovanni and David's idyll like a horrible smog. Rather than joining in their joy, we grow to hate David for his failure to take responsibility for himself and own up to his heart's caprices, even as we pity Giovanni, who has no idea where love will lead him.

And yet David does love Giovanni; we cannot help but believe him on this count. True to form, he attempts to hide his irresistable desire from Hella upon her return, until at last the full horror of his deceit coalesces before her eyes. She has pinned her hopes on him; she wants him to secure for her the life as wife and mother she has come to expect. They leave Paris for the South of France, but as an old adage goes, you can run, but you cannot hide from yourself.

In Nice, while Hella sleeps, David slips away, unable to resist his body's need. He gets blind drunk, hooks up a sailor, and then goes to visit the sailor's friends the next night. They are together two more days and nights until, sitting with the sailor in a crowded gay bar, David looks up into the mirror above the bar and sees Hella's face behind him:

> For a long time we said nothing to each other. I felt the
> sailor staring at both of us.

"Hasn't she got the wrong bar?" he asked me, finally.
Hella looked at him. She smiled.
"It's not the only thing I got wrong," she said.
(CHAPTER 5)

Giovanni's Room is a perfect novel of shame and deceit, the nails inevitably holding together the wood of the closet. It is perfect because it does not flinch, it does not spare itself any grim candor. David's confession is perhaps his one moment of honesty, yet is this enough to redeem him? People usually confess in hopes of absolution, either from simply easing their souls by sharing their horrors with another and freeing them from secrecy, or through the mediation of a priest seeking God's absent benediction. By the time David uncovers a last bit of courage inside himself, and so spills out his truth, there is no one left to forgive him.

No one but his inescapable self.

FIVE QUESTIONS

1. There are plenty of similarities between *Giovanni's Room*'s David and his creator, James Baldwin. Why do you think Baldwin chose to make David a white boy instead of a black man? What could possibly be gained by attempting to obliterate the race element from the novel? What about race with regard to the secondary characters? What assumptions do we make, and are those assumptions valid?

2. Is *Giovanni's Room* a condemnation of life lived in the closet, or does it simply serve as a story acknowledging that the closet exists? Is there anything wrong with a life lived in the closet? Is it possible to be an honest person and maintain a closeted existence? Is it anybody's business, really, how people choose to live their lives and reveal or hide their sexuality? Does society determine whether

an individual lives in the closet or not? Does David have that choice?

3. Is David responsible for Giovanni's fall?

4. Both Kit in *The Sheltering Sky* and Hella in *Giovanni's Room* seem to present themselves as "modern," self-realized women, yet they ultimately depend upon a man to give their lives meaning. Using the text to back up your argument, what does this say about them—how are they similar in this respect, how are they different? If, as we perceive them, they already have distinct identities, what is it they seem to feel is missing? Is this still a contemporary concern? Is it just a concern of women? Is it just a concern of heterosexuals?

5. Is anyone in *Giovanni's Room* an innocent? Who? How? Why? (Use the text to support your argument.)

We Think the World of You

The pane of glass sundered us, as we had been sundered by her these many lonely weeks. Out of reach still, behind it he stood, his clear brown eyes gazing into mine. The collar of his shirt was open, and the tendons of his honey-coloured neck were visible where it joined his shoulders. This warm colour was not sunburn but the natural tint of his flesh; the whole of his smooth, unblemished torso to the flat stomach and narrow waist glowed with it as though bathed in perpetual sunlight. The word Yes rose to my lips, but—

Britisher Joseph Randall Ackerley would first make his literary mark with the fluffy travel memoir *Hindoo Holiday* in 1932, when he was thirty-six. From 1935 to 1959 he served as editor for *The Listener*, a literary journal that regularly published E. M. Forster and Virginia Woolf, and also provided a nurturing home for the budding talents of W. H. Auden and Christopher Isherwood, among others.

A remarkable editor with a penchant for encouraging young writers, Ackerley as author would publish in his lifetime a few poems; a 1923 play based on his experiences as a World War I German POW, *The Prisoners of War;* and, in 1956, the endearing if singularly obsessive *My Dog Tulip,* whose central fondness would find reflection in Ackerley's only novel, *We Think the World of You* (1956).

Its title taken from a phrase bandied about colloquially throughout the novel by its lower-class players, *We Think the World of You* is the story of Frank, an upper-middle-class civil servant, drawn into a relationship he never thought he wanted with the son of Millie, his former cleaning woman. Johnny, described in the excerpt above, is a charmer—and as irresponsible as they come. His wife, Megan, has borne him a litter of children and is pregnant with another at the time Johnny is sent down. Frank and Megan despise each other, but they continue to interact because Frank has told Johnny he will look after his family while he is in jail, and Megan, though proud and devious, can't afford to turn away the help.

At the center of this delightful potpourri of dysfunctionality is Evie, Johnny's magnificent dog, whom Frank reluctantly allows into his life and then finds he cannot bear to be without. In a sense, of course, Evie is a substitute for the love Frank hoped to share with Johnny, a point of transference, a fetish. Or, more purposefully, Evie becomes to Frank and Johnny's relationship what children are to Johnny and Megan's. But all this carries with it the inference that the love Evie and Frank come to share is somehow less than these other types of love—an argument the politically correct might deem "species-ist" but which simply reads as unfair.

A year after Ackerley died, his autobiography, *My Father and Myself,* was published. Though that book has not been without its influence, it is *We Think the World of You* that for the first time carves out in fiction the curious bond many queers have found with animals, whose love—covetous but accepting—is at its best pure devotion.

Allen Ginsberg

Howl and Other Poems

I saw you, Walt Whitman, childless, lonely old
grubber, poking among the meats in the refrigerator
and eyeing the grocery boys.

—"A SUPERMARKET IN CALIFORNIA" (EXCERPT)

Born in Newark, New Jersey, in 1926, Allen Ginsberg was the son of
a poet father and a left-wing Russian immigrant mother. Educated
at Columbia University, he was lucky, as was Lytton Strachey before
him, to be at the center of a creative boom within his culture. What
Bloomsbury was to England—a redefining creative force recasting
morals and art within the greater society—the beat movement
would be to America. It is not too much to say Ginsberg was its
spirit, if Jack Kerouac was its body and William Burroughs its brain.
As Strachey would redefine the way the biography was written in
1918 with his *Eminent Victorians,* so Ginsberg would redefine poetry in 1956 with his *Howl.*

Kerouac, stud-puppet of the beat movement, who was butt-
fucked by Gore Vidal and whose friendship with Neal Casady is a
study in twentieth-century homoerotic homoaffectionalism, gave

Howl its title. And *Howl* is just that, a poetical rant against the injustices of the status quo—including homophobia—a lament resolving itself in a promise.

Ginsberg's other poetry also concerned gay issues, but rendered them universally comprehensible. His "A Supermarket in California," above, echoes Hart Crane's "Cape Hatteras." As with Crane, the old poet and the new eventually touch, and the touch is revelatory, tender. And in "America," Ginsberg, who died in 1997, utters the phrase that drives us still: "America I'm putting my queer shoulder to the wheel."

Certainly, he did, and the result was a startlingly sexy, spiritual body of work that redefined the potential of the gay poetical imagination in the latter part of the twentieth century. Ginsberg took great strides toward fulfilling that potential with his visceral faggot's *Howl.*

James Purdy

Malcolm

"A rrest that pederast!" the man said to the officer. "He attacked me!"

"Sir," Malcolm cried, addressing perhaps his "father" and the police officer together, "oh, sir, I am NOT Mr. Cox . . . I am MALCOLM!"

—"MELBA'S MARRIAGE"

What is going on here?

This can be the only possible response to reading James Purdy's *Malcolm* (1959). As slippery as an eel, existing someplace between allegory and emptiness, *Malcolm* is a book whose meaning—whose very identity—shifts with every rereading. It is a novel of identities as much as *The Sheltering Sky* is. But whose identities are its concern, and toward what end?

James Purdy was born in Chicago but moved to Ohio while still a teenager. He returned to the Windy City for portions of his education at the University of Chicago, also studying at Mexico's University of Puebla. He taught at Lawrence College in Wisconsin from 1949 to 1953, then lived abroad for a while before settling in Brooklyn Heights, New York.

His writing career was never the success that it should have been. In the 1950s he tried to find an American publisher for his first novel, *63: Dream Palace,* but without any luck. The book was published privately in the United States and then by a major publisher in England, where early devotees of his talent included Angus Wilson. *63: Dream Palace* ended with fratricide, and dealt with homosexuality and obsessive love. These proved the discomfiting signature of a talent arguably best spent showing people what it is they'd rather not see, as in his later novels *Eustace Chisolm and the Works* (1967) and *Narrow Rooms* (1978). Perhaps this signature in part accounts for Purdy's inability to realize the success that his trendy but less talented imitators have enjoyed.

Still, not all Purdy's work is in this sociopathic vein. Purdy is also a skilled deployer of the Gothic novel, using the genre to explore the Midwest, where his life was shaped. *The Nephew* (1960), *Jeremy's Version* (1970) and *In the Hollow of His Hand* (1986) are among these. He has also tried his hand at comedy, echoing Ronald Firbank in *Out with the Stars* (1992).

Purdy pursues a realism in his narration and dialogue that allows the events of his stories to completely overwhelm us, perhaps best evinced with *In a Shallow Grave,* an obsessive tale of violence and terror. Purdy is, arguably, a fatalist: Once encountered, love leads to a set end—rarely, if ever, completely happy.

Some of the best younger writers have found Purdy's work challenging but inspirational. Of these, the most successful are probably Paul Russell and Matthew Stadler. (Stadler's second novel, *The Sex Offender,* is especially Purdyesque, as it juxtaposes a plainness of language and narration against a dark, horrific background.)

In addition to novels and short stories, Purdy has published plays and collections of poetry. He has received the National Institute of Arts and Letters Award, as well as a Guggenheim Fellowship, and in 1993 was recognized by the American Academy of

Arts and Letters for his contribution to the artistry of American fiction.

> In front of one of the most palatial hotels in the world, a very young man was accustomed to sit on a bench which, when the light fell in a certain way, shone like gold.
> ("THE BOY ON THE BENCH")

The novel's protagonist is the well-built teenage (fourteen going on fifteen when we meet him) Malcolm, who sits on a bench waiting for a father he has all but given up for dead to return to him. His mother is already dead; his father's death would render him an orphan. Despite how comfortable financially he seems to be—he has been staying at a hotel on his father's credit—from the outset his well-being seems somewhat precarious. Malcolm survives only because he has kept everything in a sort of stasis by patiently waiting on the bench.

Reading *Malcolm,* it is hard to escape the thought that the father Malcolm mourns is God, even though that turns us toward the question of what Malcolm represents: Jesus or man?

Possibly neither. Possibly something else altogether. Possibly just . . . Malcolm. (Nevertheless, as mentioned at the outset, one of the startling things about reading *Malcolm* is trying to decipher Purdy's allegory, all the while never completely sure that there is one.)

Mr. Cox, a possible pedophile, is the force that sets everything in motion, urging Malcolm to leave the bench, to give himself "to life—as an older era said," and, accordingly, providing him with a series of introductions that end up overwhelming Malcolm's existence, disrupting the stasis and propelling the boy down the road of experience that will be his due.

Mr. Cox's first introduction leads Malcolm to the mortician Estel Blanc, a black man, who treats Malcolm to a sort of private cabaret performance, possibly a drag show. The show features Cora

Naldi, platinum-haired, dressed in shawls and racially indistinct. Her performance, coupled with burning incense, the chocolate they eat and the steady murmur of Blanc's voice talking all through Naldi's set, lulls Malcolm to sleep.

Throughout the book, Malcolm reveals himself as something of a narcoleptic, readily lulled to sleep by conversation. In this instance, Blanc must puzzle out whether or not he should take offense—if Malcolm lacks interest because Blanc is black or because he is a mortician.

From Malcolm's perspective, it is neither. Malcolm apologizes profusely, and Blanc eventually attributes the boy's failings to his youth, admonishing him to come back "in twenty years" and ushering him out the door into the arms of a passing policeman.

Malcolm is detained by the police, but we're never really certain why. Is Malcolm carted off because the police are onto Mr. Cox and suspect his relationship with Malcolm to be something more (or less) than providential? Is it because Malcolm has been observed successively in the company of not just pedophiles but Negroes? (For one senses that in Malcolm's world, this is indeed the term the police would use.) Or perhaps we are to understand that *Malcolm* takes place in a racist police state, such as Palestine under Rome.

Regardless, when Malcolm is released from the police station hours later, Blanc is waiting for him with the second of Mr. Cox's introductions, this one to Kermit and Laureen Raphelson:

> "So you"—[Kermit] turned again to Malcolm—"are the boy who is infatuated with his father."
>
> "I?" Malcolm pointed a finger at himself. "Infatuated?"
>
> "Professor Cox has already told us all about you," the midget explained.
>
> "But there's nothing yet to tell." Malcolm protested

against the *all,* which sounded to him both complete and frightening. ("KERMIT AND LAUREEN")

A boy "infatuated with his father"! How queer-Oedipus. Malcolm's patient devotion to his father here takes on a darker edge. But is Malcolm infatuated still, if indeed he ever was? He has, after all, left the bench. He is no longer waiting. It is difficult to say whether he is actively seeking his father in these chance encounters, but certainly, the hope survives, bobbing to the surface now and again at a word, a possibility, a mistaken glimpse. (Also worth considering by the reader: Has Mr. Cox projected such a relationship onto Malcolm and his father as a reflection of his own desires, passing his perception along to those he prepares for the son's arrival?)

At this point Malcolm is propelled by the simple fact that Mr. Cox has taken it upon himself to launch the boy's life as a sort of haphazard comet within his galaxy of acquaintances.

Laureen is blond and plump, and Kermit is something of a midget. Kermit is an artist, with fifteen cats he is devoted to, and as for Laureen:

> "How odd though that Laureen should be a . . . a . . ." Malcolm mused.
>
> "Odd she's a whore?" Kermit yawned. "Well, it's the only thing she ever wanted to be, and why she thought marriage would *straighten* her out, God only knows, especially marriage with me," and he picked up one of his paint brushes and inspected it briefly. "I never thought marriage would *straighten* me out," Kermit went on. ("KERMIT AND LAUREEN")

Determining the sexuality of Purdy's characters is difficult; he prefers offhand references to out-and-out declarations, and so we are left to make what we will of inferences like Kermit's and wait for them to be proved or disproved as Malcolm's journey progresses.

But his first visit to the couple appears to be primarily introductory, setting the stage for his return to their home after Malcolm's brief reunion with Mr. Cox. For Malcolm does indeed visit with Mr. Cox again, learning that the old man is married:

"You mean there is a Mrs. Cox?" Malcolm was thunderstruck, for it had never occurred to him that an astrologer would have a wife.

"Of course," Mr. Cox replied. "Everybody is married, Malcolm. Everybody that counts. And you will have to begin thinking about it, too." ("A SECOND VISIT")

Following this exhortation about marriage—and the growing queer resonance the term "astrologer" is coming to have in Malcolm's understanding—Malcolm, now in possession of a third introduction, again visits with Kermit and Laureen. We find that in the seemingly brief interval since Malcolm's last visit, Laureen has left Kermit. Malcolm reveals he has yet to come to terms with Kermit's being married at all, despite Mr. Cox's admonition. Kermit, meanwhile, suffers his wife's absence by hiring a delectable young gymnast manservant whose every appearance is tinged with a sly eroticism—in a certain light, Malcolm can't be sure the lad is wearing anything at all!

Moments after Malcolm is introduced to the morning servant—O'Reilly Morgan—Kermit sallies forth to contradict Mr. Cox's earlier advice on marriage. It was not marriage that brought him a better life but, rather, marriage's end. After Laureen left him, Kermit says, he "seemed suddenly to have reached my majority in age. I realized that I was beginning life at last. Alone, as everybody is."

So these are the dual possibilities in man's society: alone or married. Is this meant to indicate the options afforded gay men, especially at the time this novel was written, a decade prior to Stonewall? Even Gide married, after all, as did Wilde, and Forster's lover was married.

Already, things have begun to disassemble within the novel—marriages fail, midgets may or may not be gay—and Malcolm's comet begins to gather speed. Next he meets Madame Girard, holding court before her seemingly cowed husband and a virtual chorus of ten "tittering" young men. She has been drinking—is drinking—and accuses Malcolm of being a spy for Mr. Cox. Mr. Girard, in an attempt to change the subject, says that he has heard mention of Malcolm's father. Malcolm is happy—this is his most tangible clue so far to his father's (his lover's?) whereabouts—but his father abandoned him so long ago that Malcolm's desire to find him, though ever-present, has lost its passion.

Perhaps Malcolm represents nothing more than love itself. Could Purdy's argument be that we have jilted love in the twentieth century? Are we the father/lover Malcolm seeks? Is Malcolm a po-mo cupid for the baby-boom age? In some ways, certainly, Purdy's novel resembles another work we've read where love takes center stage: Plato's *Symposium*. In both works a single concern (here, Malcolm; there, love) is viewed from a variety of perspectives, and with resulting, diverse appreciations.

> Malcolm suddenly felt—even as he spoke to Mr. Girard—that the image of his father was slightly blurred in his own memory, and so he sipped the drink of vodka which a servant had just handed him.
>
> "I do not think your father exists," Madame Girard cried, lifting her glass again. "I have *never* thought that he did."
>
> "And what is more"—Madame Girard continued to hold the floor—"*nobody* thinks he exists, or ever did exist."

"That's . . . that's . . . blasphemy . . . or a thing
above it!" Malcolm cried, standing up.

("ADDRESS NO. 3")

Happily, this nastiness soon passes. The alcohol has its effect on
Madame Girard, and she is cooing over Malcolm's beauty and pro-
claiming him royalty, a prince, even as Malcolm is declaring Mr.
Cox a pederast—he heard Kermit refer to Mr. Cox as such, so it
must be so.

Once again, we are nudged to think of Malcolm's father as
God, and Malcolm now assumes a princely role as God's son—
Christ. Which leaves what role for the pederast, for Mr. Cox? Ser-
pent or saint?

There are other literary resonances in addition to the Biblical
similarities throughout the remainder of the book: Girard Girard,
Madame Girard's husband, is revealed as the power behind the
throne, as it were—reminding us of Kit in *The Sheltering Sky* and
Hella in *Giovanni's Room*. Girard Girard decides to leave his wife,
and she is all but destroyed, begging him to let her keep his name,
the name she has come to wear as her identity. This is her
resonance with Kit and Hella: that her façade as an independent
woman results solely from the support she has sought from the
man in her life (in Kit's case, from Port; in Hella's case, from
David).

Girard Girard poses almost as a second father to Malcolm, only
to abandon him, leaving him waiting in the Horticultural Gardens,
with the end result that Malcolm is delivered into the hands of
those who will seal his fate—echoes of Gethsemane and Jesus'
abandonment are ever present.

But for all the arguments in favor of Malcolm as an errant
Christ, there are as many arguments against. Certainly, we've addressed some of the possibilities, and there remain others. Perhaps
Malcolm is actually more like *The Odyssey* than John's Gospel in its
story of a son's search for his father. Perhaps *Malcolm* is nothing

more than a pretty little book with a crepuscular ending, and all this effort to read things into it adds up to a vast chuckle on the part of the author, a joke played upon the reader for the writer's amusement.

If the last is true, then at least we get to share in the laughter. For deciphering *Malcolm* is a large part of the fun of the book—that and reveling in Purdy's beautifully crafted prose. *Malcolm* is readily canonical because of its influence—upon Edmund White's *Forgetting Elena* most noticeably—but even without that, it remains a delightful, perturbing book about ideas, identity and nothing—nothing at all.

FIVE QUESTIONS

1. Is Malcolm believable as a fourteen-year-old boy? Why or why not? What is gained by having such a young protagonist? Is anything lost?

2. Is Purdy attempting to retell the Gospel in *Malcolm*? Why or why not? Compare the last sentence in John's Gospel with the last sentence in *Malcolm*. What other similarities are there? Are there similarities of character as well? (If Laureen is a prostitute, does her role in the book parallel that of Mary Magdalene, etc.?)

3. We mentioned the resonance of Madame Girard with Hella and Kit. Are there other resonances in *Malcolm* with works we have read (in addition to the Gospel), and if so, what are they and how do they manifest themselves? What purpose do they serve? Did Purdy do them intentionally, do you think, or unintentionally? Why?

4. Cats are noticeably deployed throughout *Malcolm*. Kermit has fifteen—including his favorite, Peter—and when Malcolm, naked, gets a tattoo, it is of a panther on his chest. Are there other images that surface with frequency or regularity or purposeful intent in *Malcolm*? What purpose do they serve? Is there any connec-

tion between them, or are their similarities completely accidental? Why?

5. Malcolm's father is as vital a presence in the novel as any other character. His absence inhabits the whole of the work. Yet what do we know of him? Who is Malcolm's father? Is he alive? Is he dead?

Frank O'Hara

Collected Poems

EDITED BY DONALD ALLEN

I feel just like Whitman said you should
and the train burrs and treadles on
diddleydiddleyGREENHORNETdiddleydiddley
—"BILL'S BURNOOSE" (EXCERPT)

Born in Baltimore on June 27, 1926, Francis Russell O'Hara grew up in Grafton, Massachusetts, and was educated in private schools. Like so many other notable poets, he studied music, first as part of his schooling, then privately. Following a two-year stint (1944 to 1946) as a navy sonarman on the destroyer USS *Nicholas,* he enrolled in Harvard as a music major. But he changed the focus of his study to English, receiving his B.A. in 1950. He dabbled in acting, published poems and stories in the Harvard *Advocate* and cofounded the Poets' Theatre in Cambridge. It was during this time that he met and befriended the poet John Ashbery and other notables-to-be, including painter and sculptor Larry Rivers. Ashbery and Rivers would provide for the musician O'Hara a launching into the worlds of literature and art, respectively.

In 1950 O'Hara began graduate studies at the University of Michigan, completing his M.A. in 1951. He won his first major literary prize, the Hopwood Award in Creative Writing, for his manuscript of poems entitled *A Byzantine Place* and a verse play, *Try! Try!* In the fall of that year, O'Hara moved to New York.

New York fueled his life and poetry. He found work in the art industry, holding a series of key positions at the Museum of Modern Art. He wrote important criticism on modern art—his study of Jackson Pollock is considered the standard—and in his vital passion for art as an admirer and enthusiast, and for literature as a creative power, he would echo the formidable Gertrude Stein. Like Stein, he played with language, finding his freedom and poetical models not in the conventional, mundane American poetry of his time but in the verse of French writers, such as the unrestrainable Arthur Rimbaud. In this sense, he was antiliterary, even as his similar passion for the new in art was at times considered antiartistic in conservative circles. He was, poetically, at once Stein, Rimbaud and Marsden Hartley.

In New York, O'Hara developed a vital social circle, stuffed with notables from the worlds of theater, art, music and literature, including Allen Ginsberg. He would often write poetry casually, dashing off a verse here and a verse there, and much of his work survives only because his friends held on to it. He wrote incidental music for plays and continued to dabble in theater and eventually tried his hand at film. O'Hara embodied, in essence, a gargantuan, absorptive, regurgitative hunger for the often-pop culture around him. He ignored boundaries and restrictions, especially when it came to writing about gay sex, and had he not been killed when struck by a speeding dune buggy on Fire Island on July 25, 1966, he might very well have found a way to harness his visual and poetical impulses to become "our" Blake.

Langston Hughes

Selected Poems

D etectives from the vice squad
with weary sadistic eyes
spotting fairies . . .
—"CAFÉ: 3 A.M." (EXCERPT)

James Mercer Langston Hughes was abandoned by his father in 1902, the first year of his life. His father left Joplin, Missouri, for Mexico, and Hughes was raised by his mother, who lived in whatever city she was able to find work, and his maternal grandmother, who lived in Lawrence, Kansas.

There would be no elite private educational academies for young Master Hughes. The African-American lad spent his early adolescence cleaning the lobby and toilets of a hotel near his public school. Despite the opportunities that came his way in later life—he was educated at Columbia University in 1921 and 1922, though he dropped out to travel—Langston Hughes would never forget what it meant to be poor and black in America.

When Hughes returned from his travels in 1926, he entered Lincoln University in Pennsylvania, graduating in 1929. By that time he had published two books of poetry, *The Weary Blues* in 1926 and *Fine Clothes to the Jew* in 1927. Fueled perhaps by the sublimation of his erotic desires, he never stopped writing and publishing, churning out the poetry for which he is best known, as well as fiction, plays, humor, books for children, biographical and autobiographical efforts, historical studies and, even, nine years before his death in New York in 1967, an anthology: *The Langston Hughes Reader.*

As the Midwest fed Inge, poverty and racism fed Hughes—but not his sexuality, at least not dominantly. Hughes admitted to only one homosexual encounter in his lifetime, with a seaman in 1926, and while much of his work is rich with a veiled homoeroticism, and he never married, there is no conclusive evidence Hughes was a lifelong cocksucker.

What is there, then?

Langston Hughes left behind a vast body of work that often lends itself to a homosympathetic reading. But this is all, and in the end the strongest argument for Hughes's homosexuality is that no one, really, seems able to argue otherwise—convincingly. He is canonical, however, for the way African-American queers—Essex Hemphill and Assotto Saint most noticeably—have mined his poetry for their own purposes. Hughes's work has become, rightly or not, the bedrock of black gay poetry in America.

The issue of race within the (Western) Canon would be problematic but for the fact that the Canon itself is not concerned with race. The Canon has predominantly and historically been the playground of the white male for no other reason than that he has traditionally had better access to the very cultural tools that inform the Canon. In part, this is why, as you read through *The Gay Canon,* you might be inclined to mutter, "Huh. Cocteau's wasn't the only white book." But inserting a work into the Canon—Western or Gay—in the name of multiculturalism instead of qualitative merit is simply wrong.

Hughes and James Baldwin, among others, are canonical writers because portions of their work boast Harold Bloom's vaunted "tang of originality." For our purposes, Hughes is canonical because he has provided a sparring partner for the (black) gay writers who follow him and who, in their response, create their own Great Books—to sit, someday, beside his within the Canon.

Joe Orton

The Complete Plays

RANCE: . . . Everything is now clear. The final chapters
of my book are knitting together: incest, buggery, outrageous women and strange love-cults catering for depraved appetites. All the fashionable bric-à-brac. A
beautiful but neurotic girl has influenced the doctor to
sacrifice a white virgin to propitiate the dark gods of
unreason. "When they broke into the evil-smelling den
they found her poor body bleeding beneath the obscene
and half-erect phallus." My "unbiased account" of the
case of the infamous sex-killer Prentice will undoubt-
edly add a great deal to our understanding of such creatures. Society must be made aware of the growing menace of pornography. The whole treacherous avant-garde
movement will be exposed for what it is—an instru-
ment for inciting decent citizens to commit bizarre
crimes against humanity and the state! You have, under
your roof, my dear, one of the most remarkable lunatics
of all time. We must institute a search for the corpse. As
a transvestite, fetishist, bi-sexual murderer Dr. Prentice

displays considerable deviation overlap. We may get
necrophilia too. As a sort of bonus.

—*WHAT THE BUTLER SAW,* ACT II

John Kingsley Orton was born on January 1, 1933, to William and
Elsie Orton in Leicester, England; he was the eldest of five children.
His father was a gardener; his mother, other people's housekeeper.
He was a mediocre student with a theatrical bent. To rid himself of
his working-class accent and a slight lisp, he took elocution lessons
in hopes of bettering his chances at acting. The gambit paid off:
Orton left business school in 1951 when he was admitted to London's Royal Academy of Dramatic Arts. He had auditioned with a
piece from *Peter Pan* that he later recalled as "schizophrenic," for
he played both parts. Like many small-town queers, Orton moved
to the big city and blossomed.

While at RADA he met fellow student Kenneth Halliwell, five
years his senior. They formed an odd couple, if an understandable
one. Orton provided Halliwell with creative youthful energy and a
physically attractive companion, for Orton was pretty much a stud,
British-style, with thick brown hair, an open face, a beguiling smile
and dark, sexually playful eyes. As for Halliwell, he provided Orton
with the education and artistic sensibility Orton had, unknowingly,
always longed for but never found.

By 1953 they were living together as lovers, a relationship that
would last until their deaths.

Their life was not a quiet one. They collaborated on a series of
unpublished novels, after Waugh and Firbank, with titles including
The Mechanical Womb and *The Boy Hairdresser.* They cut out pictures from library books and pasted them on their walls to form a
sort of mural, and defaced other library titles, converting—some
would say perverting—them into pornographic exercises. For this
the young couple were arrested and, on May 15, 1962, sent to

prison for six months. Orton responded well to the time in stir; Halliwell did not. And it is from this point that their divergence— Orton's ascendancy over Halliwell both creatively and personally— can be traced.

Orton used his prison time to write. Publicly classified by society as a "criminal" and shown its underbelly in the bowels of jail, he found himself liberated, with nothing to lose. The result was *The Ruffian on the Stair,* which the BBC bought and broadcast as a radio play within a year of his release from prison.

The rest followed quickly: *Entertaining Mr. Sloane* in 1964; *The Good and Faithful Servant,* written in 1964 but not televised until 1967; *Loot,* a failure in 1965 but a hit in 1966; *The Erpingham Camp,* another television script that aired in 1966; and the play he was revising at the time of his death, *What the Butler Saw.* Bookending these would be a novel he wrote upon his release from prison, *Head to Toe,* and a screenplay he wrote for the Beatles that was never produced, *Up Against It.* Both works were published posthumously, and *Up Against It* found brief resurrection as the title of a 1997 song by the Pet Shop Boys.

Orton's work was to the theater what Frank O'Hara's was to poetry: an enema of pure, innovative spunk. Unapologetically farcical, ridiculing the very society that viewed them, Orton's plays single-mindedly revenged themselves upon the conventions of polite theater. Nothing was unspoken, everything was out in the open— albeit behind a screen of superficial gentility and (perhaps stylistically cribbed from Purdy) a veneer of plain language that proved an effective contrast to the complex mutual manipulations of Orton's characters.

Continually surrounded by signs of his own failure as an artist and of Orton's success, on August 9, 1967, Halliwell bashed in Orton's thirty-four-year-old head with a hammer after the man had gone to sleep; he then took an overdose of sleeping pills. Orton's fabulous diaries, published posthumously, provided the fodder for Stephen Frears's excellent film, *Prick Up Your Ears*. Delicious as the diaries are, they are but ephemera when compared to the testament of Orton's plays, the literary recording of a talent that had no choice but to peak—if indeed it had—at the time of his brutal murder.

Truman Capote

In Cold Blood

B ut then, in the earliest hours of that morning in
November, a Sunday morning, certain foreign sounds
impinged on the normal nightly Holcomb noises—on
the keening hysteria of coyotes, the dry scrape of scut-
tling tumbleweed, the racing, receding wail of locomo-
tive whistles. At the time not a soul in sleeping
Holcomb heard them—four shotgun blasts that, all
told, ended six human lives.

—*IN COLD BLOOD,*
"THE LAST TO SEE THEM ALIVE"

Truman Streckfus Persons—Truman Capote—was a child of the
Big Easy, and it was in a back apartment a block away from Jackson
Square that he wrote his first novel, *Other Voices, Other Rooms.*
Born in New Orleans on September 30, 1924, Capote grew up in
Alabama for the most part. As a young man, he was educated in
New York, which afforded him the opportunity to gather literary
prizes and remain otherwise remarkably unexceptional.

But that was fine with Capote, for literature would feed him for
the rest of his life. He published his first short story, "Miriam," in
Mademoiselle when he was twenty-one; later that year, his "A Tree
of Night" appeared in *Harper's Bazaar.* The next year, Capote

would be noticed by New York's literati, as "Miriam" was selected for the O. Henry Memorial Award.

And the rocket was launched.

At first it was on a promising trajectory. Capote produced a series of remarkable novels: *Other Voices, Other Rooms* in 1948, *The Grass Harp* in 1951, and *Breakfast at Tiffany's* in 1958—the last perhaps most memorable for the film version and the fragile beauty of Audrey Hepburn.

In 1966 Capote published *In Cold Blood*, which originally appeared in *The New Yorker* and concerned a grisly murder in Holcomb, Kansas, the ensuing investigation, and the trial and execution of the killers. Written in a disturbingly still voice, Capote's prose affords us no distance from the material and at times delivers a violence and suspense that are almost unbearable. It remains perhaps the high point of Capote's career and his most bona fide influential work. Its bastard spawn is the "true crime" genre in general, and in particular, the voyeuristic *Midnight in the Garden of Good and Evil* by John Berendt. The recent revelation that Capote may have indulged in a sexual affair with one of the killers during the writing of *In Cold Blood* only heightens the dis-ease with which we read the book. It also serves as a disturbing harbinger of Capote's inability to distinguish boundaries between his work and his life.

After *In Cold Blood*, Capote's celebrity overtook his talent. The rocket imploded. The excesses of the New York party scene turned his wicked witticisms into mere bitchiness, and the last fragment of writing we have from him, an unfinished novel called *Answered Prayers*, is a flaccid attack on his celebrity friends. Its publication in *Esquire* made him persona non grata in the very circles he wrote about and depended upon, not just for material but as his society.

He died just weeks before his sixtieth birthday, on August 25, 1984.

John Rechy

Numbers

Fury is transformed in Johnny into an intense long-ing for sex. Suddenly it swells inside him. He's made it with four people (no: three—he can't count the one who only licked and kissed his body), and he's come twice in quick succession. Yet he longs again for the excitement of the act: for the precious moments when his body poises at the instant of ecstasy and then life surges in orgasm. But it's over so quickly that it's almost as if it exists only in retrospect—or antici-pation.

—CHAPTER 11

El Paso, Texas, native John Rechy studied journalism at Texas Wes-leyan College and at the New School for Social Research. He served in the U.S. Army in Germany before returning to New York, where he began to collect the experiences that would feed most of his early writing. The son of Mexican aristocrats who fled Pancho Villa's purges became a hustler, a prostitute and a drifter. His first novel, *City of Night*, published in 1963, a year before its author turned thirty, was acclaimed for its faithful representation of the life of its unnamed narrator: a hustler, a prostitute and a drifter.

Rechy's next book, published in 1967, was *Numbers*. It is the story of Johnny Rio, an ex-hustler who becomes obsessed with the quantity of his sexual experiences as opposed to their quality. Intimacy is immaterial—all that matters is the newness of yet another man's cock, a fresh notch on the metaphorical bedpost, just another number.

No novel better describes—or, more important, allows the reader to vicariously experience, as all good fiction does—the sexual mindset of many gay men in the late sixties and throughout the seventies. Support systems were few and far between for gay men, even in urban centers. You couldn't express your sexuality through "identity politics"—the option didn't exist. What there was, was core, and primal: sex. Lots of it. If you were a gay man, you probably defined yourself through sex with other men. The act became the conveyance point for identity. Getting laid was the gay agenda, and that was pretty much it.

The simplicity of this has led many to bemoan the passing of the days when sex was free and easy and all that the gay psyche required to justify its existence. There are others who proclaim that the ravages of AIDS, which brought about the extinction of this particular queer cultural dinosaur, incidentally served another purpose: enriching the queer community morally and politically even as it decimated it.

But while gay men (and lesbians) have made political progress in the years since AIDS shifted the gay moral compass to the right, we've lost the simple ability to get lost in a kind of selfish yet selfless sexual immersion. It's impossible, post-AIDS, to treat casual sex cavalierly. At some level—even for those whose denial mechanisms work at full steam—there is a haunting, cadaverous resonance that wasn't present when Rechy wrote his novel of pursuit.

For *Numbers* is a novel of the hunt. Even as the men Johnny Rio has sex with lose their identity, becoming a series of faceless (premonitions of Mapplethorpe) sexual objects, blurring into a mere series of numbers, Johnny himself becomes more solid, his identity increasingly fixed:

I'm a gay man. I fuck.

End of story.

Gore Vidal

Myra Breckinridge

T he novel being dead, there is no point to writing
made-up stories. Look at the French who will not and
the Americans who cannot. Look at me who ought not
. . . Nevertheless, I intend to create a literary masterpiece in much the same way that I created myself, and
for the same reason: because it is not there.

—CHAPTER 17

Eugene Luther Vidal, Jr., spent much of his childhood in Washington, D.C. He was cared for by his scholarly, witty and blind grandfather, Senator Thomas Gore, and Eugene would appropriate his
grandfather's surname as his own badge of identity.

Vidal was born in 1925 at the United States Military Academy
in West Point, New York. His father, an aviation expert, was an
aeronautics instructor there at the time, and would go on to be a
director of air commerce.

Young Vidal was educated at Phillips Exeter Academy, where he
attempted to write a novel about Mussolini. He proved, despite that
ambition, a mediocre student. Instead of going to Harvard when he
graduated at eighteen, he joined the United States Army Reserve
Corps. He would never go to college. Instead, Vidal served overseas
during World War II, rising to the rank of sergeant. The experience

was to provide him with the stuff of his first novel, *Williwaw* (1946).

Gore Vidal was nineteen when it was published.

Williwaw got good reviews, and Vidal moved to Guatemala to concentrate on his writing. But his second novel, *In a Yellow Wood* (1947), and its successor, the blatantly frank homosexual novel *The City and the Pillar* (1948), fared critically worse, although the latter sold well. (His publisher insisted that the book end in a horrific murder, which cheapened the work; in 1968 Vidal was able to revise and publish the novel to his satisfaction.) None of the next five novels he published were successfully received. To make a living, Vidal took a position as a television commentator and also wrote screenplays for MGM. He also wrote teleplays, one of which went on to Broadway as *Visit to a Small Planet* in 1957. He returned to the novel, at last, in 1964 with *Julian*, and the historical form (aping Marguerite Yourcenar, *Julian* is the "autobiography" of that Roman emperor) served him well. Striking closer to home for his next three works, Vidal tackled pieces of the great American myth: *Washington, D.C.* (1967), *Burr* (1973) and, just in time for the centennial, *1876* (1976). They were hugely successful books, becoming number-one bestsellers in the United States and England.

Vidal balanced these sober tomes with indulgent bits of genius he carved out between them, such as *Myra Breckinridge* (1968) and its sequel, *Myron* (1974). The 1981 publication of his novel *Creation* was meant to strike his name forever in the annals of literary history, but it was overshadowed—despite the *New York Times* hailing it as "his best novel"—by 1984's probingly researched and invigoratingly written *Lincoln*, about America's sixteenth President. He followed this up with another American historical novel, *Empire*, in 1987. In 1992 Gore Vidal made his most obvious play to outrage and offend with *Live from Golgotha: The Gospel According to Gore Vidal*, actually a narrative from the perspective of Saul of Tarsus, the man who would become St. Paul. Too eager to be blasphemous, it only irritated where it should have offended and was not the success, or the scandal, he had hoped for. In 1997 he published his dishy memoir, *Palimpest*, wherein he revealed, among other things, that he had laid Jack Kerouac.

Vidal has also published a series of fun mysteries under the pseudonym Edgar Box, as well as plays, short stories and essays. Though he settled in Italy in the 1960s and built a life there with Howard Austen, he is—brilliantly and passionately, if perhaps at times grudgingly—an American. In 1982 he won the American Book Critics Circle Award for criticism for a collection of his non-fiction writing, *The Second American Revolution*. He sporadically nurses theatrical and political ambitions, appearing in sundry films now and then. He first ran for Congress in 1960 and, as the Democratic candidate from upstate New York, received the most votes of any Democrat in fifty years, though he still lost handily. From 1970 to 1972 he served as cochairman of the People's Party. He once suffered through a personal, vitriolic debate with William F. Buckley. In 1982 he attempted to follow in his grandfather's footsteps and ran for U.S. Senator, albeit in California. In the Democratic primary for that election, he received a half million votes and finished second out of nine. It wasn't good enough.

> Myra Breckinridge is a dish, and never forget it, you moth-erfuckers, as the children say nowadays. (CHAPTER 2)

Who is Myra Breckinridge? She is, by all accounts (most especially her own), a statuesque woman. She is, also by her own proclamation, the New Woman, not to be owned by man, not to be ruled by man, but always to conquer. She is arguably one of the most indomitable personalities to emerge from the world of letters in the twentieth century, if not ever. Her novel—for it is hers, absolutely—is a triumph of comedy and some of the sexiest writing you'll ever read.

What else is there to know about Myra Breckinridge? She has arrived in Los Angeles from the East; she lives in an apartment

opposite the Chateau Marmont on the Sunset Strip. She has "studied the classics (in translation) at the New School, the contemporary French novel on my own, and I learned German last year in
order to understand the films of the Thirties when UFA was a force
to be reckoned with" (Chapter 5). She has been in love with the
movies ever since she was a child.

This led first to a crush on Lana Turner while Myra was but a
small girl. Soon enough, however, Myra's lesbian impulses happily
converted themselves into passionate desires for the actor James
Craig.

Myra presents herself as the spouse of one Myron Breckinridge,
"who drowned last year while crossing over to Staten Island on the
ferry " (Chapter 6) and who was sole heir to half a piece of property in Westwood that has been managed and developed by his
uncle, Buck Loner, a former movie cowboy gone to fat. In Myron's
absence, the property falls to Myra.

Loner—whose tape recordings form interspersed sections of
the book, and who refers to Myron without affection as that
"fag"—has established the Academy of Drama and Modeling, a
huge success with an enrollment of thirteen hundred young men
and women, some of whom live on campus but most of whom are
dispersed through the greater Los Angeles area. Myra wants Buck to
buy her interest in the Westwood property, and while the lawyers
haggle, Buck offers her a job teaching Posture and Empathy—"the
Sign Kwa Known [*sine qua non*] of the art of film acting"—at the
academy.

Myra accepts.

In the posture class I was particularly struck by one of the
students, a boy with a Polish name. He is tall with a great
deal of sand-colored curly hair and sideburns; he has pale
blue eyes with long black lashes and a curving mouth . . .
From a certain unevenly rounded thickness at the crotch
of his blue jeans, it is safe to assume that he is marvelously

hung. Unfortunately he is hot for an extremely pretty girl with long straight blonde hair (dyed), beautiful legs and breasts, reminiscent of Lupe Velez. She is mentally retarded. When I asked her to rise she did not recognize the word "rise" and so I had to ask her "to get up" which she did understand. (CHAPTER 8)

The young man is named Rusty, and the woman Mary-Ann, and the two of them will form the centerpiece of Myra's grand scheme—"the destruction of the last vestigial traces of traditional manhood in the race in order to realign the sexes, thus reducing population while increasing human happiness and preparing humanity for its next stage" (Chapter 10), acted out in miniature upon this Southern California set.

Myra's plan is to divide and conquer. Rusty she torments in posture class, afforded the opportunity to pick on him mercilessly, thanks to the asymmetrical expediency of an old football injury that never healed properly. Mary-Ann she befriends. Myra begins to schedule private sessions with Rusty, in their first go-round getting him to go so far as to strip, under the pretense of examining him for a brace. She talks to him, her voice low, and pulls his pants down to his knees until he is, at last, naked. He cries out, but doesn't say a word in protest.

Even as Uncle Buck hammers away at her past via his lawyers, in hopes of disproving her claim, Myra reveals that Myron had a penchant for rough trade. In her words, Myron was "a tormented creature, similar to Hart Crane, except that while it was Crane's kick to blow those sailors he encountered along the squalid waterfronts of that vivid never-to-be-recaptured prewar world, Myron invariably took it from behind" (Chapter 18).

Myron's favorite pasttime was finding poor (literally) straight men and getting them to have sex with him for money. The greater their degradation, the greater Myron's thrill. The ultimate high was to have them penetrate him.

Myra dotes on the popular conceit that, in fucking, it is the bottom who actually has all the power, while the top is simply deluded into thinking the power is his. For Myra, the best sex only happens when each person involved thinks he has mastery over the other. She gives a vivid example of the sailor getting blown by a drag queen. The sailor thinks he has triumphed in getting the queen to suck his dick; the queen thinks "she" has triumphed by getting the sailor to succumb to her charms, stealing from him what the sailor meant to spend in a woman. The passage also serves up a singular harbinger of Rusty's fate:

> Much of my interest in the capture of Rusty is the thought that he is so entirely involved with Mary-Ann. That gives value to what I mean to seize. If it were freely offered, I would reject it. Fortunately, he hates me which excites me and so my triumph, when it comes, will be all the sweeter.
> (CHAPTER 18)

Is Myra just some "ho" out to steal another girl's guy? The answer, emphatically, is *no*. Myra's pursuit is almost wholly anthropologically driven. It is not so much Rusty but what Rusty represents—the ur-male—that Myra wants to "seize." Mary-Ann, by default, becomes the complement, the ur-woman, yet a passive type that Myra is eager to subvert, moving the male into the passive position, liberating Woman to achieve aggressive parity with Man.

Deep thoughts for such a bitchy book. But that's part of the fun of *Myra Breckinridge*: As relentlessly comic and sexy as it is (Rusty is perhaps the most arousing vision to appear in gay letters since Ishmael and Queequeg bunked off in *Moby-Dick*), it's also relentlessly smart.

Myra's plans progress. Although Rusty has previously made it clear that he is to be the "star" in his and Mary-Ann's future family, Myra sees to it that Mary-Ann gets the first break with an agent, edging her career forward as Rusty's stalls. Over dinner with the couple, Myra hammers away at their idea of having children in a discussion about world overpopulation; having cut away at Rusty's male ego by making Mary-Ann the anticipated breadwinner, Myra is now after his *cojones,* metaphorically sterilizing him. Eventually, his ego battered and weakened, this leads to what it must: another private session, and a more thorough examination, under the pretext of a school physical. This time, Myra is bolder. Having him naked will not satisfy; she must go further.

She finger-fucks him.

This is just the beginning, though, of the seduction and rape through which "Myra Breckinridge achieved one of the great victories for her sex" (Chapter 29). Yet it is also the beginning of the second arc of the book, in which things giddily spin out. Uncle Buck presses forward with his investigation into Myra's past, uncovering the fact that not only is Myra's wedding certificate all but impossible to track, but so is her birth certificate; Myra shatters Mary-Ann and Rusty's relationship, driving Rusty toward stardom and Mary-Ann into the arms of . . . Myra?

Myra Breckinridge is a tour de force, a superb, simultaneous attack on, and defense of, America's divergent sexual mores. It is a book about what it means to be a man, what it means to be a woman and what it means to surpass the limits of the gender society ascribes to you—and how those limits seductively travel down to us via films. It is brilliant, boasting the best two-sentence chapter ever; a book that shocks you even as it turns you on, even as it makes you laugh out loud. It is a testament to the power of the gay imagination, perhaps its manifesto.

FIVE QUESTIONS

1. Is sexuality fluid?
2. What is the moral of *Myra Breckinridge?*

3. Are Rusty and Mary-Ann better or worse off after Myra whirls into their lives? Why?

4. What are your feelings toward Myra Breckinridge? Do you envy her? Despise her? Why? (Try to base your response on the text as much as possible.)

5. *Myra Breckinridge, Confessions of a Mask,* and *Our Lady of the Flowers* (among others) all deal with issues of gender as costume. How do they differ in approach, goal and execution? Is one of them more effective than the others in realizing the fulfillment of its ambition—in confronting the mutability of gender, perhaps even arguing its arbitrariness? Is gender arbitrary? Is gender—in some sense psychologically, perhaps, and given what we've just read, even physically—a choice?

Ursula K. Le Guin

The Left Hand of Darkness

And I saw then again, and for good, what I had always been afraid to see, and had pretended not to see in him: that he was a woman as well as a man. Any need to explain the sources of that fear vanished with the fear; what I was left with was, at last, acceptance of him as he was. Until then I had rejected him, refused him in his own reality. He had been quite right to say that he, the only person on Gethen who trusted me, was the only Gethenian I distrusted. For he was the only one who had entirely accepted me as a human being: who had liked me personally and given me entire personal loyalty: and who therefore had demanded of me an equal degree of recognition, of acceptance. I had not been willing to give it. I had been afraid to give it. I had not wanted to give my trust, my friendship to a man who was a woman, a woman who was a man.

—CHAPTER 18, "ON THE ICE"

Born on October 21, 1929, in Berkeley, California, Ursula Kroeber was the daughter of the writer Theodora Kroeber and the anthropologist Alfred Kroeber. She attended college at Radcliffe and Columbia; in 1951 she married the historian Charles A. Le Guin in Paris. They made a home in Portland, Oregon, and raised three children.

She has managed through sheer literary skill to be that rarest of all things: a genre writer—the genre being science fiction—who is taken seriously in literary circles. She has done this by bringing to bear the best attributes of each of the three influences that surrounded her in her life: her father's work as an anthropologist, her mother's work as a writer and her husband's passion for history.

In 1970 she won both the Hugo Award and Nebula Award for Best Science Fiction Novel of the Year for *The Left Hand of Darkness.* It was feat she would repeat, becoming the first to do so, in 1975 with *The Dispossessed.* Her work has not all been directed toward the adult science fiction market; she has also written fantasy novels and books for children.

Le Guin is a great writer because she lets her passions—artistic and political—inform but not overwhelm her work. In *The Left Hand of Darkness,* we are given a wonderful novel that is part adventure story, part social fable. Like many great novels, it has everything: palace intrigue, war between nations, creation mythology and, at its core, a discomfiting examination of love's ties to gender. This is accomplished via the Gethenians, who are humans, androgynous, generally sexually neutral, but susceptible for a few days each month to an intense rutting fervor, during which time they may become either male or female. We are guided in our contemplation of this mutability by the narrator, the Terran envoy Mr. Ai, his purpose on Gethen being to visit the two major warring nations, Karhide and Orgoreyn, and determine whether either of them is ready to join the Ekumen, a loosely theologically unified sort of interstellar confederation.

Although Le Guin, in the years since the novel's writing, has lamented that *The Left Hand of Darkness* carries too heavy a heterosexual bias, it remains a testament to the power of speculative fiction to bring us face to face with our own prejudices and thoughtless preconceptions, and to examine them fully. It is perhaps the other side of the queer sexual coin that has as one side Rechy's *Numbers,* and indeed, both share a similar central concern.

At the heart of *The Left Hand of Darkness* is the deceptively simple concept of desire. Yet while Rechy—an active participant in the all-too-human rush to set boundaries and place labels (to extrapolate for a moment, ask yourself about the importance of "gay," "queer," "bisexual" and "straight," for example, and whether you use those labels to define or limit your possibilities)—uses desire to narrow his potential, Le Guin charts her course where labels are of no use: the tidal, insistent fluidity of the heart; love.

Pier Paolo Pasolini

Poems

SELECTED AND TRANSLATED BY NORMAN
MACAFEE WITH LUCIANO MARTINENGO

Those no longer among us!
Lifted, with their innocent youth,
by a new breath of history, to other lives!
—"A DESPERATE VITALITY," SECTION 3, VERSE 1

Pier Paolo Pasolini published his first book of poems when he was twenty. They were written in the dialect of Friuli, the region of Italy where he grew up, in the town of Casara della Delizia, his mother's birthplace. Four years earlier, when Pasolini was sixteen, he had been introduced to the works of Arthur Rimbaud. It was an introduction that paved the way for the unleashing of Pasolini's nascent artistic comprehension of poetry's ability to speak the unspeakable—politically and sexually—and get away with it. He was educated at Bologna, where he had been born on March 5, 1922.

During World War II, Pasolini worked primarily as a teacher. (He was drafted into the army for a week, from September 1 to 8, 1943.) His twenty-year-old brother, Guido, was slaughtered by a Communist faction in 1945. Despite this, Pasolini signed on as a Communist shortly after his brother's death, remaining in the party until 1949, when he was expelled after his arrest for "corruption of minors and obscene acts in a public place." (On September 30 of that year he had met up with three boys and disappeared into the bushes with them, ostensibly to cavort.) Suspended from his job, his family in tatters after the war, in 1950 Pasolini moved to Rome, where his literary career began to flourish.

In part, this was because he took great inspiration from the young boys that prowled Rome's streets, most of them hustlers and petty thieves. The edge of danger he felt in their company pleased him, and he courted this risk as often as possible. Later, some of them would make appearances in his films.

In 1955 he published his first novel, *The Ragazzi*, and in 1959, *A Violent Life*. They were two parts of a projected trilogy that would never be completed. Pasolini's lust for street boys—and for the boys' capacity for sex and violence without regret—scandalized a Rome that, working in the shadow of the Catholic Vatican and Communist Moscow, demanded a happy, wholesome veneer of respectability to preserve order.

As a result of his renegade celebrity, Pasolini was drawn into Rome's intellectual and artistic community, where he was introduced to select filmmakers. He worked on screenplays, then quickly moved on to directing; his first film, *Accattone*, premiered in 1961. But his most notable film may have been his last, *Salo* (1975), in which the dying days of Italian fascism are recast within the Marquis de Sade's *The 120 Days of Sodom*.

It is impossible to compartmentalize Pasolini's passions. He gives a visceral purpose to Rimbaud's rebellious refusal to be contained. His political anger fuels his sexual outrage, which in turns fires his creative powers in hopes of releasing fury and sperm—his poems, his novels, his films. Although his anger finds a parallel in Joe Orton's plays, it is directed not against a class but against an ideology, and firmly establishes itself as the queer, shouted poetic response to that repression, paving the way for Paul Monette and other queer warrior poets that followed.

Early on the morning of November 2, 1975, Pasolini was murdered by a street hustler he'd picked up at Rome's central station and driven out to a secluded beach at Ostia. As he was an artist whose work continually challenged the authority of the brutal powers-that-be, conspiracy theories have swarmed about his death like flies on a corpse, but there is no conclusive evidence to suggest that any such theories are plausible. Pasolini died as he lived, chasing his desire on the razor's edge promised by the young tough kids he befriended and solicited for sex.

W . H . A u d e n

Collected Poems

EDITED BY EDWARD MENDELSON

. . . but round your image
there is no fog, and the Earth
can still astonish.
—"SINCE," VERSE 4 (EXCERPT)

Wystan Hugh Auden was born in York, England, in 1907 to an upper-middle-class family, his father a physician and his mother a nurse. They encouraged in their third son a love for Norse mythology, as well as scientific, religious and musical interests. He was educated at Gresham's School, Holt, and Christ's Church, Oxford, from which he received his B.A. in 1928. He spent the next year in Berlin, enjoying the cabaret nightlife of the Weimar Republic.

In 1938 he married Erika Mann, Thomas Mann's daughter. The never-consummated marriage gave her a British visa that enabled her to flee Nazi Germany. Auden spent the 1930s writing from a counter-Nazi, far-Left standpoint, but became disillusioned with the failure of his politics in action. Auden emigrated to the United States with Christopher Isherwood in January 1939. In 1946 the two men became American citizens.

Foreshadowing Isherwood's later lifelong relationship with

Don Bachardy (who was eighteen when they met), shortly after Auden's arrival in New York he found himself in love with Brooklyn's eighteen-year-old Chester Kallman. Though their relationship would be troubled—usually because Kallman couldn't bring himself to be monogamous—it would last Auden the rest of his life. (Auden died in their shared Vienna home on September 29, 1973.)

Auden taught sporadically throughout his life, at one time appointed an associate professor at the University of Michigan, and then tapped to serve as professor of poetry at Oxford University in 1956. This was the same year Auden converted to Anglicanism, for he shared Isherwood's desire for spiritual progress and fulfillment, albeit not so exotically.

Auden's poetical voice shifted through the years, a fact he acknowledged by his continued revision of even published poems and by his public disownment of a few of his earliest works that had reached print. His natural voice was fed by a religious sensibility and by a restrained, sentimental approach to love that resulted in tender pieces such as "Since," (quoted above), which is about memories, brought on suddenly, of a relationship welded solid over time. He was concerned with the union of sex and spirit, and with the place of the poet in the modern world.

A part of that concern involved being in the world, and many of Auden's poems reflect a bawdy sarcasm or fresh amusement at life's misadventures and the preening of others, as well as a simple honesty about the less poetic moments of desire:

Loneliness waited
For Reality
To come through the glory-hole.
("SYMMETRIES & ASYMMETRIES," VERSE 44)

All these concerns come into play in the shaping of his body of work, a vast corpus that shows a stunning capability to spin from intellectual appeals to the simplest truth. Ranging as it does from the most epic of concerns to the most intimate, Auden's voice as we consume his *Collected Poems* is the bedrock tone of modern poetry, plainly beautiful even when addressing otherwise inelegant moments. His work is the simultaneous challenge and support new poets—particularly new queer poets—must confront as they seek their own path, to carve out something wholly new, wholly canonical.

THE AGE

OF

CHAOS

Gordon Merrick

The Lord Won't Mind

"**B**ut you don't understand," Peter burst out. "I've got another guy. I love him, dammit."

"You mean—"

"I don't know what I mean." The tears he had been struggling against since the night before welled up once more. Once more, he struggled against them, and this time he lost. They gushed from him. He clung to the planks of the bridge and arched his neck back and opened his mouth and gave vent to the torment within him. He felt Charlie's arm around him. He felt his mouth on his hair. He was seized with a fit of trembling that shook him from head to foot. He bowed his head and choked and gasped. Slowly his body went slack as Charlie held him with both arms, pressing him close, spreading kisses through his hair.

"I'm a silly little faggot," Peter gasped when he could speak. A little spurt of laughter burst from him. "What'll people think?"

"I don't care if the whole world sees. I love you."

Gordon Merrick was a soldier in World War II, and those experiences informed his first novel, *The Strumpet in the Wind*. He wrote other novels, but he will be best remembered for *The Lord Won't Mind*. Published in 1970, it was a *New York Times* bestseller for sixteen weeks and spawned two subsequent volumes concerning the misadventures of its white-bread protagonists, Peter Martin and Charlie Mills: *One for the Gods* and *Forth into Light*.

Merrick's romantic life in some ways could be said to mimic that of his characters—he enjoyed a thirty-two-year relationship. As his novels traveled the globe, so did Merrick, dividing his time between homes in the Greek Isles and Paris. He died of lung cancer in Sri Lanka in 1988, but lived long enough to see his work become simultaneously beloved and despised by the gay culture still aborning as *The Lord Won't Mind* first hit the stands.

In its mass-market paperback edition, the book enjoyed deliciously lurid covers that weren't explicit in a pornographic sense so much as they were wholly and unabashedly queer. They were an exercise in subversion, and as such reflected the contents of the pages within. Taking its cue from the popular women's romance novels of the period—trashy, sexually fabulous tomes featuring a buxom, wasp-waisted babe on the cover together with her muscle-bound stud, neither one able to keep his or her clothing from simply slipping away—*The Lord Won't Mind*'s jacket gave us two well-built WASP-y boys, just about to hold hands, looking into each other's eyes with rapt adoration. Inside, the text was no less yummy.

The Lord Won't Mind is essentially a love story. Plotwise, it is relatively unhinged, indulging itself as it flies from plot twist to plot twist, in pursuit of the yearning, ever-burning question: Will Peter and Charlie stay together?

Really, could there be any doubt?

The result of all this is a wondrous confection of overwritten prose, deftly straddling the genres of popular fiction and erotica. Though later titles in the series lost steam, *The Lord Won't Mind* remained that most timeless of all things: the perfectly told love story, surrendering its heroes to passion's convulsions and taking us, the readers, along with them.

People love to hate this book because it spurns pretensions to high art. But that's precisely how *The Lord Won't Mind* manages to leap over more ambitious works, quickly forgettable in their sameness, and remain perfectly canonical: wholly familiar, yet startlingly strange and new.

Michel Tournier

The Ogre

TRANSLATED BY BARBARA BRAY

E tienne and I parted at the exit, and probably I
shall never see him again. When that thought occurred
to me I had a little silent sob in my throat, but I know
for certain, with knowledge from an infallible, impera-
tive source, that it is not for me to enter into individual
relationships with this child or that. What would such
relationships be, anyway? I think they would inevitably
follow the facile beaten tracks of either paternity or
sex. But my vocation is higher and more general. To
have only one child is not to have any. To lack one is to
lack them all.

—"SINISTER WRITINGS OF ABEL TIFFAUGES,
NOVEMBER 4, 1938"

Michel Tournier was born in Paris in 1924. He studied philosophy,
but began his literary career as a journalist. *The Ogre* won France's
most prestigious literary award, the Prix Goncourt, upon its publication in 1970.

The substance of the book is well indicated by its dedication:
"To the slandered memory of Staretz Grigory Yefimovitch Raspu-

tin, healer of the Tsarevitch Alexis, murdered for his opposition to the 1914 war."

Rasputin is popularly remembered as something of a monster, a sexual predator. That this reputation owes little to fact and much to the dissemination of misinformation by the ardent enemies of the last Czar of Russia is exactly the kind of truth Tournier hopes to play with in *The Ogre*. In his novel, Tournier contrasts the words of his once-married protagonist, Abel Tiffauges, with those who see in him, instead of the lover Tiffauges himself envisions, an ogre.

Without attempting to pursue the transgressive cliché in the literary sense, *The Ogre* is all the more successful in its ambition. It slides us along the knife edge of perception and guilt, thrusting light into the shadows of pat assumptions and asking us to consider what is commonly deemed ugly as beautiful. Despite having been written almost thirty years ago, it is a thoroughly contemporary novel, especially in Tiffauges' obsession with the serial killer Weidmann. Upon seeing the murderer led to the guillotine, Madame Eugénie, a boarder in Tiffauges' home he finds difficult to reject, calls out to Abel, "But, Monsieur Tiffauges, he's just like you! Anyone would think he was your brother! He's like you, Monsieur Tiffauges, exactly like you!"

The Ogre is a study of Tiffauges' slow descent into the belly of order as the Nazis come to power, and his possible redemption, not through contrived means but by means wholly natural to such a man, a monster.

But what is a monster? *The Ogre* enmeshes itself in a tangle of moral perplexities, and so asks us to address not the safe banality of evil but its insidious, multilayered nature. We like to trivialize evil, to make it a function of extremists, to distance our lives from its effect. Tournier won't allow us that delusional luxury.

What is the evil in pederasty? At what age can one be a pederast? What is the evil in fascism? What is acceptable to society on a massive public scale may be reprehensible in more intimate moments, and the reverse may also be true. Abel (in Genesis, Adam's son, murdered by his brother, Cain) Tiffauges is not an innocent serving as a conduit for the moral play of man and society. He is a complex human being, as we are, and this makes his indulgence of our darkest thoughts all the more compelling. They are irrevocably and so clearly a part of him, his—our, we must at last admit—most basic nature. At last it is Tiffauges himself who shows us by his example the only way to truly escape the black horror in our hearts, which only completes the perversity of this wonderful, dangerously erotic novel.

Compulsively readable, *The Ogre* is at once corrupting and hopeful. An international bestseller when published, it continues to exercise a wide yet immediate influence over some of the bestselling French writers of today. Michel Tournier's *The Ogre* is genuinely brave, a remarkably discomfiting achievement.

William S. Burroughs

The Wild Boys: A Book of the Dead

"There are many groups scattered over a wide area from the outskirts of Tangier to the Blue Desert of Silence . . . glider boys with bows and laser guns, roller-skate boys—blue jockstraps and steel helmets, eighteen inch bowie knives—naked blowgun boys long hair down their back a kris at the thigh, slingshot boys, knife throwers, bowmen, bare-hand fighters, shaman boys who ride the wind . . . boys skilled in bone-pointing and Juju magic who can stab the enemy reflected in a gourd of water . . . desert boys shy as little sand foxes, dream boys who see each other's dreams and the silent boys of the Blue Desert."

—"THE WILD BOYS"

William Burroughs is perhaps most famous for his novels *Junky* (1953) and *Naked Lunch* (1959), the latter adapted into a film by

David Cronenberg in 1991. He published *Junky* under the pseudonym William Lee; Bill Lee is the protagonist of *Naked Lunch* and of the Burroughs' 1985 novel, *Queer.*

Burroughs was born in St. Louis, Missouri, in 1914 and educated at Harvard. He spent much of his life abroad, most notably in Paris and Tangier. Burroughs palled around with Allen Ginsberg and Jack Kerouac, and with them shaped the language of the beat movement in the sixties. His writings echo those of his friends and vice versa. And, like Kerouac certainly, much of Burroughs' work dovetails neatly with the other work he produced— indeed, is part of the same, ongoing narrative stream. Burroughs writes from the vast storehouse of his life, from which there emerge many stories, all sharing similar points of reference and evocation.

Perhaps the keenest point of reference, the seminal spark of his entire literary output, is lined most clearly in Burroughs' own 1985 introduction to *Queer:*

> . . . the book is motivated and formed by an event which is never mentioned, in fact is carefully avoided: the accidental shooting death of my wife, Joan, in 1951 . . . I am forced to the appalling conclusion that I would never have become a writer but for Joan's death, and to a realization of the extent to which this event has motivated and formulated my writing. I live with the constant threat of possession, and a constant need to escape from possession, from Control.

The story is that Burroughs shot his wife while they were horsing around, doing a "William Tell" routine in which he endeavored to shoot objects off her head.

Self-confessed killer, addict and reluctant faggot, Burroughs put his life in his work. It was all fodder for his paper confessionals, the books that shelter his sins. Yet these are confessions intoxicated with imagination, a drunken fever contagious in the case of *The Wild Boys,* his provocative novel from 1971.

Burroughs' gay contagion of the imagination—in a parallel shockingly similar to the history of HIV—lay mostly dormant before the onset of the 1980s. Then, Dennis Cooper became its most notable scribe. "Transgressive" literature found not only its name but its voice and its forum. This period launched a spate of novels (from Cooper and others), anthologies (notably *High Risk* and *High Risk 2,* edited by Amy Scholder and Ira Silverberg, and *Discontents,* edited by Cooper) and even a publishing imprint (High Risk Books, which closed in 1996 after a ten-year run).

But what is transgressive literature? If we can argue that Burroughs' work is a direct spawn, consciously or unconsciously, of writers such as Yukio Mishima, who was capable of producing in the reader's mind images of startling sensual power and clarity (as in *Patriotism),* and Arthur Rimbaud, who ignored the boundaries set by polite society as to what was poetical subject matter and what was not (as in his sonnet "To the Asshole," which he wrote with Paul Verlaine), then what did Burroughs spawn?

Answering this question requires answering two others: What was the transgressive literature of the 1980s, and is there such a thing as transgressive literature in the 1990s?

If there is a definitive transgressive novel, it is Dennis Cooper's *Frisk,* published in 1991. Like Burroughs, Cooper reworked similar themes—men who love boys, and who also love to dissect them, emotionally and physically—in each of his novels. This produced an intriguing cumulative result for the reader: a work that was continually refining itself. For the writer, it appeared to be a process of ever more skillful evisceration. Indeed, as Cooper progressed, he collated the individual novels into a series of five. Each of the books (*Closer, Safe, Frisk, Try, Guide)* held mostly different characters and essentially different stories, but boasted ever-better deployment of similar techniques and stylistic choices—techniques and choices picked up cleanly from the pages of Burroughs, including the novelist as fictional protagonist. In *Frisk,* for example, one of the key players is a writer named Dennis:

> He licked Chretien's hole, inside out, nostalgically, almost religiously. "I . . . love . . . you," he said, not really able to help it, but smearing the words so Chretien and I couldn't hear, because it wasn't true. Then he leaned back. I guzzled awhile. Chretien rubbed his cock lazily, eyes flitting about the room. "What are you thinking, kid?" Julian asked. Chretien peered between his splayed legs. "About . . . um, you both, and me." That voice. Ugh. ". . . How I feel like myself with you," he added. Whatever that means, Julian thought. "And you, Dennis?" I unplugged my tongue. It was muddy. "Not much. Good. Great, even . . . mm . . ." My mouth squashed on the hole.

This defined transgressive writing at its nadir: men having sex with boys, murder and evisceration. The thrill—which defter transgressive writers like Cooper acknowledged in parody within their own work—was speaking the unspeakable: incest, fucking Christ, the rape of children, graphically detailed rimming turned to the eating of excrement, mutilations of people and animals, blood and semen, piss and spit, violence in sex. Transgressive literature sought to strip away the boundary that created the banned-books category of "obscenity." (This charge banned Burroughs' *Naked Lunch* upon its release, for its frank depiction of an addict's life, and its condemnation of an inherently addictive society for turning its back on and denigrating the true, chemical addict.)

Yet arguably, few writers other than Cooper managed to pull off transgressive literature, leaving transgressive juvenilia as the bulk of the work available for consideration. Transgressive literature burned itself out; as with the beat movement, its best writers— Cooper, Eric Latzky, David Wojnarowicz—were absorbed into the mainstream. In a perverse way, their mission was accomplished, yet society's mission was accomplished as well: If you absorb what is transgressive, you dilute it of any power it might have had.

And power is the issue. For whoever has power has Control. Burroughs sought to escape that Control all his life, and his continually imaginative, inventive work reflects that drive and desire. Rather than escape, transgressive writing sought to force open the limitations or subvert the criteria of Control. It did not seek to leave the playing field as much as it sought to change the rules by which the game was played. As such, transgressive work to date is notable only because it is derivative, and not canonical like Burroughs, because it sees his work as less of a challenge than a toolshed.

If there is a transgressive literature for the 1990s or beyond, it will be wholly new, and perhaps raised up by those authors who *have* read in the work of Burroughs a challenge: Stephen Beachy, Scott Heim and Matthew Stadler most notably.

They are the Wild Boys.

The camera is the eye of a cruising vulture flying over an area of scrub, rubble and unfinished buildings on the outskirts of Mexico City . . .

Close to the ground we see the shadow of our wings, dry cellars choked with thistles, rusty iron rods sprouting like metal plants from cracked concrete, a broken bottle in the sun, shit-stained color comics, an Indian boy against a wall with his knees up eating an orange sprinkled with red pepper. *(THE WILD BOYS, "TÍO MATE SMILES")*

The Wild Boys is a novel that is initially transgressive in form, making the reader ask, Is it a book or a film? What Burroughs manages is to secure the reader's visual imagination, from which he assembles his story. He wants us to encounter it as though we were watching it. He wants us not simply to understand but to see:

> Unexpected rising of the curtain can begin with a Dusenberg moving slowly along a 1920 detour. Just ahead Audrey sees booths and fountains and ferris wheels against a yellow sky. A boy steps in front of the car and holds up his hand. He is naked except for a rainbow colored jock strap and sandals. ("THE PENNY ARCADE PEEP SHOW")

Slowly, visually, we encounter Burroughs' story of a gang of Wild Boys—*The Lord of the Flies* gone punk, pigs' heads replaced with boy-cum and fucking that is magic and power. Midway through the book, another clue edges in toward Burroughs' accomplishment:

> Tonight Reggie and I had dinner with the Great Slastobitch and he expounded a new look in blue movies. "The movies must first be written if we are to have living characters. A writer may find it difficult to make the reader see the scene clearly and it would seem easier to show pictures. No. The scene must be written before it is filmed."
> ("A SILVER SMILE")

If *The Wild Boys* is a movie, is it a blue movie, a porn film? Is Burroughs attempting to recast pornography as art, the sex film as literature?

He sets up a vignette involving an older boy, Kiki, whose young cousin has just come to visit from the country. Kiki wonders from the start if the younger boy will let Kiki have sex with him. They go to a movie; they smoke pot. The kid laughs so hard he pisses on himself and then strips off the soaked pants. Kiki tickles the boy. The boy gets hard. Kiki greases the boy's ass and fucks him ten strokes; they come together. And then:

Unexpected rising of the curtain can begin with the apartment building lonely young face in the hall standing under
a dusty name . . .   ("A SILVER SMILE")

Using repetition of language to tie key moments together; disorienting the reader in time through references to the 1920s and,
moments later, to spaceships; ever ready to give itself over to whim-
sical or brutal digression, *The Wild Boys* is a cumulatively building
work, adding layer upon layer: Audrey and then John and boys who
come in "ten strokes"; sex and war and magic and dance. Burroughs is the creative anthropologist, exploring a world of his own
making, comparing it at times with our own world through the
juxtaposition of caricatures and historical memory—time periods
such as the 1920s, events such as war—and the universality of
sex.

As Burroughs adds layers of vision and work, a narrative
emerges of a pack of Wild Boys, their culture and their conflict with
the world of men in power, men who substitute sexual urgings for
violent desires: war and bloodshed. Burroughs questions the valid-
ity of established power—through conventional means such as CIA
espionage parody—and contrasts it with the boys' power, found in
sex (magic). Burroughs returns to familiar desires and themes, the
escape from Control among them, and creates a work that resonates far more viscerally within the gay heart than *Queer*. Scenes
toward the end of the book, where the reader is let into the world of
the Wild Boys to learn their rituals of life, death, love and rebirth,
are like the best sex, rooted in the sensual, but resolving themselves
in nearly insensible, breathless epiphanies, a stunning set of orgasmic revelations that leaves the reader weak yet grateful.

Queer appears almost pedestrian when compared to *The Wild
Boys*. Although more accessible because of its more straightforward
narrative style, *Queer* is also less rewarding as a reading experience.
The Wild Boys proffers happy jolts to the imagination and groin at
diverse, surprising turns; *Queer* by comparison is a fairly predict-

able yarn about a gay man in love with an ostensibly straight man willing to prostitute himself to the Queer on occasion.

Both are seminal works, for diverse reasons, but the concerns of *The Wild Boys* are more overwhelming: What is the nature of power? What is sex all about? Where is the perversity in the connection of sex and violence?

The Wild Boys tears straight to the heart of one of the greatest sources, community-wide, of 1990s gay angst: What to do with men who love boys? Yet even as the homo culture of this fin de siècle seeks to puritanically clamp down on boy-love advocates, it riddles itself with a fixation on lithe, boyish sexuality and smooth-chested youthful attractiveness—and the perpetration of same as the physical and erotic ideal apparent in clubs, on-line profiles, porn films and mainstream advertisements.

It is nothing more than blatant hypocrisy.

When Burroughs wrote *The Wild Boys,* the North American Man-Boy Love Association wasn't such a hot-button issue. Recent political advancements and opportunities have driven NAMBLA to the forefront of our attention—and made a dialogue even harder. To have doubts about the issue, in many circles, is no longer possible; at least, you are not to voice your doubts, for fear of being ridiculed, ostracized or screamed at as a pederast.

The end result, however, of this self-perpetrated duplicity within the gay community, between what it would license and what it would hold up as ideal, has only made *The Wild Boys* a more powerful work. The Wild Boys fuck with abandon, and in fucking there is power. And this is where the problem rests with intergenerational love: not so much in the ages of the participants per se but in the horrible abuse of power found in many such relationships. The present cultural dictators, gay and straight, who fail to consider or provide a place for the healthy development of the intergenerational relationship, encourage and promote the abuse of power by replacing conversation with condemnation. This hurts no one more than the younger parties in such relationships; they come to equate their sexuality with shame. This is society's crime, and its great failing.

The Wild Boys seeks to eviscerate all that, replacing the exploitation of youthful sex by the Controlling culture with a recognition of its power, indeed, its magic; power that the boys control, magic the boys create, own and define—for themselves. Reclamation.

Weirdly yet wonderfully, time has lent The Wild Boys a timeliness or, perhaps, a timelessness. For the reader of the 1990s, its pages blend the aggressive youthful energy of the urban queer—perhaps best seen in the fun-while-it-lasted hijinks of the now defunct Queer Nation—with the power of sexuality known to 1970s faggots, when you defined yourself, your community, your identity as a gay man, through sex with other men.

Both Queer and The Wild Boys and other writings by Burroughs have influenced works that came after them. Queer is worthwhile because it defines the classic situation of the gay man in love with the straight male whore and renders it sympathetic with bleak honesty. The Wild Boys is canonical, however, because it is a work of startling power, an achievement that shatters conventional answers to questions such as "What is a novel?" and "What is pornography?" And because, more than twenty years after it was written, it continues to tear at the soul of the gay community, casting light into shadows that so desperately need illumination. As empty as Queer is, The Wild Boys is visceral and, well, wild.

FIVE QUESTIONS

1. Ignoring for a moment its physical form, is The Wild Boys a book or a film? If a book, why isn't it a film? If a film, why isn't it a book?

2. Is the sex in The Wild Boys ever gratuitous, and if so, where and why? What separates those incidents (if any) from the nongratuitous incidents?

3. Is there a single primary narrative thread in *The Wild Boys*, and if so, can you trace it? What is the place of "Audrey" within the story? "Joselito"?

4. Is the violence in *The Wild Boys* ever gratuitous, and if so, where and why? What separates those incidents (if any) from the nongratuitous incidents?

5. From pages 157–161, the Wild Boys rebirth their dead. Following the text closely, where does our post-AIDS imagination lead us in considering this pre-AIDS work?

Umberto Saba

Ernesto

TRANSLATED BY MARK THOMPSON

Forgive me for hurting you. I only wanted to play,
just as you wanted to play, I know (he did not know
this at all—was sure in fact the opposite was true). If
there is still a bit of pain, remember it was me, Ernesto,
who did it to you. Then it won't hurt so much.

—SECOND EPISODE

Umberto Saba was born Umberto Poli in 1883 in Trieste. His father,
a Christian, abandoned his Jewish mother while she was pregnant,
and Saba was raised by his mother and some aunts, receiving little
formal education. He met his father for the first time when he was
twenty.

He is renowned for his poetry. In 1902 he devoted himself to it
wholeheartedly, earning additional money writing for various
newspapers as a freelancer. He served in the military from 1908 to
1909 in Salerno, then married Carolina Woefler. In 1910 she gave
birth to their first and only child, Lina.

The family lived in various places throughout northern Italy
until 1919, when Saba settled down and bought a bookshop in

Trieste. He began to take control of his poetry, self-publishing *The Songbook,* which he called "a sort of *Odyssey* of a man in our times," in 1921. It became his most famous book, and he expanded it in three subsequent editions, published in 1945, 1951 and 1961.

When the Nazis came, Saba fled; his Jewish blood left him no choice. He moved about Florence to avoid deportation, but when the war was over, he returned home to Trieste. In his seventieth year he would draw upon a friendship of his youth that in retrospect he recognized as his first love affair to feed the romantic heart of *Ernesto,* published in 1975, eighteen years after death interrupted his work on the book.

The writing of *Ernesto* consumed the last years of Saba's life, its thin screen between fiction and autobiography often broken when the poet wrote letters to friends in the voice and character of Ernesto. When Saba began to understand that he would not finish it, the realization anguished him.

Ernesto begins as the story of a horny boy who submits to sex at the hands of an older man for pleasure, only to break off that relationship when it fails to satisfy him. At the same time that he ends this affair, the boy learns he is "replaceable" in the clerk's job that allowed him to meet his lover. But it's all for the best. In the pursuit of his true devotion, the arts, Ernesto at last comes face to face with a boy who may well prove his soul mate. In Saba's never-ended story, each lad finds the other compulsively irresistible:

> Two boys passing the time on the steps outside their violin teacher's room, talking about their lessons and shaking hands as they part: it would have seemed a banal enough fact of life to any passer-by. But thanks to the particular constellation watching over them, and because of its far-flung results, this was (everything else apart) a rare encounter: an event such as happens in one country only once every hundred years, if even more.

The brutality and selfishness of Ernesto in the first portion of the novel, and the momentous impact of this tenderness, coming at what must serve as the end, renders the work Saba managed to set down before death bittersweet, hinting at what might have been, even as it momentously evokes what was.

Agustín Gómez-Arcos

The Carnivorous Lamb

TRANSLATED BY WILLIAM RODARMOR

O n that very day, I finally understood that the
bath my brother gave me every afternoon at exactly
four o'clock wasn't just my daily bath, strictly speaking, but a ritual strewn with caresses, ripe with still-
unnamed desires.

Because the bath I got at four o'clock—or there-
abouts, now—was no holiday, the way it had been
when Antonio was a strong, wild schoolboy, tender
and silent. That first day he wasn't there, I rejected for
the first time ever the view that cleanliness was among
a child's countless natural needs, which Clara had ex-
haustively and painstakingly enumerated before drag-
ging me to the bathroom. Naked in her hands, which
didn't know my body the way Antonio's did, I made it
clear that I didn't agree one bit. Filling the whole
house with my shrieks—and the bathroom with water
from the tub—I managed to so exasperate Mother that

she said something that would haunt my childhood dreams forever:

"Let it go, my dear. I am *sure* he prefers his brother's hands."

"That's right, you bitch," I thought to myself, "and you're the one who made me realize it." And I was moved by the haunting beauty of being conscious of my love.

—CHAPTER 5

Agustín Gómez-Arcos was born in Spain in 1939, but has lived in exile in France since 1968, when his works were banned in his homeland. Prior to being exiled, he had twice received Spain's prestigious Lope de Vega Prize for his work as a playwright and had published acclaimed translations of Jean Giradoux. *The Carnivorous Lamb* was Gómez-Arcos' first novel. Receiving France's Prix Hermès upon publication in 1975, it remains his most notable work.

The Carnivorous Lamb possesses a nearly uncontainable literary voice, at times tender and overwhelmingly picturesque, at times comic, at times vulgar and profane. Yet all its attributes are reconciled in the memory and speech of Ignacio, our narrator. His mother hates him, his father ignores him, and their housekeeper, Clara, at once loves and despises him. Living in the same regime that killed Lorca, Ignacio finds solace, tenderness and love without boundaries at the hands of his older brother, Antonio.

Ignacio is a creature of passion. When later Antonio writes him of his engagement to an American girl, Ignacio takes the letter, wipes his "ass with it, and flushed the traitor's document into the shit-hole forever. Everything in its place."

The Carnivorous Lamb is overwhelmingly kind, cruel, comic, kinky—and the best, most complex yet satisfying novel of filial love

ever written. In the ending moments—as peculiar as they are wonderful—Ignacio is able to realize all the ambitious promise of love
and the hope of family in what is a moment of wild beauty, as
striking as the clouds of butterflies that surrounded him when he
came to love his brother as a boy.

John Cheever

Falconer

They had known one another a month when they became lovers. "I'm so glad you ain't homosexual," Jody kept saying when he caressed Farragut's hair. Then, saying as much one afternoon, he had unfastened Farragut's trousers and, with every assistance from Farragut, got them down around his knees. From what Farragut had read in the newspapers about prison life he had expected this to happen, but what he had not expected was that this grotesque bonding of their relationship would provoke in him so profound a love.

—PART THREE

John Cheever was born in Quincy, Massachusetts, on May 27, 1912. He was the second son of older parents from whom he felt estranged even as a boy, and he was haunted by the family story that his father had an abortionist over to the house for dinner while his mother was pregnant with him. They were not wealthy; when his father lost his job as a salesman in 1926, his mother opened a gift shop to support the family, and Cheever blamed her for what he felt was his father's subsequent "emasculation."

John Cheever started sharing his stories when he was eight or nine—perhaps as a way of attracting his parents' attention—and at seventeen, shortly after being thrown out of Thayer Academy in Braintree, Massachusetts, he sold his first story to *The New Republic:* "Expelled." A year later, Cheever and his brother, Fred, went on a walking tour of Germany, and as a result, their relationship deepened. They moved to Boston together in 1932 and shared an apartment until Cheever felt their relationship was becoming too "incestuous." Cheever moved to New York in 1934, and Fred helped him financially until, on May 25, 1934, Cheever's short story "Brooklyn Rooming House" was published in *The New Yorker.* This began a lengthy and profitable association with the magazine; for years he contributed a story a month. Cheever wed Mary Winternitz in 1941. She loved him, and stood by him throughout his life, despite his chronic alcoholism, despite his bisexual bouts of infidelity. His first collection of stories, *The Way Some People Live,* was published in 1943, while he was in the army. It was the same year that saw the birth of his first child.

He taught composition classes and wrote for television after the war, receiving a 1951 Guggenheim Fellowship that allowed him to return his focus to fiction. The result was a second collection of stories, *The Enormous Radio and Other Stories* (1953), and his first novel, *The Wapshot Chronicle* (1957). The latter won the National Book Award, and its 1964 sequel, *The Wapshot Scandal,* won him the Howell's Medal for Fiction. Other novels followed, including 1977's *Falconer,* the first novel Cheever wrote after sobering up in 1975. He won the National Book Critics Circle Award and the Pulitzer Prize in 1979 for his collected stories. Many of Cheever's stories reveal his conflicted attitudes toward his bisexuality, attitudes he began to resolve around the time he embraced sobriety and, if the work is any record, made peace with before his death.

He died of cancer on June 18, 1982, and was buried in Norwell, Massachusetts.

Falconer is a brutal novel that resolves itself in eloquence. Ezekiel Farragut has been sentenced to Falconer Prison for a period not to exceed ten years. He has been given the number 734-508-32, and his crime is fratricide.

His wife is beautiful and obsessed with her own looks. She is also, quite frankly, a bitch, though it is to Cheever's credit as a writer that he does not allow his portrayal of her to seem misogynistic in a novel so steeped in a hypermasculine environment. If she is a bitch, that's all right: Most of the men around him are bastards, and although they may receive a sympathetic portrayal, they are monsters either because (in the case of the prisoners) of their incarceration or because (in the case of the prison officers) of their dulling proximity to the bestial in man. Even Tiny, the regular guard in Farragut's Cellblock F, who cans vegetables with his wife, brings Farragut gifts of leftover fresh tomatoes and allows him to slip away to make love with Jody, is still unforgettably a creature of malevolent, despicable horror. When his dinner is eaten by the semiferal cats that roam the prison, Tiny tears the head off one of the animals. It bites him badly in the process, so badly that he has to go to the infirmary.

The cats infest the prison, yet they provide the singular service of giving men otherwise isolated and alone, immersed in brutality, a tender outlet: purring, furry banks in which the prisoners invest their emotional hope and good memories. Many of the convicts have their favorites; certainly Farragut does, a cat he names Bandit because the animal has a black mask of fur across her white face. He is stroking her fur when the general alarm goes off, and at the loud noise Bandit leaps from his lap to hide behind his toilet.

Into the cellblock comes Tiny and several of the guards, all of them dressed in yellow waterproof clothing, all of them carrying clubs. Tiny calls for the men to throw any cats they have in their cells out into the hallway. The men refuse.

Tiny and the guards are there to attack the cats with the clubs.

And when the cats come toward the guards thinking they have food for them, they are brutally murdered—heads smashed, bodies split open.

The slaughter takes its toll. By the time the third guard has vomited, Tiny calls off the massacre with "O.K., O.K., that's enough for tonight, but it don't give me back my London broil" (Part Two). The door of Cellblock F opens, and the remaining cats—less than a dozen, Bandit among them—escape, prompting Farragut to pray, "Blessed are the meek."

If the violence that is within all men is given voice in *Falconer*, so is the sexual need that drives them. In particular, homosexuality bubbles to the surface in this same-gender, testosterone cauldron, and men who have known only the pleasures of the fairer sex try to reconcile themselves to each other's thickening cocks. Like Farragut, they find flashes of love with other men (Jody seems to have traded in intimacy; Farragut is not his only boy) and, simply, the release of sperm in a place called the Valley.

The Valley is a long room off the mess hall. One side of it bears a urinal; the light in the room is dim. In Farragut's chats with Jody, Jody has revealed that the prison guards are lenient when it comes to sex between the men because they figure it keeps them from rioting. But Farragut comes to the Valley most after Jody has gone:

When Farragut arced or pumped his rocks into the trough he endured no true sadness—mostly some slight disenchantment at having spilled his energy onto iron. Walking away from the trough, he felt that he had missed the train, the plane, the boat . . . What he felt, what he saw, was the utter poverty of erotic reasonableness. That was how he missed the target and the target was the mysteriousness of the bonded spirit and the flesh. He knew it well. Fitness and beauty had a rim. Fitness and beauty had a dimension, had a floor, even as the oceans have a floor, and he had committed a trespass. It was not unforgiv-

able—a venal trespass—but he was reproached by the majesty of the realm. It was majestic; even in prison he knew
the world to be majestic.   (PART THREE)

The ability to place tenderness at the heart of brutality—as in the
cat massacre—or to find majesty in a line-jerk is Cheever's simple
demonstration of his ability as a writer: Nothing is gratuitous in
Cheever's novel, everything leads to something else. Men mastur-
bating in the darkness lead to the remembrance of the majesty of
love, the orgasm shared with another when souls touch. A cat in the
lap revives in you the capacity for love. Rehabilitation depends in
part, of course, upon the vessel—Farragut—but his is an ultimately
resonant humanity, and his words, his losses, his glimpsed hopes,
are easy to tailor to our own losses and loves and dreams.

Farragut is a father, but his wife never brings their child to the
jail: She tells him the psychiatrists advise against it. Once she brings
him a letter the boy has written. Farragut is also an addict, promised his methadone while in jail, until he is deceptively weaned off
the drug during what is billed as a hard flu outbreak. Cheever,
himself addicted to alcohol, here expresses an ambivalence to substance abuse. He condemns the society that encourages the indulgence of the substance, be it the permissive Western urban culture
of the late 1950s through the '70s or—Farragut's particular hell—
the war duty that led men to do anything they could to black out
the acts of inhumanity they were called upon to perform day after
day. Cheever forgives the addict himself for his need. Addiction is
merely another human foible; the benefits of drugs—the escape, the
ability to cope that they bring—are longingly described. All of this,
perhaps, reflects the only possible perception of a recently weaned
addict toward society and substance.

Indeed, Farragut's need for the drug leads him in no small
measure to the first significant effort toward self-empowerment he
makes at Falconer before he meets Jody and before the book's eventual resolution. There is a cell lock, and Farragut panics: "How will

I get my fix?" He thinks that perhaps the infirmary will bring it up to him, but the night is long and empty for him, haunted by memories of his wife and his dead brother. In the morning there is no fix. He begins to go through withdrawal, and the intentional cruelty of it all becomes clear when deputy warden Chisolm shows up. He's there to watch Farragut go through withdrawal. They set up chairs outside Farragut's cell.

Farragut doesn't disappoint them. Sweat courses down his body. He shakes. His eyes burn, then his vision snaps. He convulses. Farragut bangs his head on the floor to find an anchor in the pain. At last, as chills set in, he tries to hang himself. When he's almost done so, Chisolm orders him cut down and allows Farragut his fix.

As soon as Tiny opens the cell door, Farragut bolts, blindly making a dash for the infirmary, where his fix awaits. Chisolm brings a chair crashing down on Farragut's skull as he passes, and Farragut blacks out. The cut from Chisolm's blow will take twenty-two sutures to close, and while recovering, Farragut decides to sue. The methadone was a court-ordered part of his treatment; Chisolm violated the court's order by withholding it. Farragut asks to see a lawyer, and when the attorney arrives, young and bearded and smarmy, he tells Farragut that if he signs a release, Chisolm won't prosecute him for attempted escape. He hands Farragut a clipboard and a pen; Farragut throws them back in the lawyer's face:

> [The lawyer] got to his feet. He carried the clipboard. He put his right hand in his pocket. He did not seem to notice the loss of his pen. He did not speak to the orderly or the guards, but went straight out of the ward. Farragut began to insert the pen up his asshole. From what he had been told—from what he had seen of the world—his asshole was singularly small, unreceptive and frigid. He got the pen in only as far as the clip and this was painful, but the pen was concealed. (PART TWO)

Farragut, in the privacy of his cell, removes the pen and uses it to write—upon the starched prison sheeting of his bed—a stunning manifesto, in which he tries to reconcile the judge who sentenced him to the arbitrary inhumanity of Falconer. Then, abruptly, he tries to reconcile himself to another torment, turning the manifesto into a hymn of romance to his wife, a cobbling together of the good memories that are all he can bear to hold on to, and to establish silence in the place of the bad memories he no longer finds himself wanting to recall.

This is before Jody allows him to fuse the happiness of love onto the frame of his present bitter reality, before he comes to understand that love isn't always about selfishness—but often is—and before he at last faces the events leading up to his brother's death. The circumstances of Farragut's fratricide are stunningly evocative of Cheever's own life: the taunt of being unwanted, a father who brought an abortionist to dinner while Farragut sat in his mother's womb. This is also before Jody and Farragut find their own separate but equal deliverances from Falconer, and before the balm of easy male friendship borne of desperation leads Farragut to:

Rejoice, he thought, rejoice.   (PART FOUR)

FIVE QUESTIONS

1. What is *Falconer* about?

2. Does Jody love Farragut?

3. Compare and contrast the fates of Farragut and Jody. Are they similar? Different? How? Why? What purpose does each serve within the novel?

4. What is Farragut's relationship with his wife? His child? His brother and his family?

5. Did Farragut kill his brother? Argue the case for and against.

Andrew Holleran

Dancer from the Dance

Everyone is the same here—suicide notes on Monday, found a lover on Tuesday, divorced on Thursday—the only things that change up here, darling, are apartments, haircuts and winter coats; and good faggots still go to San Francisco when they die. (All the more reason to, now that the Everard is gone; there is just no place to go and everyone's in a funk over it. Do you know they have fifteen major baths in San Francisco?) Write soon. I await your reaction to the novel.

Andrew Holleran is a creature in love with the idea of being a famous novelist. His name is a pseudonym, he is mysterious about his life—he may have been born in 1943—and his background. He grants a few details: educated at a prep school, then at Harvard; served a stint in the U.S. Army in West Germany; later swapped the study of law for the University of Iowa's writing program. In 1971 he moved to New York. *Dancer from the Dance* was published seven years later. Holleran published another novel in 1983, *Nights in Aruba,* and in 1995, *The Beauty of Men.*

He was a part of the Violet Quill, a group of gay writers who met a few times in 1980 and 1981 to discuss and share their works in progress, and whose members collectively have probably done more harm to gay fiction than any other force—literary, sacred or governmental. Its roster included Christopher Cox, Robert Ferro and his lover Michael Grumley, Felice Picano, Edmund White and George Whitmore.

Simply put, the Violet Quill writers' chief laudatory quality was that they dealt openly with gay subject matter. Their novels were championed not because they were good but because they were gay. (As this book has proved, gay writers produced remarkable fiction long before the Violet Quill came along.) But in retrospect, the greatest impact of the Violet Quill was the establishment of the gay ghetto in publishing, an albatross around the neck of queer letters that only now, almost twenty years hence, seems to be slipping off as its writers and those coming after them realize that the best work by gay writers has come from without the ghetto rather than from within.

Edmund White's Fire Island fantasias, while producing sometimes beautiful passages of prose, failed to equal the achievement of Purdy's *Malcolm,* which addresses similar themes. The first volume of his autobiographical trilogy, *A Boy's Own Story,* is pale and lackluster when held up to Gómez-Arcos' *The Carnivorous Lamb;* and the second volume, *The Beautiful Room Is Empty,* is itself revealed as empty when compared with the shattering prowess of Paul Monette's *Borrowed Time.* Cox's, Whitmore's and Grumley's careers were cut short by AIDS and produced little of significance; Ferro's novels dealing with families and lovers have been similarly eclipsed, like White's, by the work of other canonical writers discussed within this book; and Picano's best work, *People Like Us* (1994), was made possible only when its author was graced with time's gift of distance.

Dancer from the Dance has been held up as a faggot's *The Great Gatsby*, but it isn't. *The Great Gatsby* is a work of shimmering beauty, powered by the genuine simplicity of Jay Gatz's love for the enigmatic Daisy. There's nothing genuine about *Dancer from the Dance* except the characters' desire to wallow in pretensions. Although both works feature parties prominently in their pages, the similarities end there: Gatsby is a diamond at the heart of the novel you can't quite see clearly, it shines so brightly; by comparison, Holleran's Malone is a lump of coal.

So why discuss this book at all? Because if written as a satire, then it is indeed a good book, a pastiche of ridiculously hollow ambitions, skewering false lovers and idiots alike in rapid succession. Yet if at times it creates such frustration in the reader that he may well want to hurl the book across the room and into the fire, at other times it provokes near-obscene amounts of pity for its lost and wandering protagonist and his coterie of plastic admirers.

So we are never fully convinced that what we are reading is indeed a satire. Perhaps the novel is a tribute to an age when superficiality ruled over substance and gay men were so preoccupied with worthless pursuits that their lives were meaningless. In that case, *Dancer from the Dance* is merely another overpraised tome from the swells of the Violet Quill, a bad book, and should not only be excised from the Canon but swiftly forgotten.

Or, possibly, it should be kept around to serve as a reminder of what happens when we praise books because of their timely politics instead of their timeless, transcendent literary worth.

Edward Swift

Splendora

His knock was timid. Neither Timothy John *nor* Miss Jessie answered it. Slowly the door swung open and Brother Leggett stepped into the half-dark room. Sitting on the edge of the bed, he saw a man with short blond hair. He was dressed in a three-piece suit, his grandfather's, and was staring at the floor. Gradually he lifted his head. Their eyes met. Brother Leggett had fully expected to see Miss Jessie and had the feeling that he still might be seeing her, yet the figure was that of a man. Or was it? Angels, he had been told, were neither men nor women. For an instant he considered the possibility. Then he heard the voice, a combination of Miss Jessie Gatewood and someone else, someone he did not recognize, but felt as though he should.

"I wanted to tell you long before now," said Timothy John. "Esther Ruth, as you must realize, was my grandmother, and Miss Jessie Gatewood is no more."

—CHAPTER 18

Splendora is the name of the small town in East Texas where Timothy John Leggett grew up, teased for being too effeminate and soft, teased so badly he fled—only to return as Miss Jessie Gatewood, Splendora's new librarian, hired by mail.

The drag queen has come to be stereotypically thought of as an outrageous creature of either entertainment or prostitution; Miss Gatewood serves neither purpose. Aided and abetted by the fabulously sassy black drag diva Magnolia, Miss Gatewood is not so much the caricature of a woman as the embodiment of one—and as the town's center of attention, she wreaks her vengeance upon those who made her boyhood miserable. Yet this is not simply a novel of revenge, although it is that, and deliciously so. It is also a fable of reconciliation and, at last, a love story.

A pastiche of Firbank and Wilde, written in a voice that perfectly evokes the West Texas setting—where the new business Junie Woods plans to open will be called The Smack'n'Chew Barbecue, and where most folks gots two first names (like Timothy John)— *Splendora* predates Harvey Fierstein's *Torch Song Trilogy* by five years, creating for us the first modern drag queen to be reckoned with. But Miss Jessie is a drag queen made all the more contentious by her refusal to be pigeonholed. She exists for her own purposes, not for ours, and so she remains one of the remarkable heroines of contemporary literature, ensconced in the superbly heartfelt, often hysterically camp novel that is *Splendora*.

Armistead Maupin

Tales of the City

Mona knocked at the wrong time.

"Uh . . . yeah . . . wait a minute, Mona."

Mona shouted through the door. "Room service, gentlemen. Just pull the covers up."

Michael grinned at Jon. "My roommate. Brace yourself."

Seconds later, Mona burst through the doorway with a tray of coffee and croissants.

"Hi! I'm Nancy Drew! You must be the Hardy Boys!"

"I like her," said Jon, after Mona swept out. "Does she do that every morning?"

"No. I think she's curious."

"About what?"

"You."

"Oh . . . Are you two . . . ?"

"No. Just friends."

"You've never . . . ?"

Michael shook his head. "Never."

"Why not?"

"Why not? Well . . . let's see now. How about

. . . I'm queer as a three-dollar bill . . . I'm a virgin
with women."

"What about high school?"

"B-minus average."

Jon smiled. "I meant *girls* in high school. Didn't
you ever get it on with them?"

"All I ever did in high school was tool around
with the guys and a six-pack of Bud, looking for heterosexuals to beat up."

—"BREAKFAST IN BED"

Armistead Jones Maupin, Jr., was born in Washington, D.C., in
1944. Raised in a conservative North Carolina family, he wrote for
the *Daily Tar Heel* at the University of North Carolina, where he
was elected to every major honorary society. He graduated in 1966
and went on to law school, but flunked his first-year exams and
dropped out. He then went to work for Jesse Helms at a Raleigh
television station. Commissioned an ensign by the navy's officer
candidate school, he served as a communications officer in the
Mediterranean and in Vietnam with the River Patrol Force. In 1970,
through a series of mishaps, he became the *last* American GI to
withdraw from Cambodia. In 1971 he earned a Presidential Com-
mendation for organizing the Cat Lai Commune, ten Vietnam vet-
erans who returned to Southeast Asia to build housing for disabled
Vietnamese.

He went to work for the Charleston, South Carolina, *News and
Courier* as a reporter; hired by the Associated Press at the end of
1971, he relocated to their San Francisco bureau. He lasted five
months, then quit, finding work in a variety of jobs—mailboy, ad
exec, opera publicist and even Kelly Girl (a temp)—until "Tales of
the City" debuted in 1976 in the *San Francisco Chronicle*. The run
of the column would be collected into a series of novels (*Tales of the
City, More Tales of the City, Further Tales of the City, Babycakes,*

Significant Others), but the final volume in the series, *Sure of You*, would appear only in book form.

Although these are the works that have assured Maupin a place in American literary history, they are not his only accomplishments. Among other works, Maupin wrote the book for *Beach Blanket Babylon*, San Francisco's longest-running stage show.

Maupin has been called the American Dickens, but this owes more to the initial publication format for most of his books—Dickens' works generally first appeared as serials in magazines—than it does to the measure of his ability. Although Dickens has the greater literary gift, Maupin still has a magnificent appeal. There is no extended family whose misadventures are so beloved as those whose lives at one time or another have centered around Anna Madrigal's home on San Francisco's Russian Hill, at 28 Barbary Lane.

Relentlessly entertaining, Maupin takes cartoon sketches of the people around us—our friends, as well as those we may recognize only as people we pass on the street now and again—and then brings them fully into their own. His story? The story of our lives—and the lives we wish we led. Secretive Anna Madrigal, seductive Brian Hawkins, innocent Mary Ann Singleton, outrageous Mona and everybody's favorite queer, Michael Tolliver, entrench themselves not only in our imaginations but in our hearts. We leap from one volume to the next, from surprise to surprise, pulled along by characters we come to think of as friends. The publication of *Sure of You*, which ended the series, was a reason to swathe the house in black and tear your clothing in grief, but at last, after an impossibly successful run, we had to move on.

Maupin's *Tales of the City* manages to avoid being dated—even though it offers remarkable insights into the times in which it was written, from the seventies through the eighties—because it centers on the foibles of the human heart. And so the stories are timeless.

Timelessly good.

Thomas M. Disch

On Wings of Song

At the age of eleven Daniel developed a passion for ghosts; also vampires, werewolves, mutated insects and alien invaders. At the same time and mostly because he shared this appetite for the monstrous, he fell in love with Eugene Mueller, the younger son of Roy Mueller, a farm equipment dealer who'd been the mayor of Amesville until just two years ago.

—CHAPTER 2

Thomas M. Disch is a prolific writer with a diverse command of styles. He has published acclaimed volumes of poetry and essays; he is a dramatist; he has more than twenty novels to his credit.

Many of the more notable of these are in the horror vein, such as *The Business Man* and *The M.D.*, but Disch made a name for himself first as a science fiction writer, and it is to that genre that *On Wings of Song* belongs—or rather, transcends.

Daniel Weinreb's mother disappears when he's a boy of five, and his father takes him to Iowa. The reasons for his mother's disappearance are initially unclear, though one night Daniel overhears his father telling his grandmother that she left "because she wanted to learn to fly" (Chapter 1). Flight, in Disch's novel, is more like astral projection than what birds do: The spirit leaves the body and flies free, unfettered by fleshly concerns.

His mother returns when Daniel is nine, a bawdy creature in contrast to the plain-souled Iowans around them. In Disch's version of the twenty-first century, Iowa is a Christian Fundamentalist police state, replete with its own stamp tax; a place where radios are confiscated if they are able to receive un-Christian stations and where singing—the key to flight—is forbidden.

Daniel's mother has returned because she failed—she wasn't able to fly. Eventually the longing that separated her from her family will tear at Daniel as well, and he will find his vehicle of escape in the forbidden singing, becoming something of a pop star, hoping to fly on wings of song.

To do that, of course, he'll have to stumble, and sacrifice. He'll refine his love for singing in prison, managing to stave off his voice teacher, a fellow inmate, with Big Macs, though the guy would rather jump Daniel's bones. Soon after Daniel is released from jail, he finds himself working for the richest man in town. As handsome as Daniel is, it isn't long before he marries the man's daughter.

On the way to their honeymoon, they stop off in New York at a flight-assistance clinic, where she flies off and he—damnably—stays grounded. Her body remains in stasis, at Daniel's expense, for years, for most of their marriage. To support her, he gets a job working at the Adonis, Inc., bathhouse, eventually working his way up the social ladder of the local music circuit, becoming more and more successful as an escort, as a singer.

Will Daniel realize his mother's dream? Will Daniel fly?

While echoing Robert Heinlein's *Stranger in a Strange Land*, Disch's work is far more human—and more heartfelt. Disch never belabors his metaphors and we are moved by their simplicity. The resonance of Disch's prose doesn't need to loiter about the brain to be understood: It drives straight to the heart and soul. Disch crowds his books with moments of obvious charm—fliers are often referred to as "fairies," and there's a TV faith healer named Dolly Parsons—but crowns them with a winning spirit. *On Wings of Song* manages to evince a gay-friendly sensibility, yet it is more about transcending the limits of sexual orientation, the limits of the body escaped through song.

Many other works in the Canon deal with the establishment of a gay identity; *On Wings of Song* seeks to escape such pigeonholing. When considered alongside Le Guin's *The Left Hand of Darkness,* Disch's novel reaffirms the fantastic power of speculative fiction to flay the soft skin of the (gay) identity from the romantic musculature of the human capacity to love.

Patrick White

The Twyborn Affair

Prowse was crying, expostulating, and apparently stark-naked. Eddie's own fastidious nakedness became aware of prickling hair, tingling with moisture like a rain forest, at the same time the smell exuded by sodden human fur. He was surrounded by, almost dunked in, these practically liquid exhalations . . .

It was too much for Eddie Twyborn to endure. He was rocking this hairy body in his arms, to envelop suffering in some semblance of love, to resuscitate two human beings from drowning.

Prowse managed to extricate himself. He rolled over.

"Go on," he moaned, "Ed!" and bit the pillow.

Eddie Twyborn's feminine compassion which had moved him to tenderness for the pitiable man was shocked into what was less lust than a desire for male revenge. He plunged deep into this passive yet quaking carcase offered up as a sacrifice. He bit into the damp nape of a taut neck. Hair sprouting from the shoulders, he twisted by merciless handfuls as he dragged

his body back and forth, lacerated by his own vengeance.

—PART TWO

Patrick White, born in London in 1912, was the son of a wealthy,
conservative Australian family. His father was mellow, but his
mother was a voracious social climber, and her fervent pursuit of
status both terrified and enthralled young Patrick. Eventually the
two would have a row and carry on a lifelong feud, even as the
society she aspired to provided the backdrop for much of his work.

He was educated at Cheltenham, an English public school, and
because of his Australian background and nascent queer desires, the
experience was miserable for him. He worked for two years thereafter in Australia before returning to England to study at King's College, Cambridge. He lived in London after that, knocking about
with the theatrical crowd and other artists and writers, sleeping
around with men he met as a result.

During his military service with the Royal Armed Forces (he
was part of an intelligence unit) in Northern Africa and Greece, he
met Manoly Lascaris, another solider, a Greek, and the two became
lovers. At the end of World War II they set up house together in
New South Wales, on a farm near Sydney. They were still together
when White died in 1990.

White's novels reveal his love/hate relationship with his native
land and its people, which left him only grudgingly admired in
Australia. But the rest of the world was kinder. His novel *The Tree
of Man* brought him international fame in 1954. In 1957 he followed it up with Voss, a novel that impressed others more than it
impressed its creator. He published plays, short stories and, in 1981
(two years after *The Twyborn Affair)*, a memoir that revealed his
until then private sexuality.

White's political consciousness was a late-blooming affair. His
parents' conservatism informed his values until the 1960s, but on

December 9, 1969, he publicly came out against the Vietnam War as part of a demonstration, going on to involve himself in anticensorship campaigns, environmentalist concerns (including antinuclear activities) and the colonialist politics that dogged his country. Two years before his death, he was vocal in opposing Australia's bicentennial celebration efforts because he felt Australia should be an independent republic, and throughout his life he refused to accept official Australian awards. One award he did accept was the 1973 Nobel Prize for Literature, though his acceptance speech was deemed by many to be "ungracious."

He was averse to the homosexual "condition," seeing himself "not so much a homosexual as a mind possessed by the spirit of man or woman according to actual situations or the characters I become in my writing." *The Twyborn Affair,* his only novel dealing with alternative sexuality, clearly derives from that self-perception and, as a result, is a work of remarkable sexual fluidity, provoking us to question our perceptions and tacitly embraced rigidity. (For proof of this rigidity, we need look no further than the shabby treatment bisexuals and transgendered persons receive from many factions of the so-called gay community; they do not fit in as others think they should, and the response to them and their concerns is often far from kind or inclusive.)

The Twyborn Affair is a wise book, a sexy book, but you should expect no less from a book that proclaims, "The difference between the sexes is no worse than their appalling similarity . . ." (Part One). But this difference and similarity are at the heart of *The Twyborn Affair*—and the homosexual experience, post-Stonewall—though to date we have tended to focus on the difference at the expense of the similarity. While this may not be the specific concern of *The Twyborn Affair,* White's novel serves as a launching pad for many contemporary discussions about our perceptions of gender, gender roles and gender preferences—and how and why we argue so hard for their limitations in our lives.

Guy Davenport

Eclogues

—Thebans!

Kharon's loud shout quieted us. He was dressed
to go out. And beside him stood Getaki in all the
handsomeness of his fifteen years. He had carried the
lamb on his shoulders around the city wall that spring,
chosen for his beauty from among us in the ephebia. I
had seen Epameinondas as naked as a god with the
spring lamb on his shoulders, marching with the athlete's dignity to the sprightly hymn of the new sun,
followed by the hooded priestesses with their arms full
of first flowers, poppies and daffodils and curled is-
menes, and he was surely the most splendid of the
moskhophoroi but Damagetos with the snowy lamb
across his shoulders was the loveliest.

His hair was the color of molten bronze, the
tightly ringleted ephebaion as well, his shoulders wide,
his hips narrow as a boarhound's, his eyes bright flax-
flower blue, his lips too rich to close fully. *A boy
Pindaros ought to have seen,* the Hipparkh said on the
day of walking the wall.

—You know my son, Kharon said. I want you to
kill him.

No one breathed.

—"THE DAIMON OF SOKRATES"

Guy Davenport was born in 1927 in South Carolina. He was educated at Duke University, Merton College, Oxford, and Harvard University. In 1981 he received the Morton Dauwen Zabel Award for fiction from the American Academy and Institute of Arts and Letters. Davenport has never enjoyed popular success, although his work is adored by critics and other writers: Matthew Stadler devoured Davenport while writing his first novel, *Landscape: Memory,* and Davenport's influence shows in the superb yet approachable prose styling of Stadler's novel of young boys in love in the early years of this century.

As was once said of F. Scott Fitzgerald, Davenport is virtually incapable of writing badly. His work is smart, his playground is history, and of all the writers in the Age of Chaos, he is one of few to have energetically embraced the canonical challenge. He provides us with an excellent opportunity to examine what it means to be a derivative, yet wholly canonical, writer. Perhaps looking for a moment at the Western Canon will afford us a quick example of what such a writer might be.

The best immediate example is unarguably James Joyce. In Homer's *The Odyssey,* Joyce saw the blueprint for his own novel *Ulysses.* He created characters to parallel those in Homer—for example, Leopold Bloom is Ulysses, Stephen Dedalus is Telemachus—and set them adrift in the urban sea of Dublin on June 16, 1904. Joyce compressed the time frame—what Odysseus took years to do, Bloom does in hours—and made other changes, tweaking Homer's epic into something wholly his own. Still, if you boil the two works down to their bones, the skeletons are virtually identical.

So it is with Davenport, who here takes what is familiar and renders it almost wholly new. For *Eclogues,* the skeleton is mostly Virgil's collection by the same name, and true to their form, many of Davenport's efforts are infused with an increasing sense of the pastoral. In the book's last section, Davenport irrevocably ties his newer eclogues to those of our beloved Virgil—and to the poet himself. But Davenport's stories are canonically fed in other ways too, for he staples his prose onto the identities of notable philosophers, such as Bergson; artists, such as Picasso; and other writers: Rimbaud's and Whitman's names echo through *Eclogues*.

As with Joyce's *Ulysses* and its Homeric root, Davenport's *Eclogues* is not a mere imitation of Virgil. Most clearly, the second piece in Davenport's collection, "The Death of Picasso," is neither thematically nor stylistically similar to Virgil's second eclogue, "Corydon." Here—again, as with Joyce—Davenport has not sought to crib so much as to reinvent the work of Virgil. Davenport has successfully captured and refleshed Virgil's *Eclogues'* ancient skeleton with his own historically fixated prose. And so, Davenport's *Eclogues* is familiar—we recognize the structure—yet strange; the work produces a somewhat disorienting effect. We say, "Wait. I know you, don't I?" But we don't, not really. This is not the old, but the new. *Eclogues* lands us somewhere exquisite, between past and present, poetry and prose, altogether transforming us as we surrender to it.

In its irrefutable, passionate brilliance, Davenport's work manages to escape the dry confines of academic writing. It is not meant to be doled out in small pieces among the intelligentsia; rather, Davenport hopes to share with us—the rabble—the playfulness with which he embraces the great ideas, the challenges of our Great Books.

Charles Nelson

The Boy Who Picked the Bullets Up

Greg took one twin bed, and the soldier and I crowded into the other. I "fell asleep" immediately. After a few minutes, Greg crawled across the floor and lifted the sheet. I needed no foreplay. He set to work. I writhed dramatically. I "awakened." I waxed wroth. Greg apologized.

"I'm sorry. I don't know what came over me. It won't happen again." He returned to his bed.

Silence.

I growled, "Okay, faggot, that felt good. You may as well finish what you've started. And take care of my buddy, too."

Buddytoo had been lying quietly during the production. He was soon a member of the company. I've always wondered why you have no desire for straight guys. Besides the excitement of fucking virgin ass,

they've never heard the rumors that it's supposed to
hurt.

—"FIRST MEDICAL BATTALION, DA NANG,
VIETNAM, 28 MARCH 1967,
'MY DEAR PAUL'"

A collection of letters from Kurt Strom, a twentysomething boy
poured into the chaotic hell that was the Vietnam War, *The Boy
Who Picked the Bullets Up* is our best modern war novel. Strom is a
corpsman, a medic, and his letters are rife not only with appreciation for the manmeat he savors, men succumbing to needs born of
war, but also with the pathos of the shattered bodies and lives he
cannot repair.

Strom is complex, as any decent man is in times of war. War
demands that men perform unthinkable acts of societal transgres-
sion. Compared to brute murder, homosexuality is an easy submis-
sion. But Strom finds among his fellow soldiers not only submer-
sion in physical need but, in the face of it, emotional ardor as well.
These are often not mere sexual encounters but love affairs, power-
fully heightened against the frailty of life on the front lines of battle.

Why is *The Boy Who Picked the Bullets Up* a Great Book? Because it never flinches. As a result, it is a work of almost impossible
power. Sex and death have always been subtly entwined—the
French call the moment of orgasm *le petit mort,* or "the little
death"—but Strom in his letters exposes the connection and renders what tethers them together violently, exultantly clear: desperation. A desperation to realize orgasm, a desperation to realize life.

Nelson's second novel, *Panthers in the Skins of Men,* was a
lackluster disappointment. Perhaps this was unavoidable, however,
since *The Boy Who Picked the Bullets Up* succeeded in being that
most difficult of all books to follow up: a splinter of hope, the
defining reflection of a generation to a horror it was forced to
embrace:

I avoided paths and roads because of mines and booby traps, and because any gook who saw me would have run for the nearest VC . . . As I crept down the path, I turned a corner and nearly stepped on a little boy of ten or twelve setting an animal trap. He started to run away, but I called out softly in Vietnamese, "Do you want some money?" The boy stopped and looked at me. He smiled. "I'll give you fifty piastres if you let me play with your prick."

"No!" He giggled and moved closer to me.

"A hundred piastres?"

"Two hundred piastres?"

"Okay."

I pulled a fistful of money from my pocket. He held out his hand. I walked up to him, handed over the money and, as he was counting it, slit his throat. I threw his body into the swamp, covered the blood on the path as best I could, and hurried along my way.

—"COBRA'S FOLLY, BOU BOU PHU, VIETNAM,
12 JULY 1967, 'MY DEAR PAUL' "

James Merrill

The Changing Light at Sandover

We prop a mirror in the facing chair.
Erect and gleaming, silver-hearted guest,
We saw each other in it. He saw us.
—*THE BOOK OF EPHRAIM*

James Merrill was born into money; not for him the poet starving in a garret over crumbling sheets of verse. He was born on March 3, 1926. His father was the cofounder of financial giant Merrill Lynch. Even Merrill's Prussian-English nanny, who taught him French and German, was distinguished: She had a sister who was decorated for playing duets with Belgium's Queen Mum.

His parents divorced when he was twelve; the nanny was dismissed. When Merrill was a senior at the Lawrenceville School, his father published his poems and short stories in a collection entitled *Jim's Book*. He went to Amherst for his college education, but due to a stint in the army during World War II, he didn't graduate until 1947. In 1951, he found a publisher for his first book of poetry (appropriately entitled *First Poems*) and came face to face with writer's block while in Rome. He attempted to cure it with the help of a psychiatrist. Eventually successful, Merrill went on to publish twelve more books of poetry (not including periodic collections), two novels, plays, essays and, at the time of his death in 1995, a superb memoir, *A Different Person*.

For the first part of his life, Merrill divided his time between his Water Street home in Stonington, Connecticut, and Greece; from 1979 on, he would divide his time between Stonington and Key West, where David Jackson, Merrill's lover, lived.

Merrill never coded his work per se, but its homosexual elements became more explicit as his career advanced. Without a doubt, its crowning achievement came in 1982 with the publication of *The Changing Light at Sandover*, a collection of three books of poetry—*The Book of Ephraim, Mirabell: Books of Numbers, Scripts for the Pageant*—and a new coda, *The Higher Key*. Using occult experiments, Merrill, Jackson, and a companion attempted, beginning in 1955, to reach poets and others via the medium of the Ouija board. (The "He" referred to in the excerpt above is a "familiar spirit"; the trio have been setting up the Ouija board.) Merrill spun the work outward, from an exercise in triviality into a mystical epic rivaling Yeats in power and scope. The coda provides an opportunity to literally come full circle, repeating at its end the language of the book's beginning, a neat accomplishment that (admittedly) satisfies more than it seems contrived.

The Changing Light at Sandover received the National Book Critics Circle Award for poetry in 1983. Over the course of his career, Merrill was also awarded the Bollingen Prize in Poetry, the Pulitzer Prize and the Library of Congress' first Bobbitt National Prize for Poetry. Yet as good as the rest of his work may be, it is Merrill's epic *Changing Light at Sandover* that remains his career's best legacy: an immersive gay adventure for the artistic spirit.

Anne Rice

The Vampire Lestat

I was still sitting there, too unsure of myself to say anything, when Nicolas kissed me.

"Let's go to bed," he said softly.

I opened my eyes. Or I thought I did. And there was someone standing in the room. A tall, bent figure with its back to the little hearth. Embers still glowed on the hearth. The light moved upwards, etching the edges of the figure clearly, then dying out before it reached the shoulders, the head. But I realized I was looking right at the white face I'd seen in the audience at the theater, and my mind, opening, sharpening, realized the room was locked, that Nicolas lay beside me, that this figure stood over our bed.

I heard Nicolas breathing. I looked into the white face . . .

I think I rose up. Or perhaps I was lifted. Because in an instant I was standing on my feet. The sleep was slipping off me like garments. I was backing up into the wall . . .

I was torn forward. I was drawn off my feet across the room. I shouted for Nicolas. I screamed, "Nicki! Nicki!" as loud as I could. I saw the partially open window, and then suddenly the glass burst into thousands of fragments and the wooden frame was broken out. I was flying over the alleyway, six stories above the ground.

I screamed. I kicked at this thing that was carrying me. Caught up in the red cloak I twisted, trying to get loose.

But we were flying over the rooftop, and now going up the straight surface of a brick wall! I was dangling in the arm of the creature, and then very suddenly, on the surface of a high place, I was thrown down.

—PART ONE, "LELIO RISING," CHAPTER 8;
AND PART TWO, "THE LEGACY OF MAGNUS,"
CHAPTER 1

In 1976 Anne Rice published *Interview with the Vampire,* a literary novel whose driving conceit is aptly relayed by its title. It is the story of Louis, the vampire, as told to a reporter in New Orleans, and from it emerges arguably the most imposing character in late-twentieth-century literature: the Vampire Lestat.

Appearing as something of an antihero in *Interview with the Vampire,* omnisexual Lestat (vampires lose their ability for penile sex but develop a heightened appetite for desire, quenched only by feeding) would be the focus of the second of the five books forming The Vampire Chronicles. *The Vampire Lestat* introduces us to that antihero, allowing us to see the man, the demon, through his own sharp eyes, rounding out the reflective portrait earlier painted by Louis. *The Vampire Lestat* traces Lestat's creation—his life as a mortal, his transformation into a vampire, his education as one of the undead—and in so doing serves up a sexy, action-packed novel of morals so well written that we are never aware when, or if, we are being lectured. From the boy who was "Wolfkiller" to the rock star that is the Vampire Lestat, this is the education of a personage undreamed of by Thomas Mann or Henry James.

Lestat reappeared in Rice's next three novels in The Vampire Chronicles, but he would lose a bit of his bite, as the subsequent installments proved less restrained, less focused than *The Vampire Lestat;* the edge between fiction and philosophy dulled, and with it, our enthusiasm. Still, throughout these later volumes, Lestat continues to shine as a brilliantly conflicted persona.

The Vampire Lestat is an imposing piece of craftsmanship, the imposition upon society by one imagination (Rice) the ego of another (Lestat). A stunning literary achievement, it is one of the more obviously influential books of our time, having already spawned a school of challengers-as-imitators in Poppy Z. Brite, Lewis Gannett, Jewelle Gomez and Jeffrey N. McMahan. Yet *The Vampire Lestat* remains the real thing, a work of fiction so startlingly canonical it takes our breath away.

Paul Monette

Borrowed Time: An AIDS Memoir

F inally it was Rog and me alone, late at night in the
quiet, the way it had been all summer. Still I would not
cry, because I wouldn't let him hear sorrow. I spent all
my own endearments—*my little friend*—and sat till
four o'clock . . . I clipped a lock of his hair, which
got lost in the chaos of the following day . . . *You're
the best,* I whispered as I walked out the door, what I
always said when I left his room at night.

—CHAPTER 12

Paul Monette was born in 1945 in Lawrence, Massachusetts. His
education at elite institutions such as Phillips Andover Academy
and Yale—from which he graduated with a B.A. in 1967—was well
chronicled in his 1992 memoir, *Becoming a Man: Half a Life Story.*
It won the National Book Award for nonfiction, but the other half
of the story was never to be written, really—Monette died three
years later of complications resulting from AIDS. Almost a decade
earlier, in 1986, Roger Horwitz had met a similar fate. Horwitz had

been Monette's love since Labor Day 1974, when they met at a Boston dinner party. Horwitz was an attorney at the time, thirty-two to Monette's twenty-eight, Enkidu to Monette's Gilgamesh.

Borrowed Time: An AIDS Memoir is one of those works of literature that defies categorization; so broad is its impact that it renders any poaching on its territory a mere exercise in redundancy. Beside it, all other AIDS memoirs pale, and novels dealing with AIDS—including Monette's own *Afterlife* and *Halfway Home*—become slight echoes (with one notable exception: Geoff Ryman's masterpiece, *Was*).

Borrowed Time, then, is a definitive chronicle of the invasion of AIDS into the very fabric of our physical lives, our emotional spirit. A companion piece may be found in Monette's book of poems, *Love Alone: Eighteen Elegies for Rog*, also published in 1988, which struck the same canonical blow against later efforts to reconcile the impact of AIDS poetically. The raw power of *Love Alone* eclipses even such fine later works as Mark Doty's *Atlantis* and Thom Gunn's *The Man with Night Sweats*.

Perhaps this is because *Borrowed Time* could as readily have been subtitled "A Love Story" as "An AIDS Memoir": It is passion that drives *Borrowed Time* and *Love Alone*. Monette gave himself wholly to this writing, submitting to anger, sorrow and tenderness with equal fervor. It is the candor of these works that helps make them such defining literary moments—never once does the reader suspect Monette is holding back. Monette opens *Borrowed Time* with "I don't know if I will live to finish this" (Chapter 1), intimating that the story he is about to tell—Rog's story—could soon be *his* story, pitching the level of concern even higher for the reader. We are not idle observers of Monette's horror; we are involved, we are with him in the belly of the beast.

The fact is, no one knows where to start with AIDS.
(CHAPTER 1)

Monette recalls a Saturday in February 1982, a day spent driving down to Palm Springs. With Roger at the wheel, he read aloud an article from *The Advocate* called "Is Sex Making Us Sick?" But he reassured himself that because he hadn't had any of the diseases that seemed then to be harbingers of AIDS—syphilis, parasites, hepatitis—and because he wasn't part of the bathhouse crowd, he was safe.

These were the rationalizations we made, of course. And we continue to make such rationalizations in the face of death, any death, not just one from AIDS. We look for causes; we need something to blame, something to separate the haves from the have-nots and place ourselves firmly within the security of the latter camp.

Monette and Horwitz enjoyed a relatively monogamous relationship. In the ten years they were together, Horwitz had had perhaps a half-dozen "extramarital affairs," by Monette's accounting. Most of these happened when Horwitz was traveling out of town on business. It was Monette who had been more likely to play the promiscuity card, to treat sex as a kind of candy, an occasional (bitter)sweet treat.

Misinformation spread quickly, given its opportunity by the sheer lack of information available at the outset of the epidemic. (Gossip, like nature, abhors a vacuum.) The hoped-for distance between "us" and "them" began to take on near-tangible boundaries as people erected new Puritan moralities to keep themselves safe. But as in Poe's "The Masque of the Red Death," the murderer had already slipped inside our walls.

In September 1983 Monette and Horwitz's friend Cesar Albini is diagnosed with *it* and, in the mountains of Big Sur, Monette asks his lover:

"What if we got it?" I said, staring out at the otters belly up in the kelp beds, taking the sun.

I don't remember how we answered that, because of

course there wasn't any answer . . . But I know that the
roll of pictures I took that day was my first conscious
memorializing of Roger and me, as if I could hold the
present as security on the future. (CHAPTER 1)

This is the tenderness that lies at the heart of *Borrowed Time*. It isn't
so exalted as it is common, and for us, as we read it, it isn't strange
but comfortable, known as deeply by us as it was felt by Monette.
As with this:

How do I speak of the person who was my life's best
reason? . . . He had a contagious, impish sense of humor, especially about the folly of things, especially self-
importance. Yet he was blissfully un-frivolous, without a
clue as to what was "in" . . . Wonderful evenings were
second nature to us by then, with long walks at the end,
especially when we traveled. Days we spent cavorting
through museums, drunk on old things, like ten-year-olds
loose in a castle. (CHAPTER 1)

Memory isn't neatly confined: It prods us without regard to our
work or other distractions. The onrush of memory just above,
lurching onto the pages of *Borrowed Time*, spills directly from Monette without artifice.

Pages later: "Six weeks before Roger died, he looked over
at me astonished one day in the hospital, eyes dim with
the gathering blindness. 'But we're the same person,' he
said in a sort of bewildered delight. 'When did that happen?' "

Although there are nuggets of intimacy buried throughout, the
story of *Borrowed Time* inevitably shifts to one of illness and death,

as those around the couple sicken and die, as Roger worsens, as Paul tries to find a way to cope.

He goes to his regular doctor to get a prescription for sleeping pills, asking him for advice, but the doctor has only sarcastic trifles to offer. Stunned, Paul finds himself in the awkward position of wanting to rage at the man for his callousness but finding he can't: He still might need the doctor for something. More sleeping pills. More hope. So he buries the anger inside himself. And he feeds on it: "White-hot rage is the only thing that keeps you going, sometimes" (Chapter 4).

For many, the 1980s was a time of anger, a time of blame. While *Borrowed Time* never becomes a simple rant—it is far too complicated a work for that—it faithfully provides a record of the periodic anger that we felt at the time, rightly or wrongly, toward the medical community. We depended upon them and yet we felt separated from them. *Borrowed Time* as candidly displays our fury with the federal government and its lack of concern in the Reagan years, and with the judgmental bigots, be they Fundamentalist Christians, thoughtless heterosexuals or pious queers.

We had come to invest so much of ourselves in medical science, and yet in this case, and at this time, science proved helpless. It let us down, and we were angry. *How could you?* We paid taxes every year, but the federal government wouldn't acknowledge the crisis, and promising new drugs were stalled behind incomprehensible series of trials while people withered and died. *How could you?* Fundamentalist zealots labeled the disease "God's plague," the second destruction of Sodom, conveniently ignoring the fact that only in Western society was AIDS promotable for them as a "gay" disease. In Africa it decimated heterosexuals without prejudice, but that didn't fit their platform of hate and so it was conveniently ignored. *How could you?* Straight people, finding themselves virtually immune in the first onrush, thanks to America's rigid barriers of sexual bigotry, simply failed to comprehend what their gay friends—if they had any gay friends, for this was before AIDS slammed open the closet door with its undeniable ravages—were suffering. Inexplicably, heterosexuals maintained their claims of ignorance until Los Angeles Lakers basketball star Magic Johnson announced he was HIV-positive (HIV being the virus suspected of causing AIDS). Even then, they often responded with panic rather than with forethought, shielding their children from the HIV-positive, treating beloved family members as newly minted pariahs. *How could you?* But perhaps worst of all were the sanctimonious queers who chose to side, though they might try to deny it, with the religious demagogues, saying that People With AIDS (PWAs) were getting what "they" deserved; how could "they" have possibly thought their indulgent promiscuity and extravagant pursuit of pleasure wouldn't carry a heavy price? And so the delusionists fortified their walls, even as their hypocritical brethren began to fall sick, and they turned their backs to them as well.

How could you?

It was a time of anger, of hate and of hopelessness. New Age profiteers began to crawl out from under their rocks, scamming the hope medical science couldn't offer with wacko treatments and programs that encouraged PWAs to love their disease and think of it as something they subconsciously asked for, as a "learning experience."

Borrowed Time chronicles the exasperating medical efforts of those times, when the new drug or legitimate alternative treatment offered hope, only to have that hope shattered as the body succumbed yet again to the onslaught of this tricky, mutating virus. Flashes of the person you loved, still there, momentarily available, like pieces of a crumbling Roman fresco, slowly flaking apart.

And eventually destroyed.

Roger began to moan. It was the saddest, hollowest sound I've ever heard, and loud, like the trumpet note of a wounded animal. It had no shape to it, nothing like a word, and he repeated it over and over, every few seconds

. . . It wasn't till ten weeks later, on New Year's Day, that I understood the trumpet sound. I was crying up at the grave and started to mimic his moaning, and suddenly understood that what he was doing was calling my name. Nothing in my life or the death to come hurts as much as that, him calling me without a voice through a wall he could not pierce. (CHAPTER 12)

The serpent ate the plant of new life, and all that is left is to try as best you can to return to the world of the living, writing down the name of the lost beloved so that you may ensure he will not be forgotten, that people will remember: Once such a man lived and someone loved him.

Paul Monette was a working writer. In addition to his novels, and poems and essays that were collected and for the most part critically acclaimed, he novelized movies for Hollywood, writing the mass-market paperback versions of *Scarface* and *Predator* from their screenplays. His last effort along these lines was *Havana*, the Redford bomb, and it was published shortly before his death. Although those works do not bear upon his canonical status, a writer would be hard-pressed to find a better role model. So often, writers choose as their idol a drunken wastrel like Hart Crane or Capote; in Monette, there was a worker of legitimate talent and remarkable bravery, who, though he had every opportunity to play the dilettante, shouldered instead the ideal of the craftsman, the artist responsible to his talent, the work as the thing. The novelizations provided money to help feed the art, and they kept him writing. So what if they weren't highbrow? It was work, and in work is life, as in love.

FIVE QUESTIONS

1. It doesn't seem to matter to Monette who infected whom. Should it? Why or why not?

2. As a rule, we don't tend to blame the leukemia patient for their leukemia, but there's often a tendency to blame the HIV-positive person for their antibody status. Is this fair? Is this right? If it wasn't in the early eighties, when people could have been infected before safe sex information was known and utilized, is it now? Why? What assumptions does this make?

3. Paul Monette went on to two significant relationships after Roger's death. (The first was with another PWA, who Monette also outlived.) Does this surprise you? Why or why not?

4. *Gilgamesh* is in many ways the obvious parallel to Monette's struggle in *Borrowed Time.* Are there other echoes within the Canon, and if so, what are they? How are they formed or exploited?

5. What part of *Borrowed Time* disturbed you the most, or stays with you still, the impression you will carry away from this reading? Why? How did you respond to this aspect of the text when you encountered it? How did you respond to the book as a whole? Did you find yourself guarding against it, emotionally? Why? Did the fact that you had or had not had to deal with the scourge of AIDS or comparable diseases in your own life affect your approach to the work? How and why?

Allan Gurganus

Oldest Living Confederate Widow Tells All

Saved! Here were eyes aloose again and full of peace, a fresh start in the open air. "It worked," I spoke to his cradle. I stood there, one exhausted girl, half-laughing. He watched—a mild careful expression. His hands kept moving around in baby spasms like planning to someday somehow clap. Ned's eyes seemed smart enough, they *trusted* so. Our house was real quiet just then. Mantel clock ticking in the front room. Oh, I felt like everything was possible at last. I felt honored to be at home with a gaze this safe and sure. "I did it," I told his face in his father's cradle, "*I* did it." No shame. I wanted full credit. Ned couldn't talk yet but he could see. Me. Among others.

—"BACK TO WAR AGAIN"

Born in Rocky Mount, North Carolina, in 1947, Allan Gurganus was educated at the University of Pennsylvania and the Pennsylvania Academy of Fine Arts, where he studied painting. He served in the Vietnam War, and afterward studied writing with Grace Paley at Sarah Lawrence College, then with Stanley Elkin and John Cheever at the Iowa Writers' Workshop. He was subsequently named a Wallace Stegner Fellow at Stanford, and when his fellowship was up, he remained to teach as a Jones Lecturer.

He has since taught writing at Duke, as well as at two alma maters, first the Iowa Writers' Workshop and then Sarah Lawrence. He is a Danforth Fellow, and has twice been awarded the PEN Syndicated Fiction Prize and grants from the National Endowment for the Arts. He is a recipient of the Ingram Merrill Award, and his first novel, *Oldest Living Confederate Widow Tells All*, earned him the Sue Kaufman Prize from the American Academy of Arts and Letters for the best work of fiction published in 1989.

He followed the novel with a collection of short fiction, *White People*, which won the Southern Book Award and the *Los Angeles Times* Book Prize. He writes essays for the *New York Times*, among other publications, but he is perhaps proudest of the work he has done as cofounder of Writers Against Jesse Helms, a censorious senator from Gurganus' native state, where Gurganus presently resides in a village of forty-five hundred souls.

Oldest Living Confederate Widow Tells All is the fictionalized memoir of ninety-nine-year-old Lucy Marsden, who has seen it all. She speaks her mind clearly, often embellishing her recollections with the cutting edge of a righteous conscience.

Gurganus' novel reveals an epic vision evocative of Ovid in its collection of (often transformative) tales, and endows Lucy Marsden with perhaps the most intimate and natural voice in American letters since Mark Twain's Huckleberry Finn. *Oldest Living Confederate Widow Tells All* is in many ways a counterpoint to Margaret Mitchell's *Gone with the Wind,* with Lucy Marsden serving as a poorer Scarlett O'Hara's saner, mouthier sister—a Careen O'Hara as played by Chaucer's Wife of Bath.

The comparison between Twain (whose *Huckleberry Finn* has its own homoaffectionalist beauty in the isolated relationship between Jim and Huck on the raft) and Gurganus is apt in many ways. Both of them flout the conservative morals of their time with abandon, and use fiction as well as nonfiction as their bully pulpit. Both are often capable of moving the reader to tears as well as laughter, and of evoking that greatest of all human capabilities—for wonder.

Oldest Living Confederate Widow Tells All is a challenging, exemplary novel, showing the power of the gay imagination unconfined by the ghetto that has trapped and lessened so many other literary wunderkinds. Happily, Gurganus is not among them.

John Ashbery

Flow Chart

Patiently you again show me my name in the
register where I wrote it . . .
In riper times of trial we stayed together. But
in this kind of bleached-out crisis . . .
feeling, the best one can do is remain polite
while dreaming of revenge in another key.

Whither poetry?

In the Age of Inspiration, poets abounded, from Homer on-
ward. They were the popular artists of their day, producing pithy
epigrams alongside works of greater heft. The same could be said
for the Age of Enlightenment, with names such as Whitman,
Rimbaud and Tennyson; and later on, Hopkins, Crane, Lorca and
still others. But after the first third of the twentieth century, poetry
pretty much petered out of the spotlight. Its sphere of influence
increasingly lost out to the novel; few—Ginsberg, Pasolini and Auden among them—were able to realize the import of earlier poets.

In the Age of Chaos, the gay poet is all but extinct. Either he
has tied his work to AIDS, and been beaten to the power-punch by
Paul Monette, or he has struck off in a direction that defies classifi-
cation by the critics. And nothing has done more to isolate poetry
from the public sphere than the rhetoric of the academic poetry

critics. Their swarm grew thick during the 1960s, with the end result that ordinary people perceived poetry as something they could no longer understand, the purview of the intelligentsia. And so we turned from what frightened us toward what didn't: prose. The novel completed its ascendancy, and poetry's corpse was locked up in the ivory tower, where the flies feasted best.

But her soul escaped, and it wanders the earth as John Ashbery.

Born in 1927 near Rochester, New York, John Ashbery has created a vast body of work, beginning in 1953 with a gallery publication, with another's illustrations, *Turandot and Other Poems.* He grew up on a fruit farm in upstate New York, attended Harvard University and spent much of his adult life in either Paris or New York City. After an impressive start, with Auden selecting and preparing an introduction for Ashbery's first major book, *Some Trees* (1956), Ashbery labored in near obscurity until, in 1975, *Self-Portrait in a Convex Mirror* swept the triple crown of poetry, winning the Pulitzer Prize, the National Book Critics Circle Award and the National Book Award.

All this for the man who said in "The Invisible Avant-Garde" (1968), "Artists are no fun once they have been discovered." Ashbery would live that quote down. None of his earlier works prepared his readers for the autobiographical *Flow Chart,* his 1991 epic.

Despite its mystical overtures, Merrill's *The Changing Light at Sandover* remains a work from which we may mine a narrative. *Flow Chart* thwarts this kind of interpretation at every turn: The only possible way to consider it, to absorb it, is to view it not as poetry but as painting. This is a sensible approach, for art is arguably as important to Ashbery as poetry. In 1989 he brought out a volume of art criticism, *Reported Sightings,* having all along published important bits of criticism in prestigious journals; and he has coedited several anthologies on art. So, imagine the vast Sistine Chapel as an Impressionist effort, rendered in the intimate guise of words—impressions from a life, order replaced with mercurial, haphazard remembrances—and one is perhaps closer to visualizing the corpus of *Flow Chart.*

While many late-twentieth-century poets have allowed themselves to be swept up into lit-crit in-fighting ("New Formalists" vs. "Language Writers" vs. proponents of free verse vs. everyone else), Ashbery has remained aloof and, but for a few misses, has continued to churn out a remarkably consistent body of work. (Staggeringly, Ashbery once remarked that if it were up to him, his collected poems would not include *Self-Portrait in a Convex Mirror;* he thought it not worth preserving. But there are the awards, and the recognition, so what is a poet to do?)

Ashbery has further confounded things by publishing poetry in journals of each of the bickering disciplines, further hampering the critics' ability to define him. Grappling with this, they have all but pronounced a poetical multiple personality disorder incarnate in Ashbery, trying to split him into pieces when they cannot reconcile him into a single whole.

Ashbery deploys form (sestina, villanelle, pantoum and others) as readily as he eschews it; he appears wholly new and modern, only to turn around and invoke his heritage, acknowledging the inspiration provided in the work of preceding poets such as Andrew Marvell. (In that instance, Ashbery subverts Marvell's "Portrait of Little T.C. in a Prospect of Flowers" by simply replacing the "T.C." with "J.A.," for John Ashbery, and is on his way to a metaphysical masterpiece.)

This must seem frustrating and mysterious to the poor, addled critic. Where may he turn for explication? Happily, Ashbery himself has provided it.

In July 1957, *Poetry* magazine published a review, "John Ashbery on Gertrude Stein's *Stanzas in Meditation.*" Yale University was in the process of releasing the last unpublished works of Stein, and *Stanzas in Meditation* was their latest effort.

Ashbery's review revealed more about himself (especially in its last line) and his poetical future than, amusingly, it did about Stein. Somewhat predictably, he used art—paintings by Willem de Kooning—to help illustrate his poetical points, and demonstrated a genuine glee in Stein's use of the word "they" in her poems. "What a pleasant change," Ashbery wrote in a parenthetical aside, "from the eternal 'we' with which so many modern poets automatically begin each sentence, and which gives the impression that the author is sharing his every sensation with some invisible Kim Novak."

Bitch. But in this, Ashbery discloses why he never involved himself in the posturing that was rising in influence at the time of his review: It never interested him.

Many of Ashbery's observations on *Stanzas in Meditation* have since been applied to Ashbery himself, as when he writes:

> Like people, Miss Stein's lines are comforting or annoying or brilliant or tedious. Like people, they sometimes make no sense and sometimes make perfect sense; or they stop short in the middle of a sentence and wander away, leaving us alone for a while in the physical world, that collection of thoughts, flowers, weather, and proper names. And, just as with people, there is no real escape from them: one feels that if one were to close the book one would shortly re-encounter the Stanzas in life, under another guise.

These charges would be leveled against *Flow Chart* as critics tried to confine the poem. Another parallel to the greater body of Ashbery's work, and its focus, is easily found in his assessment of Stein's:

But it is usually not events which interest Miss Stein, rather it is their "way of happening," and the story of *Stanzas in Meditation* is a general, all-purpose model which each reader can adapt to fit his own set of particulars. The poem is a hymn to possibility; a celebration of the fact that the world exists, that things can happen.

So true of Ashbery, whose focus—even in the epic of *Flow Chart*—is on the time between events, as illustrated in the excerpt from that poem provided above. *Flow Chart* is an epic of (in)sensibility, not of drama.

Ashbery partially lists the ancestral figures he is indebted to when he writes of Stein's *Stanzas in Meditation* and, as a secondary example, of Henry James's *The Golden Bowl,* that they "are ambitious attempts to transmit a completely new picture of reality, of that real reality of the poet . . ." Other concerns that suffuse Ashbery's work—"the painful continual projection of the individual into life"—are revealed in his review, most baldly in his closing paragraph, in which he assesses *Stanzas in Meditation* as satisfactorily confronting Stein's admonition "If it can be done, why do it?" Ashbery writes:

> *Stanzas in Meditation* is no doubt the most successful of her attempts to do what can't be done, to create a counterfeit of reality more real than reality. And if, on laying the book aside, we feel that it is still impossible to accomplish the impossible, we are also left with the conviction that it is the only thing worth trying to do.

Ashbery's inspiration—his fervid joy at Stein's attempt and success—is palpable. She has hurled down a gauntlet; he will pick it up and accept the challenge, forming for *The Gay Canon* our Gertrude Stein, a force part rhythmic language, part visual art. Like Stein, Ashbery will continue to shape poetry in times to come, primarily because the challenge he sought was not to entrench, with other poets, in a set small camp but to reach out, to scrape the stars, to do what could not be done.

In the process, John Ashbery chips away at the ivory tower—aided by vigorous, popular works such as Fagles' *Iliad* and *Odyssey* translations, which remind people how entertaining poetry can be—and slowly, poetry herself begins to revive.

Keith Giffen,
Tom and Mary Bierbaum

The Legion of Super-Heroes

JAN. Shvaughn! *Damnsouls!* You've cut your hair.

SHVAUGHN. It's *Sean.* My real name is *Sean.* You didn't know *that either,* did you?

JAN. Shvaughn—Sean—Look, it doesn't matter. You just have to understand. *This*—this is *not* what's changed between us. *This* wasn't ever what we *shared.*

SEAN. Oh, come on . . . are you trying to tell me you find *this* as attractive as *Shvaughn?*

JAN. Don't you understand . . . ? Anything we ever shared physically . . .

SEAN. . . . Oh, damn . . .

JAN. . . . . it was in *spite* of the profem, not *because* of it . . . !

—NO. 31, PAGE 11, PANELS 1 THROUGH 5

The Legion of Super-Heroes began in the Silver Age of Comics (loosely confined to the 1950s and '60s), first surfacing in *Adventure Comics,* No. 258, a Superboy title at the time. The characters proved so popular, however, that they resurfaced in books of their own in several different incarnations, either under their own name or as extended guests in another title.

Set in the thirtieth century, *The Legion of Super-Heroes* allowed readers to project a fantasy of a near Earthly utopia, and then created a kind of superpowered teen UN. The Legion's representatives were culled from different planets instead of different countries, with diverse, often weird powers. (Matter-Eater Lad, for example, could eat his way through anything, while Bouncing Boy was a fat kid who could inflate himself into a ball and ricochet around the room.)

Sounds whacked? It was, and is. But it provided a remarkable opportunity for comics to address social issues.

The teen adventures continue today in two titles, a reincarnation of *The Legion of Super-Heroes* and a companion book called *Legionnaires*. The new *Legion of Super-Heroes* was launched in 1989. It was a darker time, and the kids who read the previous series were young men and women now. But in five-year interim, as the utopia cracked under worsening social changes, the characters developed sexual identities. Two of the Legionnaires, Shrinking Violet (she could shrink herself) and Light Lass (she had the power to lessen an object's gravity) were lovers. And upon his return from a spiritual quest, Jan Arrah, Element Lad (he could transmute anything into another substance), found out that his longtime girlfriend, Science Police Officer Shvaughn Erin, was actually a guy, pharmaceutically transgendered via a drug called profem. But it didn't stop there: As the above exchange shows, Jan knew and loved the man in her long before she came clean. It was a mature, defining moment in the treatment of queer concerns within the often immature pop realm of the superhero comic book.

Transgendered romance was a remarkable topic for a comic book to tackle sensitively in 1992; even today it would still be remarkable. But it should perhaps come as no surprise that two years after Jan came out, the publisher of *The Legion of Super-Heroes* reformatted the comic, launching us back into the happy world of perky teens. The subject of any character's sexual identity has been dodged thus far by the editors, who comment that the kids are too young to be so defined, though they have published the occasional queer fan letter, usually from a male reader remarking, sometimes with disturbing fervor, on how "cute" Invisible Kid Lyle Norg looked last issue.

While the potential for *The Legion of Super-Heroes* lies in its ability to expose young minds to a world without prejudice—including homophobia—the work of Giffen and the Bierbaums stands out and is elevated to canonical status because it was tenderly and brilliantly written. It provided a responsible treatment of (sexuality) issues that was neither preachy nor gratuitous but always developed as part of the story. Collected, their work could stand as a remarkable sprawling graphic novel of social commentary, the likes of which are rarely seen—with or without pictures.

Robert Rodi

Fag Hag

"I've got the *best* story," he said eagerly.

She sat up. "Oh, tell me!"

"In the men's room a few minutes ago, I ran into Lloyd Hood."

"The right-wing reactionary pig?"

He nodded. "We stood next to each other at the urinals."

"Did you peek?"

He laughed and hit her arm. "No, listen. Even better. He got all nervous, you know, all mealy-mouthed, and then he asked me if maybe I'd like to continue our discussion over dinner sometime."

Natalie felt the floor fall away. "No way."

"I'm not joking. The right wing reactionary pig is a queer." He grinned. "And I have a date with him!"

She threw back her head and emitted a peal of laughter.

—CHAPTER 10

Robert Rodi, a Chicago author who began to write fiction while working as an advertising copywriter, was born on December 28,

1956. *Fag Hag* was not his first novel, but it was the first in which he gave vent to his superb comic talent.

Fag Hag (1992) boasts a simply outlined story: Natalie loves her best friend, Peter, who's gay. Peter loves Lloyd, who's also gay. Natalie loathes Lloyd and must eliminate the two men's relationship in order to regain her importance in Peter's life.

Fag Hag has been called a camp classic, but camp is just part of Rodi's stock-in-trade, and his refusal to rely solely on that singular attitude of queer humor results in a work that is not only hysterically funny but also stylistically complex. Certainly, there have been gay writers with a comic bent before Rodi. If E. F. Benson had been writing his Lucia tales in the 1990s, they probably would have read something like *Fag Hag*. The same is true of Ronald Firbank, whose madcap plots are echoed in Rodi's novels, spinning themselves toward a conclusion that stops just short of over-the-top. Yet Rodi synthesizes his influences into something unique and wholly his own. His work establishes our standard for the modern gay comic novel.

Other writers—Charles Busch and Joe Keenan, for example—haven't managed to do this, not through any fault of their talent but through their failure to produce new work regularly. This is actually important because, although *Fag Hag* serves as the touchstone for the modern gay comic novel, all of Rodi's subsequent works—*Closet Case, Drag Queen, Kept Boy*—have refined the formula that is at the heart of their popular success, and their canonical quality.

To date, Rodi's influence has been most noticeable in the work of Los Angeles writer Christian McLaughlin, whose *Glamourpuss*, while uniquely McLaughlin's own, hews closely to the formula successfully employed by Rodi.

It would be irresponsible to end this discussion without noting that formula isn't always something to be sneered at, although many literary snobs love to do so. Shakespeare's plays followed specific formulas—the comedies tend to end with a wedding, for example—and certainly in the realm of humor, writers such as the previously mentioned Benson and Firbank also established their own sort of formula, exploited and developed by others—and themselves—along the way.

Rodi has given us not only some of the funniest novels of the late twentieth century but a model that is already serving the next generation as a successful springboard for their own literary ambitions—and our literary pleasure.

Tony Kushner

Angels in America: A Gay Fantasia on National Themes

EMILY: Looking good. What else?

PRIOR: Ankles sore and swollen, but the leg's better. The nausea's mostly gone with the little orange pills. BM's pure liquid but not bloody anymore, for now, my eye doctor says everything's okay, for now, my dentist says "Yuck!" when he sees my fuzzy tongue, and now he wears little condoms on his thumb and forefinger. And a mask. So what? My dermatologist is in Hawaii and my mother . . . well leave my mother out of it. Which is usually where my mother is, out of it. My glands are like walnuts, my weight's holding steady for week two, and a friend died two days ago of bird tuberculosis; bird tuberculosis; that scared me and I didn't go to the funeral today because he was an Irish Catholic and it's probably open casket and I'm afraid of . . . something, the bird TB or seeing him or . . . So I guess I'm doing OK. Except for of course I'm going nuts.

EMILY: We ran the toxoplasmosis series and there's no indication . . .

PRIOR: I know, I know, but I feel like something terrifying is on its way, you know, like a missile from outer space, and it's plummeting down towards the earth, and I'm ground zero, and . . . I am generally known where I am known as one cool, collected queen. And I am ruffled.

—*MILLENNIUM APPROACHES*, ACT III,

SCENE 2

Tony Kushner was born in Manhattan in 1956 but grew up in Lake Charles, Louisiana. He is the author of several other plays—*A Bright Room Called Day* and the incomprehensibly bad *Slavs! Slavs!* somehow managed to win the 1995 Obie Award, perhaps as a result of the not-yet-dimmed afterglow left by the bombastic success of his Tony Award–winning play, *Angels in America*, in 1992.

Written in two parts—*Millennium Approaches* and *Perestroika*, respectively, each a full-length drama—the plays are a monumental achievement. They are an audacious act of bravery, perhaps the most insistent product of the gay imagination to date. They are insistent because they follow through on their bona fide right to explore the difficulties of conflicted characters, playing out the slight rhinestones of our intimate lives on a grandiose, diamond scale, not only giving voice to our hopes and fears but establishing affecting resonances between our timeless spiritual concerns and our limited earthly ones—often, perhaps always, one and the same.

The central characters include Roy Cohn, the self-loathing homosexual and conservative political power broker, who died of complications resulting from AIDS in 1986, a year after the time of the play; Joseph Porter Pitt, Mormon Reagan poster boy; Prior Walter, a WASP PWA; Louis Ironson, Prior's Jewish lover; the people that surround them (friends, family, healthcare workers); and a few surprises.

Angels in America isn't simply about the differences between heterosexuals and homosexuals, nor is it a play just about AIDS. Its concern is, as with so many of the works we discuss in *The Gay Canon*, the human condition: what it is, what it isn't, what it should be. Kushner's gay fantasia is a love story, it is a story of faith, it is truth and lies, it is hope.

If *Angels in America* seems hard to pin down, that's because it is. First and foremost, it is a true epic—as much so as *Gilgamesh*, certainly, and not coincidentally, both works have abandonment as their pivot. In *Angels in America*, Joe Pitts abandons his wife, Harper, and in the process estranges himself from his mother, Hannah. Louis abandons Prior. And in the most spectacular abandonment, on the day of the 1906 San Francisco's earthquake, God abandons Heaven and, by default, the peoples of Earth.

If the intimate concerns of *Angels in America* deal with family—the Mormon Pitts and Prior's forefathers—the spectacle of it revolves around Heaven, its primary inhabitants the hermaphroditic angels. In a direct crib from Plato's *Symposium*, man comes from these angels, sacrificing his hermaphroditic capabilities for imagination. But Plato is not the only queer familiar: lines from Walt Whitman (most noticeably those that close *Song of Myself*) and Tennessee Williams, among others, dapple the text. As for the angels, Kushner bravely unites the ecstasy of religious fervor with the ecstasy of orgasm: Their harbingers are erections, their calling card the wet onrush of cumming.

In Kushner's play, who does not abandon what he or she claims to love? Belize, the black drag queen nurse, and, oddly, Roy Cohn do not. The play's heart of darkness, Cohn is at the same time its source of breaking light in the forgiveness he tears from those around him. Cohn is also the center of the play's most delightful perversity, as death leads him toward the most spectacular trial-defense client of his career.

Because of its refusal to restrain its concerns, *Angels in America* has yet to seem dated, more than a decade after its time frame, when Ronald Reagan and his legacy seem somewhat distant, but not forgetfully far away. Instead, *Angels in America* establishes itself not only as timeless but as that most successful of all things theatrical: intimate spectacle. Because of this, while reading the play is certainly a worthwhile exercise, it leaves the reader desperately hungry to see it onstage, if for nothing more than to pin down the angels of *his* imagination, to walk with Prior on his prophetic trail, to judge the abandonment of man by God, to forgive the hated.

Geoff Ryman

Was

The map showed Manhattan the town and, to the west of it, Fort Riley, the Army base. Fort Riley covered many miles. It had taken over whole towns.

Jonathan did not know there had once been a town in Kansas called Magic. There had even been a Church of Magic, until the congregation had to move when the Army base took over. The ghost towns were marked. Fort Riley DZ. DZ Milford. The letters D were ambiguously rounded.

Quite plainly on the map, there was something that Jonathan read as "OZ Magic" . . .

. . . "What's this mean?" Jonathan asked, pointing at the words.

"DZ?" the man said. "It means 'Drop Zone.'"

There were little things on the map called silos. Jonathan thought the silos might be for storing sorghum.

"At the end of the world," said the man at the Hertz desk, "it will rain fire from the sky." He still held out the car keys. "Manhattan won't know jack shit about it. We'll just go up in a flash of light."

> Not a single thing he had said made any sense to
> Jonathan. Jonathan just stared at the map.
> —PART ONE: "THE WINTER KITCHEN;
> MANHATTAN, KANSAS, SEPTEMBER 1989"

London-based Geoff Ryman is best known as a fantasy writer, but as he says in his afterword to *Was,* "I fell in love with realism." *Was* is a fantasy of several overlapping layers of fictional and nonfictional stories, each of them as real as the other. The result is a surprisingly moving novel. Surprising because, nurtured by formulaic movies—and worse, TV—so few writers seem able to create genuinely moving, as opposed to manipulative, work.

Was refuses to be categorized. It is a fantasy novel about things that never could be. It is about Jonathan, an actor with AIDS, and those who love him. It is about child abuse, when orphaned Dorothy Gael is sent to live with Aunt Em and Uncle Henry in Manhattan, Kansas, her only solace being her dog, Toto, and a friendship she strikes up, on the way to madness, with her substitute teacher, L. Frank Baum. It is a fictionalized peek into the life of Frances Gumm, aka Judy Garland. It is the story of Hollywood in the 1930s. It is a book about a book (about a film).

The lives in these pages echo each other subtly yet with purpose. *Was* is a quintessentially gay work, a perfect, almost unimaginable blend of the hard swath AIDS cuts through our lives, splashed against the chirpy backdrop of an MGM Kansas fantasia. It is about the human penchant for illusion in difficult times.

But it is, principally, a novel in which the interrelationships among the book's characters blur the edges of past and present, fact and fiction, family and stranger.

Wholly derivative yet wholly new, it is a remarkable work of art and, with Colm Tóibín's quieter *The Story of the Night,* the only novel to date dealing with AIDS that manages to rise above the impact and influence of *Borrowed Time.*

Matthew Stadler

The Dissolution of Nicholas Dee

"Wow," I whispered. The boy sat beside me, looking. He put his hand over my mouth and quieted me. I could see us both, in the light from the window. Where his legs moved into the shadow they were still visible, but only as ghosts, half-implication. Not much could be heard from below; the wind was too strong. When it died, their music and machinations rose again, lifting through the house to reach us. Oscar turned me toward him, and pushed my chest. His hand was firm and slow. I fell back against some pillows and he knelt, straddling me.

—CHAPTER 21

Matthew Stadler received a Guggenheim Fellowship for his first novel, *Landscape: Memory,* published in 1990. *The Sex Offender,* his second novel, was actually published third, in 1994; and his third novel, *The Dissolution of Nicholas Dee,* published second, in 1993.

Stadler was born on January 19, 1959. His debut novel was remarkably sensual and delicate—demonstrating the influence of the Guy Davenport prose he devoured while writing the book. Comparatively, *The Sex Offender* is a disappointment, boasting neither the style of *Landscape: Memory* nor the substance of *The Dissolution of Nicholas Dee*. The latter is one of the smartest novels of the late twentieth century; it is also possibly as defining a gay novel as Genet's *Our Lady of the Flowers,* only with Stadler's work, the concern is not the accretion of identity but the destruction of it.

The Dissolution of Nicholas Dee is an operatic adventure into the realms of love, personality, ambition and art. It is the story of a young historian, Nicholas Dee, who has spent his life shadowed and supported by the intellectual achievements of his now deceased father. Nicholas sets out to write an ambitious history of insurance and, through his devotion to the work, finds himself slowly slipping away from everything once deemed certain in his life: his father, his own position at the university. Even his capability for work falters as his ability to separate the world of the physical from the world of text ebbs.

Throughout Stadler's novel, the one constant for Dee is his sense of being; he may not be who he thought he was, once, but he is *someone.* It is this solid thread of first-person narrative that keeps the book from falling apart as it melts toward a simply stunning conclusion.

Rich with layer upon layer of meaning and possibility, Stadler's prose is a pure joy to read. The structure of the book hopscotches through the progression of Nicholas' history of insurance, gradually providing keys to his confusion. Stadler's wonderful effort is thought-provoking on aspects of art, family, commerce, health and revision. Crumbling opera houses, corrupt and perversely wealthy old men, dwarves and a "Tempest" come together in this classically written novel with a cyberpunk mentality. Virtual reality in a book, *The Dissolution of Nicholas Dee* can be a wholly interactive experience for readers successfully able to suspend their sense of self long enough to fall into the realm of the novel. For this is what *The*

Dissolution of Nicholas Dee asks of us: It demands we join Dee in his escape from the tedious, the routine.

Accompanying Dee in his dissolution is the ageless dwarf Amelia Weathered and a brilliant, beautiful boy named Oscar Vega. Dee's love for Vega—and what the lad represents—is beautiful, tender and sublime, bringing us wonderful moments rich in the sensuality and spirituality of sex and love, and in the flowing complexity of men in the role-borders between friends and lovers; fathers, and brothers. Throughout the book, Vega's identity, even his reality, is always suspect. At the end we are not sure if he was ever a real boy or always just a fantastic representational icon, a delusional artifice, a pedophile's dream: the mind of a man in the body of a boy.

Like us, Nicholas Dee exists in a complex world where glib reason and superficial logic are supported by the murky underpinnings of chaos, chance and uncertainty. Cast off from our frail moorings of conviction, our dissolution is every bit as tenuous as Dee's. (Who are we, really, without the labels we paste on ourselves?) As the reader skates with Dee upon this razor's edge of the soul, Stadler's lyrical voice lifts us beyond the realm of imagination and propels us at warp speed toward the only thing that has any meaning, the only art of any value and the only love worth having.

Part Shakespearean drama, part opera, part architectural memoir, part adventure book, part travel journal, part love story, *The Dissolution of Nicholas Dee* is an incredible novel. The reader's immersion in it echoes Dee's progressive dissolution, and by the end, we are hard-pressed to say what is real, what is artifice. Stadler's book is a singular literary achievement, a testament to the apparently boundless future of the great American novel, its promise far from played out, roomy with potential. Whatever else he may produce, *The Dissolution of Nicholas Dee* renders Matthew Stadler the best gay writer of our time.

Reynolds Price

Three Gospels

But as they landed near sunset, Jesus saw first
thing a man on the brow of the rise ahead.

The man was naked and foul with wild hair. His
hands and legs were locked in shackles, but he'd broken the chains.

A boy on the strand said that the man had been
crazy all the boy's life, that he lived in the graves, cut at
himself with flints and shells and ate raw fish which he
caught by hand.

The pupils wanted to put back out—a graveyard
dweller was impure to touch.

But Jesus jumped from the boat and walked in a
straight line toward the man.

The man held still but when Jesus neared, the
man cried, "Back! Stay back, oh God!"

Jesus came to him and held out a hand. When the
man recoiled Jesus asked him his name.

An entire tribe of demons was in him refusing to
answer. But when Jesus raised his voice to press them,
they finally said, "Our name is Legion." They spoke
like a chorus of bats in the dark that was rushing in.

But Jesus kept saying, "Out, come out" in a
steady voice.

When the demons knew they had to obey, they
spoke again and begged to be sent into some young
pigs that were rooting nearby.

Jesus nodded.

The demons flew straight into the pigs.

The pigs shied, then stampeded over a ledge to
drown in the darkening water below.

But the man that had been the Legion stood
peaceful. For the first time in his memory he was clean.

—*AN HONEST ACCOUNT OF*

A MEMORABLE LIFE

Born in Macon, North Carolina, in 1933, Reynolds Price has never
strayed far from home, barring a three-year stint as a Rhodes
Scholar at Oxford University, where he studied English literature in
Merton College. He was educated in North Carolina's public school
system and received his B.A., *summa cum laude*, from Duke University. When he had finished at Oxford, he returned to his alma mater
to teach; he continues to do so today, as James B. Duke Professor of
English.

In addition to the novels that made him famous, Price has
published plays and poetry of note. He has also produced worthy
nonfiction, including essays and a stunning memoir in 1994, *A
Whole New Life*, about his then-decade-long battle with a spinal
tumor that has left him unable to walk.

He is thought of primarily as a novelist, beginning in 1962
with *A Long and Happy Life*. Recently *A Great Circle*, his series of
three novels concerning the Mayfield family, concluded with the
return home of a PWA in 1995's *The Promise of Rest*. (The earlier
novels in the series are 1975's *The Surface of Earth* and 1981's *The
Source of Light*.) In 1990's *The Tongues of Angels*, Price tells the
tenderly beautiful love story of two boys at summer camp, a story

echoing the best of the nineteenth-century novels of friendship; despite its thoroughly modern tone, it never resolves itself sexually, choosing instead to feed on the sublimated eroticism between the pair.

In 1978 Price published *A Palpable God,* which included a translation of the Gospel of Mark, deemed to be the earliest of the four Gospels, those "eyewitness" accounts to the life of Jesus of Nazareth. The translation of that Gospel, published in 1996's *Three Gospels,* is fully revised and is accompanied by Price's new translation of the Gospel of John. (The two other Gospels, the Gospel of Luke and the Gospel of Matthew, have both come to be regarded as secondary texts.) Yet to Mark and John, Price adds a startling *new* Gospel, not some recent Dead Sea Scrolls discovery but Price's own, *An Honest Account of a Memorable Life,* a sort of compilation of previous works on the life of Jesus thrown together as raw ore, then forged by the heart's smithy that is Price's love for his much-beleaguered faith in these times. In his prefatory material, taking care to exclude himself from the blunt, blind mass of contemporary conservative Christianity, Price resurrects an ancient term, referring to himself not as a Christian but as a "member of the Jesus sect." He moves on to share with us the decades-long labors of love that form the pages of *Three Gospels.*

He brings all his talents as a novelist and poet to bear on *An Honest Account of a Memorable Life.* As a result, though his novels are remarkable, Price's Gospel transcends them through the pure distillation of his mature prowess with words. His refinements make more powerful still a narrative that has already been dubbed "the greatest story ever told" and serves in its original form as emblematic of the power of world myth to hold sway over man's soul. This is not the poetry of the King James Version, which Price admires, nor is it a mere rendering into modern English of ancient texts; instead, it is a literary transfiguration of those texts. It is also a modern man's paean of devotion to a faith whose members have, more publicly than not, turned away from its creedal dictates to invest fervor not in judgment but in love.

It is the brilliant effort of a honed talent working years to recast what is perhaps the central story of all Western culture, believe in it or not. It is a remarkable *nonrevisionist* achievement of reconciliation.

David Watmough

I Told You So

We fought over tired terrain. Once more I
accused him of disloyalty, playing Judas to my Jesus.
Again he deplored the paranoia lurking shallowly under my skin, and the self-loathing so close to madness
that only found relief in wounding words.

All dressed of course in specifics.

"You defend my brother-in-law who is a fiend;
someone who has castrated not just his son but his
whole family and turned my sister into a mindless
drudge. You wouldn't even speak out for me when
Donald spewed his hate."

"There are times when you're simply no longer
rational. You spur Jan on to babbling those inanities.
You left Donald with nowhere to go but to fight back.
He thinks you would otherwise destroy him—like you
say Jan has done to Loveday. And, Davey, the terrible
thing is, I'm not sure that Donald isn't right. Stupid,
brash, and malicious maybe—but over you he's bloody
well on target."

Finally silence between us, standing there. It is so
quiet I think I can hear the Thames breathing across
pebble-strewn mud beyond the plane trees the other
side of the road.

"This is the end then? You think we should part?"

—BOOK I, "LONDON,"

CHAPTER 3, "NERVE-ENDS"

David Watmough was London-born in 1926 to a Cornish father and a Londoner mother. His father held a variety of jobs over the course of his life, including traveling salesman, banker, farmer and innkeeper. He also served in the Imperial Camel Corps in the liberation of Jerusalem. Watmough's mother came from money, the daughter of a wealthy realtor and property speculator. Before marriage and raising three sons, she worked as an analyst in a sugar refinery, and she drove an ambulance in the London blitz. Aspects of her difficult yet loving relationship with her son David come to the fore in his 1992 magnum opus, *Thy Mother's Glass.*

Watmough's childhood was divided between Cornwall, where there was no electricity, running water or telephone, and the Watmough's home in London, which boasted all of the above and color TV. But Watmough loved Cornwall and loathed London, where he missed farmland and moor, wildlife and familial "aunt heap." He stood on the high Cornish cliffs and sobbed when he heard that World War II had begun. He knew it would change his life forever, and it did; his parents went off to join the Civil Defense, and Watmough would not see them for two years.

He was educated in Cornwall and London schools, then at the Coopers' Company School, where he and his brother were evacuated from London's East End to Frome, Somerset, during World War II. In March 1944 Watmough signed up for the Royal Navy, serving as an ordinary seaman in the Atlantic Approaches until demobilization in September 1945. During this time Watmough was arrested, tried and found guilty of sexual importuning by the civil authorities. He spent three months in Winchester Prison, followed by a further month's prison sentence by the Navy—for being AWOL!

In the fall of 1945 he entered King's College, London University, and majored in theology over a four-year period. Nine years later, when Watmough was twenty-eight, he met an American, Floyd St. Clair, at a sherry party in the presbytery of St. George's Episcopal Church. They have been lovers ever since.

Watmough's canonical works rest upon the creation of Davey Bryant, a fictionalized version of himself. The two decades–plus of novels and short stories concerning Bryant's misadventures have slowly coalesced into a singular tale about gay life in the twentieth century, "A Remembrance of Things Present" that has led more than one critic to label Watmough's oeuvre Proustian.

Certainly, Watmough boasts an enviable queer literary pedigree. In 1954 he sent samples of his poetry to W. H. Auden, who invited him to the apartment he shared with Chester Kallman on St. Mark's Place, on Manhattan's Lower East Side. Of that encounter, Watmough says, "After advising me never to write another poem, serving me dinner, getting me drunk and listening to his Bellini opera records, he took me to bed. I was quite put off by the diminutive size of his appendage and the obstinate inertia of my own. The situation made my host very cross but he forgave me and I was a regular visitor to their apartment for that year. Chester was cruising the Brooklyn Naval Yards that first evening but was usually present on future occasions."

A year later, Watmough would leave New York for Europe, carrying with him Auden's letter of introduction to Stephen Spender. When they finally met, Spender immediately took a shine to the young writer, or, as Watmough puts it, he "immediately commenced to pursue me with unflagging energy. I am not a particularly passive person (in bed or out) but I somehow managed to escape Spender's tweedy clutches until he followed me to Paris and in a seizure of lust whipped out his thing on the *Rue de Lille* and thrust it into my unwilling hand." That would be Spender's only assault on young Watmough, who, shortly thereafter, went into the hospital for an appendectomy; Spender was by his side when he awoke after surgery. The young man convalesced at Spender's home in Hampstead, where he had the opportunity to read Forster's unpublished *Maurice* manuscript. Spender and Watmough's friendship would continue through the years.

All this certainly had an influence on the young writer, and Watmough's later prose bears the impressions those physical encounters made upon his literary imagination. As a result, Davey Bryant is one of the more curmudgeonly sustained characters in modern literature, his voice contemporary yet filled with echoes of this queer bookish patrilineage.

It is in the final volume of the Davey Bryant series, *I Told You So,* that Watmough manages to outperform the work of twenty years by presenting us with the compelling story of a decades-long relationship on the rocks, all but set to capsize on the European voyage that was meant to becalm it. For diverse reasons—few writers have the insight into long-term relationships that Watmough has, by dint of his experience—these are uncharted waters. The result is both powerful and dark, and by turns bitchy, bright and loving. *I Told You So* is a stunning capstone to the Davey Bryant chronicles and provides us, in a literary voice rich with the past, a modern stunner of a novel pared to the bone, hard-wrought from histories public and private, a synthesis of everything, really, *The Gay Canon* is about: the love of men for each other, the value of history, the potential in the future.

The Gay Canon:
Suggested Reading Group
Schedule

INTRODUCTORY MEETING

Get to know each other and establish the group. Select a moderator.
Together, read through *The Gay Canon*'s "Introduction" and "How
to Read This Book," and discuss.

MEETING ONE

Read in the Tanakh, or Old Testament, 1 Samuel (recommended
translation: King James Version)
Read *The Gay Canon* on 1 Samuel

MEETING TWO

Read *The Gay Canon*, from Homer's *The Iliad* through Archilochus'
The Fragments
Read *Gilgamesh* (recommended translation: Herbert Mason)
Read *The Gay Canon* on *Gilgamesh*

MEETING THREE

Read Plato's *Symposium* (recommended translation: W. H. D.
Rouse)
Read *The Gay Canon* on *The Dialogues*

MEETING FOUR

Read *The Gay Canon*, from Xenophon's *Symposium* through Aristotle's *Poetics*

Read Aristotle's *Ethics* (recommended translation: Hippocrates G. Apostle)

Read *The Gay Canon* on the *Ethics*

MEETING FIVE

Read *The Gay Canon*, from Catullus' *Poems* through Virgil's *Eclogues*

Read Virgil's *The Aeneid* (recommended translation: Robert Fitzgerald)

Read *The Gay Canon* on *The Aeneid*

MEETING SIX

Read *The Gay Canon*, from Horace's *Complete Odes and Epodes* through Plutarch's *The Dialogue on Love*

Read John's Gospel (recommended translation: King James Version)

Read *The Gay Canon* on the Gospel

MEETING SEVEN

Read *The Gay Canon* on Michelangelo's *Poetry*

Read Christopher Marlowe's *Edward the Second*

Read *The Gay Canon* on *Edward the Second*

MEETING EIGHT

Read *The Gay Canon*, from Bacon's *Essays* through Gogol's *Dead Souls*

Read Henry David Thoreau's "Civil Disobedience"

Read *The Gay Canon* on "Civil Disobedience"

MEETING NINE
Read *The Gay Canon*, from Melville's *Moby-Dick* through Rimbaud's *Complete Works*
Read Henry James's *Roderick Hudson*
Read *The Gay Canon* on *Roderick Hudson*

MEETING TEN
Read Walt Whitman's *Song of Myself*
Read *The Gay Canon* on Whitman's *Leaves of Grass*

MEETING ELEVEN
Read *The Gay Canon*, from Tennyson's *Selected Poems* through Ellis' and Symonds' *Sexual Inversion*
Read Oscar Wilde's *The Picture of Dorian Gray*
Read *The Gay Canon* on Wilde's *Complete Works*

MEETING TWELVE
Read *The Gay Canon*, from Housman's *Collected Poems* through Kuzmin's *Wings*
Read Thomas Mann's *Death in Venice*
Read *The Gay Canon* on Mann's *Stories of Three Decades*

MEETING THIRTEEN
Read *The Gay Canon*, from Forster's *Maurice* through Gide's *Corydon*
Read Ronald Firbank's *Prancing Nigger*
Read *The Gay Canon* on Firbank's *Five Novels*

MEETING FOURTEEN
Read *The Gay Canon*, from Cocteau's *The White Book* through Isherwood's *The Berlin Stories*
Read Jean Genet's *Our Lady of the Flowers*
Read *The Gay Canon* on *Our Lady of the Flowers*

MEETING FIFTEEN
Read Evelyn Waugh's *Brideshead Revisited*
Read *The Gay Canon* on *Brideshead Revisited*

MEETING SIXTEEN
Read *The Gay Canon*, from Maxwell's *The Folded Leaf* through Williams' *The Glass Menagerie*
Read Paul Bowles's *The Sheltering Sky*
Read *The Gay Canon* on *The Sheltering Sky*

MEETING SEVENTEEN
Read Yukio Mishima's *Confessions of a Mask*
Read *The Gay Canon* on *Confessions of a Mask*

MEETING EIGHTEEN
Read *The Gay Canon*, from Yourcenar's *Memoirs of Hadrian* through Inge's *Four Plays*
Read James Baldwin's *Giovanni's Room*
Read *The Gay Canon* on *Giovanni's Room*

MEETING NINETEEN
Read *The Gay Canon*, from Ackerley's *We Think the World of You* through Ginsberg's *Howl and Other Poems*
Read James Purdy's *Malcolm*
Read *The Gay Canon* on *Malcolm*

MEETING TWENTY
Read *The Gay Canon*, from O'Hara's *Collected Poems* through Rechy's *Numbers*
Read Gore Vidal's *Myra Breckinridge*
Read *The Gay Canon* on *Myra Breckinridge*

MEETING TWENTY-ONE
Read *The Gay Canon,* from Le Guin's *The Left Hand of Darkness*
through Tournier's *The Ogre*
Read William Burroughs' *The Wild Boys*
Read *The Gay Canon* on *The Wild Boys*

MEETING TWENTY-TWO
Read *The Gay Canon,* from Saba's *Ernesto* through Gómez-Arcos'
The Carnivorous Lamb
Read John Cheever's *Falconer*
Read *The Gay Canon* on *Falconer*

MEETING TWENTY-THREE
Read *The Gay Canon,* from Holleran's *Dancer from the Dance*
through Rice's *The Vampire Lestat*
Read Paul Monette's *Borrowed Time*
Read *The Gay Canon* on *Borrowed Time*

MEETING TWENTY-FOUR
Read *The Gay Canon,* from Gurganus' *The Oldest Living Confederate Widow Tells All* through Watmough's *I Told You So*

Acknowledgments

I am grateful to the following people who at one time or another gave me advice to make this a better book. At times I listened, at times I failed to—and so they're not to blame for anything in these pages that displeases you, though I've them to thank for whatever 'tis I got right: Wendy Carter, Kevin Gardner, Steve Gere, Jim Gladstone, Phil Gochenour, Rawley Grau, Ed Hermance, Edward Johns, Maureen McClane, Mary Lou Phillips, E. Scott Pretorius, Mark Ryan, Chris Schelling, Mark A. Shaw and Amy Wuebbels. Angela Bourke, Bruce Carolan, Declan Coogan, Michael Cronin, Declan Meade, Maeve O'Sullivan, John Walsh and Michael Wynne helped me position the Introduction to the book's betterment.

My agent, John Talbot, sold this book and helped me with understanding Ashbery's wondrous *Flow Chart*. I am forever grateful and impressed. This book was acquired for Anchor Books by Rob McQuilkin. Rob lent his wisdom to the winnowing of the list of three hundred plus titles we started from, and provided incisive early editorial guidance. Siobhan Adcock edited the miserable draft copies of the manuscript I sent her with patience and sympathy. She also ran interference when I proved a putz in my understanding of deadlines, permissions and the concept of "fair use." What can I say to her but "Thank you!" Siobhan also lost many an hour with copyeditor par excellence Bob Daniels to establish a unified sensibility to the dates of works within the manuscript where diverse sources disagreed. Mario Pulice crafted a stunningly beautiful cover for the book, even as Donna Sinisgalli brought about an interior page design to match.

I am also grateful to my tutors and fellow students at St. John's College, both in the Graduate Institute and within the undergraduate program. I'm sure this book is an appalling travesty to some of them, a bastardization of everything held sacred—although hopefully the rest of them will have a laugh while reading it over beers at Little Campus.

Two resources proved invaluable: Claude J. Summer's *The Gay and Lesbian Literary Heritage* and Magnus Magnusson's *Chambers Biographical Dictionary*. And to those unnamed people who write the "About the Author" blurbs in the backs of books, my gratitude. Frequently, sources equally authoritative disagreed. I tried my best to reconcile them. In a book of this scope, it is inevitable that there will be errors of omission, or simple misinformation, though I have tried scrupulously to avoid them. If you uncover one or more of these errors in your reading, please accept my apologies. I'd appreciate it if you let me know of them, so that they may be corrected, should there be a revised edition of this book.

This book is the beginning of something. Toward that end, I'd like to thank in advance all the people who will offer up the constructive criticism that will build a better *Gay Canon* in times to come. Most especially, I'd like to thank the writers whose words fill the books discussed within these pages—for submitting to a brilliance I find impossible to comprehend, and for leaving such a rich legacy in their wake.

I thank my family for their long-standing patience. They deserve a greater reward of genius for what they have to put up with, but alas, this is the best I can do. For now.

Ciarán, "I know."

About the Author

Robert Drake is the author of the novel *The Man: A Hero for Our Time.* With Terry Wolverton, he edited the anthology *Indivisible: New Short Fiction by West Coast Gay and Lesbian Authors* and the anthology series *His: Brilliant New Fiction by Gay Men* and *Hers: Brilliant New Fiction by Lesbians,* for which they received multiple Lambda Literary Award nominations before taking home the prize in 1998. He has taught writing at St. John's College and The American University. Born in Portland, Maine, in 1962 and raised in Charleston, West Virginia, he currently divides his time between homes in Dublin, Ireland, and Philadelphia, Pennsylvania.

E-mail: gaycanon@mailexcite.com

The Last Word

Perhaps you would like to know why readers enjoy and praise my pieces at home, and ungratefully run them down in public? I'm not the kind to hunt for the votes of the fickle rabble by standing dinners and giving presents of worn-out clothes. I listen to distinguished writers and pay them back; but I don't approach academic critics on their platforms to beg their support. Hence the grief.

—HORACE, *EPISTLES* 1, XIX, 35–41
(TRANSLATED BY W. G. SHEPHERD)

Printed in the United States
by Baker & Taylor Publisher Services